Who's Not Afraid
of Martha Graham?

Who's Not Afraid of Martha Graham?

by Gerald E. Myers

Front cover photo by Dora Sanders (1957).
Back cover photo by ADF/Bruce Feeley (2002).

Dedication

to Charles L. and Stephanie Reinhart

For their lifetimes of service in inspiring and
supporting modern dance—and its philosophies too.

In Appreciation

The author's thanks go to Charles L. Reinhart, ADF's Director and my mentor during the years of my ADF participation, together with his gifted, beautiful, sadly missed partner Stephanie Reinhart, for his encouraging the book's publication and reading it closely, identifying needed corrections and revisions. But any remaining errors are the author's responsibility alone. And to Jodee Nimerichter, ADF's Co-Director, for all her initiative and concern without which this book could not have materialized. And for hours of talented work in shaping and fine-tuning the book into its ultimate form, to (volunteer) Sharon Connelly, a New York lawyer moonlighting editorially here with a former employer, ADF. Special plaudits to Concetta Duncan for her astute oversight, and to Nichole Spates for help with the original organization of the manuscript.

I would be remiss, if not arrested, not to recognize the lifelong influence of Martha Myers in introducing me to modern dance. My gratitude extends to many friends and acquaintances in the dance world who, though escaping mention in my treatise, were instrumental towards my undertaking it. Warm bows to the modern dance artists for their extraordinary achievements, including those beyond my ability to recount responsibly.

The lengthy list of "sources" for my story here attests to their importance, and preserving them for ongoing attention was a conscious objective. Writing not as a professional historian, critic, or dance authority but as an earnest advocate of the art, I am gratefully indebted to these sources. That my narrative concludes at a date several years ago explains the bibliography's end-dates.

Table of Contents

A Letter

New London
January '01

Dear Mrs. Calabash:

Happy New Millennium! *Now* it's here, at last, having deceived all those premature celebrants last December 31, 1999.

I've been thinking much about you, especially you and your friend's worries about your youngsters (still teenagers, right?) getting caught up in modern dance or what a colleague of mine at Williams College years ago called "the mudden dance." Better that than the circus, n'est-ce pas? But no, I do understand your concerns, so I've jotted some notes that may alleviate some anxieties. Your turning to me because of my many years of association with it through Martha is appreciated. And of course, as you have specifically asked about, because of my activities, especially public educational ones, that have been so warmly and professionally encouraged by the Co-Directors, Charles and Stephanie Reinhart, of the American Dance Festival (ADF). I can't assure you about the money or lifestyle that may ensue from a dancing career, but that it is certainly *not* a mindless or undistinguished thing—*that* I can prove to you and your friend! More later—Greetings to Bells and Frys, *et al.*

Regards, wherever you are,
GEM

A Rolling Recollection

A Nebraska relative, a few years ago, walked my son and me around his farm, pointing at livestock, crops, machinery, and buildings. Strolling from the flat pasture to the edge of a lush haymeadow, he exclaimed, obviously startled, "Look here! For heaven's sake, see what I've got!" My son and I stared where he pointed and our faces obviously showing our not getting it, he grabbed a tall weed announcing, "A cannabis plant! I mean marijuana!"

A patch of sedition in the haymeadow! This spot of marijuana, too small and spontaneous to alarm the gendarmes but large enough in its independence to amuse the three of us and send our thoughts, about nature's and our ways of doing things, in various directions. Our Nebraska relative hitched his overalls and beckoned us towards the house, deferring the decision to uproot or let the patch endure. But we knew he had it on his mind, that discovering its growing in the domesticated culture of his farm and under his very nose was going to nag his rethinking that culture and his relationship to it.

Each of us, if walked around our national culture of monuments, theaters, and battlefields, would likely at the edges come upon an unsuspected plot of seditious growth. Of course, to come upon it and to recognize it are not one and the same, so the summer night-strollers stopping to watch the modern dancers Merce Cunningham or Cleo Parker Robinson on stage at Lincoln Center Out of Doors may see them but without any shock of recognition. They've not yet had the "Good Heavens! It's marijuana!" experience with modern dance—a seditious patch in American arts and culture.

"Modern dance" is a broad name, theoretically protecting an artistic product impossible to define, identifiable through examples only; like low-cost dancing for near-starved performers in non-commercial theaters. What greets you from the stage is mostly unpredictable because its aesthetic is anarchic. The anarchy is usually too small and spontaneous to arouse the cultural cops but large enough to amuse some of us and send our thoughts, about art's and our ways of doing things, in various directions.

The seeds of the modern dance patch were scattered, in the 1890s and early 1900s, in the United States by soul-waving spirits such as Isadora Duncan, Maud Allan, Loie Fuller, and Ruth St. Denis whose names, like those of Josephine Baker, Gertrude Stein, and Bette Davis, symbolize personality and artistry outshining the mundane and conventional. Duncan's was an aesthetic of the sensuous, vividly illustrated by her stage image, a barefooted, uncorseted, voluptuous body barely covered by a Grecian tunic, triumphantly cavorting to, say, a cascading Beethoven symphony.

Duncan understood, long before Eric Bentley wrote, in reviewing *My Fair Lady*, that "theater is more of a directly sensuous pleasure than theater criticism would suggest...." But Bentley virtually conceded having to fight off a nagging sense of duty to call *My Fair Lady* a Broadway fluff just because of its sensuousness. For Duncan, on the other hand, sensuousness was neither fluff, nor superficial beauty, nor sexy entertainment.

Sensuousness is risky, as she knew all too well from the negative reviews of her performances that competed with the laudatory ones. Noted for her daring in life and art, playing romantic roulette or free love's gamble, Duncan is also remembered for how she died. Like Albert Camus and Jackson Pollock years later, themselves devotees of the sensuous, she ended in a car accident, her scarf caught in a car wheel. It was October 1927, a few months after Lindbergh's transatlantic flight. But granting Duncan's willingness to risk, was sensuousness, so far as her concert dancing was concerned, the real, most serious risk? Now asked, next to ponder.

Isadora Risking It

For glamour, Isadora Duncan is the preeminent modern dance founder or pioneer. Her autobiography, *My Life*, and the endless words about her, still accumulating, ensure immortality. She puts a face, body, and dancing feet on the ideological break with 19th century ladyhood. Any measuring of her achievements and legacy must take into account the risks run, and in her case there were plenty, but which should we conclude were the riskiest of all?

She was a blinking middle-class eighteen when she left hometown San Francisco for European salon-type solo dancing. Her education, worldly experience, and even dance training were too thin to be of much support. And life would be hard, suicide at times contemplated, so faith in a youthful vision of being an *artist* providing top-shelf entertainment for genteel audiences was about her only resource. How to *entertain* by dancing?

Sir John Suckling, a sort of dashing Errol Flynn and boudoir icon in the court of Charles I, had his answer and a sufficiently durable one to be quoted 250 years later in an American book *The Art of Entertaining* (1892):

> Her feet beneath her petticoat, like little mice,
> > stole in and out,
> As if they feared the light;
> > But oh, she dances such a way!
> No sun upon an Easter day
> > Is half so fine a sight.

Duncan risked disappointing the Suckling in her audience hoping for a "tease and please" performance, because she was apparently a substantial sight, round faced and roundish all around, more bare than concealed on stage, so neither her feet nor parts above resembled little stealings in and out.

Ballroom dancing in America echoed European instructions for women that might apply not only to Duncan's dancing in European Opera houses and concert halls but also to the dance schools (European and American) that she sought to establish. *A Ball-Room Hand Book*, describing 300 dances like the Waltz, Quadrille, and Prince Albert Set was published in Boston in 1858. Subtitled *Deportment and the Toilet in the Etiquette of Dancing*, it contains tips like this: "*Every lady* should desist from dancing the moment she feels fatigued, or any difficulty in breathing, for it no longer affords either charm or pleasure, the steps and attitudes lose that easy elegance, that natural grace, which bestows upon dancers the most enchanting appearance."

Duncan's dancing, many observers judged, displayed charm, elegance, and natural grace; it attracted lovers like Gordon Craig and Sergei Esenin and admirers like Rodin, Frederick Ashton, and William Carlos Williams, but an *athleticism*, that was in tune with sports and physical fitness interests, made for some heavy breathing and fatigue in her solos. So audiences accustomed to ballroom etiquette might need to adjust if in her waltzing to Strauss sheer elegance was compromised. A risk, yes, but one she comfortably survived.

Whether participating or spectating, people of Isadora's time were habituated to rules, conventions and guidelines observed in dancing. Members of an American Society of Professors of Dancing met regularly, issuing reports beginning in the 1870s, which included such as this: "The dance presented by Brother Greene was approved, but not officially accepted. Mr. James P. Brooks and others decided that the time for dancing the American Gavotte should be at the rate of 60 measures, 120 beats, 2-4 time, to the minute." Now as then, take notice, even as the 21st century shuffles on, fashions like the current vogue of "line dancing" prove, with its almost robotic precision of synchronized group dancing (often in costumes and venues that recall country square dancing), how audiences still love seeing the rules of the game stepped out in the dancing.

It was like teetering at the footlights, over the abyss of the orchestra pit, for Isadora to rule out rules, particularly those of classical ballet. Tossing aside ballet's essentials, its costumes, scenarios, five positions, and time-developed movement vocabulary of arabesques, pirouettes, bourrées, etc. because it was, she thought, unnatural and regimented, she could easily puzzle the audience trying to "get with" an obviously concentrating woman executing unrecognizable movements that often looked improvised and technically undistinctive, even at times amateurish.

Not everyone judged that Isadora had won in gambling on her discarding traditional ballet on behalf of her own freewheeling movement inventions. Anna Pavlova, while admiring her, commented "I think that my work is harder than that of Isadora Duncan. You see, she never has to get up and dance on her toes, and I do." Nijinsky and George Balanchine were never her fans, quite otherwise in fact, so "you win some and you lose some." To be sure, with admirers like Ashton, Rodin, Craig, Marie Rambert, Henry James, William Holman Hunt, and Jane Harrison, Isadora in fact won a lot. But have we spotted her biggest gamble? That, next.

Rating Her Risks

Isadora Duncan risked more brickbats than were actually dealt her. She was neither a billboard "phenom" like Josephine Baker nor an ethereal traditionalist like Pavlova. Not unattractive, she was however no show biz knockout, in fact appearing in photographs more matronly as she matured, so there was no bluffing in the sensuousness of her dancing. Her cards were on the table, some audiences reading them, others not.

Samples from those in the early 1900s who could:

Chopin! If he could have seen this child dancing, how the great master of sorrow and melancholy might be overjoyed. She is like a captive little bird in an enchanted woods; the rumble of leaves, sparkling melodies emanate from her. Skipping high up with fanning, trembling fingers, up and down, she sways rhythmically around and around…moving hesitantly, mysteriously, through anguish, ever-seeking the light yet to come into the soul. What a pure artist! (Amsterdam, 1905).

And:

No, she did not waltz, she *danced* to music of "The Blue Danube." How does she dance? I cannot describe it. I can only give you some idea by saying that she was completely free…moving gracefully, in splendor, completely unrestrained, without affection…. It was *freedom*, absolutely! That is what enchanted the Amsterdam public, prompted by a rousing ovation after the last number, Bacchus and Ariadne….

Isn't it a pleasure to see the familiar Greek dancing figures…forever returning in the refinements of a beautiful body?…those progressions of movement that make one think of a Bacchus feast depicted on a Greek vase, where you see figures thrusting forward one foot, then looking back toward the other foot raised high in a curved position behind? (Amsterdam, 1905).

But one Amsterdam writer had his doubts: "One starts reading too much into all these movements and I believe that Isadora Duncan, by giving too much mimicry, leads us astray and makes us expect meaning behind gestures whose only value lies in gracefulness, freshness, force, and external beauty."

Another writes, reviewing Duncan's 1911 performance at the Metropolitan Opera House with Walter Damrosch conducting the New York Symphony Orchestra, of the Flower Maidens' music from Wagner's *Parsifal,* seeing beauty but wondering about meaning:

This time she appeared in white gauze, beautifully draped. Her hair was caught up with flowers of pinkish hue, she evidently danced with an imaginary "Guileless Fool" standing in the center of the stage. To him she appeared with all her gestures and all her postures. It was an interesting attempt to give the spirit of the scene in the Klingsor's garden. What it meant to those who never heard Wagner's music drama this writer cannot profess to know....

(And referring to her performing to the *Liebestod* from *Tristan und Isolde*):

Miss Duncan's conception of the music did not seem to suggest a pantomimic Isolde, nor was it exactly dancing. In other words, she puzzled those who knew the music drama, and did not interest those who did not. Therefore we may ask, why?

For Duncan, answering this particular "Why?" would have been but a small part of answering "Why do I dance as I do?" And her reply to this, in words and performances, expressed her biggest gamble, the mother of Isadora risks. Sol Hurok, who produced Duncan's American tour in 1922, was a legendary impresario, a businessman who also knew her wares. Wondering in the late 1960s why San Francisco, Isadora's birthplace, did not have a memorial to her as "one of the greatest American artists," he observed (so appropriately) that, after everything had been said about her as a person and performer, "what *is* important is that she was a *philosopher,* a great artist, a great personality" (my italics).

She was most daring, as Hurok appreciated, trying to make the sensuousness of her dancing communicate an entire, philosophical manifesto. By 1920, as one writer sees it, Isadora had planted the idea, for international consideration as it were, that a lot of (unsuspected) stuff can be conveyed via the dancing body. "The whole idea of *Ausdruckstanz,* of the body as a powerful instrument of expressivity, seemed to emanate from her." Many viewers, as we know, muttered "Oh, forget meanings, just enjoy her gracefulness and *external* beauty." But others saw it differently, including Constantin Stanislavsky of the Moscow Art Theatre, who, upon seeing Isadora's outward radiation of "inner beauty," founded his famous Method that "demanded from his actors the same kind of inner compulsion that Isadora demanded from herself and all dancers."

Dance for Isadora was nothing less than "the art that gives expression to the human soul through movement, but also the foundation of a complete conception of life." Her expansions on this roamed everywhere, from Plato, Nietzsche, Darwin, and Walt Whitman, to Beethoven, Gluck, and Wagner, to anything and anyone confirming her premise that *authentic* concert dancing is so soul-revealing as to be truly religious. Dancing is a philosophical revelation, of a sacred unity of mind/body/spirit, of nature's rhythms and harmonies, of the ideals of truth and beauty, as Keats thought, found equally in the human body as on a Grecian urn.

Modern dance can trace a lot back to Isadora, the use of ordinary movements like skips and runs in contrast to ballet, the "flow" of continuous movement that the critic John Martin, for example, in the 1930s called the distinctive feature of modern dance, and innovations of movement and gesture for narrative/expressive goals. But her main legacy is a modern dance idea that, if she dancing and you watching both see to it, she can show you a *physical* performance that opens out onto a larger *philosophical*, conceptual universe than you might have imagined.

Modern dance is often said to be not a technique nor style but a particular attitude. What Isadora gave her audiences was plenty of attitude, which some greeted with ovations. "Once again," wrote an American observer, "she fully mesmerized her audience with the very perfection of pose and movement, transforming her lithe body from a physical entity into an ethereal medium for the expression of the soul of the composer." Gambling that she could actually reflect that transformation on even a bare stage was ever her biggest risk—and it is one that modern dancers, whether in the Duncan tradition or not, continue taking today.

A Letter

New London
January '01

Dear Mrs. Calabash:

I'm glad you liked the Isadora jottings and encourage me to continue—which I will! Right now! And enjoy, if you can, the fruit of your influence.

An old locker-room joke, that I'm sure never reached your ears in another room, but that, stretched a little, may have some relevance to the topic between us, posits a car stopping for a red light. A young man, hitchhiking, approaches and requests a lift. "No room," says the driver, causing the young man to ask, "Who's that in the front seat with you?" "My two sons," replies the driver, and to "Who are those in the back seat?", he replies happily, "My three daughters." "Whew!" exclaims the hitchhiker, as the car pulls away, "You know, you almost screwed yourself out of a seat!"

Mrs. C., a moral here? Think about this, that you can commit yourself to something so intensely and ceaselessly that it eventually makes you persona non grata and ousts you to another place, from where you began. It can be difficult—you know that, just ask Russell—to win increasing independence and remain in place. Win enough independence and you can achieve, desired or not, an orphanhood of sorts and all your own.

That patch planted by Isadora Duncan and others in America's cultural haymeadows mushroomed, skying to an independence that for many had a seditious look, all right. By 1910, free-spirited women like Isadora were attracting audiences in Berlin, London, Paris and Vienna as well as in New York to their dance inventions. While not exactly thumbing their noses at a gawking bourgeoisie and guilding their artistic quest for Truth, Beauty and Divinity in larger letters than Revolution or Feminism, they were of course taking on the status quo.

One of these, from New Jersey, was Ruth St. Denis (to become known as "Miss Ruth" in the dance world) who as a youngster was introduced by a dance teacher to "the individual possibilities of expression and the dignity and truth of the human body, moving in that Grecian atmosphere of grace and light." Debuting in the 1890s for a long performing career, St. Denis contributed to the voguish introduction of Greek aesthetics, formerly confined to campus classical studies, into physical education courses. The February 1903 issue of *Harper's Bazaar; A Monthly Magazine for Women*, for example, featured a Chicago-based advertisement "The Grecian System of Physical Culture for Women" and in smaller type "Taught by Mail Only and with Perfect Success"; a couple of pages later, "The May Skirt Yoke with Hose Supporter Attached." St. Denis and other modern dance pioneers, be assured, discarded more than skirt yokes and Hose Supporters; once their bodies were freed they pointed like "vanes of mission" towards bigger yokes to dismantle.

The seditious substance in the modern dance patch—let's agree, Mrs. C.—wasn't really the human body, of course, but how Isadora and Miss Ruth *thought* about it. And how they worshipped it, giving it a place at the altar! Ruth wrote in her autobiography how for years she had been unable to harmonize her intellectual and intuitive attitudes towards religion, and this inner conflict seemed to be outwardly represented by institutions. She wrote:

> The orthodox churches, the Catholic and the Episcopalian, which had rituals and color, shocked me by the horrible disparity between their aestheticism and the misery and spiritual ignorance of thousands of their parishioners.... Not until years later was I able to reconcile two seemingly irreconcilable elements which were not only present in my objective world but were also in my philosophy. For I was, you see, an artist, a lover, and a philosopher, at one and the same time.

Where did she get her solutions? From what her dancing body seemed to reveal intuitively. "In the end I was to realize, at last, that the flesh has its own wisdom, and desire its own voice of truth. I saw that I had, all my life because of my Protestant inheritance, denied this essential and elemental fact." Puritanism is wrong-headed; the human body speaks a spiritual wisdom of its own—and only dancers or those with dancing hearts genuinely know this. Admit this, however, and conventional criteria for sorting sense from nonsense are out the window!

Mrs. C., remember this as I survey for you the growth of modern dance—there's an issue here that doesn't go away. But let's not forget, either, how Isadora and Ruth tossed the dice, risking screwing themselves, so to speak, out of the seats they were riding, and inviting a gulf of incomprehension between themselves as performers and their audiences. Poignant stuff!

How's Virginia? A little more upbeat, I hope? Tell her to open the windows, let some air in. Anyway, give me your thoughts.

Regards—wherever you are.
GEM

Miss Ruth

Like Duncan, Ruth St. Denis looked to ancient cultures for inspiration but more to Asia than Greece. "Orientalism" was a popular theme in the early 1900s, dances with titles like *Cobra, Nautch, Yogi, Egypta, Radha,* and *Ishtar* attracting audiences. St. Denis danced before kings, princesses, and duchesses, verily "trailing clouds of glory," but there were problematic moments—the risks were real.

She was advertised in Paris as the "Original Hindu Temple Dance" in presenting her dance *Radha.* But it was not an authentic replication nor meant to be, the originality belonging exclusively to St. Denis's imagination whose only concern was to invent her "Oriental Impressions" concocted from the sketchiest acquaintance with the real things. It was a "modern" dance because of its personal Miss Ruth imprint throughout, not for lifting something intact from the distant past.

Radha (created c. 1906) depicted St. Denis as an Indian priestess, complete with throne and accompanying priest in a Hindu temple setting, who pleased many audiences with her subdued grace, striking costume, and the Delibes music score. St. Denis's "feminism" was evident here, since she imagined (contrary to tradition) Radha as being the virtual equal of Krishna, the god of love, and deserving reverence on her own part. Radha was "the human soul, forever seeking union with the divine, which was Krishna," said Ms. Ruth, giving this idea a ritualistic expression in her dance. But the idea, she admitted, was lost on a theater audience in Edinburgh. "When the curtain rose...I on my throne, was quite as tense and apprehensive, but for a moment there was a kind of stunned silence...it took the gallery several minutes to gather their Scotch wits together.... But finally, out of the midst of this silence, came a lusty voice, appealing almost pathetically to his fellows, "I say, boys, what's it all about?" The audience shouted, the curtain fell, the thing was done. A risk lost!

Splendid, however, were other occasions such as the 1909 Chicago Charity Ball where High Society sparkled in the audience (according to newspaper accounts, some 20,000 watched St. Denis's *Nautch*). St. Denis: "Many a Nautch girl in India had, in the palace of a rajah, gazed about her at a scene not unlike this, save that her audience, with its jewels and silks and velvets, would have been of men, and that the pierced screens of the purdah would have kept from her sight the exquisitely clad women of the zanana." This time, a gamble won!

Commenting on her touring successes, in the States and abroad, she was reflective:

> However, I cannot take too much credit, for in 1910 and 1911 any "show" that looked at all promising was avidly seized upon by theater-loving people. The movies had not yet assumed their major powers of attraction, and the public was prepared to support any entertainment which provided them with a certain standard of excellence.

She could take pleasure in raising American consciousness about Eastern culture and beauty, in correcting "our national conception of Oriental dancing [that] brought images of the Midway Plaisance at the Chicago Fair, which was not discussed in polite society." Touring was a serious business, a costly one for carrying expensive sets and costumes, and it represented significant aspects of both foreign and American cultures. Theaters around the country hosted vaudeville, theatricals, music and dance performances, and they existed in Kalamazoo and Coffeyville as well as in Los Angeles, Chicago, and New York. In Denver, too, where St. Denis performed her famous *Incense* in 1911 for an audience that included the male dancer she would wed in 1914, Ted Shawn.

Ted Shawn

The critic Walter Terry described *Incense*, the dance that left Ted Shawn "sobbing as if the soul rose out of my body when I saw the *Incense*—and never before or since have I known so true a religious experience or so poignantly a revelation of perfect beauty," as follows:

> ...The curtain rose on a dimly lit stage...a single figure came through. She bore in her hand a tray of embers and incense, and with these she offered prayers to the gods for the well-being of her household for another day. As she crumbled the incense on her tray...the smoke rose delicately, almost wispily... And as the smoke spiraled, her own arms mirrored the pattern in ripples... from shoulder to fingertips as the body swayed...matching the thread of smoke curving upward...near the peak of her dance she placed the tray on the floor, and both arms rippled as if they were not of flesh and bone but as evanescent as smoke. Quietly she picked up her tray, moved backward through the curtain, and disappeared. This was *The Incense*, the dance which changed the life of Ted Shawn.

For modern dancers such as St. Denis with a whole religious or mystical philosophy underpinning her dancing, conveying her "messages" amid the entertainment elements like jeweled costumes and Asian sets was an "iffy" business. (And the business side of it, booking agents and local producers, etc., often collided with her idealism.) She said of her audiences, attending *Incense* for example: "Of course, to some these exotic scenes were simply funny, to others they were merely a novelty, but to a small, precious minority they were the open gate to a new order of beauty, an intuitive experience unlike the run of their common days."

Ted Shawn was definitely one of that "small, precious minority" to get her message within the entertainment; or rather, for him, the so-called entertainment was a religious message through-and-through. And, in 1911, their future partnership had already been contracted.

Ted Shawn married the older and famous Ruth St. Denis in 1914, an erratic marriage to endure for some twenty years but that effectively launched his own career as a dancer, choreographer, and producer. A large, confident, handsome man, he looked less like a dancer than a banker, and given his religious bent (having studied for the ministry) together with a love of the theater, he could if alive today be a highly successful televangelist. St. Denis's marriage of religion and dance quite certainly led to their own similarly blended union.

Illustrating our earlier locker-room joking observation, how passionate commitment to something can eventually dislodge one from the place of that commitment, Shawn liked to say that because of his religious philosophy he was danced out of the church into the theater, whereas Miss Ruth with her mystical aesthetic was danced out of the theater into the church. A newspaper notice in the mid 1950s reported that "the white-haired 77-year-old performer [St. Denis] interpreted a Gregorian chant in the chancel of the Protestant Episcopal Church of the Epiphany [in Winchester, Massachusetts] before pews occupied by persons of several faiths." The church rector introduced the celebrated dancer by reading a version of the 150th Psalm: "Praise ye the Lord...praise Him with the timbrel and dance... praise Him with stringed instruments and organs."

At about this same time, about 1950, I first met Shawn at Jacob's Pillow, the dance performance and school site that he founded in the early 1930s in the rural Berkshires and that he developed into one of the world's leading dance festivals, where today its presentations of ballet, traditional/ethnic, and modern/concert dances attract large summer audiences. Shawn was a gracious, impressive master of ceremonies, most visible in introducing the evening performances and collecting supporters at napkined social gatherings, while attending equally impressively to all manner of details behind the scenes.

We sat on his cottage porch, and when I replied to his "What do you do?" with "I'm pursuing my Ph.D. in philosophy," he beamed, extending his arm for a big handshake, saying (as I'll always remember) *Philosophy*! That's what my art, dance, is all about!" As it turned out, Shawn's religion was so personally and intellectually saturated that he in effect worshipped himself out of a pew at the church, to be sustained instead by a philosophy of the dance articulated, for instance, by Nietzsche's words in *Thus Spake Zarathustra*: "I should only believe in a God that would know how to dance."

He wrote in his *Gods Who Dance*, reviewing his and St. Denis's important 1925–26 tour of Asia (the first Asian tour, he noted, by an American dance company):

America's new God will dance.... I know it, for I am American and my God dances. When my whole being is ordered, harmonious, pulsing in the sap of life, and when my intellect becomes the tool of my spirit and expresses the spirit's substance in virile grace and radiant charm—then I can speak as spake Zarathustra—"Now there danceth a God in me."

Not easy! Try it!—to articulate what, according to Shawn, Miss Ruth, and other dance groundbreakers, it is that "the wisdom of the dancing body" suggests. The dancer's body somehow pulls the mind to itself, refusing to be ignored by the mind wandering on its own. Listening to such dancers and reading their words make one guess that their intense experiencing of the body makes a mental demand, in particular that their minds take on thoughts that mirror their experienced mind/body unity that, oddly, is so commonly overlooked.

When Shawn wrote that his kind of dancers were "longing to express order, symmetry, proportion, rhythm" and that "Our new concept of God must be big enough to include all these things," we suppose he meant that as the value, say, of rhythm and proportion is emphasized through the dance experience, so ought we to *think* in ways that incorporate rhythm and proportion. Thinking, like dancing, is a rhythmic activity, and if you build upon your thinking about thinking in this way, maybe you get closer to Duncan's, St. Denis's, and Shawn's intentions—which some but hardly all in their audiences were able to discern.

Denishawn

If these first modern dancers seem in my expositions to come across as a group of loopy idealists, their minds (unlike their bodies) up in a la-la cloud-land, similar to Aristophanes's parody of Socrates, I need to correct that impression by calling attention to their *practicality* that was often shrewd, canny, almost befitting a commercial producer. St. Denis's and Shawn's marriage was also a business partnership, producing a network of performances and training schools under the name of Denishawn that would become internationally famous. The name itself names their single most important contribution, which was their *institutionalization* of the evolving new art, modern concert dance—also called at the time interpretive, expressive, or art dancing.

Ruth St. Denis put to work what she had learned from international touring about the world's dances, dance training, and performance/production requirements. She was indebted to Shawn's organizational skills in establishing the first Denishawn School of dancing in Los Angeles in 1915. The advertised mission of the school proved effective, to teach students about the central ancient role of dance in all cultures by exposing them to styles from around the world; not merely to do versions of Japanese, Egyptian, or East Indian dances but to perform their "essence or spirit"—which mattered much more than accuracy of replication. Stars of the silent screen such as Lillian Gish and actresses like Ruth Chatterton were drawn to the new school along with other expected young girls. Because the married Ruth and Ted not only looked respectable but demanded decorum and respectability at Denishawn, there were, noticeably, daughters "from good families."

By 1927, when Denishawn House was built in New York City, "the first building to be designed specifically for dance," it was apparent that American culture had grown a patch of new performing art, modern dance. Shawn and St. Denis were fabulous promoters of their art. They seem to have been *everywhere*, on the vaudeville circuit, endless theater touring whether in the States or abroad. You had to be locked in a closet not to have heard about Denishawn as the years of the Great Depression loomed just ahead.

Denishawn, with its network of dancers, schools and performance venues, institutionalized modern (individualistically expressive) dance, giving it place, continuity, and an encouraging degree of popularity. Make no mistake here, it was an *alternative* approach to traditional dancing, not something you could get in any "Mrs. X's Studio" in any American town. This was different from square dances in the village barn, or traditional folk styles like the English Morris dancers, or classical ballet, or the kind of vaudeville that evolved into musical comedy or Radio City Rockette routines. It differed from the ballroom dancing of Irene and Vernon Castle.

The Castles, their names are synonymous with American ballroom dancing that included the famous "Castle Walk," published their book *Modern Dancing* in 1914, the time of World War I. The book was in part a manual, instructing its readers how properly to do social dances such as the Polka Skip, the Hesitation Waltz, the Tango, the Maxixe, the Media Luna, the Skating Step (Before the Dip), the Eight Step, and others. It was also an exhortation, in the Castle's Foreword, to "uplift dancing, purify it, and place it before the public in its proper light." For the Castles, modern dancing was graceful ballroom expression of the music, and they lamented the "Tango Craze" around them that had begun "in the orgy that the world indulged in during the vogue of the Turkey Trot, the Grizzly Bear, and the Bunny Hug." Shuffles, twists, and jumps that had hectically infected the Two Step, Polka, and Turkey Trot were to be banished, replaced by "stately" dances that "add mobility to melody."

Ted Shawn shared the lament, regretting "The chaos of shimmy, Charleston and Black Bottom" produced by jazz music, always preferring the Castles' grace and nobility over gymnastic contortions. In fact, we have to notice here the fact that Duncan, St. Denis, and Shawn at times said or wrote things, especially when criticizing popular culture, that appear downright bigoted, seeming to express white middleclass prejudices. Recently, while producing the American Dance Festival's *Free to Dance* film/TV documentary on African American contributions to concert dance, a project with which I was intimately involved, the series producer M. Davis Lacy came upon an unknown correspondence between Ruth St. Denis and an African American younger dancer/associate, Edna Guy. St. Denis's letters draw us up short at places because seemingly on the edges of racism, and the first of the three *Free to Dance* programs (premiered on pbs nationally June 24, 2001) dramatizes the St. Denis and Guy relationship. But how now to interpret the attitudes then of these white modern dance founders is a complex matter, because they also showed interest in and concern for black dancers, as illustrated, for instance, by Shawn's supportive collaborations with Hampton Institute beginning in the 1920s. I like to think that the evidence points to our white dancers being prejudiced against certain features of pop culture rather than people, but the door can't be shut here on further discussion.

For his part, Shawn was ever the American Optimist (a not unimportant factor in his successes), declaring (apparently inconsistently as regards jazz) that "The vast mechanisms of our mills and factories are an expression of our tremendous feeling of rhythm...the extraordinary popularity of Jazz which radiating outward from America has penetrated the far corners of the earth, in the out-pouring of an exuberant and joyous vitality...it will take higher and better forms without losing its gaiety and vitality."

Denishawn's mission was more ambitious even than the Castles's. To be sure, the social and psychological benefits of good ballroom dancing are undeniable, but the modern concert dance that Denishawn represented, that would evolve into the works of Martha Graham and others, was meant to be an art whose training and performance were nothing less than one's quest for an enlightened self-realization, for an activity that feels profound enough to make life worth living. Compared to this, social and recreational dancing looked like mere diversions.

Denishawn, however, began to come apart in the early 1930s, due partly to personal conflicts between Ted and Ruth but also because it was vulnerable to the problems of maintaining a financially and organizationally secure enterprise while not surrendering its idealism. The "rumor," as Ruth expressed it, "that instead of giving our art in a pure form we were popularizing it," was distressing and symptomatic of the difficulties that led to her separation from Shawn, to her renewed focus on mystical dancing in founding the Society for Spiritual Arts (later renamed Church of the Divine Dance). Shawn redirected his career as producer in directing Jacob's Pillow and forming an all men's dance company while continuing to choreograph and perform.

Denishawn's influence lingered, however, and was important in helping modern dance to become a part of university and college campus life. Its educational mission facilitated the art's move from mom-and-pop studios in American towns, that primarily served a pre-college clientele taking tap, ballet and gymnastic classes, to campus curricula. When we remember how American campuses have largely sustained modern dance, how celebrated dancers like Paul Taylor, Meredith Monk, and Anna Halprin began their careers on the campuses of Syracuse University, Sarah Lawrence College, and the University of Wisconsin, respectively, we have to credit Miss Ruth and Ted for encouraging a campus environment for their art.

St. Denis's educational philosophy, with its striking mix of mystical idealism and down-to-earth pragmatism, was outlined in January 1931 to a female interviewer of the magazine *Needlecraft—The Magazine of Home Arts* (Miss Ruth in bright colors on the magazine cover). She expanded on her notion that artists are of two types, the inspired leader and the student follower;

that the truly great artist is a blend of both, combining natural talent or inspiration that characterizes the leader with the learning and discipline expected of the student-follower. The schools of Denishawn sought to turn out students boasting that kind of inspiration-and-discipline combination.

For the benefit of the magazine's readers, she made a homespun comparison of her dance philosophy with needlework. Like George Balanchine's later comparing choreography to cooking, or Merce Cunningham's of choreography to directing traffic, St. Denis's was meant to de-mystify, a tad anyway, the modern dancer's performance intentions. Declaring that one can develop genius just as one can perfect technique, she told her interviewer:

> All of this applies quite naturally to needlework as a form of art. Perfect your technique through following the patterns of others, but, having once perfected that technique, try creating your own design…. And if you are the type which plans and suggests, and executes day after day for a big family, turn to your needlework for stability, quiet, and comfort. Follow the directions of another for a while. In this way you will achieve balance.

The interviewer added:

> Miss St. Denis, to my mind, is one of the few highly artistic people in the world, in whom these attributes of creative genius and student technician meet and blend…. She has carried on her interpretive dancing alone, with her husband, Ted Shawn, and with the Denishawn dancers to a point as yet to be achieved by any other American dancer of her generation. In her keen and brilliant vision, KWANNON, the Chinese goddess, in white jade purity on her inlaid pedestal, becomes a living figure, moving in a stately and gracious dance where every motion is a true revelation of the Goddess of Mercy.

In 1938, Ruth St. Denis was invited to initiate a dance department at Adelphi College. Calling herself "artist-in residence" at Adelphi, she founded a dance program that continues today. In 1950, she wrote (with respect to an envisaged project on "Divine Dance"): "Today, as 'artist-in-residence' at Adelphi College, I not only have the opportunity to teach my classes the beginnings of their spiritually rhythmic education, but also to continue to inquire and explore vast new areas of bodily expression of the divine self."

Denishawn was not of course the only force to move from dance studios to campuses. Other factors, that have been extensively researched, included new emphasis on physical fitness, growth of university physical education departments, greater attention to the needs of women undergraduates, and increasing debates about the role of the arts in the curriculum. Here and there apologists for 20th century educational innovations, enlisting "progressives" like John Dewey, advocated a campus place for the dance. A landmark date in the story of modern dance's becoming a subgrowth patch in American higher education is 1926–1927, when Margaret H'Doubler, a dedicated alumna of pioneering Teachers College of Columbia University, founded the first dance major at the University of Wisconsin.

We can't but notice how female was modern dance not only during Denishawn's lifetime but beyond to mid-century. Martha Graham's company, for example, had no male dancers until the late 1930s, and there were precious few elsewhere until post-WWII. Modern dance, as often said, began and developed as a *matriarchy*, and its entry on the college scene reflected that fact. There were male spokespersons for the art's place in a liberal arts curriculum, but women, far outnumbering men as advocates and participants, effected that place for it. Even today, although the picture is considerably more integrated, the female *presence* in modern dance, on and off campus, dominates.

A Letter

New York
Feb '01

My dear Mrs. C.—

Thank you for the note received at the Club when I arrived, and apologies for this necessarily hasty response.

Tell your friend Vanessa that I'm not—absolutely not!—trying to push your daughter Vita or Vanessa's son (is it George?) into dance when they start at Wesleyan in the Fall. I'm only trying to be helpful, after you told me those kids were already gravitating towards dance, and you and Vanessa (through you) asked me if I thought this is a disaster in the making.

What I sent you, about the beginnings of modern dance, is meant simply to show how dance made an interesting and respectable entry into our culture including higher education, so after all, the kids aren't heading towards some sin-pit. The dance has some real standing these days on campus although, I admit, it always needs more, lots more support as it did in the beginnings. I have some more to write to you about that.

Stay warm! Too many cold drafts in my room here. Incidentally, are Virginia's windows up or down? Open, cold or not, the view is better, you know.

Salvos to you—wherever you are,
GEM

Dance on Campus

A Yale University freshman, I'm told, entering in 1999 could not take a course in drawing because its various sections were over-enrolled, so she settled for a course in Sanskrit instead. If my information is correct, drawing is listed in the Yale catalogue in the course distribution division that includes sociology. Given the interminable debates about the proper place, if any, of the arts in a liberal arts curriculum, does drawing at Yale token progress or not?

Charles W. Eliot, Harvard's legendary president, regretted in 1915 that although "the training of the senses" should be a primary objective in higher education, that has not happened, because generally "young men admitted to American colleges can neither draw nor sing and they possess no other skill of eye, ear, or hand." Nor, of course, the rest of the body and its skills required for interpretive dancing. As historian Frederick Rudolph observes, under these circumstances "the career of the fine arts in the course of study would be slow, halting, and ambiguous." Whether to hang some pictures might be the earliest sign of interest, but when Bowdoin College's president died, leaving his art collection to the college, the vexing issue was not where to hang them, certainly not whether to teach art, but "what to do with a copy of Titian's 'Danae and the Golden Shower' as well as someone's 'Nymphs Bathing'." To protect its students, the college sold the pictures in 1850.

Due to various factors, including increasing philanthropic support and university rivalries, the arts gradually scaled more ivied walls—so that, for example, Wesleyan University had a music department in 1925, art history the following year. Yale offered art history in 1938. Arts courses oriented towards history, fashions/manners, and taste/appreciation were more easily accommodated to traditional liberal arts curricula than studio or pre-professional "creative" sculpture, painting, film, drama, and dance. These seemed "vocational" and even today it is not unusual to see English rather than theater departments stage Shakespeare or French departments produce Ionesco.

Curricular innovations are typically "obedient" responses to popular pressures, from the student clientele and supported by key faculty, administrators, or patrons. Although the first film major was offered as early as 1932 at the University of Southern California, it took the "trauma" of the 1960s and the saturation of the culture by Hollywood and television to make it campus-prominent. By 1971, forty-seven colleges had offered a degree in film, and since then it has expanded astonishingly at both graduate and undergraduate levels—and in filmmaking as well as on theory and criticism.

Dance faced even more daunting obstacles in knocking on campus doors. Tradition had excluded it from the "fine" arts or the company of literature, visual arts, and drama. Teenagers aiming at careers in tap, musical comedy, ballet, or modern dance applied not to Bryn Mawr or Swarthmore but to conservatories and professional studios. As noted earlier, dance was established in 1926 at the University of Wisconsin, and twenty-two years later it was given for credit at ninety-two colleges. But its relationship to the curriculum was shaky, so often was it shunted off to a gym or campus corner, nurtured best by physical education departments. Some thirty years ago, about 110 colleges/universities offered a dance major, and 77 of these were located in physical education departments.

Physical education leaders never tired of preaching "Sound mind, sound body," citing in support such as Plato, Locke, Jefferson, and Nietzsche. And this helped to diminish the resistance to growing the seditious patch of modern dance in academic groves. Seditious? Really? Yes, if it is seen, as it so often was, as a recreational distraction, taking the student's eyes off the serious targets, the arts and sciences that are supposed to prepare you for successful careers. And even if you allow women their romps, how in our culture can you do the same for men?

This was Ted Shawn's challenge in the early 1930s, teaching in the physical education department at Springfield College, following the disbanding of Denishawn schools. His touring experiences with all-male dancers convinced him that, despite the on-tour financial reversals due to the Depression, audiences could be cultivated for male dancing. "Though I, the first American man to make the art of dancing his life-work, had made good, there was still a prevailing prejudice against dancing for men," and to the extent that this prejudice has been dented, Shawn deserves a big slice of the credit.

Prior efforts at Springfield College had failed, like those of the coach of their famous gym team to teach his athletes a Spanish dance called *La Senorita* and a football dance to mazurka music, so Shawn's first maneuver was to surprise the athletes with basic dance exercises more strenuous than those for football, wrestling, and basketball. Slyly, he had them doing *pas de basques* and *pas de bourrées* "which they would have resisted had they known the proper names and usual milieu of the movements." These were worked into dances like rowing a boat, using a two-man saw, scything a field, and "I used simple Negro spirituals for music that the students loved, since every man has a deep religious feeling which seeks expression." Subsequently,

Shawn presented (a "first") a two-hour all-male performance in Boston that received a "rave" review by the influential critic of the Boston *Transcript.*

Shawn's most famous and durable choreography for his Men Dancers was *Kinetic Molpai,* created in 1935 and periodically revived, notably in 1972 by the Alvin Ailey American Dance Theater at New York's City Center.

The title comes from the Greek *molpe,* meaning the ancient Greek harvest celebration when the men "threshed the grain with their feet and when they danced their thanks for nature's largesse." The dance, according to his program notes, was an exploration of Love, Strife, Death and "that which is beyond Death."

Whether or not the audiences always got the concept, what they saw in the performances of *Kinetic Molpai* was strikingly athletic, dancing by men "bare-chested in belted trousers," virile enough to silence accusations of "sissiness" or effeminacy. Much of the movement was a back-and-forth interplay between eight men as chorus and Shawn as leader whose expressive gestures connect in successive sections with Love, Strife, and Death, and at the vigorous celebratory ending "all kneel to the leader, who stands at the center of their file." The physicality of the piece is presented through tossing of men from one group to another, individuals performing whirling spins, high leaps, and extended leg balances. The critic Don McDonagh, also quoted above, writes: "The piece was very popular, and the gesture of arced parallel arms over the head became a personal trademark for Shawn, and drawings of him in this pose turned up regularly on his programs."

Life's seemingly unavoidable paradoxical marriages of the sacred and profane, the tragic and comic, majestic and ridiculous, popped up in Shawn's dances, mixing his philosophical religiosity with commercial show-biz tactics. Like Isadora Duncan, he sincerely wanted concert dancing to represent the "natural" in body and movement, so nudity on stage despite its controversiality ought to be encouraged. But this "exhibitionistic" proclivity plus the faux-Spanish, faux-Indian, etc. sets, costumes, and steps of his Spanish flamencos and his popular *Cosmic Dance of Siva,* choreographed during a tour of India, looked like pure kitsch to his critics. Shawn's description of *Allegresse,* a "sort of bacchanale" loved by audiences on a long Follies tour, illustrates the show-biz side of his otherwise ministerial philosophy of dance:

> Its ensemble group included six girls in extremely transparent violet chiffon; two girls in leopard-printed silk leotards; three men, including one, in the briefest of G strings; and Ernestine Day, swathed in an orange chiffon scarf over bare-skin fleshings. In the finale, lighted to look like a pagan fountain group, Ernestine, perched in a flower-ladened basket, was held high by the three men. That number wowed every Follies' audience.

Gerald E. Myers

Shawn's ability as producer and advocate of this new interpretive/modern dancing, with his charismatic personality, despite what many deplored as a lack of "taste," was an essential element in the art's growth on and off campuses. Careers for men and women began to open up. But the next generation of modern dancers, while extending Shawn's lofty concepts of the art, would tamp down his show-biz tricks and his body-beautiful displays. His body had come damned close, many thought, to outstripping his mind, and that had to be remedied—especially if those classics classrooms were not to be disrupted.

Body-Wrapping

Vince Lombardi, the famous coach of the Green Bay Packers professional football team, is reported, at the beginning of the season's schedule, to have lined up on the field his fearsome-looking players, all recruited for being the beefiest and most physically terrifying available, and, staring at them like a TV army sergeant, shouted: "O.K., men, from now on it's all *mental*!" Play well? Then *think* well. Gotta have the right attitude, the right mind-set!

"Wrap your body with the right mental stuff" applies to dancing, too. Audiences new to modern dance, finding it elusive, are helped by learning about its *mental wrap-around.* Because, in general, it is this that distinguishes modern theatrical dance, beginning with Duncan, St. Denis, and Shawn (and of course the others too many to treat here), from other dance styles. The individuality of the choreographer takes center stage in modern dance, so how that individual *thinks* her dancing, how she wraps a *conceptual* shawl around her shouldered movements, is essential to grasp in some degree—or the elusiveness takes over.

"All art is conceptual," a claim that I happen to associate with the artist Sol Lewitt, that others associate, say, with Marcel Duchamp who, looking back at his *Nude Descending a Staircase* and *The Bride Stripped Bare By Her Bachelors, Even,* wrote: "I wanted to go away from the physical aspect of paint-ing. I was much more interested in recreating ideas in painting…. I was interested in ideas—not merely in visual products. I wanted to put painting once again at the service of the mind."

Conceptualism returns us to the 19th century Hegelian aesthetics that was sustained by Benedetto Croce's writings, wherein the concept of the artwork is valued more than the physical object itself. However much you may want to side with Duchampian theorizing here, to downgrade art's physicality, you obviously can downgrade only so far, *somewhere* short of the artwork's total evaporation!

Accept conceptualism and you return to something else, the re-instatement of the artist/author and her intentions/ideas. For almost a half-century notions like the "intentional fallacy" and "death of the author" have been the fashionable ones. Formalist aesthetics, that accompanied tight textual analyses, typified not only by the New Criticism of the 1940s but by most literary criticism since then, also by advocates of abstract or non-representational art that lends itself to "art for art's sake" briefs, argues for the art-work's standing alone out there and, if such is even required, speaking on its own. At the very least, fashion had it, anything and everything said about an artwork must be found *within it* and nowhere else.

Since modern dancers everyday are still taking Isadora Duncan's risks, of seeking audience communications but typically with only their physicality showing, how does their art relate to conceptualism? Pretty closely, like kissing cousins, I think—provided that we insure a Duchampian reversal such that the valuing of the intentions and ideas "behind" the dancing results in *upgrading* its physicality. After all, who can gaze upon Duchamp's porcelain urinal signed "R. Mutt" and titled *Fountain* (1917) with less rather than more affection after "getting" its ironic conceptual fountainhead?

Dance critics, like the performers they critique, take risks, too, in guessing at what mentally or conceptually wraps around the dancing. Clive Barnes, for instance, once hesitated before Erick Hawkins's dance *Black Lake*, writing that it has "some effective dramatic moments…yet…gestures are heavy with meaning, and only the meaning seems light"; and that, despite Hawkins's known preference for seamless fluidity of movement, in this dance he is "less concerned with flow, and more with kinetic incident."

Without a good sense of its conceptual wrappings, a modern dance performance can indeed seem heavy with meaning but the meaning itself too light and floaty to be anchored by the critic's perception. Erick Hawkins, as choreographer and performer, appreciated the problem (although whether he solved it, we'll leave to the reader). Consider what he said about his dance *Naked Leopard* that was presented on the same program with *Black Lake*:

> I shall try to convey in words the pearl of great price in the awareness of the human body. It is the hardest thing in all of dance teaching to talk about, or to convey to a student. But it is quite exact. It is mysterious but not unknowable. [It]…is the sensation in the center of gravity of the body, the center of the structure of the skeleton, the center where the largest, strongest, truly integrating muscles lie—in the front.

And, for any reader who unsuspects the kind of intimate relationship that the dancer feels between anatomy and artistry, Hawkins adds this:

> Those of you who ever saw me dance my solo, "Naked Leopard," can perhaps recall the red felt rectangle shape which covered me…right at the place I have described as the center of the body. It was pure intuition, as I designed the costume, that led me to put the single important red area of color where my sensation of the body was centered.

...You may have seen a striking photo of me from the dance, at the end, where I am walking forward. The photo shows the *significance of this consciousness* and I have always been astonished that the photographer could catch it. (my italics)

You might have warmed to the sight of Hawkins striding forward at the end of *Naked Leopard*, but he would have you believe that, had you watched with his *concept* of it in mind, your temperature would have happily risen reliably higher. I think he would have us believe, too, that for conventional academic readings of dances, his red patch of a costume was of a truly seditious nature.

A Letter

My Dear Mrs. Calabash:

Yes, I realize that the stuff about *conceptualism* might confuse you, but give it more thought, and maybe it'll come clearer. But you are dead-right, about how dancers—like your daughter, you say, and Vanessa's son—are so much into the body, always moving and exercising, etc.

What brings those young people to modern dance classes? Who knows? I don't certainly, except to say that it is not some one thing, like Freud's "narcissism"—or any other "ism." But you're right, any explanation remotely correct must focus on *physical stimulation*, the body's impulses. I've collected, below, what some students at a private New England liberal arts college, also at a Midwestern public university, maybe some 15 or 20 years ago, wrote about it. You and Vanessa, it occurred to me, might be interested. I've also indicated which statements were made by male students, the others all female. So take a look!

> "The human body is a marvelous instrument and can be made to do incredible things. Now in dance class I'm beginning to think of myself as two beings, body and mind. The body becomes an instrument in creating what my mind has conceived. I guess what I'm developing is an ability to look at myself objectively."

> "I love the feeling of being able to close my eyes and move as the sensations produced by the music occur. I also love the feelings of closeness that I get from the group. Although I only know a few people, I feel very close with everyone—as if we have all shared a very special experience and in a sense I think that we have. And I look forward to expanding concepts of movements and their meanings."

> "Using the body in the physical discipline of dance has strengthened and 'grounded' me tremendously, so that I am now more capable of actually

materializing many of the lofty thoughts about healing and service which I've been speaking of for so long. Grounding is where it's at."

"I am a poet. Am eager to experiment with the spontaneous image. The image that the body can create (not to mention my sore muscles at the point). To support my idea, I am using the Chinese written character, William Carlos Williams, and Ezra Pound."

"Being a visual person, I really like to wear leotards to see, or least be aware of my limbs. My stockings don't have feet, so with slippers on, there is a nice pattern, a negative and positive that make me aware of my feet (they are 6 feet away!). Also, with leotards, I become a silhouette. A 2 dimensional *visual* image…a very funny image!"

"As a fine arts major, my interest in this course is mainly to become more aware of my own body and the way I subtly may be communicating to others through it. I appreciate all art forms and wish to understand more fully the dance in its relation to time, energy, space, movement, and our society."

"I'm a pre-architecture student. My curriculum includes mind bogglers like Physics, Statistics, Computer Science and Urban Planning. Dancing allows me to release my anxieties which I get from these other courses. I guess I just love dancing." (male)

"I've hit upon one of the motivational aspects of my enjoyment of dance. In my lower back, I experience discomfort, pain, and tension, extreme tension. Throughout the dance class when I'll stretch and work on isolation of my movements, and a large part of my thought will work towards clearing my whole spine, emphasizing my neck and lower back. I usually reach a point where I have relaxed the tension. The satisfaction involved in the final relaxed state and in the working process towards that goal is fantastic. A large part of my vocabulary of movements stems from my lower back out." (male)

Thoughtful statements, don't you think, Mrs. C.? They get into the body and its movement, all right, but they also get a lot of complexity out of it, too. See what I mean by dance's *mindfulness*, remembering *that* is also a bodily thing.

As always, wherever you are—
GEM

A Letter

New London
March '01

Dear Mrs. C.—

Thanks for the response! Glad you liked those student quotes, thought you'd be interested. Did Vanessa look at them?

Yes, you're right, these were all liberal arts undergraduates, and pre-professional or professional dance students might express themselves differently, maybe more matter-of-factly. But, in general, I don't think there's all that much difference. Get them thinking about it, and most dancers can get pretty profound, sorting out their motivations, feelings towards body and movement, etc.

Don't be surprised to hear them, if encouraged, exploring how dancing helps self-discovery, other person-discovery, non-verbal communication, and so on. Or as one of the samples I sent you shows, there is the communal or "together-ness" element. Reading it, I recalled a middle-aged woman on Long Island who told me that, living alone day after day, she sometimes made a point of lightly touching the arms of the check-out clerks at the supermarket, just to feel once again some human contact. Maybe, Mrs. C., *bonding* is more intense in dance than in any other art.

The communal nature of dance has caught the attention of the eminent American historian, William H. McNeill who contends, in his recent *Keeping Together in Time; Dance and Drill in Human History*, that shared rhythmic movement in dance and military drill has always been a powerful cohesive community force. He says, "keeping together in time arouses warm emotions of collective solidarity and erases personal frustrations as words, by themselves, cannot do." Maybe you should take a look at McNeill's book.

You know the name, Joe Klein? He wrote *Primary Colors* (about Bill Clinton, presidential campaign), is a hard-nosed journalist, at *Newsweek* I think. By accident, perhaps three or four years ago, I saw him on C-Span and referring to McNeill's book as being relevant to our times, when societal "fragmentation" increases. Klein later surfaced again recommending McNeill's book in *The New Yorker*, September 27, 1999.

Incidentally, do Roger and Clive still talk? And here's to opened windows for you-know-who!

Regards, wherever you are,
GEM

P.S. I'm continuing my story for you, next installment maybe next week.

Body-Democratization

As the modern dance patch crept from its plantings in physical education departments into the intellectual groves of academia, its mental wrap-arounds became ever more apparent. The college campus differs of course from a Los Angeles professional ballet studio or a Boston conservatory; on campus it can be expected that the young dancer's wit, imagination, book-learning, and attitude count as much if not more than god-given physique. A "democratization" of the body, abandonment of the "ideal" figure, is one of the modern dance's notable achievements. Evaluations of the dancer's body departed from those common in ballet, as is illustrated by this taken almost at random, by Theophile Gautier in writing about the famous Fanny Elssler:

> [She] is tall, supple, and well-formed...delicate wrists and slim ankles...legs elegant and well-turned...knee-caps are well defined...the whole knee beyond reproach...

> [She] has rounded and well-shaped arms, which do not reveal the bone of the elbow.... Her bosom is full, a rarity among dancers.... Neither can one see moving on her back those two bony triangles which resemble the roots of a torn-off wing.

> As to the shapes of her head, we must admit...not as graceful as it is said to be...superb hair [but]...the dark shade of her hair clashes in too southern a manner with her typically German features; it is not the right hair for such a head and body...her eyes, very black, are inconsistent with the nose, which, like the forehead, is quite German.

"All bodies welcome!", however, is the modern dance chant, especially from its bases on campuses, as well downtown urban lofts and off off off—you name it—performance spaces. The "plumpness" of Isadora Duncan and other deviations from a so-called norm—short, lean, squat, tall, angular, round, etc.—on the bodies of early modern dancers, continue to be represented in such contemporary companies as Paul Taylor's, Bill T. Jones's, and Jawole Zollar's *Urban Bush Women*. The widening of the kinds of bodies admitted to dance in turn produced a broadening of the mental dimensions that can be attributed to those bodies.

An important but mostly forgotten woman who straddled the educational and professional dance worlds was Bird Larson, who met an untimely death in 1927, the same year as Isadora Duncan's. Larson first taught in Barnard College's physical education department, also corrective gymnastics at Columbia's Teachers College, then for professional dancers at New York City's Henry Street Playhouse. Her students included notables like Anna Sokolow, Franziska Boas, and Esther Junger. Larson developed a training system that took students from natural movements through gymnastics to expressive/musical dancing. Prior to Ted Shawn and Ruth St. Denis, she composed religious dance rituals for Manhattan's St. Mark's Church.

A notebook (undated but probably about 1925) by one of her female students (who later became a leader in American physical education) reveals the "thoughtful" character of Larson's daily studio classes. Working from rhythmic exercises, the student wrote "she gave us ¾—(1) We walked it (no music) thought of some ¾ and changed on our direction with phrases of what we're thinking. (2) Then we walked note pattern of ¾ *in our minds* note values by feet and phrases by change of direction" (my italics). This hints at what dancers mean by calling themselves "thinking bodies." Of course, being mentally alert or doing some thinking hardly distinguishes modern from ballet or other styles. Moreover, as one entry in the student's notebook indicates, Larson cautioned against too much thinking getting in the way.

In my freshman year at college, I was supposedly a fine baseball player but, one day having made an inexcusable error, the coach yelled, "Myers, your problem is you think too much." So non-dancers sympathize with Larson's warning or with the kind of disturbance, described in Heinrich Von Kleist's *Puppet Theatre*, that self-consciousness can produce in motor behavior. When it comes to moving your body from here to there, neatly, when and how to think and when and how not to, is a very practical issue and one that dancers learn to resolve in very practical ways. The Larson notebook indicates how the student's initial thinking about how to execute certain movements was to be gradually replaced by automatic performances. The students rehearsed "forward and backward flexions of the spine," "on side flexions," and "rotation" with the "extremities" (legs and arms) simply following. These notebook entries confirm what was once written about Bird Larson: "The forward flowing movement from the base of the spine, the changing movement center in the torso, the pelvic rotations seen in modern dance, were independently by her, without distortion."

Bird Larson told her students two other things that illuminate not only hers but other dancers' view of where the "thoughtful" fits into their physical exercises and performances—keeping in mind that modern dance's habitual objective is "entertainment-plus" or something "more" than mere diversion.

An entry in the notebook reads, "Must have a working Philosophy of Life—which will help you each day. *Arrive at something*. This day isn't the day, nor tomorrow—It's *accumulation* of days that counts. Your average that counts." Larson meant, I take it, that the concert dancer needs a philosophy or background thoughtfulness that guides her use of rhythm, dynamics, and dramatics. It is not a constant, conscious analytical process that is required, rather a back-of-the-mind grasp of why one is dancing at all, or why, say, one is dancing with Merce Cunningham rather than David Parsons, with Trisha Brown rather than Sally Silvers. For the choreographer even more than the performer, this background of thoughtfulness, as our story continues to suggest, plays a conspicuously significant role.

Secondly, Larson warned against the banality of dance movements that merely illustrate ideas, of permitting ideas priority over movements. For instance, "If [you] do not give movement first then when the idea of being oppressed (given first) then the person will lift *all in one piece* or will be inhibited and won't want to do it at all—*movement first then idea*." I take from the rough notebook entries the view that the best ideas in dance *emerge from* prior movement impulses, patterns, or improvisations. Weak choreography, as Larson cautioned, often shows as a fragile set of steps/gestures that are top-heavy with ideas but that remain mostly invisible in the choreographer's mind.

A landmark and better remembered figure in early educational dance was Margaret H'Doubler, a friend of Bird Larson, who began in physical education and, from 1917 to the 1960s, taught at the University of Wisconsin. There, in 1927, she established the first university dance major, so that her influence is hard to overestimate. One of her students was the distinguished Anna Halprin who says:

> Of course she was always interested in movement as an expressive medium for communication and was never interested in style and patterns of movement… when you learn patterned movement, you're so involved in learning the pattern that the tendency is simply to cut off the feeling aspect.… I'm not referring to a kind of free-style self-expression. I mean just the feeling that's inherent when you clench your fist in anger, or stamp your foot, or jump in exhilaration.… And when you become aware of the movement and the feeling it's evoking, you begin to have the freedom to use it consciously and excitingly, and that's when you begin to become an artist in your material.

Years after her college days, Halprin paid tribute to H'Doubler: "I still feel I'm her student and I'm still learning." H'Doubler's dance philosophy, reflecting the transition of modern dance from physical education to its own artistry, focused on the notion of art as *organic unity*. This was a lively idea at the time, in 1940 when she was writing about dance as a creative artistic experience, borrowing prestige from "progressive educational" thinkers like John Dewey and his still-influential *Art as Experience* (1934). "Wherever there is life," H'Doubler wrote, "there is an organic tendency to form," implying that human gravitation towards formal unities is a biological, evolutionary product.

This gave H'Doubler a philosophical/scientific basis for her analyses of dance that emphasize its intellectual implications and thus its credentials for admission to the university curriculum. Seen evolutionally, dance is at first mostly sensory, its pleasure being the sensation of moving, so here training and thought are irrelevant. "Little by little the evolving self outgrows this stage.... *The mind's need for order* begins to assert itself and must be gratified. And so we enter the second stage." Movement then becomes more disciplined, more thoughtful, more expressive of mood and ideas. In this second stage, she wrote, "Dance is growing up."

Then, as dance moves yet to a third stage, "mind becomes intellect," developing the capacity to select and articulate meanings. "In this stage the dancer organizes his movement in order to give his meaning form." The mature dance artist takes the sensory movement sensations of the first, plus the disciplined movement training of the second stage, and formally integrates them into an organic art work where each element aesthetically dovetails with the others. These three stages, for H'Doubler, are not necessarily discrete and successive but in Hegelian fashion may be synchronous, and "the problem of creative dance teaching" is one of stimulating the student to appreciate how these three stages exist with each leaving its traces during the "upward" progression through all three. Here, then, is an example of how apologists for the "democratization" of the dancing body also costumed it theoretically—and so persuasively that it began to look, increasingly, like American higher education's youthful, adopted art.

A Letter

New London
March '01

Mrs. C:

This afternoon I was weeding in the garden, and a friend of ours, knowledge-able about gardening and dance, stopped by. She's been gravely ill, in her sixties somewhere, but is astonishingly alert, bright, and curious—infec-tiously so. Trimly attractive, black Italian hair tied high, she looked down at me, weedily occupied, laughing when I replied "Writing on modern dance" to her "What are you doing besides weeding these days?"

"Gerry!" she exclaimed, looking very sharply at me, "You know what to say about Martha Graham, don't you?" I answered "Sure! I'm starting with contrac-tion-and-release, as you'd expect." She targeted me with an even more acute gaze. "What are you gonna say about it?", and when I hesitated with "Well…," she burst "Naw! You, you males, don't begin to know what it's all about!"

She struck a really impressive posture, then planted both hands on her pelvis, followed by some equally impressive rapid thrusts. "It's about female orgasm, Gerry, that's what Martha Graham was all about. You saw it in class, in performance. She was telling the world—'This, my friends, is what my dancing is telling you about.'"

I stayed silent, so she continued "Then you know what happened? José Limón took the orgasm and the pelvic contractions and release—up into the chest area! That's what happened to it in male dancers' hands. So what do you think of that?"

Gosh! I had to confess, that having never thought of Graham and Limón in quite that manner, I was more than a little excited by her hypothesis. She laughed—loudly—repeated the pelvic demonstration, bent over and plucked a couple of weeds, advised me how to improve on my way of doing it, and went on her way, seemingly very happy.

Her name? Joan. I think you'd be taken with Joan, Mrs. C., now and then, I mean.

That garden conversation reminded me of something I'd once read, in a 1930 (October) issue of *The Dance: Magazine of Stage and Screen.* It was this in the publisher's "To the Readers of the Dance Magazine": "Some dance halls of today are cloaking the oldest of professions under the guise of the oldest of arts. An investigation of such conditions is under way for future detailed discussion in these pages. This racket merits merciless exposure, and the decent dance halls which still exist must be set apart."

Maybe it alls hangs together somehow, Mrs. C., maybe that's what Joan is getting at, too. Graham and Limón were cleaning things up—of course, each in his/her own way—de-cloaking dance's thrust and setting those decent dance halls—really apart?

Just another tidbit, a crumpet for tomorrow's tea.

Good night, Mrs. Calabash, wherever you are,
GEM

Martha Graham

1926—what we know as the 20th century was barreling out of the station that year. The China Civil War was erupting, Stalin was beginning his power base in Russia, Goebbels led the Berlin Nazi Party, and Hirohito became Japan's Emperor. Erwin Schrodinger and Max Born were developing quantum mechanics, John L. Baird demonstrated his television, and Enrico Fermi's techniques for predicting subatomic particles were formulated. Fritz Lang made his influential German science fiction film *Metropolis*, Ernest Hemingway published *The Sun Also Rises*.

The Gershwins' musical *Oh, Kay!* opened on Broadway with Gertrude Lawrence singing "Someone to Watch Over Me." A. A. Milne created Winnie-the-Pooh. Bobby Jones won both the British and U.S. Open, Gene Tunney upset Jack Dempsey for the world heavyweight title, and Helen Wills Moody dominated women's tennis. Theodor H. Van de Velde, in his *Ideal Marriage; Its Physiology and Technique,* candidly described sexual activity "suggesting a focus on foreplay and simultaneous orgasm, a shift in sexual attitudes." And after a court battle, Constantin Brancusi's sculpture *Bird in Space* was admitted to the United States "as an art work rather than as a taxable, otherwise unidentifiable imported chunk of metal."

It was also the year that Martha Graham debuted with her own program, assisted by three young women dancers, at Manhattan's Forty-Eight Street Theater. She presented eighteen short pieces, some derived from her Denishawn years and some strikingly original, to musical scores by such as Franck, Schubert, Brahms, Debussy, Scriabin, Ravel, Satie—and her pianist/accompanist/composer/mentor/lover, Louis Horst. No money at hand, she could do this only because the managers of the Greenwich Village Follies, for whom she had performed for two years, leased her a theater at cost, and because a woman friend (who had never seen her dance) pawned her sole valuable, a jade necklace, worth $1,000 for the cause.

Thus began a modern dance career, as usual on a shoe-, or in this instance, a necklace-string, and arguably the most celebrated and mythical of all concert dance careers. Working until her death in 1991 at age 96, having choreographed some 200 dances, Graham fascinated her watchers with how her "genius" and "fanatical theatrical need" fed each other. She subordinated her life to art, Louis Horst once remarked, while for others like himself it was the reverse.

The Graham story has been many times told, how she was born in 1894, into a Pennsylvania middle-class family, her father a physician/psychiatrist whose Scotch-Irish grandfather came to America and founded Pittsburgh's first bank. Her mother's pedigree apparently included Miles Standish and *Mayflower* pilgrims, and as practicing Presbyterians, the Grahams shied from "frivolities" like dancing.

The family moved to California when Martha was fourteen, where she saw Ruth St. Denis perform in Los Angeles, decided "then and there" (as seems to happen with many dancers) upon dance as her future. After graduating in 1916 from a non-traditional arts-oriented college called the Cumnock School of Expression, she was accepted at the new Denishawn School in Los Angeles. For several years she was a Denishawn dancer, leaving in 1923 to join *The Greenwich Village Follies*, performing musical comedies for which the Denishawn vaudeville touring had prepared her. When she left the Follies to make her choreographic/performing debut in 1926, she began what many have called the "true" beginnings of modern dance.

Graham's choreography and dancing were hugely *controversial*, a seeming hallmark of most if not all modern dance. Her obeying as it were Ezra Pound's injunction "to make it new," and via an astonishing intensity of purpose and performance, resulted in lots of attention. A diminutive (5'4" and slender) but striking figure, both on and off stage, she was not considered in her Denishawn years to approach the beauty or romanticism of Isadora Duncan and Ruth St. Denis. Not strangely perhaps, because the kinds of movements that she chose for herself were percussive and jerky rather than serene, conspicuous torso contractions and releases rather than flowing lines, laborious fallings to the floor and risings from it instead of the held verticality in ballet—hence unattractive for many audiences.

Martha Graham recalled, years later in 1968, how a woman came backstage and upbraided her for deserting the glorious days of Ruth St. Denis. "You have destroyed all the beauty you were raised in.... When will you stop?" Martha replied, "Not as long as they come to see me. I was dancing anguish, torment, and hysterical gaiety. That was new to her, and unpleasant." Graham told how, on a Southern States tour, she was performing her famous *Lamentation* (1933), a few-minute solo on a bench (on a small stage in an exclusive women's club), where swaying and manipulating an encasing fabric costume she became the very picture of agonizing grief. But then "one little old lady got out of her chair and walked straight down the aisle. She put her hands on the platform and looked at me. Then she turned around and walked out. Well, it took a little bit of trouping to finish the dance...."

Interestingly, *Lamentation* that is often revived as a landmark modern dance work was a favorite of Louis Horst's, Graham's closest advisor. For him, it was her "dance of sorrow" or "the personification of grief itself." The dance's power came from its eye-catching choreographic/theatrical originality and Graham's own high-intensity performance of it. Compared to most dancing including Denishawn showbiz styles, one might join puzzled audience members in asking of it, given its cloaked and bench-locked writhings, "Is it really dance?" But, of course, once a thing is offered and daring you to ask, "Is it really art?," "Is it really poetry?," "Is it really dance?," you can pretty safely predict its making an aesthetic and cultural splash.

A Letter

New York
April '01

Dear Mrs. C.—

Got your note at the Club, thanks! And glad you like my diggings in that
notebook of a Bird Larson student. Am especially pleased that daughter Vita
tuned in on that—any reaction from neighbor and neighborly (I hope!)
George?

These musings on Graham that I'm sending you take us into the heart of
our subject, so I truly hope they hold your attention. They bring back so
many memories for me, having seen Graham dance over all those years. But
frustrating, too, 'cause in those days I never contemplated writing now what
I am for you, and too many recollections are fragmented, making me rely
on others' first-hand observations. Of course, wife Martha is an indispensable
resource.

Back in The City makes for recall, too. Yesterday I walked by the Apthorp
apartment building at Broadway and 79th, where we lived in the late Sixties.
Tanaquil Le Clercq, once married to Balanchine but tragically paralyzed
with polio, also lived there, and we used to see Balanchine, Graham, and
others coming to visit her.

Maybe I'll write you again before finishing the Martha Graham jottings,
I don't know. Meanwhile, stay warm, it's a cold wind out there, all around.

Best to you—wherever you are.
GEM

Gerald E. Myers

The Stage is Graham's

Martha Graham and modern dance became virtually synonymous from the late 1920s through the 1950s, because she and her dancers grew the art like no one else. Opportunities for training and performance expanded and so did dance careers. It was *hard*, however, little or no funding, living in those walk-up cold water flats, rehearsing nearly everyday, but some years with very few theater performances. It was for many dancers more a lifestyle than a performance career. Better (though never great) times, from their check-books' perspective, were still in the future, especially in the mid-Sixties with the establishment of the National Endowment for the Arts and its stimulating other funding sources.

The dedication of Graham and her dancers was phenomenal, not only to the daily rigorous physical training—of lifts, plies, jumps, back falls, etc.—but also to a dance philosophy that was authentic-from-the-heart, so non-commercially uncompromising as to be potentially if not actually downright unpopular. Graham as performer, mentor, teacher, and advocate could be "fearsome," a woman more adept at seething than soothing. Her example was infectious.

A legendary dancer in her own right, Sophie Maslow (who danced with Graham from 1931 until 1944) observed:

> I studied at a time when we chose the way we wanted to dance. No one earned a living dancing, aside from a few dancers in Broadway shows.... It was not a question of what jobs were available.... It was a matter of what was right for dance. We didn't want to be embarrassed by being in poor productions. It was better not to work....
>
> But in Martha's works, not only was the movement important to me, but her philosophy as well. She seemed to feel the pulse of the time—the anger, sharpness, aggression in life at that time—things that were part of our lives, and she seemed to be able to put those things into an art form and communicate them.

Dear Mrs. Calabash:

I want to interrupt—forgive me!—first for a word about the Martha Graham personality. Paul Taylor, I think, once described her as a whole theater on two little legs when she approached you.

You could be forgiven, I want to tell you, if in the presence of Graham you felt a novel insecurity. Have you ever had your looking-at stared back-at, by lidded eyes that wait to see you?

Somehow, this seems to me not unconnected with the rise of modern dance in the 1930s. But that's as far as I can go with it here.

Yours, wherever you are—

GEM

Other factors, in addition to Graham, of course contributed to dance's growth. John Martin, for years the most influential critic and modern dance advocate in his columns for *The New York Times*, wrote on May 27, 1928, that this was the most significant year thus far in the history of dancing in America. There were important ballet productions, including the premiere in Washington, D.C. of Stravinsky's *Apollon Musagète* with choreography by Adolph Bohm (after which Stravinsky offered the score to Diaghilev, who assigned the ballet to Balanchine), debut performances by "moderns" such as Doris Humphrey, Helen Tamiris, Charles Weidman, Hans Wiener (later know as Jan Veen), and La Meri. Although incomplete, the list indicates how Graham's as well as dance's stature was enhanced by the sheer amount of dancing taking place. Why? Well, there is a saying in the antiques business that the more shops on the block the better; the cluster attracts more customers and, consequently, distinctive or better quality wares have a better chance of being recognized.

Other developments in the Thirties, especially the success of Lincoln Kirstein in bringing George Balanchine to America to establish what would eventually become the New York City Ballet, plus what Hollywood and Broadway offered, gave dance a more expansive public face. The 1930s also witnessed an increasing American pride in its own cultural achievements exemplified in dance by separate proclamations from Martha Graham and Lincoln Kirstein, that modern dance and ballet would no longer merely echo foreign models. Graham's choreographies, accordingly, such as *Primitive Mysteries, American Provincials, Chronicle, Frontier, American Lyric,* and *American Document* focus on American themes. Each of these can be analyzed for its American subject and style, but even after such analyses, questions remain about how they show themselves to be "American."

A distinguished critic, Deborah Jowitt, has written that, paradoxically, although Graham is called an originator of *American* modern dance, she actually composed few thematically-American works, developing her movement vocabulary from her own motor impulses plus what she had absorbed from other cultures. Graham's way of "borrowing," Jowitt notes, is laudable because her creations provide "an object lesson in the uses of the past, for her style has never looked eclectic, has never looked anything but authentic and wildly original."

Graham herself acknowledged the difficulty of identifying what is "American" about her dances. Her words in an interview:

> It is hard to define the American characteristic. It is less easily recognized than the Spanish. My dances are not easily recognized as American from my costumes because we have no traditional costume. It must be recognized as American either through the subject matter or through a tempo, rhythm, and attitude towards space which is peculiar to America and, while not so quickly recognized, is unlike any other country on earth.

> I have occasionally used woodwinds, brass, and percussion as best suited to the expression of the American idiom. America has a characteristically percussive beat, a rhythmic interplay rather than a richness of melodic line. To some people this music may sound strident, to others it may be refreshingly free from a heavy accent on the rhapsodic quality.

Years later, in 1961, Graham stated in another interview what, despite her reservations about the name, "modern dance" meant to her. "Modern dance isn't anything except one thing in my mind: the freedom of women in America—whether it is Isadora Duncan or Ruth St. Denis or Clara Barton. It comes in as a moment of emancipation." Putting aside specific themes of such dances as *Frontier* and *Appalachian Spring* (1944), I guess that she stated here not only what "modern dance" meant to her but also what, in its overarching sense, its being "American" meant; i.e., women's emancipation!

Responses to Graham's dancing, on her departure from Denishawn, were mixed, as were John Martin's *New York Times* reviews of her performances in 1928, "She is far more eloquent...when...lyrical rather than when she is dramatic...when her primary concern is decorative she achieves the happiest results" (February 13, 1928). Such comments must startle anyone acquainted with Graham's lifetime dedication to dramatic choreography and opposition to merely decorative dancing, notably exemplified in her later works based on Greek myths. But later that same year, Martin praised her for revealing an improved projection of the "*inner mood*...in her newer dances she has deliberately sought out ugliness and clothed it with deep and satisfying beauty" (my italics). Here, in 1928, Martin pinpointed modern dance characteristics that have sustained its rewarding controversiality.

Graham's solos at the time were also social/psychological comments, bearing such titles as *Petulance, Remorse, Strike, Dance of Death, Tragedy*, and they reflected her transition from Denishawn folk/character dancing to something more like German Expressionism. She said, "I was through with character dancing. I wanted to begin, not with characters, or ideas, but with movement.... I wanted significant movement. So I started with the simplest—walking, running, skipping, leaping—and went on from there. By correcting what looked false, I soon began creating. I did not want it to be beautiful or fluid. I wanted it to be fraught with inner meaning, with excitement and surge. I wanted to lose the facile quality."

Points here, apparently, to be noticed: Begin with movements, improvise with them, and discover what ways of moving seem "true" for you. Start on your own body and then go on to ensemble choreography. Discover further how the truth connects with your deeper feelings and what they suggest for ideas and inner meanings, how these can be expressed by your favored ways of moving. This is a "hard-work," not a facile process, so the result of performed dance deserves to show the effort required, as it also deserves to show the "dark" or "ugly" as well as the prettier sides of the things that you choose to express.

Certainly, not all of Graham's works were of an Adams Family variety. From the beginning she experimented with the full range of the art, from the lyric to comic and light-hearted as well as to the heavier and dramatic. Yet, she will always be remembered for her "long woolens" (costumes) dancing of the 1920s, as she acknowledged in 1941 while preparing her audiences with more "color, warmth, and entertainment values" in her premiere of her *Letter to the World* piece based on Emily Dickinson's life that came across impressively—but not without its grimness.

So, with its abandonment of Denishawn showbiz and beautiful movements, instead often equating artistic success with audience unpopularity in the old avant-garde spirit, Grahamesque modern dance invited jokes and criticism, often harsh. Michel Fokine, the legendary Russian-born choreographer immensely influential in the development of the 20th century ballet, clashed in public forum with Graham in 1931, saying to her, "You must admit this modern dance is ugly," to which she replied, "Yes it is, if you're living in 1890." Fokine is also credited with this as a summary of the new modern dance: "Ugly girl makes ugly movements onstage while ugly mother tells ugly brother to make ugly sounds on drum."

Revelation of self and self-nourishing convictions, instead of beauty and other standard audience gratification, still motivate many a modern dancer (if not most), so, the jokes, puzzlement, and recrimination continue—along with the admiration, fascination, and interpretation. A scent of this airs in A.L. Kennedy's prominently noticed novel *Original Bliss*. A mature couple, beginning an affair during a visit to Germany, go at the man's urging to a modern dance concert in a small unpretentious auditorium. He tells his companion, "But it *will* be modern dance. It always helps me think. I have no idea why and not the vaguest desire to find out." The dancers, he adds, are from Finland and he expects their dancing to be a distraction. "And it really will help my mind to clear. I use it a lot."

The couple—Edmund and Helen—watched "while a huddle of slender young women circled each other out from the wings and stood. They shuddered as a mass. They stood…all of the dancers tugged at the lengths of muslin which had been keeping them more or less wrapped. The cue for their closing blackout was apparently the unveiling of the final pair of breasts." Helen and Edmund left before its conclusion, using the performance for testing-each-other banter. It was bad dance, Edmund declared, but "That's what I love about bad dance, it's utterly, utterly meaningless and wonderful to think against," while "checking her [Helen's] face to see…what she would agree with, trying too hard." But she puzzled and amused him, responding, "But on interesting themes," and they continued, at the dance's expense, their mutual probings.

Mrs. C.—

Another interruption! No time yet to digest the preparations for a separate letter…

See if you can get hold of a copy of Kennedy's book. She's a Scottish novelist and attracting attention these days, and take my word, she's an Original. Blissful, I can't say…

I find her Helen and Edmund episode interesting enough to pass on to you, because—this will sure sound strange to you—I see that fictional couple as a kind of mirror-image of the dance performance as they saw it. They're in a tugging dance of their own, fraught with confusion, uncertainty, and contradictions, maybe eventually unveiling themselves to each other. But more relevantly, they remind us of many a concert dance audience whose fascination with the art (good or bad) is intertwined with their puzzled response to it.

You see, Mrs. C., in its presence, modern dance audience members often collide with themselves, become question-marks to themselves, and why it should have this effect—whether on Fokine or Helen and Edmund—leaves one wondering, endlessly intrigued! But, there again, that's what the "cutting edge" of any art is like—right?

Forgive the interruption, or do you like it this way? Let's make it soon—from you or me, either way.

GEM

Louis, Too

The strongest, burliest advocate of modern dance could not by sheer brawn *partner* it out of the gym into the fine arts building, nor could the most eloquent of Demosthenes's students just soap-box it into that prestigious campus edifice. Since Martha Graham's dance theater, building on but departing from what Isadora and Denishawn had done for the educational role of dance, was especially influential in ushering modern dance into American university life, beyond the confines of the gym or field house, we may infer that she helped the cause neither by physical technique alone nor solely by lecturing/preaching.

Graham's dance theater had an "intellectual" tone that distinguished it from its predecessors. This was due in substantial part to Louis Horst, who had joined Denishawn as a musician after various West Coast jobs as a pianist, often in wrong-side-of-the-tracks venues, and who left Denishawn with Graham to become her devoted mentor and lover. His influence as Graham's composer, accompanist, conductor, and all-around intellectual advisor, until their separation in the late 1940s, was widely recognized, and Graham was among those acknowledging his influence after his death in 1964 at age 80. Horst as Graham's compatriot was a major force not only in her career but also in modern dance's. He can be partially credited for the art's movement towards greater discipline, intellectual as well as physical.

The Foreword to Louis Horst's *Pre-Classic Dance Forms* begins with this:

> ...it is generally recognized that America's dancing began with little regard for the formal aspects of the art. Little in the dancing of Isadora Duncan can be credited to conscious structure. Her dance composition was an emotional delivery, sensuous rather than sensible.... The Denishawn School, though completely divorced from the romanticisms of Isadora, was no less influenced by the [French] impressionist and symbolist currents. Formal design in dance composition did not come to the fore until 1926, 27, 28, with the appearance of Martha Graham, Doris Humphrey and Charles Weidman as soloists on the American dance scene.

When asked, in the late 1940s, to summarize his contribution to modern dance theory and practice, Horst said, "A consciousness of the importance of *form*, and a *survey of the textures and influences in all of the modern arts*, and the *relations of these to modern dance*, specifically" (my italics). This was his basic reiterated pedagogical message to legions of students who took his legendary courses in pre-classic dance forms and in modern dance forms (both represented in short books, *Pre-Classic Dance Forms* (1953) and *Modern Dance Forms in Relation to the Other Modern Arts* (1961, rev. ed. 1987). The pre-classics course, as the Foreword's author notes, "developed a sense for dance form among the young aspiring choreographers; it developed a restraint in dance compositions, an *intellectual approach* to the creation of dance—and still does" (my italics). In the second course that looked at modern dance's relations to the other arts, he said things like: "To compose is not an inspirational experience. Composition is based on only two things: a conception of a theme and the manipulation of that theme." And, opposing the romantics and intuitionists, he cited, for example, the artist Paul Klee's declaring "One must know a great deal and be able to do a great deal, while creating the impression of its being innate, instinctive."

Horst and Graham were well aware of the "modernist" trends in the arts— cubism, constructivism, expressionism, formalism, etc.—that gave, they thought, their dance predecessors an outdated look. The Bauhaus's Gropius in architecture, Duchamp, Picasso, and Klee in painting, Scriabin and Schoenberg in music, or Eliot, Pound, and Gertrude Stein in literature— these and numerous others represented the 20th century search for new forms. Form was the key word in Horst's aesthetic, in his concept of the most effective music-dance relationship.

Dance and music, he always held, are truly independent arts, but as musicians can learn from dancers in collaborations, so dancers can learn from musicians and their theory/practice. Too much dance, Louis taught, is only "musical visualization" and is drowned by the music, whereas in "pretty pictorial dances" the music gets lost. As a beginning, dance students should study pre-classic musical forms like the pavane, sarabande, minuet, etc. for learning how they may use music as accompaniment, and as a model for giving ample form to their movement inventions.

An important new feature of Graham's dances was drawing upon original or commissioned scores, including Louis Horst's. In addition to himself, Louis and Martha favored composers like Villa-Lobos, Henry Cowell, George Antheil, Paul Nordoff, and Norman Lloyd. Insisting on a carefully delineated relation between the choreography and the score, and mostly eschewing musical styles ranging from jazz to symphonic, Horst was a stern disciplinarian in the Graham school classes. Preferring simplicity in dance music and a formal match of this in the choreography, he contributed to Graham's so-called "stark" or "spartan" dancing.

Louis forced students to inhibit spontaneity and intuition, settling for "what feels good," in making dances, and to stop in their tracks and analyze what they were doing, a process that many found frustrating to the point of tears. They were encouraged to come with their own motivations and ideas, but he demanded disciplined, formal translations of these into physical steps/gestures. However wonderful the aspiring choreographer's intentions might be, these still needed the right formal *embodiments*, and achieving this requires *thinking* along with intuition or inspiration.

Horst's aesthetic, with its prescriptions and taboos about music and dance compositions, whether instructing an ABA or sonata pattern or to avoid jazz and operatic accompaniment, inevitably seemed arbitrary and authoritarian, leading to rebellions such as were mounted by John Cage and Merce Cunningham in the 1940s and after, and that are nowadays commonplace. Compared to the austerity of Louis's aesthetics, contemporary approaches both to choreography and musical accompaniment are anarchic. As for the choice of form in modern dance today, pretty much anything goes! So, of course, don't be surprised when you hear pendulum watchers grumble, "It's time to bring Louis back"; meaning that artistic creation always involves breaking rules, and what may be needed today are something like Louis's rules to rebel against.

Whatever one concludes about the merits or otherwise of Louis's doctrines, one must acknowledge his nudging modern dance closer to academic study or intellectual involvement. The questions—How have dance and music related historically? How in our rapidly changing culture do and should they relate today?—connect the analytically-minded dancer with longer looks at music, theater, literature, painting, etc., past and present. And the Louis-Martha collaboration raised, as not before, the question, What is Modern Dance?, and in so doing gave the art a revolutionary intellectual thrust.

Graham-based Thoughts on Dance

Martha Graham made regular "takes" on the culture around her, was responsive to the other arts, and read widely. Her interest in Jung's psychology, in his theory of cultural archetypes and collective unconscious, has been noticed, because in her literary or dramatic works she meant her characters to be archetypal rather than specific, and the emotions expressed to be universal (their "essence" distilled), not idiosyncratic. But she constantly warned against "literary" readings of her dances, urging audiences to heed less the literary background and more the dancing itself. What to think of this?

John Martin muddies the waters further for us when writing about Graham in the mid-Forties.

> It is useless to look for objective theory in a style as completely personal, as completely outside the realm of the intellectual.... Graham has become one of the most potent in the entire world of the dance, yet she has done so without establishing any systems, any generalities of procedure, that are applicable to art as a whole or to its continuity of development. Her greatness is in an almost unique sense her own.

Whether this verdict rang truer in the Forties is perhaps a fair question, but that it has been disproved since, through the endurance of the Graham School and Technique as well as her choreographic repertoire, is beyond dispute. But what about Martin's flat denial of "intellectuality" in her works? Again, I confess my concern on the issue, because too often the career of modern dance is detoured by seeming determinedly anti-intellectual. Some years ago, when Lynne Cheney was chairing the National Endowment for the Humanities, she asked us if the rise of illiteracy in America and the recent dance "explosion" were causally related, a question she was led to ask after reading an article in an influential publication that suggested such a relation. The charge of anti-intellectualism only gets in dance's way, promoting an image of school drop-outs who never read or allow their heads a thorny thought. If we can justifiably enlist Martha Graham and others as anti anti-intellectualism, that should help the art's cause on campus and consequently elsewhere where it counts.

Louis Horst liked the dance theorizing of Susanne Langer, distinguished philosopher and author of several important books, including *Philosophy in a New Key* (1942) and *Feeling and Form* (1953) that echoed ideas of German thinkers like Friedrich Schiller and Ernst Cassirer. Langer frequented the American Dance Festival at Connecticut College before it moved to the Duke University facilities in 1978, and her ideas on dance were partly due to this association, to conversations, for example, with Pauline Koner, leading member of the José Limón's company. The bulk of her thinking, however, was taken from her intimate acquaintance with music, in tandem with philosophy.

Langer's theory was based on the notion that what the arts present are illusory or imaginative, and dance, too, is best described as a "virtual" thing that features virtual or illusory interactions of "powers or forces" that are produced for the viewer by the dancing on stage. Although choosing to bypass scrutiny of this, I share Horst's appreciation of her bringing dance into the intellectual arena. But I regret that, when I knew Horst (due to my wife Martha's ongoing acquaintance after studying with him), we never explored Langer's theory together. We touched on dance philosophies now and then but, both being New York Yankees fans, I fear our talks were more on baseball.

Permitting dance an intellectual pedestal remedies the ancient failure to admit it to the realm of the *fine* arts, so far as Western tradition goes anyway; Eastern and non-European traditions are another matter, insofar as they perceived dance and music to permeate their cultures so intimately that calling them "*un*-fine" would be as offensive as startling. Another philosopher, to be commended for acquainting himself with dance towards correcting its intellectual neglect, is Canadian Francis Sparshott. He writes about dance's exclusion from the system of *fine arts* as they were conceived in the 18th century:

> At its center were the "sister arts" of poetry and painting, representing to eye and ear respectively "beautiful nature," the ideal reality of which the perceptible world is a blurred copy. Painting is institutionally as well as theoretically inseparable from drawing, as drawing is from sculpture and architecture, and invokes an underlying geometric order. Poetry is institutionally inseparable from music and drama, and invokes an underlying algebraic order. That is the developed system of the fine arts, and there is no place in it for dance.

Despite the efforts, since 18th century theorizing about the fine arts, to give dance its deserved place, the struggle continues even as it wins now and then on campuses such as New York University, Ohio State University, University of Michigan, University of California at Irvine, among others. "We're at the bottom of the totem pole!", dancers and dance teachers complain as they seek funds, jobs, and performance outlets, whether on campus or in urban professional settings.

Why has dance been excluded from the fine arts, ranked along with landscape gardening in Hegel's 18th century classification? Numerous answers have been offered, but one factor stands out. Our Western intellectual tradition extends the Greek or Platonic subordination of body to mind into medieval and modern ideologies. In Thomistic philosophy, for example (whose influencees include James Joyce), the arts that are from the human body, attuned to the eyes and ears as "distant" receptors, such as music, painting, and poetry are allegedly less bodily involved, thus *fine*. Dance's handicap is its physicality, with its non-verbal "silence" often equated with intellectual emptiness.

Whatever John Martin meant by his seeing an absence of intellectuality in Graham's dancing, I think the art's cause is better helped by insisting instead on the intellectual richness of its physicality, of the interpretive possibilities to which the physical movements of dance are susceptible. And this, we've maintained, is one of modern dance's major contributions. Duncan, Denishawn, and others encouraged such insistence, on what is to be learned, not only narrowly about dance but more widely "life and the human condition" from learning to think more originally, imaginatively about the human body, its movements, and their occasions for inspiring unsuspected insights.

Agnes De Mille, impressed by Graham's new way of thinking about the physical aspect of dancing, illustrates what I call its intellectual richness, its invitation to interpretation. She wrote in the 1950s:

> In ballet movement, the arms and legs are used as separate revolving members on a steady spine. Ballet is largely a series of poses, linked with the lightest and most flowing movement; it strives always to conceal effort. Graham's novel approach was in thinking of dance as movement. This was also the core of the von Laban-Wigman school but Graham had never seen them. Graham thought that effort was important since, in fact, effort is life, and that the use of the ground was vital rather than the escape from it. And because effort starts from the nerve-centers, it follows that a technique developed from percussive impulses that flowed through the body and the length of the arms and legs, as motion is sent through a whip, would have enormous vitality. These impulses she called "contractions." She also evolved suspensions and falls, utilizing the thigh and knee as a hinge on which to raise and lower the body to the floor, thus incorporating for the first time the ground into gesture proper.

De Mille's was only one voice in the international choir singing Graham's praise as innovating "probably the greatest addition to dance vocabulary made this century," as seeing to it that the core of choreography and concert dancing is movement itself. What De Mille praised Graham for was exactly what years before John Martin, and being very intellectual about it, praised as modern dance's distinctive contribution; i.e., discovering distinctive move-ment as the very *substance* of dance:

> Previously movement was only incidental. In the classic dance what counted primarily was poses, attitudes, and prescribed combinations of them. The movement that united them was unimportant.... In the romantic develop-ments [Fokine in the Russian Imperial Ballet, Isadora Duncan and Denishawn in modern dance's beginnings] it was the emotional idea that was the centre of interest. This was conveyed largely by means of the music.... Movement resulted, of course, but it was not seen as the material out of which the dance was to be made.

Although it may seem like thumping the obvious to stress, with DeMille and Martin, that movement is the core/substance of concert dancing, you realize upon seeing dances consisting of isolated steps and gestures that the ongoing *flow* of Graham's movements makes for another kind of artistry. Moreover, compared to predecessors, her dancing was "abstract" because it was neither pantomimic nor (usually) representational/realistic. And insofar as it was, she said, inner moods (or the "graph of the heart," "landscape of the soul," slice of life, etc.) that were what her dances expressed, they could be called, like the paintings, say, of Pollock and Rothko, examples of *abstract expressionism.*

Of course, when you make the substance of your dance an ongoing flow of unrealistic, unfamiliar, or abstract movements, you elevate the communi-cation risks of Duncan and St. Denis to new highs. John Martin, for one, claimed to be unworried about this in the early Thirties. Impatient with the layman asking, "What, please, does all that movement mean?," Martin replied, "My dear man, if I could tell you what it means, there would be no need for so-and-so to dance it. He might much more easily write it to you."

This kind of answer to the poor layman has been popularized throughout the arts, but, although its bite is appreciated, I believe its abruptness, its own crypticness harms rather than helps the art. Overly simple and facile, it needs considerably more filling-out. Another response is just to deny there being a problem at all, "nothing puzzling here." A Graham press book of the 1930s took that tack: "Many dancers go out of their way to be esoteric, mysterious, and to cultivate something of a cult but not Martha Graham. There is no hidden meaning, no surrealistic implication in any of her dances. She believes in the simplicity of movement. Movement so simple that it can speak a language directly to the spectator." The hyperbolic "spin" of this has to convulse the many who know about the Graham cult that did ensue and the haze of meanings that hovered interpretively over her dances.

John Martin, again, saw few audience issues with modern dance's abstract expressionism: "This does not make dancing singularly remote or esoteric. No art can be described, explained. Dancing has its effects on the spectator by means of very simple processes.... If the movements are not representational, what happens?... Through kinesthetic sympathy you respond to the impulse of the dancer which has expressed itself by means of a series of movements."

Martin used the term "metakinesis" for the process by which, he argued, the dancer's movements transfer their intentions to the comprehending perceptions of the spectators in their theater seats. He apparently believed that this process is more or less instinctive, a part of ancient tribal dancing, as a kind of "kinesthetic bonding" between dancers and audiences that endures to make even modern dance's unfamiliar movements comprehensible. "But," wrote Martin, "no conscious use was made of metakinesis until the modern dance arose."

Despite its partial aptness, I think Martin's "metakinesis" is too limited a concept for explaining dancer-audience connections, that the difficulties for successful connections are fiercer than he wanted to admit. Most concert dances are too complex—visually, aurally, kinesthetically, and conceptually—to be somehow "grasped" via an alleged kinesthetic receptor. For my part, what the Graham-Horst and modern dance aesthetic contributed, in its advocating abstracted movements for expressive and dramatic ends, was no "simplification" of things. Rather, they presented audiences with a new "problematic," one of *interpretation*. And this shoved the art in an intellectual direction.

No one exceeded Martha Graham in stimulating the interpretation of dance movements, in making these into a collective problematic—for the dance world and the rest of us to ponder. Graham's former dancers seem more interested in their recollections, in her movement inventions than in her ideas about the cast of characters in her repertoire. They tell how specific movements originated in dances, then retained in class exercises as "technique." Bessie Schönberg recalls: "In class, we did *calls*, a twist in the torso in a percussive movement that pulled one arm up as if to call someone to follow. They are circular movements, in part. The audience was supposed to finish the circle for themselves."

Graham's famous "contraction-and-release" principle is said to have occurred to her in the late 1920s, important also in freeing her from Denishawn habits to invent her own dance vocabulary. It came out of her discovery of how anatomical changes in one's body happen when alternately one breathes in and out, and of how these could be exploited expressively/

dramatically. That image—of Graham scooting across the stage, spasmodically contracting and releasing her torso, acting out an avalanche of emotions in the most eye-riveting ways—that image never fades away.

Sophie Maslow gives us another sample of what Graham's classes were like, of their physicality that led to so much interpreting of body and movement:

> *Turns* were learned in a sequence that includes a preparation, a half rotation or turn, and a full turn. The eyes do not "spot" as in turns in ballet, and the body moving from low to high positions forms the turn. The body begins in a tipped position parallel to the floor in *attitude* (one leg bent at the knee and raised to 90 degrees.) The force for the turn is a twist in the back—the spiral—that makes the body turn.
>
> The head floats around with the body, as do the arms. The arm opposite the lifted leg is raised, then the arms open to the side. From the *attitude* position, the pivot occurs when the body is raised and the lifted foot is placed on the floor. This movement can occur without a turn, as in a preparation, or in half- or full-turn series. The tempo is a slow four counts.

The centrality of the physical technique and the "problematic" of deciphering its sense when choreographically employed can be illustrated by any number of Graham's dances, but arbitrarily, we can take her 1947 *Night Journey* (to a score by William Schuman and sets by Isamu Noguchi) as an example. Based on the Oedipus and Jocasta myth, it was the third in what was called her Greek cycle of dances. Although I saw this work along with many others of hers, I wasn't watching intending to write about them, so my memories of Graham—swooping in low half-turns, percussively darting in alternating directions with tiny quick steps, hesitating with striking back falls—are untrustworthy guides, so I rely on the words of writers-at-the-time.

When the dance opens, we are supposed to know that Graham as Jocasta has just learned the awful truth, that she has married her son who had unintentionally murdered her husband/his father. Horrified, she runs with chest and shoulders contracted, head carried forward, and arms groping for some kind of support. We are to understand, as the dance proceeds, that she relives the series of events that seal her fate, her meeting Oedipus (of whose real identity of course she is ignorant), their courtship, their marriage, then the horror of the truth told by the Seer.

As was her practice, Graham depicted the myth's events abstractly or symbolically. Noguchi's props contributed to the effect, the steps gradually rising to the marriage bed that symbolize the stages in Oedipus's wooing of Jocasta. There is the Seer with his staff as the emblem of fate, the six-girl chorus of social censure, and the rope that joins Oedipus and Jocasta that in the end hangs her. Especially interesting is that, while much of the story's telling depends on these symbolic helpmates as well as prior acquaintance with the Greek legend, "her own dance movement," the critic Frances Herridge (whose description of *Night Journey* is relied upon here) wrote, "reveals her emotions in recalling the past. She sees Oedipus simultaneously as child and husband, as hero and murderer. His love-making now seems crude and defiling. She shows this in one instance by having him put his leg around her *shoulder*, his foot against her *breast*." Writing this, at the dance's New York City premiere, Herridge judged that, particularly in one section, the choreography succeeded in avoiding pantomime while achieving dramatic effect. When the curtain fell, the audience's applause broke slowly and "mounted to sincere bravoes. It was literally a stunning work."

Another critic, however, writing earlier at the Massachusetts world premiere of *Night Journey*, was less enthusiastic. Ruth Lloyd, too, liked Noguchi's decor, Schuman's score, and the costumes. Oedipus was an impressive sight in "unconventional scarlet shorts with diagonal straps across his bare torso," Jocasta in a "beige gown with scarlet touches in the bodice," the Seer "in a Greek-style robe of golden brown," and the girl chorus in black. But when we come to the "core-dancing" that is meant to express Jocasta's "graph of the heart" (inner moods), Lloyd wrote: "In little runs and darts of anguish, in small, vibratory motions and large extensions, Martha sought, *unavailingly*, to tell us of Jocasta's suffering. Only in the curious duet with Oedipus, insinuating in its contrasts between maternal affection and marital love, was the horror of the situation brought home" (my italics). But, to be noted, Lloyd acknowledged that when *Night Journey* was presented with changes at the 1948 Broadway season, it was "rumored" to have improved.

When the heart of the dance is non-pantomimic or abstract movement yet meant to be expressive/dramatic, the "problem of interpretation" is bound to arise, as it did for audiences facing *Night Journey*. Full appreciation of the problem led Balanchine to say dryly, in effect, that dance has enough difficulty in depicting a sisterly relationship, so forget sisters-in-law, etc. But Graham was undaunted, illustrated again by her most ambitious evening-length *Clytemnestra* of 1958. Interpretations and critical reviews were mixed, yet despite the robust audience-challenge, "the initial audience sat spell-bound through the unfolding of 'Clytemnestra.' But at the end of each stanza, the Graham devotees arose as one to cheer. It was an epochal occasion for modern dance fans. A new milestone in the development of this form."

The relationship between the Graham physical technique and its expressiveness retains its interest for the inquirer. Mindy Aloff, a few years ago, wrote about it:

Consider a single detail: the way the [Graham] dancers hold their heads.... The dancer's spine is a plumb line that seems to begin, as in classical ballet, at the base of the skull. When the face is lifted, exposing the throat ecstatically, the action is never an isolated physical event. It is invariably the result of some other change, occurring elsewhere in the body, that takes the spine momentarily off plumb: a contraction, a spiral turn, a back fall, a looping recovery. Whatever happens, the face remains composed. *To track the transitory emotions of the dance one seeks out the torso and limbs, whose motivating energy the movements of the head project.* (my italics)

The Graham-Horst legacy is memorable, complex, endlessly discussable. But what I think is not always appreciated, and is therefore trumpeted here, is its demonstrating how, like the other arts experimenting, its own medium of physical movement is "rich for interpretation." The capability of electrical dancing to stimulate thunderous differences in critical verdicts, debates in interpretation—of course, about context, decor, costumes, music, etc., but especially about the "movement-core" of a dance—placed it on a par with avant garde literature, music and the arts generally. No "problem of interpretation," no intellectual stimulation, no significant art! Martha Graham, we see, took care of that.

A Letter

————

New London
May '01

My Dear Mrs. Calabash:

Thanks! For your liking my Graham notes. Sorry for the late response, but I fell over my neighbor's dog. Not his fault, we were playing hide-and-seek. I was the one who got too frisky, skinned some parts, had some hide of my own to seek.

If you think my "story" thus far eases your worries about the kids trying out modern dance, just wait till you catch up with what's ahead. You will like Doris Humphrey—next—if I'm not mistaken. Her name never got out beyond the dance world like Graham's, but she's important! Some say that choreography as a discipline was born with her!

Oh, by the way, stop fretting about J.M., and *please!* maybe it was she, the ballerina, who married *down*. Would *you* want an economist, and with all that other stuff going on?

Kisses—*formal,* of course—to Vanessa!

Goodnight and take care, wherever you are,
GEM

Doris Humphrey

On little dancing feet, the art of modern dance continued to de-fog American intellectual awareness of itself, mainly on American campuses. In 1979, the dance critic and historian, Marcia Siegel, taught an entire course on Doris Humphrey at New York University's Graduate Dance Department, causing one awestruck student to ask, "You mean like a course in Milton?"

Doris Humphrey may never challenge Milton's ranking, but she is top-shelf in 20th century modern dance history. Alongside Martha Graham, Charles Weidman, Helen Tamiris, and the German expressionists like Mary Wigman and Hanya Holm (who settled, influentially, in the States), Humphrey was a leader of the 1930's concert dance movement. Born in a Chicago suburb in 1895 to middle class parents, she began her dance career in 1913, joining Denishawn in 1918, going on her own in the late 1920s, establishing a distinguished reputation as a choreographer, performer, teacher, mentor. Despite severe health problems, she sustained her choreographic and teaching career until her death in 1958.

The 1930s—world population approaching 2 billion, the Spanish Civil War, New York City's 102-storied Empire State building, the FDR political era, the great Depression, rural America still awaiting electrification, Hitler assuming power in Germany, Stalinist purges in Russia, John Lewis and founding the C.I.O., Italy annexes Ethiopia, Jesse Owens dominates Berlin Olympics, Picasso paints *Guernica*, Amelia Earhart and plane are lost, WWII approaches and with nuclear weapons. And a small band of dedicated non-commercial dancers, almost all women, move away from pageantry, showbiz, and scarf-waving towards stricter choreographic standards.

Doris Humphrey, like Martha Graham and Louis Horst, stressed the need for dance *theory*, about form and choreography, and this by itself took modern dance to a new intellectual level. It was in the 1930s that choreographic theory became an established modern dance ingredient. Why was this needed, and why did it happen then?

Humphrey answered that, because dance is so bodily physical, dancers mostly thinking in and with their muscles, the "person drawn to dance as a profession is notoriously unintellectual." Nor had theoretical hypothesizing about dance been encouraged.

Tradition had suffocated innovative thinking in the Italian and French schools of ballet until shaken up by the "modernism" of Duncan and St. Denis, as shown by Michel Fokine's revolt "against the stilted and artificial ways of the Russian Imperial Ballet and School. He declared that dancers should look like human beings, that technique should vary according to the theme, and that music and décor should correspond in style to the period chosen." But, in Humphrey's judgment, this beneficial reaction within ballet did not produce choreographic theory, and as modern dancers still relied, too comfortably, on intuitive inspiration, the needed thoughtful re-conceptions of where concert dance could effectively go were lacking.

Why did the need to be met begin in the 1930s? Humphrey's answer:

> It seems to me that the social upheaval of the first world cataclysm was, more than anything else, responsible for the emergence of a compositional theory. The shocks reached all the way down to the thoughtless lives of dancers, especially in America. Everything was re-evaluated in the light of the violence and the terrible disruption, and the dance was no exception.... In the United States and in Germany, dancers asked themselves some serious questions. "What am I dancing about?" "Is it worthy in the light of the kind of person I am and the kind of world I live in." "But if not, what other kind of dance shall there be, and how should it be organized?"

Humphrey recognized that the times required a new "thoughtfulness" of dancers, that they needed both a theory of movement and a theory of choreography for building on initial motivation and talent. Because of the art's growth in secondary and higher education, dancers teaching in the schools and colleges had to compose for student recitals, theater and musical collaborations, and this demanded training not only in physical technique but in dance-making (compositions). Humphrey understood how the majority of her own students would resist theorizing, asking silently if not aloud, "Why this? Come on, let's move!," but, deeming it her moral/educational duty, she persisted.

And her successes, we need quickly to add, while due in good measure to her teaching effectiveness, were mainly owing to her reputation, rivaling Graham's, as an artist/choreographer (and earlier as performer). She is remembered for creating landmark works from the 1920s to the 1950s that include *Air for the G String, The Shakers, New Dance, With My Red Fires, Passacaglia and Fugue in C Minor, Story of Mankind* and *Days on Earth*. In addition, she assisted and choreographed for her partner, Charles Weidman, also for the José Limón company. (If this were a comprehensive rather than highly selective history, Weidman as an influential, serious but also comic concert dancer, a rarity in itself, would receive the attention deserved). Conveying her choreographic theory/practice through such mentoring/coaching, both visibly and behind the scenes, she was an enormous force in moving younger dancers from "just dancing" to "thoughtful creating/performing."

It was in more detachedly analytical, spelled-out terms than Graham's that Humphrey formulated her theories of movement and choreography, that continue—because making explicit and conscious what for the talented dancers were often unconsciously inspired motivations—to be referred in current analyses of the art. Getting her dancers into thoughtful frames of mind, of developing conscious motivations in creating and performing, was a major objective. Dancers with fine physical technique, she said, are a dime a dozen. "For my taste, something must be added to make this display worthwhile, and that something is motivation."

Modern dance choreographies typically reflect the temperamental and physical personalities of their performers, and more often than not the choreography mirrors its maker's personal movement style. Dancers like Graham and Humphrey began as soloists, creating on their own bodies, and their choreographic choices reflected themselves even as these were more "objectified" through subsequent ensemble creations. As Graham's style has been labeled "contraction-and-release," Humphrey's is known as "fall-and-recovery." Margaret Lloyd on this:

> She [D.H.] had yet to find the way the human being moved when not pretending to be something or somebody else. To do this she must look to her own body. Conducting her research before a mirror, she found a physical expression of the essence of struggle at once. While seeming to stand still her body swayed ever so slightly, making minute motions just to maintain balance, letting go to see what would happen, she began to fall, more and more rapidly as she went down. In an involuntary effort to save herself she saw that the resultant movement made a design, and with the finish of the fall came an accent. The recovery brought a new design, with new accents.... This was a brand new point of view (or action), a motivation entirely different from that of any other dancer, modern or otherwise. It was a re-application of certain laws of physics to dance.

Like all literate dancers, it seems, Humphrey read the philosopher Friedrich Nietzsche, especially his *The Birth of Tragedy* where he proposes that great art like classical tragedy is born from the tension between the Dionysian principle of "intoxicated inspiration" and the Apollonian principle of "serene reason." Tension and balance, Nietzsche liked to declare, are required for life itself, and Humphrey saw an application for this to dance. Nietzsche wrote suggestively through aphorisms and epigrams, being tersely provocative rather than long-winded, a feature that artists generally have found congenial.

Humphrey, in tune with Nietzsche, described her fall-and-recovery thesis dramatically. It was, she said, "an arc between two deaths," meaning that at one movement end is a death, where total inactivity and no grappling with gravity exists, and at the other movement end is another death, where gravity totally conquers and all kinetic resistance is spent. Tension, opposition, resistance, balance, fall, and recovery are all essential for the "aliveness" of dancing. However one assesses this manner of thinking about physical movement's sensations and behaviors, that it offers dancers new motivational choices and postures/steps/gestures options is clear.

Humphrey was forced by severe arthritis to retire as a dancer in the mid 1940s although continuing her career as choreographer and teacher, so her own dancing has few eyewitnesses. What we seem to learn about it from those few observers and surviving films is that her style was natural, calm, confident, and rhythmic. Marcia Siegel finds that in a film of an early Humphrey dance she relies on a swing movement with its "release and recapture of weight," of runs, skips, sways and turns; and changing dynamics, alternating between movement acceleration and deceleration.

Some dance writers have contrasted Humphrey and Graham, emphasizing how Humphrey seemed "cooler" or less intense than Graham, more pragmatically concerned with design, dynamics, and rhythms than with Graham's dramatic expressiveness. José Limón said she "moved like a gazelle," and Agnes De Mille, while preferring Graham's personality-saturated dancing, acknowledged Humphrey's "smooth and facile," technically flawless style. Some have judged Humphrey to be the most astute craftsperson in modern dance, making well-crafted dances, with well-defined beginnings, middles, and endings, to music by Ravel, Bach, Milhaud, or to words and sounds without music.

All observers note the inevitable rivalry that separated Humphrey and Graham, and DeMille even suggests that the comparison giving the nod to Graham "broke her heart." Although seeing numerous performances of Humphrey's choreography, I never saw her dance. But because my wife Martha had studied with her and was a friend of two dancers, Lavinia Nielsen and Lucas Hoving, who were close to Humphrey, I was introduced one evening at her Manhattan apartment for a discussion of dance aesthetics.

That evening (around 1950, I think) afforded me the chance to tell her, for example, how much I liked her dances such as the *New Dance* trilogy and *Passacaglia.* She smiled and elaborated a bit on these and other of her works. It was a very pleasant occasion and, as a graduate philosophy student I much appreciated her taking time with me, especially since she clearly was a professional woman impatient with wasted moments.

We spent some time on the purpose of a dance, partly because, after a deliberate pause, she said firmly, "It's to communicate a personal emotion," and because I wanted to hear more on that. One could argue, I suggested, that her statement might resemble Tolstoy's aesthetic theory (sometimes called the "infection"-theory) that the artist's purpose is to infect (communicate) an audience with an intended specific emotion. But doesn't this open the possibility (however stretched) that a new drug, say, could produce that emotion, thus becoming an adequate substitute for the dance as the emotion-producer, and robbing the dance of its vaunted artistic autonomy?

She was sharp, acute, and analytical in our discussion, carefully listening and totally composed, true to her reputation as a formidably intelligent woman. My questions and "logic-chopping" were deftly, directly fielded, and she saw no real problems in my worries, on her view, about dances losing ground to drugs. She was more interested, and interested me, in what was happening then in modern dance, the trend towards "non-expressiveness" and dancing (movement) for its own sake. *This* did worry her!

I found Doris Humphrey reserved but gracious, a look-you-in-the-eye plain-spoken conversationalist, throughout open, courteous, and generous in granting me an audience. I never *really* talked with Graham, muttered words and side-glances more my style with her, I guess because my wife had been her student and the recipient one day of a famous Graham face-slap that was delivered when she thought you needed prodding. And those lidded eyes! I never found comfortable access, as I did with Humphrey, to Graham. But from what I've been told, "Who, after all, is not afraid of Martha Graham?" Or, by extension, of modern dance?

Gerald E. Myers

A Letter

New London
May '01

Dear Mrs. C—

Good! Real pleased that Doris Humphrey appeals to you. I've some more to go with her, so hope you continue liking.

So Vita and George are now asking, which colleges? I thought Wesleyan was in the bag, but minds change, especially the young ones. More suggestions? Ohio State might work, and Hollins in Virginia is a smaller place with a good dance program. Depends on where they want to be. But let me know if more suggestions are wanted.

Yes, Graham could be intimidating. I never knew what to say to her. Then, I assume because of Louis Horst's ongoing encouragement of my Martha, Graham maintained a certain curiosity about her. We were shocked when, on an award-receiving visit to ADF at Duke University in the early 1980s, she remarked from the stage that she was delighted to "be back," see old friends, including Martha Myers. We were startled, because there had been no meeting with her, and in the dark of evening how with her aged eyes she could have espied us defies explanation. But then, of course, *she* defies explanation.

Anyway, you egg me on, pleading for more "personal touches" in my historical jottings. I'll try…

Remember what your favorite philosopher always says—a thing is what it is, and not something else. Take care—

Goodnight! Wherever you are.
GEM

Thinking With Humphrey

A colleague teaching at a New England liberal arts college told me years ago about lecturing to a class of undergraduates on Hegel's philosophy, a notoriously difficult subject. A student, wide-eyed and waving his notebook, approached the lectern at the lecture's conclusion, exclaiming to my colleague: "Hey! I REALLY like Hegel!" "Why?" my friend asked, "Do you understand him?" "Well, I don't know about that, sir, but golly, how that man could think!"

When Doris Humphrey wrote *The Art of Making Dances* in 1958, just before her death (the book published posthumously), she wanted her dancers/readers to think—but pragmatically, not for its own sake. She wanted them to see how a dance is a *conceptual thing*, not simply a physical doing, in effect replying to W.B. Yeats that, yes, you can tell the dancer/performer from the well-crafted dance/choreography. You ought to think out a dance from its center to its corners, from its inception to its development to its conclusion. Your mind can grasp its overall configuration, as Mozart claimed to "hear" an entire concerto "all at once."

Efforts like Humphrey's go some way towards meeting the complaint from the other arts, particularly music and literature, that dance has no body of theory behind it. Erecting dance for conceptual analysis, as Humphrey did, incites intellectual interactions between dancers, other artists, critics, and theorists. It can boost dance's status by showing that theory is built into a dancer's training, that this involves more than, as one college president not long ago is reported to have said, "all that jumping and kicking their legs over there in the gym." Theory, however, that repays, has cash-value was Humphrey's concern; head-thoughts that help a young aspirant to put a dance together. Learning to make your movements manipulatable to and by your thoughts, that can be of great practical value, and an example relating to Humphrey comes to mind.

Years ago, in the 1950s, I became interested in the nature of metaphor, and surprisingly little beyond Aristotle, I.A. Richards, and a few other contemporaries was available on the subject. Since then, literature on the subject has blossomed extensively. "Metaphor" seems to have replaced "symbol" and "representation," and almost everything but especially art works, including dances and concertos, show up these days as metaphors for something or other.

Back then, one question I pondered is whether metaphor is exclusively verbal, solely a figure of speech (language). I put that question to the late Pauline Koner, a founding member of the José Limón company and Doris Humphrey associate and she unhesitatingly replied "Metaphor is not only verbal, it occurs in dance, too." She told me about once getting stuck in making a dance, finally asked for Doris's help—the account of which she has more recently described in her autobiography *Solitary Song*.

Koner's dance *The Visit*, of 1950, called for a sequence between her and Lucas Hoving depicting a conversation, but Koner foundered on how to indicate this without miming it, without being too literal. Humphrey rescued the situation by noting that in a conversation the speaker dominates, the listener is sub-dominant. "So," she said, "why don't you progress on a diagonal across the stage, the speaker/dancer walking/standing, the listener/dancer moving in a low crouch, both facing each other, and then intermittently reversing their roles so that one is up, the other down, and so on." This worked for Koner who writes: "It was the first time I understood how Doris analyzed a realistic situation, digging for the inner reactions, then stylizing these into movement. This was dance, not mime."

It worked for Koner because she had been led by Humphrey to think metaphorically, to think of how a conversation can be variously conceived, beyond what is commonplace and "all too familiar." The hit-upon movements, of Koner and Hoving crossing the stage on a diagonal with each other alternately dominant and sub-dominant positions, became a movement metaphor for an ongoing conversation. Metaphor is thus a dance strategy, not only a linguistic device, so my question was answered—case closed!

As my wife's notes taken in a Humphrey composition class indicate, she stressed the need for an original ("real-life") source for a stylized (non-mimetic, non-literal) movement or gesture that is meant to be emotionally expressive. "Abstracting from" or "stylizing" everyday behaviors had become a basic modern dance principle. Martha Graham's *Lamentation* of 1930 mentioned previously, where she writhes on a bench in an enveloping costume that sculpts her movements, exemplified the principle. The critic Anna Kisselgoff recently described it as "a purple-shrouded figure…an assemblage of planes…less a woman mourning than an abstract embodiment of grief; 'the thing itself' as Graham called it."

But, as Koner discovered, finding effective movement abstractions of real-life things can be frustrating, and Humphrey told her composition classes that they try, too often, to stylize or abstract before having an original basis for it. Her advice: "Go back to the original [e.g., shaking hands, bowing, trembling, etc.]. Do it naturally or realistically first. Analyze its dynamics, rhythm, weight, design, and its different meanings." As she put it in *The Art of Making Dances*, using work as her example, "to express the essence of work, the dance movement must contain certain characteristics which are embedded in the original action."

Humphrey's book sets out guidelines on props and sets, use of words and music in dance, dynamics (gradation in tension, speed, direction, etc.), rhythm, and form. Several chapters are given to design that contain engaging ideas about symmetry and asymmetry of movement, opposition and succession, movement phrasing, and use of stage space. Although she seems to have regarded her guidelines as objectively regulative, I doubt that any one of them has gone unchallenged. On the use of space for stage exits, for example, she held that, when we see Adam and Eve in José Limón's *Exiles* slowly exit downstage as they depart Paradise for a world of suffering, we identify with them personally "as our first ancestors. An upstage exit for these two would have made the whole thing seem mythical; we would not have had a sense of immediacy." Well, maybe so, maybe not. Still, the aspiring choreographer, whatever she makes of this Limón example, will agree with Humphrey's summary statement here: "The whole lesson to be learned here is that stage areas will support and enhance various conceptions, or they will negate them, and it is necessary for the choreographer to make *conscious choices*" (my italics).

Humphrey's emphasis on dance-endings was legendary, claiming that a good ending is forty percent of the dance's effect. Why? Because its last impression is the audience's strongest. She was in her aesthetics an Aristotelian, as we have said, advocate of the well-crafted dance with a defined beginning and middle—and a crafty ending. Today, in our so-called post-modern (or is it now post-postmodern?) era, when the well-crafted concept is largely scorned, "the good ending" rule gets dismissed. For my part, however, I tend to side with Humphrey here, thinking of how one of my favorite choreographers, Talley Beatty, a few times, disappoints with "weak" endings, that stutter or seem just dropped in, for a couple of his otherwise most exciting dances. No, all endings are not equal.

Speaking of Talley Beatty, the great African American performer/choreographer, I think it interesting to note that he shared with Humphrey a profound concern for group vs. individual relationships and dance representations of these. I mention this because of a longtime conviction that concert dance, of all the arts, can most effectively depict the more poignant, subtle aspects of individual isolation, group exclusion, harmonious togetherness. Even in upbeat "dancey" dances like Paul Taylor's *Esplanade*, for example, the undramatically presented aloneness of the remaining dancer downstage, watching her fellow-dancers exit, can tug at your heart. One of Humphrey's class assignments was to experiment with ways of relating a single figure to the group, for example depicting a lone individual making a political proclamation and the group's reaction. Much has been written about how Humphrey's own choreography reflected her concern for dignity and justice in group-individual interactions.

Doris Humphrey has been applauded here for making modern dance more of a "thinking person's" art, for giving it greater intellectual stature. But a couple of cautionary notes—*The Art of Making Dances* should be read not as a set of rules but as a remarkably provocative array of ideas about how to *conceive* and thus *perceive* dance movements. We can call hers a distinctive "philosophy" of dance, at the same time remembering her also stating, "You cannot philosophize in dance. This is for words...." And she always warned against the "over-intellectualizing" that accents what is more in the head than in the movement impulses; a balance of mind and muscle, as always, is the desideratum. No, you cannot philosophize in dance, but yes, and this she taught, you can philosophize about it, hence drawing to it the intellectual attention it deserves.

A Letter

Durham, NC
June '01

Dear Mrs. C.—

You're recovering? Nasty late-season flu everywhere, I know. Hoping my annual shots protect!

Am here, where ADF (you know, American Dance Festival) uses Duke University's facilities, is planning another project. Here is where I started, back in mid '80s, with ADF on The Black Tradition in Modern Dance programming. Remember—I sent you our publications, reports, etc. about what we did over the years—institutes, tours, panels/demonstrations, etc. Of course, the big culminating event is the national PBS/TV airing of our 3-hour film/TV production *Free to Dance*, evening of June 24th. Yes, I know, you'll have to miss it, but we'll get you a tape.

Anyway, working with the Black Tradition project was a great experience—I learned a-plenty of fascinating stuff, about African and Caribbean roots of African American dancing, the Plantation South, minstrelsy and vaudeville, on and on. As I told audiences while we toured coast-to-coast, the story of how African Americans contributed to modern dance's development is intellectually rich and exciting, also emotionally touching. It deserves a prominent place in college curricula. Our goal was to move towards that, to make both the dance world and the general public more aware of the (neglected) achievements by African American dance artists.

And how much I enjoyed all the black dancers, directors, presenters, scholars, critics, and others that were met. Too many to even try to mention—although I have to tell you about Joe Nash. He was my constant colleague for those some 15 years, touring the states and planning/talking in between, at ADF/NC or at home in New York. Joe had danced in the 1940s with Pearl Primus, Donald McKayle, in *Showboat* on Broadway. But, in addition, he became a self-taught dance historian after retiring from performing. He's a walking encyclopedia, especially about dancing by American Blacks, is regularly honored for what he has done for dance history, and I'll always remember how he and I shared a "humanities" interest in modern dance, in its aesthetic and cultural place in American society.

What I'm sending you next are jottings about that Black Tradition experience. You have to understand that, if I were composing a real or standard history, it would need a different look/approach. Each choreographer, for instance, would get a separate section. But I'm compacting it all for you not as a historian but as a participant in a very special project. It gives, I trust you'll agree with me, another kind of intellectual dimension/context to the story of modern dance.

Incidentally, if you should want—for yourself or the kids—deeper looks at Dunham, Primus, Ailey, McKayle and others—I can refer you to recent books by Richard Long, John Perpener, Jennifer Dunning, and Brenda Dixon Gottschild. Given time and health—and the right kind of encouragement (no hint, really)—who knows? Maybe I might try a longer, deeper look myself.

Good! I thought you'd like the Humphrey thoughts. But of course sorry as always about the inevitable omissions. Had to neglect two men of importance associated with Doris—Charles Weidman and José Limón. Weidman's contributions of comic touches to modern dance were special, also serious works like his *Lynchtown* in 1947. Limón, whose company continues nobly, is a landmark figure. His choreography, like *The Moor's Pavane* of 1949, *The Traitor* of 1954, and *Missa Brevis* of 1958 are classics. Sorry! Can't do it all, and no point in windy justifications. Arbitrariness always wins—don't you know?

Really hope you like the next stuff. Don't think for a moment that Clive and Roger will like it. But be sure to put it under the noses of Vanessa, Vita and George—after all, they're whom I'm, I mean we, are trying to reach—Yes?

Take care and recover, wherever you are,
GEM

Katherine Dunham and Pearl Primus

Women, as we have seen, set modern dance in motion, and women set Civil Rights in America in motion. Martin Luther King, Jr. and other men, as African American commentators have noted, joined in, when needed, what Black women had initiated. Racism in America prevented facile integration in the arts, including modern dance, so it too remained largely white and sadly out of bounds for most African Americans aspiring to the concert dance stage.

Two African American women—Katherine Dunham and Pearl Primus— in the late 1930s and especially in the early 1940s, began dismantling the "No Admission, All White" signs blocking the entrance of black dancers to modern dance studios and theaters. It is a complex, controversial history of why blacks were excluded, of what factors other than the prevailing national racism were responsible. One hesitates before pointing fingers at specific individuals or organizations and calling them bigoted, because we are reminded that "their times" were different from ours and, moreover, it is not so easy to get a confident reading of why and what they believed.

Nevertheless, among the regrets felt in looking back at pre-World War II dance in the United States is this: how unfortunate that observers and critics at the time were unable to recognize dancing by blacks as a part of the emerging experimental art form, modern dance. The tendency was to categorize such dancing as "Negro" or "ethnic," a compartment apart from the modern dance of Duncan, St. Denis, Shawn, Tamiris, Graham, and Humphrey. In 1940, the most influential critic, John Martin, enthusiastically reviewing Katherine Dunham's Broadway debut, predicted "a bright future for the development of a substantial Negro dance art," meaning in part that this special Negro or Black dance is "debonair and delightful, not to say daring and erotic…it is not designed to delve into philosophy or psychology but to externalize the impulses of a high-spirited rhythmic and gracious race." How (unintentionally) condescending this sounds to black artists, Martin likely never realized.

There was much at stake in how you were categorized as a dancer, for financial and moral support, for admission to desired companies, studios, and performance venues. So long as you bore the label "Negro," "Black," and "Ethnic," your chances of joining the new concert dance were dim. Your audiences would be expecting something from the traditions of vaudeville, burlesque, minstrelsy, and earthy down-home tomfoolery. Get acquainted with the story of how African Americans eventually won their struggle to be acknowledged as *genuine modern dancers*, and meet another civil rights episode, that happened, in the performing arts, before World War II and before the Sixties.

Katherine Dunham and Pearl Primus, as earlier versions of Rosa Parks but in the arts, altered the look, the vocabulary, and the context of concert dance. Don't underestimate the aesthetic challenge facing audiences where black bodies took the stage and moved not only in new ways but often in ways resembling ballet and the new modern of Graham and Humphrey. A different look, and as we discovered in our national touring with a black dance company, a look that some American audiences still need to adjust to, on the concert stage.

They expanded the modern dance vocabulary or inventory of steps, gestures, and movement patterns. This resulted from their use of researched "roots" in traditional African and Caribbean dancing and blending these with movements typical of ballet and modern dance—Dunham having her training in Chicago, Primus in New York City. The blended or "fused" products, from these different styles, required special training. Dancers had to learn how to isolate movements in different parts of the body, how to perform polyrhythmically, how to accent the body's weight, how to exploit rather than combat gravity as occurs, say, in attaining the desired lightness and verticality of ballet. And attitudes, hard to describe but embedded in this different movement idiom, have to be acquired.

When interpreting dances, subjecting them to critical and intellectual scrutiny, you generally need some knowledge of their context, "where they're coming from." The Dunham-Primus context clearly differed from St. Denis's and Graham's, including a whole cultural background that was African American as well as African and Caribbean. Its complexity increases when to the dance, dramatic and musical styles inherited from such a (largely misunderstood) cultural background are added the ingredients of ballet and modern dance. To be fair, we note that white critics, of course aware of their minimal acquaintance with the "African American context," were often understandably hesitant about that context's dances, hesitant to "intrude" into the "Other's" territory. But, over time, the fascinating richness of that different context would be researched and displayed for the enrichment of American arts and letters, including modern dance and its intellectualization/interpretation.

Katherine Dunham, born in 1909 to working parents in a Chicago suburb, took to dance (ballet and modern) and theater as a youngster. She was bright, energetic, beautiful, intellectually curious, proud of her brother Albert who became a philosophy professor and taught with Alain Locke at Howard University. (She and I had discussed the possibility of publishing certain writings by Albert, but neither she nor her associates had located them.) Studying anthropology at the University of Chicago, encouraged by her famous professor, Melville Herskovits, she researched dance/arts/culture in Jamaica, Martinique, Trinidad, Haiti, and Brazil.

The combined influence of Chicago-based ballet and modern styles, on the one-hand, and Martinique-based on the other, are reflected in an enduring creation of hers called *L'Ag'Ya* (1938). A vibrant theatrical piece, filled with Caribbean colors and costumes, it depicts male rivalry, through martial arts movements, for female attention. Other major works include *Rites de Passage* (1943) and *Shango* (1945), dances that adapted Afro-Caribbean puberty, fertility, and cult rituals. In 1950, looking more homeward, she choreographed *Southland*, of a "defiant" tone that focuses on the American South and its history of lynchings and related outrages.

An important ongoing Katherine Dunham legacy is the physical technique she put together. "She had to create a new dance technique that would encompass the many movements and uses of the body that did not exist in Western dance except in the social dances of African American people. She is often credited with singularly enlarging the movement vocabulary of modern dance more than any other choreographer. She is also likewise often credited with forming a basic technique of Broadway and Jazz Dance as we know it today."

The Katherine Dunham dance technique is the only African American dance technique that is established with an ongoing international following, predominantly in black populations that include America's many historically black colleges/universities. All or most dancers have some familiarity with the techniques associated with Martha Graham, Doris Humphrey, Lester Horton, José Limón, and Erick Hawkins, but for probably the majority of white dancers, apart from hearsay, the Dunham training is an unknown. Yet into her 90s, she continued to develop it at annual workshops at her headquarters in East St. Louis.

The Dunham Technique distinctively blends the isolated movements of different parts of the body, coordinating them polyrhythmically and often asymmetrically. It also features the "get-down" powerfully athletic quality of Afro-Caribbean dancing, mixed with modern and balletic influences. *Choros* (1943), for example, is a Brazilian quadrille that has four joyful dancers executing rapid balletic steps to a samba beat. Importantly, learning the technique is, like the creativity of choreography and performance, "a way of life," the reflection of an overarching philosophy that extends beyond aesthetics.

The body and its movements are the site "of it all," the place where mind, body, and spirit become one, where the physical and emotional become indistinguishable, and often where one's own identity is to some extent discovered/created. *That* is certainly where the Dunham dance aesthetic is anchored. She says, "Dunham Technique is more than just 'dance' as bodily executions. It is about movement, forms, love, hate, death, life and human emotions.... Dunham Technique, which has been called a way of life, is about life in the Universe."

Dunham will always be remembered for her theatricality, of full-theater dancing with eye-catching costumes, sets, and ear-catching music and drumming, whether on the concert stage, on Broadway in *Cabin in the Sky*, or in films such as *Stormy Weather*. Her theatrical flair was abundantly evident in the tribute to her in 1987 in New York City by the Alvin Ailey American Dance Theater as the *Magic of Katherine Dunham*.

The glamour and showbiz glitter of her productions, of her own striking attractiveness, are only a part of the legacy, for there are mind-catching qualities as well. Her dances are usually narrative, reminding of past rituals and their present relevance, often radiating the message that one's inner self is found or constructed through dancing that is historically and culturally informed. Her dances usually wear a mental wrap-around, and for understanding this as with most modern dance, audiences will need both more information and more viewing experience.

Because of her conviction that concert dance is much more than physical stepping, that it is the presentation of ideas-in-movement, she naturally emphasized the intellectual dimensions of dance, retaining her own associations with Southern Illinois University, choosing the title *Katherine Dunham Centers for the Arts and Humanities* for her East St. Louis headquarters. When John Houseman went to ADF in Durham, NC, in 1986 to present her with the prestigious Samuel H. Scripps American Dance Festival Award, he told stories about his acquaintance with her years before in Hollywood, including how Charlie Chaplin honored her in the last party that he gave before "exiling" himself from the United States. Hearing Houseman tell this, I thought that, as the sentiments of Chaplin's "little tramp" shone through his walks and prat-falls, so for Chaplin the range of Dunham's cultivated sensibility shone through her turns and jumps.

Which modern dancers, not seen, do you most wish that you had? Katherine Dunham certainly, but also her celebrated contemporary Pearl Primus. Given the many first-hand descriptions of her dancing that I've heard, also recollections by a few elderly New York City women accidentally met, plus attending recent re-stagings of her famous solos, I have some idea of what I missed. Missed in Primus was not the glamour of Dunham but rather sheer power, athletic and dramatic. Those who were there say her leaps were so strong and high that she literally "hovered" before landing, that her runs and lunges were panther-like, her swoops and turns like mini whirlwinds. Rumor has it that she once held (still does?) the female high jump record at Hunter College, where she graduated with a degree in medical science, later turning to dance as a career because of racist barriers for pursuing one in medicine.

Primus's dynamic, the dramatic personality behind the leaps and swoops, was *intense*. This intensity was for her, as it was for Martha Graham and others throughout modern dance history, essential to her dance aesthetic; the physical feat in and of itself matters little, but it matters enormously when manifesting inner attitude or spirit. In conversations I had with her during the late 1980s and early 1990s, she often criticized the tendency she perceived by contemporary dancers to settle, say, for a "bland" technique, high leg extensions and aerobic movement sequences, or women "heroically" lifting men, but all without any hint of personal motivation for the heroics.

Primus, ten years younger than Katherine Dunham, was born 1919 in Trinidad, then moved with family to New York City. After Hunter College, she began a dance career through a scholarship received in 1941 at New York's "rambunctious" New Dance Group. This was an important "downtown" modern dance organization in the 1940s that, in representing the radical and political left as well as immigrant and trade-union folks, furthered the course of modern dance as an art with a social conscience. Although Martha Graham, Doris Humphrey, and others were, by comparison, politically reserved, their dancers sometimes showed up as "activists" in the New Dance Group's productions. Two examples were Sophie Maslow and Anna Sokolow, both influential landmark figures in modern dance history who, alas, can only be mentioned here, that being all the cramped space these "jottings to you" will permit.

Pearl Primus, in gratefully accepting the support of "white moderns" like those at the New Dance Group, was an African American equally concerned with social issues. This took her, my dance friends say, on a long "personal journey" of which her dances represented lengthy stretches. In 1943, she created *Strange Fruit*, one of the most famous in dance history, portraying a lone woman's anguished reaction to witnessing a lynching of a black man. In Primus's mind, I'm told, the imagined woman could be black or white. A dance interpretation of Lewis Allen's poem, known by many through Billie Holiday's vocal version, *Strange Fruit* is a searing piece that ends with gestures and demeanor implying a defiant "We shall overcome!" even as the poem's words continue to haunt:

> Southern trees bear a strange fruit
> Blood on the leaves and blood at the root
> Black bodies swinging in the southern breeze
> Strange fruit hanging from the poplar trees...

That same year, 1943, she created three other outstanding solos. *The Negro Speaks of Rivers*, to a Langston Hughes poem, and inspired by the suffering of Negroes along the Mississippi, it is a meditation on how rivers have historically defined cultures. *Hard Times Blues*, to accompaniment by Josh White, is another "protest" dance, on the plight of Southern working blacks, that includes the blues and spirituals. *African Ceremonial*, based on a Belgian Congo fertility ritual that Primus (like Dunham, she was an anthropologist as well as dancer) had researched in pursuing anthropological dance studies in West Africa, represents Primus's fusing traditional with modern styles.

Subsequent to her African sojourns in the late 1940s and afterwards, Primus composed African-based, including Watusi, dances that enlivened Western awareness of African traditions, alerting it as well to expanding notions of what "modern dance" could be. Like Katherine Dunham, she reshaped the modern dance theater through the prominent display of Africanist elements—costumes, drums, polyrhythms, traditional/ritualistic movement motifs with their various themes/narratives, and communal high-energy that invites, across the footlights, the audience's near-participation. These elements, where fused innovatively together and with New York-based modern techniques by a personal Primus imprint, no longer count as "Negro," "Black," or "ethnic" but as the "real articles," genuine examples of modern dance along with Graham and Humphrey. The personal choreographic imprint on experimental movements unreliant on a codified dance vocabulary puts them in the modern dance camp.

For many in the dance world, Primus is remembered primarily for her solos, more for the "personal journey" and self-discovery that she experienced in studying dance-and-life both in the United States and West Africa. She was less theatrical than Dunham, more of a loner, without the entourage that usually surrounded Dunham. Nor did she leave anything to be called a Primus Technique. But modern dance is applauded for encouraging individualism, in quest and creativity, and Primus by example gave the art a boost in that respect.

Perhaps more than any other dancer of her time, Primus called attention to black oppression in the United States and the need to address it artistically as well as politically. All the more interesting, because this was a time, from the Thirties to Forties, when American dancers and artists generally were intent on shedding European influences on behalf of locally-generated creations. Composing solos like *Strange Fruit*, working out and through her emotions and attitudes as a black woman living in a nation where lynchings of blacks had an underground legitimacy, was a way of answering "Who am I?" Primus's West African study of dance provided a rationale, because there "People use their bodies as instruments through which every conceivable emotion or event is projected. The result is a hypnotic marriage between life and dance. The two are inseparable."

Primus emphasized, in my conversations with her in the early 1990s, the "big" objective of concert dancing, that she found in African professional dancing. "He [the professional dancer] is told that he is not one, but that he is the entire group. His body is an instrument with which he can speak for his people." The dancer's role, pictured large, is no less than to reveal the "oneness" of all humanity. The communal character of dancing, that embodies tradition within individualized creativity, reminds us of continuities between past and present and between "them" and "us."

Like Katherine Dunham, Pearl Primus practiced and taught a kind of dancing that is as much an intellectual quest as it is a physical activity. History, cultural studies, the other arts, anthropology, and the humanities belong somewhere in the dancer's mentality, whether in the fore or background. Fittingly, Primus was a visiting scholar at Pratt Institute in the 1970s, a professor of ethnic studies at the Five College program (Amherst, Hampshire, Mount Holyoke, Smith and University of Massachusetts) in the 1980s. Unlike Dunham, however, Primus, who died in 1994 has not received the interpretive attention that she deserves. Some day surely, not too distant one hopes, this will be remedied.

A Letter

————

Durham, NC
June '01

Mrs. C.—

Good! You're fully recovered, and now I have a touch of it, the flu is every-where, and I had the shot—*it's unfair*!

But I'm so pleased—Vanessa, Vita and George—you too?—are really grabbed by my notes on Dunham and Primus. It *is* fascinating material, and so is what's coming next—on my national touring with ADF's Black Tradition in Modern Dance projects. I do regret just skimming the surface of those experiences, so much to tell—but can't be helped. Maybe, though, this will stimulate more looking-into by you and the others.

My room here has a view, overlapping tree tops making a seamless green canopy. Here is strange, Durham and ADF and connecting with the whole African American thing—odd, here is where my passage to Africa began!

I love the image of you, in the lounge on the sunporch, reading these jottings. Don't be offended, but that's a better image than of your being in the next room doing such. Distant companionship—isn't that what we're all about?

Take care, my dear communicant,

Wherever you are,
GEM

A Project—Dancers Modern and Black

"Why Dayton?", a man called out from the post-performance audience in Atlanta "Why Dayton?", asked a post-performance audience member in Salt Lake City. "Dayton? Why Dayton?", queried a woman at a theater in Portland, Oregon.

These occurred in the early 1990s at question-and-answer occasions when the Dayton Contemporary Dance Company (DCDC), an Ohio modern dance ensemble of some sixteen dancers, toured nationally in project collaborations with the American Dance Festival (ADF), located in Durham, NC, and using the facilities of Duke University. These two organizations began, in the late 1980s, dance-and-humanities programs that combined theater performances, scholarly commentaries/public education forums, and local community outreach activities, aimed at showing how significantly African American dance artists contributed to the development of modern dance. Unfortunately, both the professional dance world and the general public are ill-informed on the subject, so our objective (my role, director of the humanities side of the project) was largely remedial. We started with touring historically black colleges in North Carolina during ADF's summer season, to acquaint students and faculties with their own dance heritages, and the results achieved then led to five intense years of national touring and intermittent dance-and-humanities programming from about 1997 to the present.

Founded in the late 1960s, DCDC was created through the vision of Jeraldyne Blunden who directed the company until her untimely death in 1999. She was an African American woman who got her initial dance training in hometown Dayton, venturing on her own as a teenager in the summer of 1958 to ADF where it then resided at Connecticut College in New London, a major step in pursuing a long career as dancer, choreographer, teacher, and company director in Dayton.

"Why Dayton?"—"Because that's where we're from!" Jeraldyne would reply. And when a questioner persisted, "That's o.k., but I mean, wouldn't you sound more glamorous, sell more tickets if you had a hotter name like… well, you know what I mean?", she would shrug a good-natured response:

"We're loyal to our town that's been good to us, we want everybody to know that we're a top-notch dance company from a top-notch town." Her modesty on these occasions, especially in post-performance informal exchanges with enthused audiences around the country, was always a winner, her "Thank you all" much appreciated by the many who were primed to applaud again.

The ADF traces its history to 1934, when it began with Martha Graham, Doris Humphrey, Charles Weidman and Hanya Holm as a summer site outside steamy New York City, in Bennington, Vermont, for rehearsals, try-out performances and student classes. Like other dance festivals, notably at (Ted Shawn's) Jacob's Pillow and at (Hanya Holm's) Colorado College, ADF nurtured the growth of the modern dance patch, largely by becoming an influential liaison between the professional and educational dance worlds. Since most of the festival students were (and are) college students, they have helped substantially over the years in discovering natural bridges between the two worlds, and as a result modern dance increasingly professionalized its intellectual side and, equally importantly, intellectualized its professional mission. At ADF, a tradition of intellectual exchanges continues between artists, scholars, critics, students, and audiences from the world over.

ADF's goal of supporting modern dance through a mix of functions—commissioning new choreography, training new generations of students, presenting theater performances, preserving dance performances (and other important activities) through film/video/archives, and implementing public education programs—dovetails neatly with DCDC's of performing superior examples of modern dance, including those by African Americans who followed the "break through" achievements of Katherine Dunham and Pearl Primus. For this joint touring project—The Black Tradition in American Modern Dance—DCDC, a predominantly African American troupe, had the dancers, the artistic directors, and their performance reputation, while ADF had the resources for organizing and supervising it, including the selection of participating dancers and scholars/analysts comprising an ongoing arts-and-humanities team. Together, their objective was, by combining performance and commentaries, to bring modern dance and its all-important African American presence to as much public attention as possible.

Hell'o Mrs. Calabash:

Stop for a moment—these notes surface so many memories, of so many rewarding experiences. You know what I think about most? About how the African American dance world, including the DCDC dancers and my humanities colleagues, "took me in," guiding my directing the humanities side of the project. Having retired as a philosophy professor at the City University of New York, as you know, I could afford to take on the assignment with its not undemanding schedule.

We were presented at campuses like Northwestern, Vanderbilt, Berkeley, Florida A&M, at Martin Luther King, Jr. Centers and downtown arts organizations in cities like Pittsburgh, San Diego, Milwaukee, and Huntsville, Alabama. Although originally designed for adult audiences, our project was increasingly invited for younger ones, so we modified our historical/cultural/humanities commentaries for secondary and even elementary schools in various states. In addition to historically black colleges/universities, we toured Native American reservations (Apache, Zuni and Navajo) in New Mexico. And this I particularly enjoyed, romanticizing the experience because of some American Indian background of my own, while driving one of the vans up and down the New Mexico Landscape.

Since our project focused on important dances by black choreographers, dances in danger of being forever forgotten, to present them for audiences around the country, to preserve them via film and video, and to contextualize their historical and cultural significance for audience education/appreciation, DCDC performed dances by Donald McKayle, Talley Beatty, Eleo Pomare, Ulysses Dove, Bebe Miller, and others. And of course we showed films or videos of Dunham and Primus. Everywhere we went, our show was received as "fresh and fascinating," many an audience exclaiming, "Never seen dancing like this before" and "Never heard a story like this before."— Reinforcing stuff, Mrs. C.

Which I need from you, too. Maybe soon?

Dancing salutes to you, wherever you are,
GEM

Touring Rainbow *and Black Classics*

"We could do that, too," a Navajo woman exclaimed, after watching Donald McKayle's "classic" *Rainbow 'Round My Shoulder*, created in 1959. The dance depicts the hardships of black men on a Southern chain gang. "We could make a dance about our history, about the terrible Long March," she continued, her friends from the reservation nodding in agreement. So we talked hopefully about collaborating on a project that would reflect American Indian experiences as *Rainbow* does for African Americans. Regrettably, the opportunity never occurred.

A pity, because as we saw (only a few years ago) on the New Mexico reservations, youngsters were being encouraged to experiment creatively in writing (fiction and non-fiction), in studio art where they did more, say, than traditional sand-paintings. The prospect of bringing modern dance choreographers to the reservations for guiding Indian youngsters in creative dancing while conspicuously avoiding any tampering with their traditional and often sacred dances, was (and is) appealing. It is appealing because the youngsters, notably on the Apache reservation in Dulce, staring vacantly as they upped-and-downed their yo-yos, became alert, animated while watching DCDC perform and lead them in classes. So no trouble here in fantasizing how their lives might be invigorated by a program of creative movement/dancing.

Rainbow 'Round My Shoulder has been described as "the most powerful" of modern dances. Seven bare-chested black men, linked (suggestively rather than literally) together in a chain gang of the type occasionally still seen in the South, leap and shout their suffering to the accompaniment of heart-stirring traditional/folk vocal music. The single female dancer, entering at different points in the twenty-plus minute piece, on each appearance being a different fantasy or remembered woman by the chain gang, is a gossamer-like complement to the sweaty, pounding out-sized movements of the seven males.

The dance ends tragically, a gun-shot is heard offstage where the audience has seen a gang member try to escape, and the stricken man stumbles onstage to collapse, and, as the lights darken with the curtain about to descend, the female figure moves into the spotlight and slowly circles her arm in the air—conclusion. Years after creating *Rainbow*, Donald McKayle commented, somewhat surprisingly given the dance's unusual focus on male dancing, that he realized in retrospect that its theme was "woman, the inspirer." When I queried him recently about that, he smiled his staying with the comment. Maybe, to prove the point, McKayle has re-worked the dance in workshops, as once in Argentina, for an all-woman cast.

When DCDC performed *Rainbow*, on another ADF occasion in Moscow, Charles Reinhart reported that the Russian audience sat in stunned silence at its conclusion, then a few minutes later, burst into huge applause. Another bit of evidence for dancers' favorite theme, the art's universal communicability. When dance's capacity to capture special nuances of the human condition such as the "American Black experience" comes up for discussion, *Rainbow* is naturally cited as a perfect example.

We were out to make the case, while touring the nation during the 1990s, that *Rainbow* and other major works by African American choreographers deserve attention in the university curriculum. However the history of modern dance and its place in American culture is presented, it ought to include its "black tradition" that extends back into the 1920s. Our case was made easier by the fact that Donald McKayle and the others had already made it for us; what remained was wider dissemination of their dances, and of their belief, like Dunham's and Primus's, that into the dancing is built a sustaining philosophy of life.

Donald McKayle was born in 1930 in New York City, to transplanted West Indian parents, studied at the New Dance Group with Pearl Primus and Sophie Maslow, among others, learning ballet, Haitian, Hindu, tap and modern. He debuted as a choreographer in the late 1940s, toured as an impressive virile (six-footer) performer with Martha Graham in the Far and Near East in the mid-1950s, continued his Broadway experiences as dance captain in West Side Story in 1957.

Since then, his has been a brilliant career in concert dance, musical theater, film, television, and club acts, where the quality and versatility of his achievements have earned him pages of honors and awards. Modern dance has always remained his first love, but, as he will tell you, his work in that area has benefited through lessons learned from Broadway, Hollywood, and other more popular venues. Add to the above McKayle's role in connecting dance in professional and educational settings. A Tony award winner for directing and choreographing *Raisin* in the 1970s, performing over the years with Bill Cosby, Harry Belafonte, and the Temptations, he was also once the School of Dance's Dean at California Institute of the Arts, currently holding a distinguished professorship at the University of California at Irvine. He demonstrates convincingly how modern dance, in addition to gracing the gym, studio, and theater, fits the seminar room's intellectual interests, the interpretations that are historical, sociological, anthropological, religious, philosophical, and aesthetic.

For general audiences, dances by African American choreographers are often as "problematic" as any others, and, given their burden of sometimes conveying complex narratives and philosophies, we encountered audiences asking "What is that dance really about?" Provided with program notes, audiences had no problem with the general drift of *Rainbow 'Round My Shoulder*. But unless those notes were elaborated, our pre- and post-performance discussions with audiences assisted their understanding and appreciation substantially. The title meant more to them when we explained how McKayle had in mind the rainbow-like glint made by the pick-ax when swung by the prisoner over his shoulder, and how the rainbow also serves as a metaphor for freedom, hope, and the like.

Our audiences needed help in realizing that the female dancer, in her successive appearances, represented the men's fantasies or memories of sweethearts, wives, mothers. And they, like I from conversations with McKayle, appreciated learning that, despite the dance's tragic finale, he conceived the female dancer's spotlighted entrance on the darkened stage, standing quietly and slowly circling her hand high in the air, to signal trust in a redemptive tomorrow.

The theme of "We shall overcome" is not confined to civil rights marches; it occurs throughout African American arts, and the tone of "affirmation" whether obviously or subtly inserted as in *Rainbow*, tends to characterize the dance aesthetic of choreographers like Donald McKayle. It is conspicuous because the negative side of the "black experience" conspicuously shows in dances by black choreographers, challenging the choreographer's personal courage or resoluteness as a bulwark part of his artistic imagination. Bear this in mind when you read or hear Ronald K. Brown or other contemporary artists of color refer to themselves as "spiritual warriors."

The African American presence on the modern dance stage was increasingly visible when McKayle created *Rainbow* in 1959. Talley Beatty, a Katherine Dunham protégé, had earlier made his mark in 1947 with his *Southern Landscape*, a powerful and complex dance about Blacks and the American South after the Civil War, and he continued as one of our leading choreographers until his death in 1995. Major works included *The Road of the Phoebe Snow* (1959), to Duke Ellington and Billy Strayhorn music, and *Come and Get the Beauty of It Hot* (1960), to scores by Miles Davis and Gil Evans, a six-episode high-energy, sexy work that concludes in a Spanish Harlem ballroom.

Alvin Ailey, born in Texas and later moving successively as an adult to California and New York City, who would become the best-known African American choreographer, created *Blues Suite* in 1958. In this, you see Saturday night small-town folks loading up the evening with blues music, languorous dancing, and sexual send-ups, to Jimmy Rushing's "Good Morning Blues." In 1960, at age 29, Ailey presented *Revelations*, his most celebrated work, that is often said to be the most famous, most seen (world-over) of all modern dances.

A three-section work, choreographed to sung traditional Negro spirituals, *Revelations* is an exhilarating, colorful dance of spirituality. Ailey's childhood experiences in a Texas black church are echoed in the women's Sunday-style walks and gestures, in their yellow dresses and straw hats, and exaggerated fanning themselves in the remembered Texas heat. The revivalist excitement of the concluding "Rocka My Soul" is infectious, propelling audiences out of their seats to clap in unison with the dancers, to sway with their rhythms, to join the big communal smile. Ailey was not represented (except for film clips and discussions) on our touring because his was an ongoing company, his works in no danger of being lost because they were regularly presented both at home-base in New York City and on international tours. (Nor, as we often had to explain, did we represent Arthur Mitchell and his Dance Theater of Harlem, because our project focused on modern dance, not ballet.)

Talley Beatty's dances were prominently displayed on our touring, popularly received as exciting jazz-based dancing, although Beatty shared the reservation of other professionals about the meaning of "Jazz" and whether his idiom is better described as "modern" that adapts vernacular/jazz movements. His *The Stack-Up* (1983), to music by Earth, Wind, and Fire, Grover Washington, Jr., and the Fearless Four, is a firestorm of movement, about as galvanizing as it gets, and it proved a crowd-pleaser. Joe Nash's description gives its flavor:

> At the intersection of uptown Metropolis, street people of every size, shape, and character are constantly on the move. There is the wino stumbling along and muttering to himself. There are the hustlers, gamblers, pimps, street gangs and panhandlers. People rushing to their "9 to 5" pretending not to see the lost multitude in their midst. Young men and women walking their walk-bopping. There are the strollers, loafers and haranguers. There is the drug dealer scanning the scene for victims…urban jungle…. This is the setting for Talley's dance of action.

Another Beatty piece, totally different from his "jazzy" group works and always a hit on the tour, was *Mourner's Bench*, a four-plus minute section, nowadays usually performed alone, of his 1947 *Southern Landscape*. This work expressed Beatty's reactions to accounts in Howard Fast's book *Freedom Road* about the violence suffered by Southern Blacks following the Civil War.

Mourner's Bench is a solo rendition of those reactions of fear, anger, grief, prayer—and you can add to these when you see it. A description that I have given it is this:

> This dance, presenting a trousered youngish male, naked to the waist, on a plain wooden bench, and reacting with a mixture of grief, anger, and foreboding to something obviously disturbing but unidentified except in program notes, resonates emotionally with audiences when performed to the exacting standards set by the choreographer. The dancer balances precariously on the bench, then stretches full-out across it and rolls his body along it in rapid wheeling movements, rocks suspended on its ends while spasmodically contracting and releasing the upper torso, then spins out tall from the bench for a desperate embrace of freed space, provokes gasps during his "hinged" fall to the floor, followed by a slow folding of his body into the fetal position, the conclusion. *Mourner's Bench* beautifully illustrates how an intensely physical dance, balancing on the cliff between dance and gymnastics, can be eloquently emotional. You see the physical feats on the bench and you get a sense of the feelings, not in themselves tangible or touchable like the physical body on the bench but just as real in giving the dance its identity. Because mourners' benches are part of church history and because of what is implied by the dance's context when fully explained, the feelings of this dance deserve to be called spiritual.

In mentioning again the complex and controversial subject, of concert dance's "problematic" or challenges to audience interpretation, let us agree at the outset that for some audiences some dances "come through" clearly and immediately—although why and how in specific cases this is the case may challenge explanation. With others, I have had to dissent too often, when verdicts, either "It's clear" or "It's puzzling" are heard, to believe that the dance-problematic can be explained away. That is why, on tour, I pleaded with local presenters before we arrived to program pre-performance discussions, preferably for an hour prior to curtain time. Providing audiences beforehand with a context, of information and interpretation about the dances to be performed, often makes the difference between rewarded and cheated viewing. (If such providing ever hurt, I never heard of it.) I shall always remember how in Kohler, Wisconsin, where the presenter decided against a pre-performance presentation, an audience as white and polite as could be desired showed its total cluelessness regarding the "black classics" performed by the Dayton Contemporary Dance Company (DCDC).

Our audiences were grateful for pre-performance discussions preceding their watching *Mourner's Bench*, provided with clues both to its general structure and some details. Its emotional impact was the stronger, the better the understanding of it. Dance teachers also noted that, brief and compact, it is a first-rate instructional example of how unadorned movement by itself can be remarkably dramatic/expressive; an example of how technically exacting, virtually gymnastic movements can twist your innards, moisten your eyes.

A persistently interesting aesthetic issue was raised by *Mourner's Bench*. Remembering that Talley Beatty, a black man, originally performed the solo figure grieving (etc.) on the bench, forever making the dance a black's reflection on black history, would your eyes moisten if a white dancer performed it? This question was forced on us because Talley had selected a white member of (predominantly black) DCDC to dance it "simply because he does it better than any of the others." But, despite Talley's rationale and the further reason offered, that the dance has not a confined racial but rather a universal significance, audiences could remain troubled.

When we showed a video of *Mourner's Bench* performed by the white DCDC dancer, after explaining its historical "black" context, to program officers and staff at the National Endowments for the Arts and Humanities in Washington, in the early 1990s, some audience members openly confessed their disappointment, having expected a black performer in "this, of all dances!" A few years later, in Indianapolis, we showed that same video as part of a discussion on dance and spirituality, including the attitudes of Black Churches towards modern dance. "No spirituality there, we don't see it!", exclaimed some attendees, including a black minister. Yet, the next evening, when a black DCDC dancer performed it, those same attendees reacted altogether differently. "Ah, now we see it, yes, that's got spirituality alright."

Other black choreographers represented during touring were George Faison, Ulysses Dove, Kevin Ward, Dianne McIntyre, Bebe Miller, Debbie Blunden, Donald Byrd, and Ronald K. Brown. Eleo Pomare, distinguished choreographer and influential figure in black dance history since the 1960s, was often represented by his *Les Desenamoradas*, an adaptation of Lorca's *The House of Bernada Alba*, and *Missa Luba*, a complex religious reflection that blends dance reminders of Catholic and African rites/rituals. These were in addition to other "classics" by Donald McKayle such as *Games* (1951), about kids' games and life in New York City streets, and *District Storyville* (1962), on the birth of jazz in that storied section of New Orleans.

Looking back, it is fair to say, we believe, that the ADF Black Tradition project, of almost two decades, with its various formats including regional, national, and international touring, and culminating in the film/TV series *Free to Dance*, was remarkably successful.

Large numbers of audiences saw these major works by African American choreographers, these works have been preserved, black dance companies that include the Cleo Parker Robinson Dance Ensemble in Denver and Joan Myers Brown's Philadanco in Philadelphia in addition to DCDC have a richer repertoire to show, and a huge amount of public education programming, including publications widely disseminated, has been accomplished.

Plenty of work remains to be done, as will always be true of efforts in the arts. We could wish that our audiences, on tour, had included more blacks, that presenters in fewer cities would tell us, "This is really a ballet town, but we hope for a decent-sized audience," that our efforts had been more uniformly successful in generating interdisciplinary faculty participation on the numerous campuses visited, and that a larger number of young African American students/scholars, expressing their intention of doing research in our project's subject matter, could be counted.

The role of African Americans in developing modern dance—there is a big story here, only hinted at in my condensed review above: so many important choreographers, dancers, companies, and teachers not mentioned here and how they have made dance a local community resource, its discipline and creativity countering drugs, street violence, etc. Add as examples to those mentioned previously Ann Williams's Dallas Black Dance Theater and Lulu Washington's Dance Theater in Los Angeles. Such community companies/schools/performance spaces, whether in Dayton, Kansas City or New York City, and most invisible to popular perception, are all-important to the cause of concert dance, in training young dancers, supporting and encouraging choreographic creativity, and in providing those hard-to-get performance opportunities. How dance functions both as an artistic and social/psychological resource, in non-black as well as black communities, makes for an inspiring story that, through televised documentaries and other methods, should be told to the country.

For the majority of audiences, modern dance by African Americans is a "high" art form when compared to MTV, rock concerts, and the like; meaning by "high," I suppose, less visceral, less raucous, less sexy, less hyped, less produced for bobby-soxers and teenagers; more subdued, thoughtful, smaller-staged, more problematic, less fearful of boredom, but really scared of commercialism. All the same, within the dance world, I think, that the role of African Americans is diminishing former tall-fence distinctions between "high" and "low" art is acknowledged.

Dancing rather more literally than Doris Humphrey, more vernacularly than Louis Horst-Martha Graham would allow, in depicting scenes from the street to music by Duke Ellington and John Coltrane, and in mixing autobiographical/confessional texts with movement, black choreographers have made concert dance seem less high-strung, more accessible. I occasionally said to audiences, when touring ADF's Black Tradition project, that it is doubtful, without the African American dancers having set the precedent, that we would see Twyla Tharp dancing to Frank Sinatra songs. I also, tongue in cheek, asked not be quoted publicly on that, being too hypothetical for evidence for or against. But, I confess, the hypothesis keeps returning, won't leave me alone.

Something else that keeps returning is a remark made by Bill Moore, black dance critic and member of our project humanities team, in the early 1990s during a performance-and-commentary stop at Northwestern University. Bill, a laid-back affable chap, caused a smile in half-seriously offering the comment that Northwestern's campus buildings, as we approached them looked "awfully aristocratic and forbidding" and from "another era." We had been talking about why it seemed that white critics and audiences were often put off by blacks' dancing, and, after a pause following his comment about the buildings, Bill stopped, looked me in the eye, asking "Why, Gerry, can't they accept *our reality*?" That remark/question keeps returning, one moment seeming banal but the next revealingly true.

It is more difficult to accept the other's reality than you might suppose. As I learned during the years of the project, sometimes our unconscious biases elude our conscious perceptions of ourselves, and some of the strongest and most elusive of these are our *aesthetic preferences*—about bodies, faces, audiences, music, rhythm, lines, patterns, colors, stories, plots, violence, sex, birth, death, life, reality. So much of what one calls reality, positively or negatively regarded, is defined by our aesthetic prejudices; about what is beautiful, attractive, desirable, valuable, laudable, etc. It is one thing to understand more or less abstractly that one is probably biased aesthetically, but it is quite another to have such biases surface, be experienced and recognized, maybe to be later exorcised or at least modified.

A trivial thing, but I actually ceased to feel de-privileged when black audiences shouted responses during performances to the "calling" dance movements on stage. In many and more profound ways I learned, in learning about the black tradition in modern dance, that once you ask, "Am I accepting the other's reality?", your aesthetic sensibility can go adventuring.

A Letter

New York
August '01

Dear Mrs. Calabash:

Shame! Shame! Anytime you want to reprimand me for going overboard, O.K. with me. And *maybe* I was a bit expansive on the African American matter. But, please! Accusing me of letting my "black dance belt overfloweth." I can't believe you authored *that*!

But you have no idea of how much I had to omit, about our Black Tradition project. Most people don't have the opportunity to see the same dances repeatedly, to read and re-read them like books or re-visit them like paintings, and it was a real discovery, during those years of touring, to get to know certain dances so well that I could anticipate the next moves, compare performances with previous ones, acquire that (indescribable) sense of how a dance's myriad details collectively embody its overall concept.

After Joe Nash, I learned more about the black tradition from Donald McKayle, in conversation and watching his dances. He's hard to match, for sheer intelligence, wit, articulateness, and the most amazing memory. Donald is open, expansive, always composed or so it seems, and noticeably unassuming for a person of such celebrity-level accomplishments.

Talley Beatty, on the other hand, was on the coy side, somewhat elusive, reserved, smiling mysteriously as he deflected questions he felt were too direct. He was one of the most sensitive, poetic dancers I've met, given to quoting T.S. Eliot and others in his low murmuring melodious voice. I got well acquainted with him during the years before his death in 1995, especially in the summer of 1991 when Dr. Richard Long, of Emory University, and I directed an ADF Institute, funded by the National Endowment for the Humanities, on the black dance tradition and its place in American culture, for an audience of college/university teachers. Talley sat in on most of our daily sessions, regularly participating in the seminar discussions. It was apparent, from his contributions there as in his choreography, that within himself he carried, somehow so singularly that you took notice, a wounded bafflement that humanity can be so hard on itself—racism of course being a constant example.

Once in Atlanta, where our touring project and Talley's receiving a Living Legend Award (along with Max Roach and others) coincided, I asked him if his *Mourner's Bench* solo (1947) echoed at all Martha Graham's famous *Lamentation* of 1930, where she had been so expressive alone on a bench. Had he ever seen a version, filmed or live, of *Lamentation*? He smiled, looking at me sideways, muffled an answer that I think was "No," then said abruptly and loudly enough to hear distinctly "There are those contractions, you know." And that was it.

Bye! Leaving with our group here to bus it to the Joyce Theater for a Donald Byrd performance. He told me, I think, that he's been reading Jean Baudrillard, who I hear is pessimistic about what will post postmodernism—French, you know, so I guess you're not interested.

Tell Vita and George "Congratulations!" I'm all smiles that they "got" my jottings on the "black modern dance tradition"—even if the jaded Mrs. C. flounders. Anyway, tomorrow back to New London, to the lighthouse!

Take care, lighten up.

Wherever you are,
GEM

P.S. I'd bet my subscription to *TLS* that you'll Love Erick Hawkins who's up next.

Erick Hawkins

When Erick Hawkins, age 85, died in 1994 the curtain fell on one of the more curious and controversial modern dance careers. Given the amount of uncertainty or outright disapproval distributed over the years about his choreography and philosophy of dance, one might have been surprised at how the dance world turned out full force, and seemingly reverently, for his memorial service at Manhattan's Joyce Theater. Those in attendance could agree, whatever else might be said, that with his death a large empty place in modern dance history had been created. Anna Kisselgoff, in her *New York Times* obituary notice, observed that but a few weeks earlier Hawkins had received the National Medal of the Arts from President Clinton at the White House.

The "unusual" featured Hawkins's long, distinguished career. He was born in Trinidad, Colorado, a one-main-street town just north of the New Mexico border (where an ADF/DCDC tour made a memorable lecture/demonstration stop in the early 1990s, with our "same art" connections to Hawkins recognized by local attendees). His father, a Western inventor, had he foreseen the outcome of his son's going East to Harvard, might have sent him Pacific-ward instead for his collegiate years. Though he suddenly adopted dance as his profession in the 1920s upon seeing, while still an undergraduate, a New York City performance by the German expressionists Harald Kreutzberg and Yvonne Georgi, his own subsequent choreography veered away from such expressionism towards what could be called "American" themes and styles.

Tall, lean, athletic, craggy-faced, handsomely packaged, Hawkins began in ballet with the encouragement of George Balanchine and Lincoln Kirstein, but soon moved to modern dance, joining Martha Graham's company as its first male dancer in 1938. He and Graham married in 1948, that relationship ending six years later. In private conversations, I several times heard him speak more candidly about the extent of what he considered to be his own unacknowledged contributions to such Graham dances as *Deaths and Entrances* (1943), *Appalachian Spring* (1944) and *Night Journey* (1947). And though in these conversations always polite and deferential in referring to

Graham's and Balanchine's achievements, he rather pounded the theme on which he more sedately wrote, that both traditional ballet and modern dance such as Graham's were too hard on the human body, and his fierce belief here was largely founded on his own injuries to knees and back.

When Balanchine declared "Ballet is Woman," alas he spoke accurately, Hawkins observed, because ballet is made for the woman on toe with the male dancer merely a supernumerary. Ever aware of his role as a pioneering male dancer, who had interrupted and altered the all-female Graham enterprise, Hawkins objected to the artificiality and tautness, as he saw it, of balletic dancing that stereotyped both male and female ways of moving. He thought modern dance, especially Graham's, suffered from excessive emoting, and its contraction-and-release technique was no better than ballet in its reliance on "tight muscles that don't feel." "De-contraction," on behalf of relaxed movement, was used as a name for the alternative technique that Hawkins developed and that became his choreographic and performance trademark.

Hawkins credited Isadora Duncan with discovering the right vision of the body and its function in dance, so a résumé of his aesthetic strongly resembles Duncan's. She was one of the few in Western cultures, he wrote, to appreciate how the human body is a "worthy and loved and equal partner with the 'soul-mind'" and only when the "body was re-recognized and freed could a new art of dance arise in the West." He elaborated:

> Isadora Duncan was the first dancer in the West to intuit a kinesiological truth: that human movement starts in the spine and pelvis, not in the extremities—the legs and arms. That is: human movement, when it obeys the nature of its functioning, when it is not distorted by erroneous concepts of the mind, starts in the body's center of gravity and then—in correct sequence—flows into the extremities.

And:

> ...she conceived the essence of movement to lie in transition, not in position. When she says "Study Nature," she means "flow organically," in arcs, like the spring of a cat, the wiggle of a water moccasin, the gallop of a horse, the wave on a beach, the toss of a ball, the bellying of a sail—not like a man's mind-contrived, inorganic machine, which essentially cannot move but only take positions.

Whereas for many choreographers the goal is to make the dancers' *effortful* movements look like what they are, emphatically effortful, Hawkins's objective was to make his dancers' *effortless* movements look exactly so. Like John Cage and Merce Cunningham, focusing on dance as poetic movement,

Hawkins found Zen and Eastern philosophies relevant to his intentions. Beverly Brown, a Hawkins dancer and recognized spokesperson for his theory and training, connects Isadora Duncan's "natural dancing" with Zen's message of "learning to dance without forcing the movements to happen, but rather by letting the movement happen, by letting 'It' dance in the dancer's body." Hawkins and his longtime musician-partner, later his wife, Lucia Dlugoszewski, (who died in 2000) liked to compare dance to Haiku or Japanese aphoristic poems that lyrically invoke Nature in some respect.

The intellectual context for Hawkins's dances was made more complex by his idea that his artistry was an American locus for blending Eastern and Western philosophies. Personal experience contributed of course to his theorizing but so did what he called "scientific investigations" of the body, which he found especially in Mabel Elsworth Todd's well-known book on body mechanics, *The Thinking Body* (1937). Hawkins and others liked her message that topped the nitty-gritty details of body mechanics: "Living, the whole body carries its meaning and tells its own story, standing, sitting, walking, awake or asleep. It pulls all the life up into the face of the philosopher, and sends it all down into the legs of the dancer." Western physical education scientific investigations that buttressed this sentiment were welcome mixers with wisdom from the East.

Lucia Dlugoszewski was remarkable, for being Hawkins's music maker, for what was know as her "timbre piano," but also for her grasp of his thought. This was especially apparent after his stroke and speech hesitancy, when she would close awkward silences by speaking for him. And on occasion she could clarify his meaning, as she does in writing that the philosopher F.S.C. Northrop's "great philosophic insight" was to appreciate how the "nirvana" of Hindu and Buddhist religious traditions is the harmony of nature intuitively experienced as oneness. Northrop called this the "undifferentiated aesthetic continuum," a special kind of experience so direct and immediate that it precludes conceptual or perceptual distinctions/differentiations. Northrop was a Yale University philosopher who authored in the 1940s *The Meeting of East and West*, for some years a widely consulted book on the two disparate cultures. A decade later, he wrote the *Logic of the Sciences and the Humanities* that included ideas on aesthetics found attractive by Hawkins.

As Dlugoszewski notes, an implication of the Northrop reading of Asian thought is to "demonstrate the exact difference between the psychological and the aesthetic in direct experience. This insight is now shared by Western science." Whether or not Western science, perhaps represented by some who stress the limits of science and reason, shares this insight, it is clearly an all-important concept in Hawkins' dance philosophy, in its divergence, say, from Martha Graham's. The idea here is that, as (allegedly) first understood in

Asia and now confirmed by Western science (including Todd's *The Thinking Body*), there is available to us a kind of aesthetic experience that is quite different from ordinary emotional experience. For one thing, it is said to be "ego-less," is free of subjective clutter as a "kind of clear field of sensation." I think it evident that Hawkins's personal quest was for serenity (harmony, truth, beauty) and release from conceptual/cerebral confusion. So he called the human body a "clear place," meaning in my reading that the dancing body affords serene experiences but, moreover, inspires or "clears" the way for a unifying philosophy of Nature and our place in it. This helps us to understand why the participants in a 1972 Hawkins-led workshop at Oakland University in Rochester, Michigan, were especially grateful for the "philosophical insights" learned there.

Hawkins's belief that the experience of dancing can provide a philosophic window on nature, life, etc., that in collaboration with science and philosophy it can supply precious insights, is apparent in his writings but was made even more apparent to me in conversation whenever I brought up Northrop's name. I had met Northrop and talked to him about Hawkins at an East-West Philosophers Conference in Hawaii in 1959. He was delighted that a leading choreographer had embraced his ideas publicly and in practical, working ways. Hawkins was particularly fond of Northrop's distinction between the "first" and "second" functions of art, the first being simply sensuous display (of colors, sound, movement quality, etc.) or immediate appeal to the senses, the second being the meaning or conceptual implications of the sensuous display. This second function, Hawkins argued, is too often missing in contemporary arts, listing Pop Art as one of the villains responsible for this. He often cited the painter Robert Motherwell and the composer Virgil Thompson as his colleagues in creating "positive" art that performs both functions simultaneously.

Is it possible to choreograph mentally, in advance, before worrying the performance details? I believe Hawkins would have to answer "no," since his choreography was formed on and around his central concern, which was *movement quality.* He wrote that "the important essence of all dancing is movement quality, and its excellence or lack of excellence. I quickly discovered that the wondrous, immediate knowledge of existence that you get in the pure fact of movement can come only if you find that inner quality. I soon realized that pure movement is decorative, instead of significant [art's "second" function], if the inner quality is lacking."

Hawkins's dancers often refer less to his choreographic configurations than to the (inner) kinesthetic sensations experienced through his careful instructions. I'm looking this moment at a photo of a Hawkins dancer, sent by her to my wife some years ago, taken in a 1980's performance of his 1962

Early Floating. She inscribed on the back of the photo "I like this photo.... I think it reveals a delicacy that's been hard for me to achieve." Refinements of movement quality, leaning towards the gentle, delicate, natural free flow—those were the Hawkins desiderata.

Erick Hawkins risked what Isadora Duncan, whose dance theory and practice he much admired, had earlier risked—and what modern dancers generally are committed to gambling—an audience failure to see the philosophy (content, subject-matter, meanings, etc.) in the dancing; the abstract (concepts, ideas) in the concrete (physical steps). An unusual aspect of Hawkins's career was the change-of-mind verdicts made by critics, more approving of works in his later years. Keeping in mind that Hawkins had choreographed his first dance, *Show Piece*, in 1937, we can appreciate why Clive Barnes wrote in 1973 that "oddly enough" he would *now* name Erick Hawkins to the number of "new significant modern-dance companies."

And Deborah Jowitt in 1997: "When I first saw *Early Floating* in the '60s, it didn't mean much to *me*.... Now I see *Early Floating* as the expression of an idyllic sensuality." Even devoted followers confess to having been turned off when first encountering Hawkins's dances, before undergoing subsequent conversions. How to explain this? Possibly the result of changed expectations and allowing one's watching to have the serenity of absorbing the even-tempered movement qualities on stage. That can happen, I attest to it.

Although his dances were suspended from lofty philosophical heights, Hawkins invented a variety of works, some comic (notably, clowning in his amusing *Parson Weems and the Cherry Tree*), others lyrically meditative, anecdotal, ritualistic, ceremonial, or purely poetic. *Early Floating* exploits Hawkins's use of unusually lyric arms, features small movements like raising an arm or swishing a foot across the floor that seems to say "exquisite is the detail." As usual, Lucia Dlugoszewski's music and her performance at her prepared "timbre-piano" contributed to its effect. (Hawkins' was highly respected for his unwavering insistence, despite the costs and problems involved, on live music for his company performances). Glide and flow, Hawkins trademarks, marked the moves of this dance's quartet.

Here and Now with Watchers (1957), one of Hawkins's most praised works, consists of smooth-moving solos and duets by two oddly costumed dancers who look like alien creatures, at first alien to each other, eventually passionately united. Knowing the Zen and other influences at work here, one can view the dancers as human manifestations of nature's openness to being explored through movement. Another memorable dance, *Eight Clear Places* (1960), is described by Don McDonagh as a "succession of tableaux featuring his dancers holding poses for long periods of time and flowing easily to another pose, then exiting. Masks, floor-length robes, and highly stylized props complete the mixture of Oriental tone and Western dance dynamics...more in common with Eastern conceptions of time than Western."

McDonagh notes that this dance is another instance of personalized ceremonial dancing "saturated in obscurity, and little attempt is made to form the direct transitional links that would elucidate the intent of his dances." For Hawkins, I may add, the poetic qualities of the movements can only be grasped intuitively, thus defying narrative translations or elucidations. Intuition typically motivated the "poetic rightness" in his choice of costumes, masks, sets, and movements. Hawkins, as noted earlier, wrote about his solo Naked Leopard, "It was pure intuition, as I designed the costume, that led me to put the single important red area of color where my sensation of the body was centered."

The dances and rituals of Southwest American Indians were important influences on this choreographer from rural Colorado, but again, their influence in Hawkins's dances was mostly indirect, rarely if ever literal. *Plains Daybreak* (1979), named a masterpiece by some but less favored by others, inspired by Indian rituals and creation myths, is a strange, unrecognizable movement-world. Eight dancers wearing headdresses and animal-like costumes move under Ralph Dorazio's "sculptured sky," suggesting a congenial togetherness that is interrupted by the First Man (originally danced by Hawkins). Ritualistic passages such as hunting, exploring, and paying deference to the earth ensue, and in the end First Man and animals, symbolizing nature's harmony, consolidate a peaceful togetherness reminiscent of the scenery in Edward Hicks's nineteenth-century *Peaceable Kingdom* paintings.

It was, I believe, another Indian-inspired dance of the 1970s, *Black Lake*, that came to mind when my son and I visited Wounded Knee, the South Dakota site where almost 200 Native Americans were massacred by U.S. troops in 1890. On leaving the reservation area and its conspicuous poverty, uncertain about which road to take back to the main highway, I called out from the car, for directions, to a young Indian walking through a field of tall grass. He stopped, facing our direction, and wordlessly executed the most eloquent arm sweep that ended in pointing where we should go. It reminded me, if memory was on target, of movements in Hawkins's Black Lake.

Like Isadora Duncan, Hawkins's way of celebrating the "naturalness" of the human body was to dance it nude or nearly so, discarding his oft-used costumes and masks. An example is his *Of Love and Angels of the Inmost Heaven* (1972). Admirers of this said, as they had of his solo *Naked Leopard*, that a kind of "innocence of the sensuousness" shone through, and that despite the controversies nudity arouses, "truly facing Hawkins's unclothed 'angels,' neither cupids nor saints but men and women glorious in their vulnerable and newly-seen flesh, instills in one a like kind of passionate awareness."

On the other hand, many objected to the "tensionless" and "nothing is happening" moments, to the repetitions of "melting jumps" and subdued turns and bends, so they found the nudity troubling. These included the perceptive critic, Marcia Siegel, who wrote:

Philosophically, Hawkins's explorations have led to a paradox. In trying to see the dancing body as a thing in itself, possessing an intrinsic beauty provided it is being faithful to its own natural rules, he comes closer than perhaps anyone to the "objective" goals of modern art, music and literature. But he is assuming that we can see the naturalness and the pure beauty as anyone performing his technique can feel it. He asks the audience to separate the literal fact—that real persons, male and female, are doing real actions with inevitable resonances in our own experience—from the aesthetic fact—that these persons can be perceived for their form and harmony alone. Instead of suspending our natural affinity for these dancers and placing audiences at some less personal distance, as Hawkins would like us to do, some of his viewers, myself included, find in their nearly naked, hairless bodies engaging in soft, gentle play not a more human humanity but one that is somewhat deficient.

If we wanted proof of the risk that Hawkins took (the general modern dance risk, I reiterate, in staging his philosophy of the dance), here we have it. If professional critics don't "see" it adequately presented, the choreographer can only pray for a kindred soul somewhere in the audience. Restraint, as I see it, was a necessity in Hawkins's aesthetic, and while ministering to the enjoyment of some, it clearly restrained that of others. This is not to overlook buoyant moments in his dances, that often seemed to reflect the buoyant temperament of Lucia, his partner, such as occur, say, in his 1981 *Heyoka* (Sioux Indian word for "clown"). This dance is broad-humored, clownish, with runs and jumps in loud-red leotards, but even here the overall effect is subdued, restrained. Why?

Naima Prevots, reviewing a Hawkins performance, has perhaps the answer: "Hawkins is using these clowns as a means of pointing out to us the balance of life, the ridiculous part of the serious and the poetry in both." So the underlying seriousness insures restraint. *Heyoka* came to mind while watching, during our ADF/DCDC tour of New Mexico and near Gallup, the Zuni ritual in the plaza that began with clowning (often poking fun, we were told, at other tribes) that was followed by traditional dances. The clowning, as in *Heyoka*, was buffoonish/oafish but contained and, frankly, for me more obvious than funny. The members of the reservation, who knew every movement's meanings, were clearly but quietly amused, smiles but no uproarious laughter. The clowning opening in *Heyoka*, as in the Zuni ritual, is followed by the company's entering for serious dancing; in Hawkins's words, "through their fooling around," the clowns "open the people to the poetry of the dance to come."

Erick Hawkins may be remembered as a kind of Matthew Arnold or Lionel Trilling of concert dance, a *moralist* in the arts. As Anna Kisselgoff appreciated, "Ethics and aesthetics were inseparable for Hawkins, and uplift was his message." Choreographer and choreography could enjoy the advertised "freedom" of modern dance but only to the point where moral restraints took over. I recall, when we held an ADF symposium in the early 1980s on Duke University's campus, that Hawkins began by asking the audience, "Have you considered the moral implications of our being here, in effect sponsored by a tobacco fortune?," his intensity making us all uneasy enough to wonder for a moment whether we should immediately disband. He expressed a similar concern about the moral need to control one's own health when he and Lucia visited my wife recovering from a hip replacement operation in a New York City hospital.

The moralistic tendency seemed at times to clash with his oft-repeated attacks on Puritanism, especially for its alleged put-downs of the human body. A tough tight-rope to hike, between aesthetics and ethics, without falling off. This was perhaps Hawkins's greatest risk. But he never faltered in taking it, as the crowd at his memorial service must have understood. His sense of mission seems to have been too confident to permit faltering, a mission that he expressed in a 1983 commencement address at Western Michigan University when receiving a Honorary Doctor of Fine Arts Degree:

> I believe the art of dance…is of great significance for the inner life of individuals and for the joint cultural life of our society, and that…it can build up the spirit.

> To quote a man very wise in the traditional metaphysical aspects of human knowledge, our task is to "Spiritualize the body and to corporealize the spirit." The art of dance, as I envision it, includes the two sides of this coin.

Gerald E. Myers

A Letter

New London
August '01

My dear Mrs. Calabash:

Hallelujah! Erick H. is a hit with you and Vanessa! What about the kids? Did they read me on him? You don't say, so I wonder...

I knew you'd like the Hawkins aesthetic, art on a moral/intellectual highroad. And especially his use of F.S.C. Northrop, transforms the structure of dance into *significant form*—yes, I know.

Let's see, is today Monday or Tuesday? Ah, yesterday it was that I re-read your one reservation about Erick, suspicious about his relations with Martha Graham. Sorry I can't help you on that. He never told Martha (mine) or me anything intimate about it, and though Louis Horst had some harsh words towards him, supposedly from Graham's side, Louis was hardly neutral, so...

Gotta close—but, Mrs. C., you have to appreciate how pleased I am that my theme in these jottings is coming through, that you (and Vanessa) are becoming ever more comfortable with the prospect of Vita and George trying out this art form. After all, it's not a life-and-death choice for them, just an artistic one. Whoops! I didn't say that right—not right just after Erick, right? Oh well... You fix it, I know you can.

I've been meaning to ask—do you think intuition and introspection are the same thing? I've always gotten interesting answers whenever I've asked that, which is why I'm asking you.

Take care, good night, wherever you are.
GEM

Alwin Nikolais

Time magazine (May 20, 1966) carried an illustrated sub-column titled "Alwin in Wonderland" on its Music page that included:

As vaudeville shows go, it might have been conjured up by Ed Sullivan on an LSD binge. Right there onstage in living, quivering color, a formation of UFO's performed an aerial ballet. A chap in fluorescent lemon leotards wrestled with a space-age cobweb. Next came a drill team of Martian types outfitted with glowing lampshades, then seven creatures in baggy sacks who squiggled like giant amoebas in heat—all to the other worldly twang, ratatat, whiz and kapow! It was called *Vaudeville of the Elements*, choreographer Alwin Nikolais' latest excursion into the twilight zones of modern dance....

More than dance, it is an ingenious melding of motion (often frenetic), shape (usually grotesque), color (always striking), light (constantly changing) and sound (super-stereophonic) into new and fresh dimensions that bedazzle and often trick the eye.... In the final act, the ten-member company, chattering like chimps, cavorted about the stage with sections of aluminum tubing, which they suddenly fashioned into a 16-foot high Tower of Babel with flags emblazoned IBM, A.M.A., and CBS. The results were at once fast, funny, and evocative of glimpses of man as both the victor and victim of his environment.

A performance in Alwin Nikolais's permanent home, "a small (348 seat) theater nestled between a drugstore and a Jewish bakery," and run by the Henry Street Settlement, a neighborhood social resource, was the occasion for *Time*'s coverage.

In 1961, a reviewer of two new Nikolais dances, *Nimbus* and *Stratus*, and comparing them to his well-known earlier works such as *Kaleidoscope, Prism* and *Allegory*, wrote:

In the Nikolais scheme, dance has exactly the same, but no more importance as sound, color, and design.

His dancers are magnificently trained and can perform any movement asked of them, but they are never asked to be human. No emotions are involved. His dancers are part of a pattern and color scheme. There is no margin for human error, and this tightrope awareness of danger is part of the fascination.

When five girls in leotards and tights sit on short columns and slowly manipulate hoops with their feet there must be no slip or the pattern is ruined. There is no slip.

About the 1966 performance of the *Vaudeville of the Elements*, a reviewer, observing that according to Nikolais's program notes the "elements are the toys of man and man is the toy of elements," concluded (not without a tinge of frustration, I think) that how to interpret "elements" here "seemed of little moment when viewing a work designed more for entertainment than philosophical rumination."

In 1969, another reviewer volunteered that we can look at Nikolais's works as "pure sensory luxury," of color, sound, movement:

> You can wallow and dig, with your sense and with Nikolais to guide you. Or you can, as I was this time, be sternly philosophical. When you choose this path, consciously turning off the Moogy sound or determinedly peering beneath the light sorcery…you discover what you've always suspected. The Nikolais Dance Theater requires intelligently trained bodies…but it does not offer them anything particularly significant in the way of movement.

Yet another response by an audience member welcoming "depth dimension" in dance and finding it in the least expected places:

> …for example, in the mystical levels of Alwin Nikolais' *Sanctum* or *Imago*… I am disturbed enough by unexpected relationships…to ask the question why?… A confrontation by a figure, personal or impersonal, caught in some shape of cloth between heaven and earth, acutely aware of a universe, catches me, as it were, "off guard." The presence of the unexpected…forces the audience to see life "as if for the first time"….

> Take the still figures in *Spectrum*, who move and do not move. They are still points, but they are active and alive to their environment. The spectral, sheeted dancers in his *Spectrum* remind me of how the Biblical poet looked at nature and saw "trees that clap their hands."

And this reviewer is reminded here of T.S. Eliot's line in his *Four Quartets*:

> …at the still point, there the dance is, but neither arrest nor movement…. Except for the point, the still point, there would be no dance, and there is only the dance.

The above responses were chosen more or less at random for indicating the "look" of Nikolais's dance theater and the variety of critical reactions it can produce. They also point to the "problematic" or interpretive issues presented by his dances, including their philosophical complexity that some favored, obviously more than others. Nik, as the dance world called him, choreographed a vast range of dances, from the 1930s to his death in 1993 at age 83. His creations, of movements merged into a "total" and "magical" theater, every element of color, lighting, and sound being his inventions, dating from the 1950s, constitute the major Nikolais legacy.

A Connecticut native, Nik was early drawn to anything theatrical, then in the 1930s, attending the summer Bennington School of the Dance (ADF's forerunner), added modern dance to his interests in music, lighting, puppetry, etc. Louis Horst and Martha Graham were influences, as was Hanya Holm and her mentor Mary Wigman (both legendary figures in modern dance history, but due to the arbitrary options imposed by content/space limitations, are regretfully unattended to here). Curiously, although Wigman and Holm at the time represented German Expressionism, what Nik took from them mostly excluded that kind of emotion/expressionism; instead, he liked Wigman's use of percussive music and Holm's "de-personalized" movement technique that also incorporated improvisation.

Nik's association with Hanya Holm continued both in New York City and at Colorado College where in 1941 the Hanya Holm Summer School of Dance was founded, to endure for 43 years and which "at its demise in 1983, was the longest-lived institution of its kind." It was here, in 1949, that Murray Louis as a student met Nik, and their famous partnership (choreography, performance, teaching) began. The Colorado venture became the third major summer school/festival, besides Jacob's Pillow and the American Dance Festival (ADF), that would foster modern dance's growth and influence its development on American campuses. Nik and Murray were prominent campus influences over the years, and I remember the warmth with which they were greeted by university dance educators at summer sessions of the National Endowment for the Arts' Artists-in-Schools Dance Component that was administered by ADF's Director, Charles Reinhart.

Because of the Holm/Wigman connection, and because of the "metal technology" or "teatro magnetico" quality of his theater pieces, Nik's inspirations were often traced to the Bauhaus, Oskar Schlemmer, and others. And to the lighting-and-dance experiments of Loie Fuller, Isadora Duncan's contemporary, who today receives deserved renewed attention for her pioneering role in modern dance's early development. Nik's comments on such matters, delivered with his usual candor and wit, when receiving a Dance Magazine Award in 1968, are informative:

> I suppose you all know this award is given for dehumanization. If you have read the reviews of my works over the past fifteen years, you certainly know that I'm considered the best dehumanizer in the business.... I seem to have a diabolical talent in obscuring the dancer in my choreography....

...it was thirty years ago that I started in the concert dance field, and it was twenty years ago that I started at the Henry St. Playhouse. About fifteen of those thirty years were spent in shaping a philosophy, or battleground, that would determine the...choreography which I did.... Fifteen years ago in modern dance we had not yet emerged from the foetal, fertile, phallic stage.... So, in the ensuing years, I fought off Freud, I fought off Buck Rogers, I fought off spacemen, I fought off Loie Fuller, and I fought off the Bauhaus and even Oskar Schlemmer.

The philosophy of dance that Nik evolved is as distinctive as the *Gesamtkunstwerk* or total dance theater that he invented, although how to relate the two is not so obvious. I had long known about Nik's fondness for the "abstract" in dance, of his departing farther from the "literal" than predecessors like Graham and Humphrey. And for years, especially since conversations when Martha Myers and I met with him during the production of Thirteen/WNET New York's series *A Time to Dance* (at WGBH-TV in Boston), I had imaged him as a "son rebelling" against the modern dance matriarchy.

But it was not until 1980, in discussions with him at ADF in North Carolina, that I quite realized how fierce was Nik's rejection of the "psychologism" he attributed to female modern dance leadership. He emphasized his own anti-Freudian and anti-psychoanalytic-confessional sentiments. He lamented the loss of respect for "the unique gesture." As I understand this, he meant that you ought to choose this rather than that movement/gesture, in a classwork or performance context, because it is peculiarly apt or significant in that particular context. Artistic talent is what discerns which movement/gesture in a particular context is unique to it. In Nik's eyes, even as early as Graham, and certainly subsequently, movements/gestures in modern dance were popping up arbitrarily all over the place, thus looking capricious, unmotivated, insignificant.

In expressing his fondness of the abstract or the non-psychological, he acknowledged his immersion in the details of motion, shape, space, and time, a happy alternative to an ascending narcissism, as he saw it, in modern dance. He was not guilty, as had been charged, with disliking emotion in art, only preferring emotionalism when it was not the origin but the result of theatrical manipulations of motion, space, time, lighting, shape, etc. He once wrote:

I have particular points of view about the difference between the male and female mind in respect to abstraction, but I had better not get involved. What I'd like to point out is that the male is far more inclined toward the abstract, and the field of dance is overpoweringly female and matriarchal. I hope fervently for the time when the socio-dynamic climate will re-establish the male in a more just position in the modern dance world.

As noted earlier, but needing elaboration, I for a long time took from Nik's writings and conversations the image of the "sons' anti-matriarchal rebellion," by Nik, Murray Louis, Erick Hawkins, and Merce Cunningham, as representing the post-WWII shift in modern dance away from Graham's psychologism to (often male-generated) abstractionism. I often emphasized this in informal discussions, including those about why African Americans generally adhered to narrative/expressive dancing when their white contemporaries, during the Sixties and beyond, went for abstraction and movement for its own sake.

People in the dance world to whom I offered this idea tended, however, to be underwhelmed by it (just why, I never found out), although women (whether dancers or spectators) seemed to smile or nod assent more regularly than men (odd, I agree, so maybe my sampling was poorly conducted). Perhaps the male dancers I talked to, remembering how Hawkins, Nikolais, Cunningham, Paul Taylor, and others had on many an occasion commended their female predecessors/mentors, thought my use of "rebellion" was too harsh. In any event, I was thus led to calling it my "quirky" bit of theorizing until recently when I found it (independently, of course) expressed by Sally Banes in her *Dancing Women*.

She quotes the same passage (as above) from Nik, although in omitting his opening words about having a particular point of view on gender-based aesthetics about which he had better shut up, she risks conveying the depth of feeling here. She adds (controversially, I believe) José Limón, Alvin Ailey, and Paul Taylor to the "rebellious" sons list; "often they were the *rebellious* sons of the *domineering* mothers (aesthetically speaking)." Given Banes' very distinguished career as a dance writer/theorist, maybe my harbored notion is not so quirky, and for all I know maybe among dance historians is more or less a commonplace.

The preceding is important, because Nik's male rebelliousness was the most outspoken and intense, more openly calling our attention to an apparent "gender-divide" that continues as a strong undercurrent in the modern dance world today. Moreover, this sentiment of his explains, if or if not justifying, his moving to the abstract and building from there a complex dance philosophy.

It took years to evolve, but that process was already underway when in 1937 and watching Hanya Holm's famous *Trend* performed in Bennington, he got the images "where the mass of dancers, just by raising one hand together, blew off the whole top of the universe." A certain gesture, unelaborated emotionally but impressively unique in the context, had a blasting effect! Dynamite! A lot could be learned from that!

Of all the formulations of Nik's philosophy, the one that I find most revealing, that tells you why he so firmly censored psychologism and especially "egoism" in concert dancing, is his four-page paper, "The New Dimension of Dance." You learn here that "abstraction" means "transcendence" through art, transcending the all-too-familiar/everyday into new realms of experience that are only reachable via mathematical and technical methods; science has made "abstract communication current and plausible," and it has "brought man into symbolic communion with the unknowable."

This is the attitude of a man who sees the abstractness of mathematics, logic and science as "liberating" from the self-drama or self-preoccupation of everyday life and its lamentable mimicry in too much contemporary theatrical dancing. Liberation occurs in focusing on the qualities of sound, lift, color, and motion, then discovering their "poetry" and their eventual human/emotional effects; without relying on prominent intrusions of the dancer's ego or personality. In allowing emotions, Nik cautions that they, too, must be "abstract"; they include feelings of heavy, light, thick, thin, large, small, fast, slow, etc., akin to certain sensations of color or sound, "yet by themselves do not qualify into that category of emotions which may be identified as grief, anger, etc."

Nik's "new" abstract-minded choreographer has to be more than just a choreographer. That is partly the consequence of having to treat all elements non-literally and co-equally—costumes, sound, lighting, props, and motion. As someone once wrote or said, Nik needed to be the whole show—composer, designer, electrician, choreographer—almost to the point of presiding in the box office and showing you to your seat. You had to watch him engaged in backstage operations to appreciate the technician he was. Knowing his anxiety about backstage details, I once had to resist telling him that my 14-year-old son, a totally inexperienced emergency substitute, had (successfully) operated a follow-spot for Nik's company performance that night.

Nik was the most "philosophical" modern dancer I ever spent time with, his words flying over my head abstractly and speculatively but always arrestingly. His language was almost as invented as his dances. He acknowledged that, besides being called Buck Rogers, Space Man, etc. for his stage arsenal of masks, props, and mobiles, he was even (rarely) dubbed an "existentialist." That is due, I suppose, to words such as these:

> He [the "new dancer"] is ready to raise the self out of the pedestrian diathesis, and to reshape it into those forms of motion which translate his discovered poetic substance.... It is part of the constant reaffirmation that reflects the *timeless and spaceless divinity of being*. It is the *undercurrent of life itself* into which the artist dips. (my italics)

The dances must first of all recall Man through himself. Here the psyche in full spirit demands that the body *uphold the primal nature of Man, within the content of his specific being.* This specific self…does not relate to the unusual attitude of the proud-pigeon hero…. This is the creature through which the dancer speaks—the one who within himself is kindred to the substance of art. (my italics)

I have emphasized above the "existentialist" words that remind me of the philosopher Martin Heidegger's "revelations of Being" and the like. I don't know the extent of Nik's acquaintance with philosophy, including Heidegger, but what is evident is his conceiving modern dance (in league with the other arts), in departing from the literal/representational in favor of the abstract, as capable of relating a transcendent realm of "Being," of which his own finite self or being is a small part. You may ask, "Can't' this be expressed less densely, more clearly?" Nik's answer was "No!," and in lending wavering support, I add that Reality and Being are no easy things to articulate.

Did Nik expect his audiences to "see" all that philosophy in works such as *Kaleidoscope, Prism, Imago,* and *Vaudeville of the Elements*? If so, you may say, he takes the cake as risk-taker. But in fact, Murray Louis informs us, he entertained no such expectations, as we realize once we distinguish between him as teacher-philosopher and creator of abstract theater:

With an artist like Graham, whose technical approach to movement was so clearly incorporated into her choreography, it was not difficult to know what she taught from what one saw on stage. This is not the case with Nik…. What is done on stage is Nik's personal vision. He shares this only with his audience. He imparts none of this to his students. On stage he creates theater, in class he teaches dance. His approach to dance in the classroom is of classical purity. His insistence on motional revelation and its clarity of articulation is relentless.

Murray Louis knew him best, so we follow him in distinguishing the versatile Nik as creator, teacher, and philosopher. And as realist, in all likelihood he never expected his audiences to "see" his dance philosophy moving on stage; nor did he want seminar-style "intellectualizings" by either his dancers or audiences. Given his extraordinary talent for *image-making* on stage, images gushing fireworks, he certainly discouraged intellectualizing of the sort that hindered *image-watching.* Still, I have to believe, from what he told me as well as from his published words, that he hoped his audiences would be *led,* by the impact of his performances, to at least a beginner's sense of the kind of philosophy that motivated these performances in the first place. Without doubt, his dances were designed to stimulate the sense but the mind as well, otherwise no "new" dance as he called it. And of course to stimulate our minds not just anywhere but in the direction of his own philosophy—so risk preserved!

Nik's imaginative talent, its wildness, is abundantly evident in works like *Noumenon Mobilus* and *Tent*, but for those unacquainted with his theater pieces, it is hilariously illustrated, for the reading, in his response to a request made in the mid-Sixties for a description of how he would (or not) choreograph the Prodigal Son theme (which he promised he would "never" do). These excerpts give you its flavor:

> The son would be in a bulk of bright yellow material against a panel of lavender. The mother would be a huge, amorphous swath of purple; the father on stilts in an elongated blue. The brothers are bound together in a single large sack of rust-colored stuff, with their heads almost buried in it.... All this could be accompanied by suitable electronic sounds, in the nature of clashing steel, reverberations, feedbacks, switch clicks, with an obbligato of finger-nail scratching on a blackboard....

> There is the possibility of a dada...approach to this scene...a naked female with one foot in a steaming pot-au-feu and the other fitted with a bicycle wheel. On her head is a weathervane, and she holds a 1916 Baedeker in her hand. The mother keeps pouring whitewash over her son's head, and tries to towel it off while prancing violently.... Put all this together with the title *The Prodigal Son*, and it is bound to be meaningful to someone, and even several—if not all.

A risk Nik was willing to take was the possible inability of his audiences to thrill, as he did, to a sensuous mélange of motion, color, sound, etc. that to some degree depends on grasping the abstract configuration or scheme that makes that mélange coherent rather than simply chaotic. That abstract or de-personalized configuration, as we've seen, was for Nik essential, and the reality of the risk he took, is indicated by again citing Murray Louis.

Louis tells of seeing Balanchine's *Agon* with the critic John Martin shortly after its premiere, that Martin was annoyed by how the dancers performed it, adding too much, as he saw it, of their own personalities. Martin said that Balanchine himself felt the same way. Louis then took Nik to see *Agon* who agreed with Martin and Balanchine. Louis comments: "I couldn't understand how these three guys, independently of each other, had the same reaction while I thought the dancers made the ballet. They were strong, personality dancers then—clever, witty and hip, and they brought the piece to life. Today much of what those dancers added is part of the choreography of *Agon*. So much for you three guys."

In the early 1980s, when I mentioned to Nik how a certain dancer had reacted to a negative review, he replied that it was "tough" because "for most of them dancing is so personal." I venture that what his "total theater" sought was not total de-personalization but the experience of being a "deeper" person through exposure to its magic of "abstract sensuousness." We have to see him in the "abstract expressionist" vanguard, one of the first in 20th century modern dance to understand how motion, lines, shape, etc., lifted or abstracted out of familiar into non-representational contexts, have the power to stir novel emotions, our minds to novel conceptions of dance and art. That power of the abstract in art, so widely assumed nowadays, is just a brute fact, beyond dispute.

The durability of Nik's achievements was evident during 1992–1993, when Rutgers University conducted a 25-year retrospective of his and Murray Louis's dances. Some dozen or more of their works were reconstructed, including Nik's *Imago, Tower* (from *Vaudeville of the Elements*), *Tent, Four Brubeck Pieces*, and *Bach Suite* by Louis. A conference on issues relating to dance reconstructions, including those of Nik and Murray, was held at Rutgers in 1992. As a program brochure states, Nik pioneered multimedia dance performance, with side lighting, side projections, electronic music, among other strategies, and now "His developments in these areas are used by the full spectrum of contemporary dance and theater artists. With his long-term collaborator Murray Louis, Nik has shaped the way we see contemporary performance today."

A Letter

New York
September '01

My dear Mrs. C.:

The kids are wonderful! So pleased I am that they got something from our meeting. Vita is such a pretty young thing, and George seems as sensitive as he is sensible. They are two *civilized* creatures, and I'm sure that the dance can only help, can't possibly hurt *those* characters!

And they liked that brief video of Nik that I showed them. Your reaction—I'm not surprised, not at all, too macho. I was prepared for how you'd feel. Don't think I'm not sympathetic. Because I like Nik, admire him and his work immensely, but because of Martha's and my "comradeship" with so many in the dance world, we have to sympathize with all those feeling there's a gender problem. You're not alone in your feelings on this.

Just yesterday, Jennifer Dunning, in *The New York Times* reported on the problem ("Dance Notes," September 3, 2001). A recent study by what's called the Gender Project concludes that "modern dance is now a man's world, at least in New York City." The numbers of dancers presented, receiving grants, getting publicity, etc. show this, but why and what should be done about it? These questions are being tossed about for airy debates, as of course you'd expect.

But this isn't just a "now" problem. John Martin wrote in 1961 that the gender role in modern dance had radically changed: whereas early modern dance was "almost exclusively a woman's art...the bulk of [this] season has definitely been male...it has not been a conspicuous improvement artistically." ("Dance: Muscling In—Male Performers and Choreographers Monopolizing the Modern Field," *The New York Times*, December 17, 1961).

Women so far outnumber men in dance—as performers, audience, presenters, contributors, etc., so it's a problem that's not going away. What's the solution? Mrs. C., you tell me!

Please don't brood over my sketch of Nik. A pity you never saw his dances, 'cause they'd be more vivid for you than the philosophy. But, please, don't discount the philosophy, it's *really* part of those dances, so if you've understood anything at all in my sketch, you've "seen" *something* of those dances, the thought that's *in* them.

Thank you, my dear, for arranging that chit chat with Vita and George (when do I meet Vanessa?). Warm greetings to them and to you wherever you are,

GEM

Merce Cunningham

Dances that cause us to ask "What is that dance about?," then on top of that "What is modern dance anyway, what is its purpose and raison d'etre?," criss-crossed the New York City dance scene after WWII. When dances seem to question themselves or the art they exemplify, they immediately stimulate intellectual inquiry. An abundance of these, mostly by white choreographers over the past fifty years, has made modern dance an ongoing subject of debate and deliberation.

The almost countless dances of Merce Cunningham, that illustrate the point, have created a half-century's supply of pleasure, worship, debate, and deliberation. They have been the avant-garde rabbits in the race to show what modern dance is or is not all about, more often than not eluding the critics, scholars, and paparazzi hounding behind. Those dances have inspired films, articles, reviews, forums, books, semi-imitations, and documentary studies, so that, even without the additional influences of distinguished con-temporaries, Merce Cunningham's choreographies would have made mod-ern dance a thinking person's art. So much has been said and written about Merce, as the dance world knows him, that all I can bring to the table are certain emphases and footnotes.

Now in his eighties, active as ever, Merce is a transplanted New Yorker, having left his native Washington state to join Martha Graham's company with which he performed from 1939–1945. At Graham's suggestion, note-worthy because of the open hostility that reportedly existed then between the two worlds of ballet and modern dance, he also took classes at the School of American Ballet. The balletic influence is evident in his work both as performer and choreographer. A spectacular dancer, celebrated for his ele-vation, speed, agility, and sprite-like charisma, he brought a male stardom to modern dance that many assumed was reserved for classical ballet.

Cunningham's career, as is well known, is interwoven with John Cage's, musician and composer as influential in his field as Cunningham in his. Both men met in Seattle in the late 1930s and began their legendary collaboration until Cage's death in 1992. What they achieved together (and independent-ly), as interactions with the other arts and especially music and painting, in defining 20th century avant-garde theory and practice, is monumental and beyond summary here. What, however, has to be mentioned is that the distinctiveness of Cunningham's dances and their underlying aesthetic owes much to the collaboration with musicians like Cage and Morton Feldman, to artists like Robert Rauschenberg and Jasper Johns. Once other artists, critics and scholars started exploring the nature of that distinctiveness, Merce's works increasingly penetrated American and international intellectual awareness.

The Cunningham-Cage collaboration re-emphasized modern dance as an experimental art. Unlike Martha Graham, Katherine Dunham, José Limón, and Donald McKayle, for example, the collaboration experimented mainly with movement-on-its-own rather than movement-as-representative. During the post-war years and since, while others including African American choreographers extended modern dance's tradition of inventing movement for "expressive" purposes, Merce's dances were praised or pondered for being abstract, (allegedly) non-expressive, movement for its own sake. While representing a wholly different dance theater from Alwin Nikolais's, Merce and Nik did seem to give their art a tandem push away from the *psychologically* to the *abstractly* expressive.

It is worth noting that Merce has often reiterated, sometimes as annoyed by the charge that his aesthetic is "non-expressive" as Nik was on the issue of "de-humanization," that theater dancing will always impress some viewers as being emotionally expressive and revelatory of personality. That *they* the viewers rather than Cunningham the choreographer make the call about what the dancing expresses or reveals—how democratic is that?—is all that his aesthetic demands. The choreographer puts the dance out there, gets credit for the time, energy, and talent to make the thing, but as a novel entry into our experiences we have to make of it what we can.

To do that, to make of it what we can, but relevantly not recklessly, I say that we are helped by knowing something about his theory and practice. My watching a Cunningham dance is usually enlivened by retaining in the background of my consciousness certain well-known principles of his modus operandi. These include creating dances independently of musical/sound accompaniment, perhaps not fraternizing them until the initial performance; using chance (e.g., flipping a coin, clicking a computer, etc.) for deciding certain features (length, steps, exits, entrances, etc.) of a dance; unconventional structuring, the dancers performing simultaneously but seemingly disconnectedly, and no identifiable progression from beginning to conclusion. For some, the effect is of isolated, energetic movements within a static and unobtrusive theater setting, pictorial elements alternating with each other in a stationary frame.

But, like myself, you may want to bring, mentally tipped, lots more to backdrop your viewing a Cunningham concert. Read about how the intellectual atmosphere of the Cunningham-Cage collaboration reflects ideas of Buckminster Fuller, Marcel Duchamp, Marshall McLuhan, D.T. Suzuki, Arnold Schoenberg, James Joyce, Milton Babbitt, Erik Satie, Edwin Denby, Andy Warhol, among others—and you sensitize your *viewing mind* to Merce's offerings. But there is a paradox here, which is appropriate, because Cage and Cunningham always found paradoxes delightful.

The paradox is that the more you roam what Merce and Cage said about space, time, causality, the arts, and life itself, the more you are somehow returned, from these mental excursions and their temptations to generalize/universalize, to the *particularities* of a Cunningham performance—the specific qualities of a side-jump, of a battement tendu, a tour en l'air. All the intellectualizing associated with the Cage-Cunningham aesthetic, after all, starts from and returns to performance details, and although that aesthetic may burgeon in the theorist's cerebral space, in Merce's theater it miniaturizes into a laser-like illumination of *this* and *that* detail of a dancer's performance.

Merce nodded approvingly when I once ventured in a conversation how clearly, almost starkly, each movement of each dancer stands out in his pieces, to be sharply perceived. But, oddly, those same movements would probably remain blander and more indifferent to my perceptions were it not for the intellectual pointers I had garnered through acquaintance with the Cage-Cunningham guiding ideas. Among those (legendary) audience members who could not "get it" and walked out of a Cunningham concert, there were many, I have to believe, who would have stayed in their seats, had they the benefit of the conceptual framework with which to identify (if only in their own terms) what was occurring on stage.

The Cage-Cunningham way of looking at things is flavored with wit, humor, mischievousness, pomposity-busting at every turn, process favored over product, questions-and-answers typically reversed, and Zen-like delight in coming upon still another contradiction. I was part of a conversation with Cage in the mid-Eighties that touched on the relations of art to life, and, with his usual grin and eye-twinkling, he said we first had to get straightened out on the nature of "Being." Hoping and expecting him because of his Eastern philosophical interests to be amused by it, I piped up, "What about *Non*-Being?" He didn't disappoint, smiling broadly, eyes rolling, silently clapping his hands he replied, "Ah! That's even better!"

Stories about Cage's "outrageousness" or artistic unconventionality are legion, but a recent example being reported by the media (September 6, 2001) is the beginning performance, lasting 16 months in silence, of a Cage organ composition meant to take 639 years before performance completion.

Beginning in silence at a church in Halberstadt, Germany, the performance will be extended at another church west of Berlin. Only the organ's bellows had been built as of late 2001, which was fine since the first three notes were not to be played until January 5, 2003. Meanwhile, the sounds of air coursing through the bellows marked the time between 2001 and 2003. Sounds of the completed organ will presumably mark time's passage for the performance's remaining 637 years.

Merce told me, in another conversation some years ago, when I asked about the influence of philosophy in his work, that Cage more than he had read in that area. I had in mind Cage's fondness for Haiku (unrhymed Japanese lyric poems having a fixed 3-line form consisting of 5, 7, and 5 syllables, respectively), but without further words from Merce about this, I like to think that his dances reveal a *Haiku* likeness. Cage applauded this: "Haiku requires of us that our soul should find its own infinity within the limits of some finite thing." The semi-theological idea here, that the finite can incarnate infinity or that smallness can encapsulate bigness, that the minimal lines, say of a Matisse drawing, can express maximally, I think applies to Cunningham's choreography.

A lot of "heady" stuff is compressed into Merce's movements' sparseness; dramatic flourishes and fancy elaborations of steps and patterns are excluded. The choreographic approach is always economical, all the more appreciated when the concepts of time, space, causality, chance, structure, etc. behind it are understood.

The apparent simplicity of the movements belies the complexity of thought responsible for them. A reviewer of Merce's creation, *Way Station*, performed at ADF's 2001 season, appreciates the point:

> The middle of *Way Station*…a woman enters slowly from off stage left, walking, not quite tiptoe, on the balls of her feet…still extended, she proceeds to take in the world around her with no small degree of fascination, head erect, slowly turning…. As she looks at her own arms, legs and torso, the same rare air of discovery intensifies. At points she seems to be measuring gravity itself. She deliberately articulates and extends each extremity individually, observing its responses, with what appears to be intellectual interest….

> From individual investigations of space, gravity, self, and others, dancers develop and explore duets and trios that assess the possibilities of contact at the body's articulation points. The slowest of these axial sequences suggest living Alexander Calder mobiles….

> Fifty years out, his [Cunningham's] technique is astounding and his dancers breathtaking. Still the attractions of his works are *unapologetically intellectual.* (my italics)

Gerald E. Myers

The review bears out Merce's thesis that ostensibly abstract movement is also expressive, and it occurred to me, watching again his dances performed at the 2001 ADF in Durham, North Carolina, that characterizing them as exemplifying movement-for-its-own-sake can be misleading, not only because it can be expressive but because it is theatrical. His dance movements serve a traditional objective, to be transformed from the ordinary to the magical/theatrical. Merce's dance is a spectacle, visual and aural as well as kinetic.

This is evident in the new *Way Station*, with James Hall's striking costumes, Takehisa Kosugi's "live electronic" music that defies description, and Charles Long's decor of three "Tripods" (skinny, multi-colored surrealistic reminders of garden archways?) through which dancers enter and exit. As it is in the popular and revived *Rain Forest* (1968), with the spectacular combination of Andy Warhol's decor of "silver clouds," huge, lustrous aluminum-looking pillows, and Aaron Copp's lighting (Copp also lighted *Way Station* to great effect).

Movement counts spectacularly too, in these dances, old and new; meaning that, if you expected exquisite dancers to perform exquisite but "deadened" movements, you should have been surprised. Numerous movement passages in *Way Station* and *Rain Forest* stimulate interpretations of meaning, of expressiveness, while knowing full well that you'll never locate such in Merce's expressed intentions. Something in *Native Green* (1985), also on the ADF program, caught my attention; namely, its movement dynamics. By alternating slow and quickening movements in the given context, the dancing process itself conveyed alternating moods of relaxation and urgency. I was struck by how, without any acting, miming, or special changes in the dancers' demeanors, the quickened movements by themselves created a sense of urgency, an "abstract" urgency, I add, because it lacked any real-life sort of context.

Returning to the *Haiku* concept, I think that as composing a poem to strict Haiku requirements represents a puzzle-challenge, so for Merce and Cage, musical and dance composing are puzzles or task-challenges. The attention thus paid by both men to technical and minutely detailed items is quite startling. Henry Cowell, Cage's teacher and major musical influence himself, wrote about Cage's compositional methods, and you get some very small sense of it in this:

> Cage's method of employing the *I Ching* [ancient Chinese method of throwing coins, like dice, for chance numbers] to ensure that his compositions are "free of individual taste and memory in their order of events" is based on a complicated system of charts. These govern "superpositions" (the number of events happening at once during a given structural space), tempos, durations, sounds, and dynamics; and all the charts are derived from tosses of the coins.

Similarly, what I may call the method of "charting chance" is used by Cunningham in making dances. Remy Charlip, distinguished dance artist and former Cunningham dancer, describes how the piece *Suite by Chance* was composed in 1954:

> It is a long dance in four movements to music for magnetic tape by Christian Wolff. For this dance, a large series of charts was made: a chart numbering body movements of various kinds (phrases and positions, in movement and stillness); a chart numbering lengths of time…; a chart numbering directions in space (floor plans).
>
> These charts, which defined the physical limits within which the continuity would take place, were not made by chance. But from them, with a method similar to one used in a lottery, the actual continuity was found…. At important structural points in the music, the number of dancers on stage, exits and entrances, unison or individual movements of dancers were all decided by tossing coins…. There are familiar and unfamiliar movements, but what is *continuously* unfamiliar is the *continuity* freed from usual cause and effect relations. (my italics)

As Merce looked happily to chance, that others might avoid like the plague, for help in inventing dances, so he later seized upon the computer, anathema to others more soulful, for assisting the choreographic imagination. In recent years he has used a computer program called Life Forms that enables him, for example, to computer-generate movements, store them, then combine into movement phrases. Images can be examined from various angles, the timing of movements can be changed so that, for instance, you can study how the body, in slow motion, metamorphoses from one shape to another, and so on. Praise the computer, says Merce, for its inventiveness, of presenting possibilities of movements ("impossibilities," exclaim some excessively challenged Cunningham dancers) that otherwise would never occur to the choreographer.

On several occasions I have tried to draw Merce out on why he admires the critic Edwin Denby's dance writings, and each time he emphasized his appreciation of Denby's poetic ("beautifully precise, not fancy") formulations. Denby's poetic way of thinking and writing about dance, I am persuaded, provides audiences with the appropriate approach to the art, at the very least serving to alter our literal staring to poetic seeing. The Cunningham-Cage aesthetic, in echoing Denby's, deserves to be called a modern-day "Poetics."

John Cage, in the 1940s, called attention to a special component of their Poetics, the concept of *clarity*. This is interesting, because clarity distinctively characterizes how Cunningham dancers perform—clean vertical lines,

Gerald E. Myers

pointed feet, quick brisk steps, still moments, etc.—also because James Joyce, a favorite of Cage and Cunningham, took the concept of *claritas* from Thomas Aquinas's aesthetic theory in composing his final, briefest version of *Portrait of the Artist as a Young Man*. For Joyce, at that period in his career, clarity and verbal economy go together, and, as we have seen, for Cage and Cunningham economy verging on minimalism is standard practice.

In 1944, Cage argued that modern dance had lost clarity; yes, in *Frontier* Martha Graham had achieved it but certainly not in her *Deaths and Entrances*, and the problem menaced the art generally. Rhythmic structure was on Cage's mind; its clarity being "cold, mathematical, inhuman, but basic and earthy." For artistic effectiveness, however, it needs a playful, even tense wedding with grace that is "warm, incalculable, opposed to clarity and like the air. Grace is not used here to mean prettiness; it is used to mean the play with and against the clarity of rhythmic structure." This tension or give-and-take between clarity and grace makes for the best art—dance, music, and poetry included.

Eight years later, in 1952, Merce showed how his concern for clarity, well known for applying to his dancers' steps and posture, extended to the dancer's space. This is important because "the moving becomes more clear if the space and time around the moving are one of its opposites—stillness. Aside from the personal skill and clarity of the individual dancer, there are certain things that make clear to a spectator what the dancer is doing." Space (and time) is one of those things, but unfortunately, Merce suggested, modern dance "stemming from German expressionism and the personal feelings of the various American pioneers, made space into a series of lumps, or often just static hills on the stage with actually no relation to the larger space of the stage area...too often the space was not visible enough...."

In 1958, Cunningham created his landmark *Summerspace*, a dance to music by Morton Feldman, costumes and decor by Robert Rauschenberg. *Summerspace* illustrates Merce's poetic-philosophical musings about dance-space. The dancers are costumed in pointillist designs matching the vast backdrop, so that while standing still they seem to fade into it but while moving come into clearer visibility. Space thus becomes something not only stepped through but stepped into and out of, and the dancers, whether jumping, running, or turning, seem mostly isolated from each other, balletic forms in a languorous summer space that are themselves summer-delicate, anything but winter-lumps on stage.

To appreciate how Merce's choreography and dance technique have spawned a remarkably dense discourse, a constellation of concepts about space, etc., one is helped by learning how his associates, former dancers, and observers characterize his works and their underlying aesthetic. Their recollections and anecdotes are entertaining, about early touring in a bulging Volkswagen microbus for relatively few and debt-yielding performances at colleges, but they are also valuable for showing how new ways of intellectualizing concert dance accompanied Merce's studio and theater experiments. For his dances but also for their stimulating conceptualizations that enriched general artistic as well as dance discourse, Merce has been regularly honored, including his Honorary Membership in the American Academy of Arts and Letters, MacArthur Foundation Fellowship, Kennedy Center Honors, and France's Legion d'honneur and the Samuel H. Scripps American Dance Festival Award.

When talking with Cage about the arts, Richard Kostelanetz suddenly said to him, "I get the impression that this evening we're talking less about theater or music than about philosophy," and Cage replied, "That's because the boundaries have gone." Eliminating suspected boundaries between dance/music and intellect, between artistic doing and inventive thinking, is an achievement of the Cunningham-Cage aesthetic. American intellectual as well as artistic traditions have been permanently re-directed as a result.

You can unravel a lot of philosophy out of E.H. Gombrich's aphorism that an artistic painter tends "to see what he paints rather than to paint what he sees." So we can uncover an intellectual hoard by thinking-through Merce Cunningham's invoking Gertrude Stein in claiming that the grammar of movement does not *represent* meaning, it *is* the meaning; and his saying, perhaps in response to critics wondering whether only the physical matters in his dances, "For me, it seems enough that dancing is a spiritual exercise in physical form, and that what is seen, is what it is".

A Letter

Dear Mrs. Calabash:

I think of ("see," I mean) you in that deck-chair looking out like Cyrano on those leaf-strewn lawns, seasoning your meditations. From my window I see Autumn's browns and reds reflected in the calm harbor here. That's what I see—no response, please, leave it *there*.

There? There! The *thereness* of things, I think of this when thinking of Merce Cunningham and John Cage. Because this "found" and thus "artistic" feature of things is what they present us so distinctively. But what is it? Hard to say, hard to understand, and that has got to please them enormously.

The existence of your chair, Mrs. C., its "thereness"—you can point to the chair, its shape and color and the rest, but can you point also to its existence/thereness? I guess not. We of course see the chair but not something additional, its thereness. How can that be, since the chair's existence/presence/thereness seizes our attention? How can it seize our attention if we can't point to it? So the thereness of things that we can't doubt, we can't understand.

Cage adored what he couldn't understand. An example is his short radio play *James Joyce, Marcel Duchamp, Erik Satie: an Alphabet* (1982) that is currently touring with Cunningham performing in it. Performers, noises, lights, antics, a madcap hour-plus of incomprehensible and all grinning their *thereness*.

"Thereness" distinguishes the undecorated, starkly figured steps/moves of a Cunningham dance. Why stand and applaud them? Not because they're there, rather for their thereness. *That* (but what is it?) seizes our attention, making for clear perception but opaque understanding.

There, Mrs. C., all decked-out, what think you (and Vanessa) of this encomium to the Cage-Cunningham aesthetic and its embrace of paradox?

Good night, wherever you are.
GEM

Paul Taylor

Paul Taylor, who in 2000 met his 70th birthday head-on and head-up promising to keep his gift-bag full of dances-to-be, is acclimated to hearing himself described as "the world's greatest living choreographer." For winning, over almost a half-century, the combined applause of critics and public audiences, he hears himself described accurately. Honored, medaled, and for posterity recorded all ways possible, Taylor is not only a modern dance icon, he is an American institution.

Audiences here and world-around greet the touring Paul Taylor Dance Company like a happy band of American troubadours. Fortified by a canny management team, released thereby to focus on their art, and confident in how their reputation has preceded them—all the result of admiration, loyalty, and affection for Taylor and his achievements—the company dancers blow into town and on stage *infectiously*. They bounce, squat, soar, and lope like their leader whose full round face you see as still boyish and openly congenial (but more, you learn, to see than to be seen), the dancers, whatever their age, exude youthful exuberance. They smile their enjoyment of giving the audience a contagious dance-life to the accompanying and usually enchanting music. If less than fifteen or twenty dancers, they yet present a Big Show that guarantees audience animation. But they also exemplify modern dance's being more than entertainment alone, often reminding us of the murkier dimensions of life that tug at our interpretations.

Paul Taylor is physically a large man, six-feet plus and sturdy muscular and whose choreographic imagination is even larger. His dances range from the plotlessly pure and lyrical to mixes of comedy, mayhem, dance noire, to suggestively narrational or demi-dramas. A former swimmer, he invents dances that are athletic, and that athleticism, transformed aesthetically, eliminates the need for the prescribed steps of ballet or of other forms including prior modern dance. An amateur painter, he choreographs with a keen eye for the pictorial—costumes, sets, and movement patterns in his work.

The Bigness that one associates with Taylor is due in part to his astonishingly prolific ingenuity, also to his wanting to embrace the scope of American history and culture. In this respect, he joins the ambitions of Martha Graham,

Doris Humphrey, and Charles Weidman in the 1930s. The Bigness of America, its spread-outness in time and space sufficient to sprout big contradictions, is redolent of human existence itself and tailor-made for the witty, ironic perspective of this modern dancer choreographer; and that infuse his works with a mentality that attracts critical and intellectual explorations. Examples include *From Sea to Shining Sea* (1965), *American Genesis* (1972–73), *Speaking in Tongues* (1988), and *Company B* (1991).

From Sea to Shining Sea, as Taylor writes in his autobiography *Private Domain* (1987), can be considered social satire, a wry portrait of "old Miss America's wrinkles" via choreographic references to the statue of Liberty, Pilgrims and the Mayflower, Iwo-Jima flag raising, Betsy Ross, among other historical landmarks. A dance panel in Washington, appalled, judged it anti-American and recommended to the State Department its removal from international touring programs. But the State Department, as Taylor himself apparently agrees, concluded that the dance's critical view of the United States is "an affectionate one and that its slings and arrows are outweighed by its being a worthy example of artistic freedom here...."

Although I have never exchanged with Taylor, personal acquaintance restricted to brief social acknowledgements, I have over the years absorbed numerous impressions of him from a few who know him well, in addition to what he has said in interviews and his writings. One strong impression is that, despite his sometimes blunt criticisms of American culture, he seems to feel deeply rooted in and attached to it. He indicates, for example, in *Private Domain*, that while touring abroad he remained mostly immune to foreign dance and artistic influences, always pointed inside back to these shores.

About *American Genesis*, an evening-length allegorical dance, Taylor comments substantially in *Private Domain*. His initial idea was to inject the Bible into a reconstruction of American history, from the colonial period through the Revolution, the Western expansion, to the Civil War, and to "braid them into corresponding biblical days of Creation, Fall, Fratricide, and Flood. All was to be presented as one eternal single-stranded conflict and shown in dance images that made double, even triple, cross-references." About the motivation for this and other "researched" dance scrutinies of his American heritage, he says, "A part of America's history that particularly appealed to me was a combination of puritanism and free spirit, a paradox that, by the way, was a large part of Martha's [Graham] own character and a warring part of mine."

The plot of *American Genesis*, employing reminders of earlier styles such as the cakewalk and minstrels, is about as thick or dense as one can get (see *Private Domain*, p. 333–334, for Taylor's own involved analysis), so you have to guess that allusions to Noah's children fly way over the audience's heads and those to the Flood seep way under their seats. Although many Taylor dances (another prominent example is the 1980 *Le Sacre du Printemps* [*the Rehearsal*], exciting and provocative despite its outrageously complex plot) can be identified via what they are "about," their "aboutness" can, as we see, be obviously elusive, running the traditional risks of modern dance. Such elusiveness can't be praised or condemned in itself. Depending on the context, the performance circumstances, the kind of audience present, etc., that elusiveness can be either a liability (distracting, frustrating) or an asset (stimulating, provoking interest).

Because of its calling to mind, like Graham's *Appalachian Spring,* the role of evangelical religion in America, *Speaking in Tongues* (to music by M. Patton, designed by Santo Loquasto, and lighted by Jennifer Tipton) is distinctly American-rooted. Concerned with religious hypocrisy, set in a Southern town, with such dramatized roles as the "outsider" who is stoned by the others, the piece opens with a barn dance. When it was revived for performance at New York's City Center, Anna Kisselgoff wrote in 1995 that as a "heavy-duty" piece it treats "the darkest of emotions," ending with folded chairs atop the dancers' bodies on the floor in a "mass death image"; the hour-length work evoking a "community whose surface gaiety covers up seething passions."

Company B is a Taylor "hit" of 1991 that moves to nine songs by the Andrews Sisters, a three-sister act that broke up in 1968 but is still remembered for its melodic associations with WWII and the 1940s. Their pictures, of three uniformed women with 1940's rolled hairdos smiling and saluting while performing for the troops in Europe and Africa during the war, adorn veterans' walls to this day. So *Company B*, in resounding songs like "Rum and Coca-Cola," "There Will Never Be Another You," and "Boogie Woogie Bugle Boy (of Company B)," creates an atmospheric interpretation of past and present, nostalgic but concretely (and perhaps relevantly) in the "now" of those vigorous dancing bodies on stage.

Company B is another ambivalent look at our history, on the surface rollicking to the "feel-good" songs of the Andrews Sisters but underneath betraying war's ravages. Women skip and run for soldiers' eyes but also abruptly collapse, and couples make buoyant but ultimately futile advances to each other. Laura Shapiro took note of an important bit in *Company B*, what is discernible in many Taylor works:

> Some of the most glorious dancing to be seen anywhere bursts forth in the male solos Taylor has made for "Company B." Andrew Asnes in "Tico-Tico," dashing and suave but with an undercurrent of anguish; Patrick Corbin in "Oh Johnny, Oh Johnny, Oh!," his eyes glittering as he drinks in the bevy of women around him and rips into a series of dazzling spins; and Jeff Waddlington, the

"Boogie Woogie Bugle Boy (of Company B)," cool and sharp and gaudy—these men hit the stage with an honest blast of masculinity that's thoroughly refreshing, and so is their attention to the subtleties involved in a bit of jazzy posturing, or a touch of impudence.

When Taylor launched his career in the 1950s, dancing with Martha Graham, how to dance as a male became a nagging question. He writes that Graham's (archaic) idea of a man was of a flat, two-dimensional figure; her men were "usually stiff foils, or something large and naked for women to climb up on. A few of us would like to be more 3-d and think that less beefcake would be a good idea, but have been *scared* to say so" (my italics).

Was Taylor part of the "male/son rebellion" against Graham and the preceding modern dance matriarchy? To an extent, but not much. Apart from feeling the need to redefine male dancing and to puncture Graham's pompous rhetoric (Taylor and others are amusing on this), he actually extended her expressive and theatrical aesthetic. Although he gained prominence in 1957 with a group of daring unconventional dances that challenged the status quo and that have been duly noted by dance critics and historians, he has since sustained his predecessor's practice of keeping dance expressive and dramatic, while experimenting and ever modifying former styles and predilections.

Taylor resisted the unplanned ("chance") and non-expressive aesthetic that emerged from the Merce Cunningham and John Cage partnership. He confesses in *Private Domain* to being puzzled by those favoring dances that are allegedly about nothing at all, since "Merce danced his own roles dramatically. Each of his movements, be they sharp or soft, shouted or whispered, startled or stealthy, clearly meant something to him...in *Untitled Solo*, an obviously psychological study, he was communicating personal but unspecific conflicts."

While also valuing ordinary movements like running, walking, and jumping, Taylor resisted the non-expressive aesthetic of loosely organized dance groups in the 1960s and 1970s known as the Judson Church dancers. He also remained conspicuously apart from their egalitarian or radically democratic philosophy insofar as he defended the "well-crafted" dance by a choreographer who exercises firm artistic control. And unlike those "revolutionaries," he pursued choreography that would be publicly accessible rather than directed primarily towards an audience of "insiders."

Taylor is less concerned than others about distinguishing between modern dance and ballet, partly because of his own balletic training including Antony Tudor's influence, and having performed in a Balanchine-choreographed solo in 1959 for *Episodes*, a collaboration between the New York City Ballet and the Martha Graham Company. He seems to prefer being mindful of the commonalities, not the differences, between the two dance forms, in addition to showing an impatience with "fancy" wordy attempts to demarcate them. Early in his career, while touring with Graham in Japan, when asked how to define modern dance, Taylor answered—quite unlike the others' responses including Graham's—"It's like this…. You know ballet? Well, modern's just the same, but uglier" (perhaps recalling Fokine's notorious comment that we noted earlier). He found it interesting, as he saw it, that Graham's choreography had become more balletic in the 1960s than it had been in the 1940s.

Versatility rather than a narrowly defined aesthetic is Taylor's trademark, one that definitely includes the ugly. *Churchyard* (1969), that looks like a community's moral and behavioral deterioration, is an example. So is *Big Bertha* (1971), an unforgettably unsettling 20-minute piece (to the music of a band machine and a garish cut-out set by Alec Sutherland) that shows a family on a carnival outing and going bonkers after throwing coins into Big Bertha, played by a tall dancer representing a machine that looks insanely like a dominatrix. It ends with the father raping his daughter. And dances like *Insects and Heroes* (1961, music, by J.H. McDowell, set by Rouben Ter-Arutunian) and *Cloven Kingdom* (1976) are among those that, with memorably suggestive movements, gestures, and costumes starkly remind us of our animal nature.

In addition to the theatrical, Taylor has worked less dramatically, where the experimental dominates. His 1968 dance *Public Domain* is an example. Marcia Siegel writes that, spoofing chance styles and opening with Tchaikovsky's "Swan Lake" second act overture and closing with Brahms's "Variations on a Theme of Haydn," and everything from the Gregorian chants to polkas to Elizabethan music thrown in between, *Public Domain* is really an exploration about dance itself. *Polaris* (1971), to music by Donald York and designed by Alex Katz, is another example. Its first section has five dancers in bathing suits in a kind of at-the-beach mood. Its choreography is repeated in the second section but with replaced dancers in the same costumes. This section's lighting is lowered, the music's tone alters, and the atmosphere when curtain falls is no longer light but duskily ominous. A proof, if needed, that movement's context makes all the difference!

Discussing this dance recalls an essay "Down with Choreography" that Taylor wrote in 1966. Writers on dance, he observes, discourse on everything, dance theories and history, music, costumes, choreography, and the audience, but they neglect the most essential of all, the dancers:

The finest choreography in the world does not mean a thing if the dancers are not suited to it and they look terrible.... A dancer is occupied with placement, stage spacing, the quality of a leap, the softness of a foot...but actually what we see is more than a foot or a curved back. We see an individual, and we see what that individual is.... A person is going to be revealed. Vanity, generosity, insecurity, warmth are some traits that have a way of coming into view.

So, for a change, up with performance and down with choreography! The focus is on *the body and its movements*. Theories and choreographic ideas are fine insofar as they highlight the dancer's qualities of movement, I take Taylor to mean, but too often the former become the focus themselves. Beware of the impulse that is conceptual and that diminishes the motor/physical. In the 1950s, during his avant-garde collaborations with John Cage, Jasper Johns, and Robert Rauschenberg, and absorbing the influences of their arts, Taylor located his own artistic self in another medium, body/movement exploration.

"I grew up watching for the *telling movement*," he has written, "both animals' and humans', as I suppose, but have never known for sure, all children do" (my italics). He studied ordinary, natural movements, drawing stick-figure images of legs standing, squatting, kneeling, etc. He learned that a kind of "body logic" exists, that *posture* for example amounts to gesture. "Discovering how to hold still and yet remain active in a way that looks vital is the most difficult of all." Since postures lose their distinctiveness when displayed in rapid succession, surrounding each of them with stillness rescues their gestural individuality.

Taylor allows himself some subtleties in thinking about the relation between natural and staged movements. Alluding to Graham's famous statement "The body does not lie," he calls this wishful thinking, adding that although a natural movement such as a pedestrian's smallest gesture can be telling, "The most communicative dances...are based on physical truths that in the making have been transformed for the stage into believability by the artistry of calculated lies." Evidently, artistry here blends with artifice that blends into a kind of "believable lie."

For the stage, learning how a move is to be performed is not easy; just being natural is usually insufficient. "For instance, the light turn of a head, the heavy drop of an akimbo arm, the slowing down of a run into a walk. When done right, there is much appeal to the tilting of Toby's shoulders as she stands with her weight on one leg, and the soft settling of Cynthia's arms as she folds them...—also, when the girls gaze downwards, the lovely arching of their necks." The shifting postures in his *Events I* (1957), Taylor tells us, convey a restless waiting, so when the dancer Donya finally walks off, "she is not merely moving to a different spot—she is *leaving* Toby." Context helps to give this effect, be it the music, costume, set, or in this instance "the sound of wind adds to the tension."

But some kind of balance between a dancer's natural ways of moving and the choreographer's transformation of them for staged performance is required. Taylor came to appreciate this early, discovering how the choreographer's attempt at "objective" control is limited. As the dance's context develops, unforeseen movement connotations, emotional and dramatic, leak through. Each dancer's idiosyncratic ways of moving leak through the choreographer's artifice, his attempt to transform them unfamiliarly. Taylor concludes: "By failing to find a completely objective approach, and by failing to disguise the dancer's individual body language, my awareness of the communicability of dance has increased."

Writers on dance, agreeing with Taylor's own admissions, highlight the fact that his movement vocabulary, so rich and varied in its expressiveness and dramatic range, is yet so minimal. Arlene Croce wrote in 1982: "As a choreographer, Taylor has the largest and clearest rhythm, the fewest shapes and steps and postures, since Michel Fokine." This is true, for instance, of Taylor's most famous piece, *Aureole* (1962), that is pure or lyric dancing to music by Handel and designed by himself. Although none of the steps are balletic, its flowing lyricism, the baroque music, and the white costumes for three female and two male dancers have led to its being called a "white ballet." It is perhaps the modern dance most widely seen (excepting Alvin Ailey's *Revelations*), since, as has been reported, it has invited over 100 licenses in more than 50 countries.

Taylor had Louis Horst in mind when inventing *Aureole*, in his limiting the dance's steps to a few basic ones that, like themes, would vary in speed, order, directions, etc. "My favorite step in *Aureole*—a certain run with flyaway arms—is a direct and intentional steal from Martha's *Canticles for Innocent Comedians*. It may be a little off, but it's the closest I could come."

Although his hat is tipped here to Horst and Graham, *Aureole* was in what some called its "old-fashioned" look and reliance on Handel an intentional, successful challenge to the devotedly "modernist" aesthetic of the American Dance Festival in New London, Connecticut that had commissioned it. A five-section work, it features athletic lunges, jumps, hops, and runs that are lyrically modulated. Numerous entrances and exits are used, Taylor has said, to give the illusion of both a larger cast and an expanded space. It concludes thrillingly, the dancers repeating exciting moments with arms stretching high, spinning, rolling, leaping—guaranteeing audience ovations.

Aureole is sheer dancing, yet as Taylor writes: "Even in this 'pure' piece, feelings are foremost." This is especially true of a duet that he composed for himself and Elizabeth Walton, and a solo adagio for himself that is done

Gerald E. Myers

almost entirely on the left foot; high-flying thoughts and images that might be called its "meaning," he tells us, accompanied its performance. Yet, the solo's most difficult part was the simple entering walk in silence from the wings to stage center. "No matter how often I've practiced it, this easy walk scares me to death. It's going to strip me of dance steps to hide behind and leave me stark naked." (Let's not forget this when we speak of the "risks" run in concert dance!)

A major reason for Taylor's conspicuous role in bringing modern dance into American intellectual awareness, in elevating its status to equal the other arts, is his popularity. Not only dance fans, including other dancers (who make up much of the modern dance audiences), and arts lovers on the campuses where the touring Taylor company is a fixture, but a general public has found his works accessible even where their "meanings" are problematic. That accessibility may trouble some, given modern dancers' inclinations, as we have seen, to be suspicious of popularity, of its representing surrender to commercialism.

Then we discover that Taylor himself is troubled by *Aureole*'s popularity, a dance that he had compared to "child's play." He tells us that "yet for all its success, perhaps because of it, *Aureole* filled me with resentment. I was wary of it. It caused me to see a time coming when a choice would have to be made—to remain on the comfortably safe side of the doorway to success, or to pass through it and into a tougher and lot less familiar place." Subsequent to 1962, as his more complex, darker, and stranger dances show in abundance, he made that latter difficult choice many times over.

Taylor's interest in music and the visual arts, his collaborations with musicians like John Cage, David Hollister, J.H. McDowell, Morton Feldman, and others, and with artists like Robert Rauschenberg, Rouben Ter-Arutunian, Alex Katz, and John Rawlings among others, have influenced the artistic dimensions of his pieces and, in so doing, attracted numbers of artists to his performances. Collaborations with celebrity fellow-dancers like Nureyev and Baryshnikov were of course additional audience draws. About music, we should note, he has much to say on its importance for his work and the care given to his musical choices—which is apparent to any follower of Taylor company performances.

He began, in 1961, a new dance called *Junction*, which was to be about musicality, about how movement and sound interact. The aim was not to visualize Bach's "exuberant sound" but to contrast and interact instructively with it. "By alternating contradiction with agreement, I hope to establish structural tensions and unexpected contrasts." Having watched many a Taylor program over the years, I recall numerous dances largely through musical as well as visual and kinetic associations, and though this might seem to be obviously expected, the fact is that not all choreographers affect one's perceptions and memories in this manner.

Taylor's recent creations to jazz are novel interactions between movement and sound. Remembering that one of his early dances, *3 Epitaphs* in 1956, was done to historic New Orleans jazz, at a time when jazz was mostly foreign to the modern dance aesthetic, we can think of his *Piazzolla Caldera* (1997) and *Oh, You Kid!* (1999) as continuing an inquiry into jazz's kinship with modern dance, both devoted for instance, to freedom of experimentations.

Piazzolla Caldera has been praised for capturing the essence of the tango and, eschewing tired imitations, takes it into unexpected movements and semi-dramatic episodes. *Oh, You Kid!*, to the accompaniment of Rick Benjamin's Paragon Ragtime Orchestra, is a "researched" and complex romp through American social musical/dance styles. It is a dance whose movement-and-music interactions, representing slices of American culture, warrant careful re-seeing and reinterpreting. As, of course, do all worthwhile dances since one or two "readings" can never catch it all.

Esplanade (1975) is one of Taylor's most appealing dances, and one's memory of it may retain mainly its buoyancy, exciting floor slides by the dancers towards its conclusion and with the exhilarating thrust of Bach's music. But important undercurrents can easily go unnoticed or unremembered. Charles Reinhart, Taylor's first manager and now ADF's Co-Director, calls our attention to how *Esplanade*, a joyous dance employing natural movements like running and jumping, has a middle "family" section where the dancers reach out to each other but never quite manage to touch; a wistful moment that tempers the joyousness, a question-mark punctuating the exuberance.

The Taylor company performed *Esplanade* along with *Syzygy* (1987) and *Arabesque* (1999) at ADF summer 2000. I recall a reviewer commenting that if *Aureole* is Apollonian, then *Syzygy*, to commissioned music by Donald York, is Dionysian because of its frenzied movements. This dance also illustrates Taylor's care for movement details, the dancers shuddering their shoulders when entering, while sliding on the floor, their bodies always alive one way or another, taking on odd shapes and viscerally responding to the comet-like musical cues.

Arabesque is in five sections to music by Debussy and, though more tranquil than *Syzygy*, is like it and *Esplanade* in suggesting shifting, uncertain human relationships. If you look for a touch of wistfulness in all three, it can be found in various places including the dancers' conclusions. *Esplanade* and *Syzygy* end with a solo "alone" dancer on stage, and *Arabesque* approximates a similar effect save for the full cast being on stage, by having only one dancer actually moving at all as the curtain falls.

Concert dancing, as I have volunteered previously, is especially adept at depicting group-versus-individual scenarios, and when Taylor's friends tell you how much of a "loner" he is, how being a depression-era kid who longed for a normal functional family led to his becoming a cultural misfit, you find it increasingly easy to discern the lonelier outsider moments (intended or not) in his dances.

He tells us a lot too, in his autobiography *Private Domain*, a truly remarkable story, not simply of what, where, and when but of the imaginative, thoughtful insides of this intensely physical choreographer/dancer. It is a book that, like his dances, endows his art with intellectual seductions that we readily associate with poetry and painting, less readily with dance. College-like curiosity may be unnecessary for infusing dance with a thoughtfulness akin to the intellectual, but it can help. Taylor was at Syracuse University and 22 when he turned to dance, later noticing that so many of his dance peers were also former collegians. Modern dance and the modern campus have more in common than he or others had quite realized.

Perhaps the most remarkable pages in *Private Domain* recount Taylor's final dancing in 1974, in his *American Genesis* at the Brooklyn Academy of Music. Despite debilitating illness and injuries, he performed nonstop for 90 minutes, fighting off the inevitable fainting at the end, taken then by ambulance to the hospital. The nightmarish experience on stage, trying to remember cues and summon the strength to continue dancing, is wonderfully written. For a closer look at the dancer's special mind-body unity, read these pages!

Of all intellectual challenges that modern dance presents, the most interesting is learning how to unravel meanings upon meanings from the moving human body as your starting-point. Paul Taylor: "A dancer's true voice is his body." And for that body to speak effectively, the mind hitched to it "must be inundated by words to do with dance, for without a thought on dance and a dance to dance they're [dancers] left with nothing but a lot of talk." The body and its movements embody the thoughts, and a tradition from Isadora Duncan to Paul Taylor embody thoughts ranging from highly personal takes on the art to generalized philosophical theories. It may be a detoured route from body to theory, but it's there.

Anna Halprin

Anna Halprin is possibly, of all modern dancers, the one that is simultaneously most influential within her profession but least-known to the public. This is less the result of personality, which in her case is warm and outgoing, than of dance philosophy which in her case is strikingly unconventional even for a dance-world renowned for being unconventional.

Born in Winnetka, Illinois in 1920 (advertising her age is an aspect of her dance philosophy), Halprin recalls having loved dancing from childhood. How should one dance? Her early answer to this was influenced by her legendary teacher, Margaret H'Doubler, at the University of Wisconsin. H'Doubler emphasized a biological approach to dance, advocating the study of anatomy and kinesiology long before this became a curriculum standard.

H'Doubler and Halprin were not drawn to the biological roots of dancing for their own sake, rather for their clueing dancers to how movement can be an expressive medium for communication. Movement styles and arrangements—in short, movements-as-artifice—interested them less. H'Doubler and Halprin sought "natural" movements, those that are biologically appropriate to the nervous system, bone structure, and muscle action that allegedly express and communicate directly or "naturally."

Halprin writes that for H'Doubler (and herself):

> ...the stress in movement was on understanding your body as action and, at the same time, being able to appreciate feedback, so that the relationship of the feeling to the movement was complete. Now when you learn patterned movement, you're so involved in learning the pattern that the tendency is simply to cut off the feeling aspect...the feeling that's inherent when you clench your fist in anger, or stamp your feet, or jump in exhilaration. These are all natural and the most expressive movement we do. And when you become aware of the movement and the feeling it's evoking, you begin to have the freedom to use it consciously and excitingly, and that's when you begin to become an artist in your material.

Process more than finished product has occupied Halprin's interests and—what most non-dancers have yet to grasp—her process (and typical of her art) is one of bodily exploration for discovering new worlds of sensations and feelings. And, of course, given our bodily selves, such discovery is all the more stimulating because it feels like self-discovery. The person for whom dancing is a constant activity of self-revelation is likely to find prescribed steps and patterns much too constricting, whether in ballet, prior modern dance, or any other dictating source. Halprin is evidently such a person.

She tried New York City after graduating from the University of Wisconsin, getting acquainted with modern dance of the 1940s—Graham, Humphrey, Weidman, and Limón. In 1944, she danced in Humphrey's and Weidman's *Sing Out, Sweet Land.* When this had its New York performance, the critic Edwin Denby wrote that if one compared the "heavy accents and strained postures of the dancing" with the "limpid, relaxed, and delicately elastic rhythm by which Burl Ives, the balladist, sings his songs, you notice how 'inauthentic' the dance effects are."

Whether Anna Halprin shared Denby's verdict here, I don't know; in any event, she has described reacting to New York's concert dance as "feeling unrelated to what was going on in my life as a wife, mother, woman, and a person who loves the earth. I felt that dance had become too cerebral.... I like to feel the ground under my feet and the trees around me and be able to look up at the sky and know that I'm an extension of nature and that I can express this as part of my everyday living."

Halprin, take notice, complained that dance in Manhattan had become too "cerebral," so we ask, what is her attitude as a dance artist towards the intellectual? In the late 1960s, she said:

> I've already accepted the process as the purpose. In this sense it's nonintellec-
> tual. I don't get all sorts of intellectual theories that this dance work or this
> new piece is this blah blah blah....The process is the purpose; let it be, let it
> keep growing, and something will happen. And what happens generates its
> own purpose...in this sense it's nonintellectual and very nature oriented.

The sentiment here, reminiscent of Isadora Duncan's and Erick Hawkins's encomia to the "natural," gets the nod of dance artists who play up the intuitive and instinctive, playing down the analytic and discursive. The rhetoric in which the sentiment is couched, seemingly anti-intellectual, can be off-putting for would-be sympathizers wanting dance to be on all fours with poetry, drama, music, architecture, and the visual arts—arts where the mind and its intellectual pleasures find hospitable homes.

But, as often happens in dance-talk, seemingly anti-intellectual locutions are misleading, and this is especially true of Anna Halprin's. Her practice is actually surrounded by theory, her intuitions by intellectualizations. Her dance philosophy, likewise, really asserts that you best dance/practice intuitively *if* you *think* about it in the best way.

Thinking about it in the best way, forming your practice in class, workshops, or on stage with the most helpful concepts, is no simple matter for Halprin. In addition to H'Doubler's biological/scientific approach, Halprin has noted other main sources of her ever developing structure of dance concepts. To her husband, Lawrence Halprin, distinguished landscape architect, she owes her ideas about "dance space" and artistic creativity. When they moved to California's Bay Area in 1945, she began a career with West Coast scenery as her beloved proscenium. Among dance's celebrated spaces is the tree-canopied deck, at the foot of Mt. Tamalpais, designed by Lawrence Halprin for dance performances (including orchestra space).

Another intellectual influence was Dr. Fritz Perls, famous Gestalt psychologist who had fled Nazi Germany, and after coming to the United States in the 1940s established institutes for Gestalt Therapy in New York, Cleveland, and San Francisco. The Gestaltist principle, that the whole (a unity) is more than the sum of its parts, appealed to Halprin seeking a sense of her body "as a totality." Even more, one guesses, Gestaltist emphasis on "connectedness" reinforced her searching out the connectedness of mind, body and spirit. And to disclose the connections between one's diverse and partial thoughts, especially those about concert dance and its implications.

Gestalt therapy, as represented by Fritz Perls, must have appealed to Halprin, championing self-discovery via excitement. The human organism's special energy, what the philosopher Henri Bergson called *elan vital, libido* by Freud, and *orgone* by Wilhelm Reich, Perls called *excitement.* This is experienced as "rhythm, vibration, trembling, warmth," connecting us via our sense and motor systems to the world, so that the heightened subjective awareness produced by excitement is simultaneously objectively related.

The biological marriage of excitement, emotion, and movement is remarkable; excited, our aroused emotions metamorphose into motor movements. "We cannot have sex without sexual rhythm and movement; we can't grieve without our diaphragm shaking and tears being produced; we *can't* be joyous without dancing" (my italics). So the therapeutic value of this biological marriage, with a special function for dance indicated here, I presume, caught Halprin's favorable attention. Gestalt therapy is the dancer's polestar, in the mix, both subjective and objective, produced by being *actively aware.*

Anna Halprin, now in her 80s, is one actively aware person! Petite, trim, tensely alert, the smile-up she gives you is warm, amused, maybe mischievous. Wanting to teach your child the meaning of "animated"? You'd do no better than to point to the compact intensity of the constantly excited Halprin, enthusiastic about dance, life, the Gestalt Totality, or Nature itself.

The unfenced nature of dance fits perfectly with Halprin's free-spirited imagination, so collaboration with other artists comes naturally. She credits such visual and musical artists, other than her husband, as Walter Gropius, Robert Morris, La Monte Young, Luciano Berio, Morton Subotnik, and Terry Riley with broadening her dance philosophy. She prizes what she calls "collective creativity," what gets invented or discovered through collaborative excitements. "Processing" with other artists yields a more inclusive inventiveness than what the solo imagination can produce. She confesses to feeling more comfortable in the theater than in the dance world, because in our Western culture the former is more "inclusive" than the latter.

Halprin's intellectual energies are further illustrated by her publishing six volumes on her work, including *Movement Ritual* (1981), *Circle the Earth Manual: A Guide for Dancing Peace with the Planet* (1987), *Dance as a Healing Art: Returning to Health with Movement and Imagery* (2000), and *Moving Toward Life: Five Decades of Transformational Dance* (1995). As the titles intimate, her creativity has blurred hard distinctions between art and therapy, art and ritual, or, as she might add, art and life. Given what has already been noted here, this comes as no surprise.

From 1948–1956, in San Francisco, Halprin co-directed a studio in the modern dance tradition, and as the only West Coast dancer, she performed at a New York Dance Festival (an American National Theatre Academy event). In photos of her dancing then, for example in a piece titled *The Prophetess*, she seems to retain a traditional concert dancer look. But what she saw on the East Coast left her unimpressed, and she returned home resolved to risk new directions. As dancer, teacher, choreographer she founded the San Francisco Dancers' Workshop that would support avant-garde art through experimental collaborations by artists and psychologists. Its company performed nationally and abroad, becoming widely recognized as a new center of creativity.

Improvisation was the workshop tool in Halprin's objective to surpass stereotyped danced mannerisms whether individualistic or traditional modern. Like Merce Cunningham and John Cage, she discarded customary cause-and-effect relations, for instance working for a time separately from the collaborating musicians when creating a dance.

She says of this period in her career:

I began to chart movements…everything became arbitrary.… I have a great chart on which I've taken every possible combination of movements, put them all on sheets of paper and given them numbers. One sheet had to do with flexion and different joints; another had to do with extension. I would pick some elements and make a pattern. I tried to do them and I got into the wildest combinations of movements, things I never could have conceived myself. All of a sudden, my body began to experience new ways of moving. We applied this in bigger compositional ways. We would experiment with all the elements we worked with, even combinations of people. Even though I got the composition system formalized, we still worked it out with improvisation.

The experiments led to staged dances. *Birds of America* in 1960 was fifty minutes long and took about three months of workshop composing. Uncomfortable with the theater stage and searching for a partial substitute/solution, Halprin at the last minute thrust a bamboo pole in each of the dancers' hands and, for fifty minutes, they performed holding bamboo poles. Two years later, the Halprin workshop created *Five-Legged Stool*, a two-act full-evening work. This was "new" in juxtaposing independent elements—sound, voice, text—and in having a painter as co-choreographer.

Halprin wanted the dancers in *Five-Legged Stool* to keep bringing objects out and depositing them, so her painter-partner presented her with forty wine bottles, saying "I want you to bring these in." Halprin liked this because "I had also gotten attached to the idea that I wanted people to have tasks to do. Doing a task created an attitude that would bring the movement quality into another kind of reality. It was devoid of a certain kind of introspection."

The concept of "task" is notable here because it shows Halprin's constant concern with getting beyond mere self-expression; with heightening self-awareness, yes, but with expanding it through outward relations as are implicated by performing tasks. The task, of bringing and placing overhead all forty wine bottles, in its challenge to balance, stooping and rising, was difficult. And from that experience emerged the lesson that the choice of a task amounts to the idea of the movement that performs it.

I once asked the director of a well-known performance art venue in Manhattan how he defined "performance art." He immediately replied "it's the performance of a task." In the early 1960s, Halprin gave momentum to what became a national development of performance art, although in casting about for a name other than "dance," she sometimes dubbed it "kinetic theatre," among other labels.

Between 1965 and 1967, Halprin came up with 12 versions of *Parades and Changes*, a work that has recently been re-created and in the dance world is commonly identified as a landmark dance/theatrical event. Its specific elements, including length, scenarios, and number of dancers vary, depending on the performance occasion. Its use of nudity (for expressing the body's spirituality, an idea Halprin got from Perls's Gestalt therapy workshops) and outrageous episodes such as dancers engaged in slow-motion dressing and undressing, playing in and tearing up sheets of brown paper, storming wildly around the stage, changing costumes, bringing props on and off, etc., made it instantly notorious during its European tour. Although distinctly critical

Gerald E. Myers

of the piece, Clive Barnes found things to praise in his review of the first New York City performance in 1967, observing that the "kids get stark naked," romping in masses of brown paper; "...churning their way through great mounds of brown paper was enormously effective."

Parades and Changes was regarded by many as a perfect reflection of America's turbulent 1960s and of what dance, once it became performance art, should look like. If proof were needed, it could be found in the New York City police's efforts to arrest Halprin when the work was performed there in 1967 at Hunter College. A reviewer of the revival performance, summer 2000 in San Francisco, wrote that "It remains as striking a stage image as I have seen, at one with the best in the Living Theater, the Open Theater, and early Robert Wilson." Having seen it, albeit under different circumstances, in 1997 at the American Dance Festival, and thinking how the 1960s are still alive in it (and us), I concur with the reviewer's verdict.

For Halprin, *Parades and Changes* as well as other of her creations like *Animal Ritual* (1971) and *Imitations and Transformations* (1971) are short runs in a life's journey. Where to? To "body consciousness," she says, to an uninhibited "celebration and spirituality of the life force." The acting-out exercises of Perls's workshops, each participant having for example to act out polarities (e.g., first topdog, then underdog), were movement exercises that for her avoided "head trips" and rationalizations; the good result was that "[we] could experience ourselves nonverbally. All these approaches reaffirmed my own vision of linking the theatrical experience and the life experience." Dances like *Parades and Changes* illustrate her conviction that "each performer could only essentially perform him or herself. Each of us in our own art," even though for full development the individual needs the "reality of a group situation where more lifelike experiences and diversity could be confronted and checked out."

The group or communal element was always an essential part of the San Francisco Dancers' Workshop (disbanded in the late 1970s). Besides the workshop collaborations, audiences became participants, several hundred persons for example at the San Francisco Museum of Modern Art. Later, in the 1970s, Halprin developed *Citydance* that became an annual dance event in the San Francisco streets involving hordes of people from sunup to sundown. Following the Watts riots in 1967, she worked with an all-black group for a year. This resulted in a dance, *Ceremony of Us*, based on the dynamics of a confrontation that she had arranged between all-black and all-white groups. Here group art and group therapy become one and the same. Invitations to extend such work to other areas and groups added to the Workshop's influence far beyond the West Coast.

In 1972, when Halprin was using internal imagery as part of a holistic approach to unifying mind and body in specific ways—called the Psychokinetic Visualization Process—she was stricken with colon cancer. Prior to this diagnosis, she had drawn an image of herself unable to dance, and taking this plus having drawn a round ball in her pelvic area as a danger signal, she consulted her doctor who diagnosed her colon cancer. After operations and recurrence, she returned to dancing, use of internal imagery, and of developing accompanying theories and methods of healing (which, if not curative, do improve one's condition). In the process, after discovering that the name on her birth certificate was Hannah Deborah, she changed her first name from, in her own words, the "Anglo-Saxon 'Ann' to the much more Jewish 'Anna'. I was Ann Halprin until 1972."

She developed a process—Five Stages of Healing—adapting it for helping people with life-threatening illnesses, often in communal contexts in the form of ritualistic, group healings. She comments:

> In 1981, I began to create large-scale rituals…and I always applied this process of drawing and dancing as a way to generate what I call resources. By 1989, one of the largest experiments using this process had evolved into *Circle the Earth: Dancing with Life on the Line*, a large group dance for and by people challenging AIDS. The Five Stages of Healing were the guiding structure for this dance.… I am so captivated by the discoveries that happen in the visualization process and in this road map for the healing journey that I often forget to tell my friends…that after this dance my cancer went into remission.… The process of healing rests within dance, an ancient practice with wonderful possibilities for us today.

In 1978, Halprin founded the Tamalpa Institute, a movement-based organization offering training, community, and healing arts programs. It provides training in Halprin's Life/Art Process that employs dance and the expressive arts for creative, healing objectives. It has published her *Dance as a Healing Art; A Teacher's Guide and Support Manual for People With Cancer* (1997).

Halprin's prodigious and talented energies have initiated, organized and presented an astonishing array of processes and products. In addition to what has already been mentioned, they include work with children, with the Pomo Indian tribe on the northern California coast, and "the world's people." In 1995, as a Jewish woman, she was invited by the International Peace University to stage a "big" dance event commemorating the 1945 Potsdam Treaty, and in an auditorium adjacent to Hitler's suicide bunker.

As Janice Ross reported this, Halprin's Berlin dance, *Planetary Dance: A Prayer for Peace*, "investigates the sentiments of the performers as they try to find personal meaning in the concept of 'peace'." Some 300 to 400 participants, after an introductory half-day workshop, performed in her *Planetary Dance*. Given that the dance was conceived as Halprin's search for an appropriate contemporary ritual, "Berlin in 1995," Ross added, was an "ideal locale" for staging it.

Halprin has been influential in specific ways, in using dancing theater therapeutically, in using it for community building, for enlarging its own artistic capabilities. More generally, and reflecting the social restlessness and revolution of values of post-WWII America, she influenced the dance and artistic worlds in challenging the "establishment" and stressing anew the values of individualism and democratization. At one time, yes, the modern dance movement was "real," she says, "where Martha Graham, Doris Humphrey, Charles Weidman, and Hanya Holm revolted against ballet, and the Denishawn...developed another style...based on their personalities, it was subjective and idiosyncratic. Their followers imitated them and soon we had companies of look-alikes."

The intensity with which Halprin made movement experiments into life-experiments attracted the curious and the like-minded. Merce Cunningham and John Cage were among the visitors to the Halprin dance-deck in the woods. More directly influenced, in addition to her West Coast associates, were younger dancers such as Simone Forti, Meredith Monk, Trisha Brown, Yvonne Rainer, and Kei Takei. These all became name-performers, partly through a talented rebelliousness like Halprin's that is our next section's topic.

Halprin, like most if not all modern dance leaders, is distinctive for her ideas on how to *think* about dance, not only how to do it. She opens our eyes to how the art can be viewed afresh through the mind's eye, and as a result it becomes increasingly important intellectually; dance becomes a subject-matter to be turned over and around in one's mind, as one concept of it after another gets explored. Halprin has appropriately received many honors and awards, among them in 1994 a honorary degree of Doctor of Fine Arts at her alma mater, The University of Wisconsin. The award, one surmises, was due in part to recognizing how she had made dance a life of the mind as well as the body.

Her career of thinking about dance is set out in her collected writings and in film documentaries. Present at the American Dance Festival (ADF) to hear her talking to students and teachers, I was struck by the infectiousness of her personality and sense of mission; that can be indicated but hardly duplicated in documentaries. And this is true not only of Halprin conversing but of her performing too.

Joining Halprin on stage at ADF a few years ago, as a colleague/moderator for her lecture-demonstration, I watched her close-up explaining and demonstrating a solo *The Grandfather Dance*. Mixing spoken memories with vigorous movements, squatting, jumping and stomping, slapping knees, sometimes resembling Russian folk dancing, she took us into images of her grandfather praying and its impression on her at age four. "He was a Hassidic Jew who would pray by singing, jumping up and down, and flinging his arms in the air. He had a long white beard and I thought he was GOD and that GOD was a dancer. To this day, I still have vivid images of his religious ecstatic dancing."

The audience, when her ADF performance ended, rose spontaneously in standing ovation. It had been a genuinely "moving" experience, due partly to the sight of a woman approaching 80 dancing so vigorously, but also due to appreciation of the warmly witty mind that gave the dancing a special appeal. *The Grandfather Dance* is physically demanding, for anyone at any age, but, having a text, it is also a mental exercise; reversing the usual order, you in this instance have to believe it to see it!

Judson

In the early 1960s, a radical dance movement took flight. Called the Judson Dance Theater, after Judson Memorial Church in Greenwich Village that hosted its performances. Called simply the Judson movement in the years that followed, and although like all artistic eruptions eventually surrendering to history, it still influences. Its leaders still perform, however differently from some forty years ago.

The movement, said to represent Minimalism, Postmodernism, and numerous other "isms" that fashioned the 1960s and 1970s, has been widely reviewed and analyzed. In addition to regular press coverage, notably as a "Downtown" phenomenon in *The Village Voice* as well as in *The New York Times*, it has received careful analysis by dance critic Don McDonagh, even more by dance historian Sally Banes. For many dance buffs, Judson was the most exciting happening in late 20th century modern dance. It was exciting to see, but this seeing was all wrapped up in new and exciting ways of thinking about the nature and purpose of concert dance.

Compared to the dance establishment, the group with its rambunctiousness and manifestos, like earlier Futurists and Dadaists, revamped and chortled as they "officially" severed ties with that establishment. They bring to mind the New Dance Group's rebelliousness in the 1930s, but unlike that group less politically and socially preoccupied. Yes, they were socially sensitive, yet overall they only faintly resemble the radically activist "children" of the Sixties.

It was not until almost the end of the Sixties, attending a few Judson group performances, and memorably going with Don McDonagh to Judson Church for a performance evening that honored the publication of his book *The Rise and Fall and Rise of Modern Dance*, that I became more distinctly aware of this "break-away" dance movement. So my impressions of the Judson dancers are based on their later work seen, on what they have said and written, on what has been said and written about them. My sense is that they were primarily reacting as artists against a reigning modern dance aesthetic than as activists or revolutionaries dancing out their political/social convictions.

Their champions, such as Jill Johnston, Don McDonagh, and Sally Banes, like the so-called "postmodern" dancers such as Yvonne Rainer, David

Gordon, Steven Paxton, and others, agreed that modern dance leading up to the Sixties had become stagnant, authoritarian. Post-WWII American population, including that of artists and dancers, had grown in impressive numbers, so there was a sufficient supply of "youngsters" ready to espy both stagnation and "parental" resistance to sharing power. Modern dance, by the late 1960s, helped enormously for new funds and public prestige by the founding of the National Endowment for the Arts and its spin-offs, had become an art-world of its own. Now a distinct profession, with its rewards of grants and performance opportunities to distribute, the questions of whether it was living up to its legacy of innovation and individualism was bound to invite scrutiny.

Yvonne Rainer's scrutiny provoked a bored "No!," or rather, in a kind of Molly Bloom stream-of-consciousness, a string of "no's." She declared in 1965:

> *No* to spectacle no to virtuosity no to transformations and magic and make-believe no to the glamour and transcendency of the star image no to the heroic no to the anti-heroic no to trash imagery no to involvement of performer or spectator no to style no to camp no to seduction of spectator by the wiles of the performer no to eccentricity no to moving or being moved.

Rainer baptized her "No's" in one of the movement's most influential dances, her *Trio A* (originally titled in 1966 *The Mind is a Muscle, Part I*). This 4.5 minute "single-phrase piece" was originally performed, in Woody Allen style of sneakers and daily clothes, as three simultaneous solos by Rainer, Steve Paxton, and David Gordon, and is described, for simplicity's sake as one solo, by Don McDonagh as follows:

> A woman stands with profile to the audience and swings one arm across her stomach and the other simultaneously behind her. Smoothly swirling her arms, she joins hands and frames her head. The flow of movement continues in an unbroken and uninflected stream following the weight of the gesture rather than any emotional determinant. She taps one foot in a smooth arc and then the other, extends out to the side and makes tiny circling motions....

> She sits and rolls over backward, rises to face away from the audience, wiggles a bit, and, turning in profile, she adjusts a little like an athlete ready to compete. She bends all the way forward, spreads her legs, and then drops into a squat to thrust a leg to the side. A sequence of rolling like a log is started, and she stops to offer a little spasmodic variation followed by bouncy leaps, and with her back to the audience she tilts her head to the left, arcs her body to the right, and concludes on the balls of her feet.

For casual viewers (though clearly not limited to them), this is pretty tame stuff. Relentlessly unemotional and undramatic, determinedly unspectacular, the dance's "constant flow," McDonagh comments, "makes it so enjoyable an exercise." So, if you are fascinated by the human body in action as Rainer and all dancers are, *Trio A* can be mesmerizing in its tameness. *And* because, though physically tranquil, it fiercely challenges your mental and perceptual skills to see what's there, to see among other things how the dancer's mind works muscularly, is in fact a muscular thing.

Rainer has written about *Trio A*, its elements and mode of composition, and you have to study that in detail to appreciate its remarkable complexity. Reflecting the influence of contemporary artists, including Robert Morris and Robert Rauschenberg with whom she worked, she conceived *Trio A* out of an envisaged set of relationships between minimal sculpture and contemporary dancing. She made a "chart" of such relationships where, for example, under *Objects* the "role of artist's hand" and "hierarchical relationships of parts" correspond under *Dances* to "phrasing" and "development and climax."

Convinced that the 1960s called for dancers who are "neutral doers" (whose personalities, unlike Martha Graham's for instance, are sacrificed to their actions), and who abandon technical virtuosity and display of specialized bodies, Rainer and the other Judsonites turned to ordinary movements/activities—standing, walking, running, eating, carrying bricks, showing movies—the goal "to be moved by some thing rather than oneself." Not only was the authority of the modern dance establishment to be resisted, so was the self-serving authority of oneself (narcissism).

John Cage once observed that "there is in Rauschenberg, between him and what he picks up to use, the quality of *encounter*" (my italics). I guess that the Judsonites and others of the Sixties sought encounters that took them "out of themselves," into what felt like neutral, objective turf, challenging the dancers' mental muscles to respond creatively. Why are you (Paxton, Forti, and others) just being yourselves? That was often asked of the Judsonites, and Rainer's response was "I was more involved in experiencing a lion's share of ecstasy and madness [in some sense, one supposes, outside one's narcissistic self] than in 'being myself' or doing a job." So, for Rainer anyway, it appears that settling for ordinary movement did not in fact equate with just being one's ordinary self.

Encounters could be had by "picking up" an object or a task of some sort, and Rainer analyzes *Trio A*'s "movement-as-task or movement-as-object." No pauses between phrases are major features. The phrases might be "right leg, left leg, arms, jump," but each phrase merges indistinctly into the next, giving the (filmic) impression of the body constantly in transition. This is reinforced by not allowing any phrase to be more emphatic than any other.

Given no place for pauses between phrases, no rest for the weary, *Trio A* displays the dancer's endurance. "The irony here," Rainer says, "is in the reversal of a kind of illusionism: I have exposed a type of effort where it has been traditionally concealed and have concealed phrasing where it has been traditionally displayed." Another feature of this dance is avoidance of repetition. Why? Because Rainer wanted *Trio A* to be "about" itself, to self-comment as it were, about the real difficulties of "seeing" a dance.

As dancers and students of the art rightly stress, the details (rhythm, weight, color, space/time dimensions, posture, direction, etc.) of movement sequences occur too quickly and voluminously for easy seeing. A dance is hardly visually absorbed on one viewing, and Rainer wanted *Trio A* to be both culprit and witness to the fact. "My *Trio A* dealt with the 'seeing' difficulty by dint of its continued and unremitting revelation of gestural detail that did *not* repeat itself, thereby focusing on the fact that the material could not easily be encompassed."

Yvonne Rainer, Steve Paxton, David Gordon, and the other Judsonites, as much as any 20th century dance movement, brought the art into America's intellectual awareness. They startled audiences with their breach of expectations, saying "no" to meaning, expressiveness, display of technique, and anything else that a traditionally-minded and ticket-paying person might expect. But for many, especially the arts community, their ways of flaunting "ordinary" movements transformed them into *encounters*, delightful, whimsical, impudent, totally out-of-the-ordinary.

For myself, the identity of *Trio A* is wrapped up with Rainer's conceptions of it. To see (not just stare at) it requires a certain frame of mind, a set of concepts that give sense to its visual and kinaesthetic stimulations. I'm unable, for my own take of *Trio A*, to come up with better conceptions than offered by its creator, so I'm left with a dance that cannot be identified apart from its *intellectual* complexity. Sure, for whatever reasons, I could be stubborn, turn away and wave off that intellectual complexity as so much nuisance, and not budge from a single bare-boned, stripped-down description of *Trio A*'s movements, one after another; and say that I have identified the dance. But if you admit that such a description is only "bare-boned, stripped down," then you're admitting that something, that has been stripped down, has been omitted from your "bare" description. And that something, of course, is the interesting rest of the dance that can be identified only via concepts such as Rainer's, or others that you might prefer. Again, the point is that the dance as *seen* by you is largely (and properly) what you *think* it is.

Years past, I confess to being mildly amused by an apparently inverse relation between minimal (Judson-type dancing) and critical/scholarly writing about it; the more minimal or skinned-down the dancing, the fatter the writings about it looked. Those skinny-looking dances seemed to cry out for flesh-giving characterizations by sympathetic observers.

When Sally Banes, in thinking about *Trio A*, wrote that she found the philosopher Martin Heidegger's essay "The Origin of the Work of Art" useful, I privately smiled that this was rather a stretch, not just endowing but bloating the skinny thing with excessive flesh. But now I think differently. Heidegger, Banes wrote, "reflects on the art-work's source, rejecting the idea that it originates in the artist...the origin of the work of art is in art." In Heidegger's words, "art is by nature an origin: a distinctive way in which truth comes into being that is, becomes historical." The upshot of this about *Trio A* for Banes: "The artist remains inconsequential as compared with the work, almost like a passageway that destroys itself in the creative process for the work to emerge."

Given Rainer's plea, cited above, for self-effacement in the creative process, and the idea that encounters engendered by objects and tasks help to make the art-work, Banes's placing her in Heidegger's company is appropriate; moreover, it forces upon us the realization that the *intellectuality* (despite vacillating statements by the Judsonites on this) of Rainer and colleagues had become a hallmark of the Sixties' new modern dance. The risks involved, of presenting works that internally compete for both revelation and concealment, rival those taken by Isadora Duncan and other predecessors, but Rainer and her co-riskers seemed to relish every minute of it. But no, not every minute, for there were moments of doubt and internal disagreements typical of artistic movements under sail. And, despite the Judsonites thrilling in challenging audiences, the audience's return challenges could be chilling. Steve Paxton recalled that some of the Judson performances ranked among "the most embarrassing moments of my life" because people "would boo and shout."

Another leader of the 1960's movement, and still prominent in the dance/theater scene, is David Gordon. Unlike Rainer who grew up in San Francisco, aiming to become an actress but turning to dance (with some Anna Halprin influence absorbed early in her career) after moving to New York, Gordon is a native New Yorker who began his dance training at Brooklyn College. Like Rainer, he studied briefly with Martha Graham and other modern dancers, but, always conspicuously independently-minded, soon backed away to join the Judsonites, later with an evolved group called the Grand Union. With his wife/dancer Valda Setterfield, he continues to work as one of the field's most innovative performers.

An early work called *Random Breakfast* (1963) set the Gordon tone. Outrageous images—resplendent woman dancer stripping to G-string, male running about and uttering instructions for making a dance, woman napping on floor in fur coat and bikini outfit, showing up later as a nun, man at the conclusion with top hat, listening to Judy Garland's "Over the

Rainbow"—adding up to a wrinkled squint by Gordon at the seriousness with which concert dancers are wont to take themselves. Nor did he miss opportunities, as in his 1978 *Not Necessarily Recognizable Objectives,* to glance quizzically at his own creations.

In the late 1970s, Gordon accepted Sally Banes's characterizing his work, whether called dance, dance theater, or performance art, as being artworks that analyze and criticize entertainment. He agrees with Banes that in his pieces he "accumulates and organizes multiple views of a single phenomenon into one composition." And he happily acknowledges that he always looks for trouble, considering himself a trouble-maker because, after all, what else is art's function? Comfort-seeking students, as you might surmise, are not the company he seeks.

After launching in 1978 his own David Gordon/Pick-Up Company, he became increasingly productive and on a larger-than-Judson scale. Works of startling originality were created for the Dance Theater of Harlem and American Ballet Theatre. In 1988, he presented a "big" complex called *United States* at the Brooklyn Academy of Music (BAM) that combined music, movement, text, and a recording of a discussion with Robert Frost about poetic creativity. The program listed successive scene locations as Minnesota, New England, New York, San Francisco, ending back in New England.

A (naturally) controversial offering, *United States* marked Gordon's drift towards theater and spectacle to which Rainer had said "no." This drift, towards what seems more theater than dance, continued with the impressive and widely discussed *The Family Business* of 1994. Interestingly, Rainer had left dance years before (in the 1970s) for film-making, leaving the impression that, for these two Judsonites anyway, their yearning for drama and spectacle exceeded the capacities of dance. If so, where was the incapacity, in dance itself or rather in their concept of it?

Gordon described himself in 1981: "I am this thing called a post-modern/avant-garde experimentalist. That doesn't mean that I don't want my share of romantic images which have affected me in certain ways…. *Bayadere* is one of my favorite ballets. I think it's one of the most avant-garde goddamn things I ever saw." If Anna Kisselgoff's recent review of Marius Petipa's 19th century ballet *La Bayadere* indicates where majority sentiment resides, then, as we might expect, Gordon takes up residence on the other side. Kisselgoff wrote of the ballet staged in Boston by the Boston Ballet that not even the impressive dancing "can save this white elephant of a ballet from itself," and despite the Boston Ballet's good efforts, being a dance that "has to succeed in spite of itself," those efforts were "only partly persuasive." Declaring it to be his favorite ballet, Gordon had to know, would get him into stimulating trouble.

Gordon and fellow Judsonites brought an updated "braininess" to dance, attracting intellectual interest on campuses as well as in lofts and cafes. What is dance? What is art? Can a dance be totally non-expressive? Can you be said to "see" a ballet performed in pitch dark? How much respect is due these questions individually is problematic, but once raised they generate numberless others, and taken together they do indeed test the muscularity of one's mind.

Gordon maybe outruns all competition in blending a movement theater that is satirical, ironic, self-referential, and always trouble-making. His is a singularly merciless wit, capable of wilting the entire *Seinfeld* gang in one swoop. This impression was reinforced years ago when I moderated a session, Gordon participating, on the state of modern dance that was held at ADF in Durham, North Carolina.

At ADF, we avoid the label "postmodern" dance, because we take the Judsonites and like-minded to belong to the modern dance tradition, where they began and developed their own reactions. Modern dance is a brand name, of an art that uses movement for endless reaction/innovation, so "postmodern dance" misleadingly suggests that the art of Graham, Ailey, and others is dead or wholly discontinuous with what self-described postmodern-ists are doing. More practically, modern dance presenters worry that funders, with "postmodern" buzzing in their overly busy heads, will reject their cups-in-hand, understandably not wanting corpses for clients.

Our reasoning, however, left Gordon unpersuaded, as I remember, con-sidering himself a postmodernist and, so far as modern dance goes, a novelty bred from scratch. As a practical matter, now that postmoderism is often outdated by post-postmodernism, also that writers increasingly acknowledge the jargonish and amorphous nature of such labels, the issue seems obsolete with fewer experimental dancers being label-insisters.

When we switched the session's discussion to dancers' training, Gordon strongly advocated an intellectual requirement. Incidentally commending ADF for its humanities programming, he stressed the need for dancers to be curious beyond dance, to read, visit museums, be informed, enliven their minds. It is widely reported that Rainer, Gordon, and some colleagues are not sleek body-types, not "natural" dance-bodies (as conventionally defined). They typically behaved on stage like (and with) untrained dancers, encouraging the entry of those thinking "Hey! *I* can do *that!*," thus democratizing modern dance even further. But what also needs recognition is that, as the Judsonites relaxed the dancer's physical requirements, they upped the mental ones.

The Judsonites have long had their critics who, regarding minimalist expressionless dancing, trace their disliking it to its betraying a kind of intel-lectual interference by choreographic ideas that, while alive and well themselves, deaden the dancing. Tobi Tobias recently reviewed in *New York Magazine* a re-appearance by Lucinda Childs, a Judsonite who, finding more support there had moved to France. While not unappreciative of the way Childs has four work-clothed men in her dance *Radical Courses* (1976) use Child's signature "light, brisk, precise steps" through various stage routes, maintaining a steady pace without music or much movement variation, Tobias is ultimately dissatisfied. Such minimalist dances are "so restricted, so uncompromising...large doses can alienate the viewer by allowing him to realize how much of life's abundance is being denied. Child's original principles were bracing and admirable, but dancing, the art of human bodies in motion, rarely captivates through an idea alone."

Yet, as non-Judsonites such as Sara Rudner and Dana Reitz, in collaboration with master lighting designer Jennifer Tipton, have thumpingly demonstrated, minimalist performances can be maximally gratifying. A "hit" of the 1994 New York season, staged at the tiny Kitchen in Chelsea, was their *Necessary Weather* piece. I remember the keen interest shown by the dance/ artistic world for that concert, reserved chairs for Jerome Robbins, Paul Taylor, and the like.

Necessary Weather was an hour of movement reticence heightened into moody mystery by the here-and-there but always in-charge moving lights of Jennifer Tipton's. The two dancers, wearing loose and see-through white shirts and trousers, as I recall, simply walked—journey-walked—with occasional bends or bows, with pauses counting as provocatively as in a Pinter play. No music, total silence, the lights the loudest elements in the performance. While one walked, often on a diagonal, the other might be stationary, and an effect of this in sequence was to suggest an underlying relationship between the two women dancers that would remain unarticulated, suggested only.

The dancers' space, where they were motivated to walk, stop, advance, recede, was defined by the lighting that sometimes cast a circle or a rectangle, or, blotting out all else, pinpointed brightly a single place or dancer. As this collaborative gem illustrates, an understated *structure* of interactions between movements and lights—nothing more—can be deeply moving. Sometimes, all that's needed, for thrills and more, is for things to come together as they do or are made to do.

Your despairing of dancing that says "no!"—to plot, expression, emotion, drama, technique, virtuosity, and personality—can be rescued by espying its *structure*. But, alas, without tutoring experience of some sort, you can look but never locate it. And that is noteworthy, because the design (sometimes called "scores" by Anna Halprin, Steve Paxton, and others) of the dance, its blueprint (that may permit some improvisation or performance refinement) of steps, space-time sequence, etc., is what the choreographer often cherishes most. I have watched choreographers, both minimalist and others, look with intensifying pleasure as their (often painfully worked out) design or structure comes sequentially to life in performance. "Ah, the structure!," they exclaim, smiling happily.

Often, the clearest case of choreographer and spectator not seeing the same thing is when the thing is the dance's structure. This is frustrating when the structure is "there," not just in the choreographer's head, when "design is the art," as someone said, "that is hidden in plain sight." The choreographer can relieve our frustration by pointing to the dance's design of spatial and rhythmic patterns, movement phrases some repeated and some not, arrangements of dancers in alternating duos and trios, dancers' legs and arms in opposition and then in sync, and so on. Such elements, and only these, plus the movement qualities given to them by the actual performing, are quite enough to enthrall the minimalist choreographer, and us, too, if we persevere.

Structure in dance can be a very satisfying perceptual discovery. Complex and often elusive, its importance can hardly be exaggerated. Recently, watching a rerun of the 1936 film "After the Thin Man," starring William Powell and Myrna Loy, I rolled over when an attractive woman is shocked to learn from detective Nick Charles (William Powell) that all of her activities in her apartment had been eavesdropped by a man in the apartment above; and she responds in hushed voice to the detective and his gawking lieutenants, "Holy smoke!" The campy inanity of her response recalled another, an audience member exiting the performance of *Necessary Weather* and saying to another, "Now *that* performance you have to see to really appreciate it!" Something relevant never got said there, an absence that often bedevils talk about dance structures.

One who talks very carefully, very deliberately, about dance is the oft-honored Judson ringleader, Steve Paxton. Looking back on those days when as a wide-eyed and inquiringly "innocent" from Arizona he met the New York modern dance world, he seems surprised that his and the Judsonite "experiments" (he sometimes calls them "bumblings") mushroomed into a major movement that now commands celebratory revisiting. At ADF, in 1994, in conversations with 55-year-old Paxton, I found him intensely thoughtful, verbally cautious, seeking accuracy of statement to match—visible in his frowning and gesturing—the sincerity of his intentions.

Artistic, a fine gymnast, Paxton is a striking physical mover. So, after he studied a while with Martha Graham and others, his being invited to join José Limón's company in the late 1950s and Merce Cunningham's in the early 1960s was already in the cards. He was drawn to Cunningham (and Cage, Rauschenberg, *et. al*) partly because Merce was a dance-world "scandal" who, according to a leading Limón dancer at the time, "deserved a spanking." Paxton's memories make for good stories, of nine persons and all their stuff packed into a Volkswagen bus for performance touring, four-month on-the-road-bookings at times, and unstiffening for performances more likely held in college gyms than theaters. But among the rewards, besides the Cunningham company stimulations, was Paxton's downtown Manhattan three-room apartment's monthly rental of $19.84!

For Paxton, like other Judsonites, Cunningham's use of chance ("tossing coins") for choreographic decisions was appealing, as was Merce's nonchalance and apparent "non-extraordinary" movement style. But in the end even Cunningham's company proved to be too traditional, in retaining an authoritarian structure and requiring trained (quite extraordinary, often balletic) dancers. Paxton's resolute egalitarianism won out, he left—for Judson and himself.

Dance historians remember Paxton's 1961 dance *Proxy* and the 1967 *Satisfyin' Lover* for challenging concert dance conventions in featuring unspectacular off-the-street ("boring," said the disappointed) movements like ordinary walking. The 1967 dance had a written score or instructions, allowing some improvisation and individual motor mannerisms, which was implemented/performed by a huge assortment of people alternating between simply standing, turning, walking, sitting. Why? To tap into the medium, human movement itself, and see what it yields. To tap into what is important, after all, in ourselves—the ordinary—and see what happens. The risks? Maybe too little yield, too little surfacing,

Paxton sometimes reduced (for some) the risks of being boring through using Judsonite "Improbables." He once plucked chickens as co-performers, commenting on one such occasion that although, sadly, the actual performances went badly, they'd had a really good rehearsal. Eye-catching objects like an ordinary chair except made of cake served as props that excited both audiences and fellow-Judsonites. When one reads about the Judson group interactions, they seem to have egged each other on, clapping hands when a colleague came up with the newest outrageousness, like young hikers thrilling to each sighted shift in their landscape.

Flat is a "minimalist and intellectual" 1964 dance by Paxton, remembered for its non-momentous walking, his taking off a business suit, hanging the clothes on hooks taped to his body, and sitting in various ordinary postures. The latest and surprising resurrection of this work is performed by Mikhail Baryshnikov at age 52, as part of the White Oak Dance Project's "Past Forward" that celebrates the Judsonite movement. Baryshnikov praises Paxton for being a "dancing existentialist" akin to Kafka, Beckett, Ionesco, and Sartre; his ball-park meaning, I speculate, being that the seeming meaninglessness or flatness of *Flat* is nevertheless given a ghost-like significance by the character of its performance.

Paxton says that at the dance's completion the viewer "knows something very intimate about the person that doesn't show through the clothes. He's covered up again, so it's like a secret has been revealed and concealed." Here, again, we have Rainer's idea of a doppelganger dance, employing the contrary movements of concealing and revealing. It might be hard for Paxton or anyone else to say exactly what "intimacy" of person we learn about in *Flat.* Maybe it is just his elusiveness? Which would be okay—just as Baryshnikov who, in declaring "That's Steve. He's the most elusive person I ever met," seemingly finds that not merely okay but to be a delightful peering into what is intimate about the Paxton person himself, whether on stage or off.

After the early 1970s when he moved to Vermont, Paxton worked even more independently, founding what is probably his most enduring dance innovation, Contact Improvisation (CI). One can see this as a natural outcome of his initial gymnastic skills and subsequent explorations of dance-sports connections. Akido, a Japanese martial art with special movement qualities that Paxton investigated, influenced his concept of CI.

CI began as a duo or partnering activity, featuring improvised movement sequences that are triggered by initial physical contacts between two participants. The initial contacts can be grasping of hands, jumping onto the other's shoulder, rolling over each other, twisting a partner around one's hips, and so on. As happened, duos can be expanded into larger groups. Originally conceived for studio experimentation, CI elements can be seen nowadays within concert dance, or CI can be a full evening in itself. In one form or another, CI has become enormously popular and influential, leaving little modern dance training and performance untouched by it.

Watching CI in action is often like watching martial arts in action, vigorous but controlled physicality of interacting bodies being the hallmark. Many dancers love to do it, all day all night, and to observe it, part-day part-night. What I find fascinating are less the improvisations, although to be sure these can be stimulating, than the dazzling array of *ideas* and *conceptualizations* of it that its practitioners carry in their heads. They weren't being cute when they subtitled their journal *Contact Quarterly,* "A Vehicle for Moving Ideas." I can only refer you, for getting a sense of how CI's devotees tumble out endless and engaging notions of what they're doing from their tumbling with each other, to such sources as *Contact Quarterly* and, say, *Sharing the Dance; Contact Improvisation and American Culture* (1990) by Cynthia J. Novack.

Starting with certain convictions about democracy, egalitarianism, the arts and society, and hoping for what psychologically and creatively, movement experiments such as CI may discover, these improvisers generate an amazing variety of ideas ranging from the obscure and fragmentary to the scrutable and philosophical. Novack, for example, speculates that CI's advocates, drawing upon 1960s and 1970s experiments in dance, theater, sports, and therapy, were "trying to realize a *re-definition of self within a responsive, intelligent body*" (my italics). She and others emphasize the development of *trust*, glaringly needed when you're relying on your CI partner to keep you from breaking your neck, and of what unfolds from that in deepening appreciation of human relationships.

The concept of the "responsive body" is central to Novack's analysis of Contact Improvisation. The self is defined as "the responsive body" and also as the responsive body listening to another responsive body, the two together spontaneously creating a third force that directs the dance. "The boundaries of the individual are crossed by 'seeing through [via] the body' and 'listening through the skin,' allowing the dance to unfold."

And you have to connect with the fuller meanings of the responsive body. Abandon simplistic descriptions of interpretations of the human body that too often satisfy non-dancers or even those dancers who treat the body only as a utilitarian tool. Rather, according to Novack and others, it vibrates with multiple meanings, and ideally it "represents honesty, reality, spirituality, and the suppression of selfish, egotistical striving…the responsive body is the person" and "allowing it to act is felt to reveal the individual in a profound way."

Images and sensations, *the materials of ideas*, bubble up from the CI practice of feeling, say, another's weight and then one's own response to that. The produced sensations may themselves produce, for example, erotic images. But Lisa Nelson, well-known CI advocate, writes:

> Actually, for me, the sensation is the image.… To me this is what dancing is… the thrill of seeing sensation manifested in anybody's body is what I think dance is.… All the sensorial images are experienced physically—the visual images, for example; in the way I'm looking, the feeling in the muscles around my eyes, my posture. Reading my physical sensory experience in this way…gives shape to my desire, it directs my imagination.

For Paxton, compared to the early Judson days, the creativity of CI "isn't mental so much as it is submental.… Even in Judson, I was the one who was doing the submental work, so I guess it's natural I would be involved in Contact." The meaning of "submental" is unspecified but I take it to convey not the psychoanalytic unconscious but rather the *emergence* of mentality (ideas, concepts, etc.) from the physical processes of CI. And I surmise that compared say, to Yvonne Rainer whom Paxton admired for her "intellectuality," which might precede and guide the creative process, he considered his own intellectuality to be not causes but effects of contact improvising.

Merce Cunningham once said, Paxton recalls, that the choreographer's job is the traffic cop's of keeping people onstage from bumping into each other; whereas I, he smiles, have made a career out of having people bump into each other. Not the whole story, however, because in the 1980s and 1990s he surrendered to the desire to "make art" again, to dance more balletically and *extending* arms and legs accordingly. He has composed some 200 solo improvisations to Bach's *Goldberg Variations* and *English Suites*, prompting Trisha Brown, he reports, to call them Paxton variations.

Looking back, Paxton muses softly, modestly about modern dance and his role in it. Still the Arizona quester, he surveys this historical terrain as the kind of savannah he believes humans were meant to gaze at rather than the TV tube, and he seems to discern dominant continuities. He sees his own career, including Judson and Contact Improvisation, that features modern dance's insistences on innovation, as continuing that tradition. Talking to ADF students during the summer of 1994, he urged them to study the art's history, explaining how he had been impressed not only by the choreographers but also by the philosophies of dance and body-mind that stand out in modern dance's relatively brief history, since the 1890s.

The Judson movement, that carries on modern dance's experimental/individualistic tradition, remains influential in presenting human movement as an "alternative" path to keener self-awareness, to a firmer philosophical outlook for oneself. Since this, throughout history, represents a major intellectual objective, whether in the sunny corners of the college campus or on the shady side of city street, we can understand why many turn from strictly cerebral types of instruction to pursuits like Contact Improvisation for shaping their ideas into a kind of overall *Weltanschauung*.

Eastern philosophies encourage this concept of the intellectual (when they are not misleadingly interpreted as being aggressively anti-intellectual), and Deborah Hay, active in the spotlight since her Judson days, is one so encouraged. Baryshnikov, commenting on a new duet created by Hay for both of them, praises her "internal commitment in improvisation." And the writer Wendy Perron adds: "Hay, whose face is a cross between Martha Graham's and that of a timeless butoh dancer, exudes an internal authenticity—serenity through turmoil, one might call it."

Terms like "internal commitment" and "authenticity" convey the flavor of the Hay aesthetic. Although not a practicing Buddhist nor schooled in its thought, but having experiences through dancing that are similar to "the experience of beginner's mind in Zen Buddhism," she recently authored *My Body, The Buddhist*. Her book, she states, "describes innate skills and basic wisdom that bodies possess but that remain untranslated because as a culture we tend to hide in our clothes. Unrecognized is the altar that rises with us in the morning and leads us to rest at night. The book's intent is to open some trapped doors that prevent awareness of the body's daringly ordinary perspicacity." This sentiment represents a good chunk of the Judson movement and of modern dance history, and if you bet on its longevity, you should come out ahead.

A Letter

Dear Mrs. C.—

You say it all for us. This "war against terrorism" won't share the foreground. Since September 11th and the destruction of the World Trade Center, justifying one's daily self-attendings won't work, so proceed as usual, unjustified. If we could, if we must, in another time and context, let's dig around it for our deeper selves.

My first return to the City since September 11th, but I'm not up to gazing at Ground Zero. And untempted to peek at our old digs on 14th street. I see from here where Twin Towers are now occupied by dark skies.

These dark-sided days must surely register with Paul Taylor. He says his dances are not autobiographical. They mirror what he notices around him, conceding that how he notices things—often heavy, dark, ugly—can be partly credited to his personal takes on the world. His is a practical philosophy, approaching each choreographic assignment/theme from its particularities, not from some Big Theory. When the musicologist Joseph Kerman asked a composer friend for a profoundly insightful analysis of what it is like to compose a concerto, his friend's brow furrowed, then he replied, "The first problem is how to start the sucker." Paul Taylor, I believe, would like that! Anna Halprin's "communal" philosophy of dance veers towards the sunny side of the street, moving hopefully over its dark potholes, though duly noted. A big philosophy with big objectives, both theatrical and therapeutic, its influence on the Judson movement and so-called postmodernists includes revived interest in myth and ritual. Deborah Gans comments provocatively that such contemporary dance "differs from traditional ritual in the content of the common vocabulary of simple movements: it eliminates the duality of the mundane steps and their spiritual intent. Repetition and unison lead not to transcendence but to an affirmation of the power within their material bounds."

If desired, Mrs. C., I'll send you Gans's essay, worthy of your spared attention.

I agree with you, Halprin and Taylor are contrasts, but don't overlook how both acknowledge, dancingly, life's duality. I assume their approving Susan Sontag's siding with Oscar Wilde's "A truth in art is that whose contrary is also true."

You'd never quote Wilde, so I did it for you. But only because most "serious" modern dancers I know are on his side, too—on this matter, I mean, of "truth" in or about art.

It's a formal issue for song writing, too. Carly Simon says, beware of too much rhyming both interior and at phrase's end. It dulls the listener into fantasizing "everthing's O.K. with the world." Not good, so "Some emotions are better left unrhymed."

No better note to leave you on, 'til next time. Goodnight, wherever you are.

GEM

Meredith Monk

As 2001 began, it was announced that some fifty-two composers, boasting association with New York City, would be celebrated in a nine-concert and three-symposium Lincoln Center Festival. Milton Babbitt, Elliott Carter, Lukas Foss, Philip Glass, Ned Rorem, and Charles Wuorinen were honored, and so was—prominently pictured—Meredith Monk. What makes Monk's selection unusual is that, for many of us, she is primarily a distinguished modern dancer/dramatist whose works typically incorporate her own music.

But her three-part Festival retrospective, *Voice Travel,* featuring her as both conductor and composer, recalls how her voice has always been an independent faculty, never merely a dance addendum. A reviewer of "Solo Landscapes," the first of the three Festival programs, praises Monk's vocal flexibility, ranging from wordless plosives and hums to wails and plaints, to songs with her own piano accompaniment. As I was reminded in her recent demonstration at Connecticut College, Monk can hypnotize you with "otherworldly" incantations, or more familiarly entertain and amuse with fetching lullabies or comic sendups sung at the piano or on a "Jew's Harp."

You, Mrs. Calabash!—*You* hardly need to hear me trumpet again the theme of these jottings to you—how modern dance has expanded our intellectual horizons through combined physical and conceptual explorations of the dancing body and its experiences—but you do need to hear, or rather you will want to hear, about Monk's way. It's different, very.

Back in 1996, at ADF's January Intensive Program that was held at Hunter College, we listened to Monk tell the students about her "Eureka!" experience that occurred a year after graduating from Sarah Lawrence College in 1964 and then dancing (without much singing) in New York. It is an experience she has recounted on many occasions. She was tinkering at the piano, playing with her voice, then suddenly thought something like this: the voice is like the spine, having a whole life, and like one's whole body can traverse landscapes, invite adventures, and audition as both choreographer and choreographed. The voice, consider it not merely as a bodily part but as an extended body that dances, too. Coming from a musical family, trained in music almost from infancy, she hit upon an "archaeology" of an old associate and instrument—her voice—that would take it and her beyond the traditional confines of music and dance.

Although the range and complexity of Monk's music, and of its audience effects, defy facile summary, the music critic John Rockwell is helpful in noting that Monk's method involves generating a "gently rocking ostinato on a single instrument...and then to sing over it," creating a tension between the simplicity of the instrumental part and the complexity of the vocal part.

Monk's musical pieces are usually wordless, as Rockwell observes, relying on sheerly aural and structural values. The literally "nonsensical" Monkian sounds, as in her 1977 *Tablet*, are indeed suggestive, perhaps of "chattering gossip, or fervent rhetoric, or anguished waiting" that, like James Joyce's impressionistic people-sketches in *Portrait of the Artist as a Young Man*, point us to poignant "universalities" in human experience. In her dances or dance tableaux, Monk's musical voice is the "body" that dominates and sets our minds to wondering.

Like many modern dancers, maybe increasingly since the Sixties, Meredith Monk does not resemble the sleek natural dancer, ballerina or otherwise. She imposes her vocal self on her movements rather than vice versa. Physical coordination, she tells us, was a youthful problem, so it is understandable that she sought an art that would surround physical movement with her remarkable musical, dramatic, and creative talents.

Petite, girlish, with a strikingly expressive oval face, gazing at you from above an unassuming physical posture, Monk offstage is a portrait to look at. Onstage, she is a compelling performer who takes you into a world that is only half-real and therefore haunting. The image she presents as a performer, from her solo *Education of the Girlchild* (1972) and earlier, is often that of a questing wanderer, a questioning vagrant on life's highway.

When she leans out at you, her eyes competing with long black braids for our eyes, her voice rising eerily, her milkmaid's body tilting or shifting intermittently, she is a picture of friendly, sometimes funny vulnerability. Watching her, I'm prey to revived images of Judy Garland, Carol Burnet, Bert Lahr, and Buster Keaton (whom Monk admires)—and of Imogene Coca from the old Sid Caesar television shows. I'd never have the courage to make these associations public, had Monk not endorsed them herself during our conversation at ADF 2001, exclaiming for instance "Imogene Coca! She was wonderful," in acknowledging how the comparison might be made.

When Monk began her career in the mid-Sixties in New York City, she joined the experimentalism of the Judsonites and their pursuit of The New. Wanting to "make things," she says, not content to be a company performer, she was encouraged by the "happenings" and daringness of the Judsonites, as she was by a West Coast sojourn with Anna Halprin. This experience, too, was important towards crystallizing her own artistic inclinations.

My first acquaintance with Monk's work occurred in 1969, at New York's Billy Rose Theater where, as one reviewer put it, Monk staged more a "happening" than a dance concert. What everyone remembers from that were the cartons in the theater lobby that revealed, when you peeked through the holes, squeezed-in-persons reading with flashlights or contentedly nibbling. Why? Well, why not? And therein lies the rationale.

On stage, as a man slowly filled a plastic tank with water, Monk as a Marie Antoinette look-alike matched the slowness in her walk across. Two performers jumped into the tank, splashing water wildly, for their own and (for some, anyway) the audience's amusement. A lot goes on in a Monk dance or tableau, too much to absorb in a single viewing, but I do recall how that evening in *The Beast* Monk strode about in high heels, then climbed to jump off some wooden structures, to a recording about mountain heights. Another female strider—blonde, older, and in street dress—moved to center stage and announced to our by-then-belief-suspended-senses "I'm Meredith's Mother."

Monk laughs, sometimes indicating "How could I?" on the few occasions when I mentioned the event to her.

Unforgettable, in outline anyway, was Monk's outdoor production, *Needle-Brain Lloyd and the Systems Kid: a Live Movie*, at the 1970 summer American Dance Festival at Connecticut College. This event is historically significant for representing the increased prominence of avant-garde dancers at the trend-setting Festival, newly directed at the time by Charles L. Reinhart. They in effect challenged the tradition of Graham, Humphrey, Weidman, and Limón. *Needle-Brain Lloyd*! Like others in the crowd on Connecticut College's campus, I watched it fascinated, amused, startled, fatigued, admiring and puzzled. *This is dance?*

Involving some 150 performers, the piece began in the afternoon at the college arboretum and after an hour moved to the college green overlooking New London harbor in the distance. The second part commenced on the green in late evening darkness, concluding with the performers followed by the audience shambling the return to the arboretum. It was impossible, given the shifting distances and multiplicity of action/actors, to discriminate all the elements of this marathon movie, but selected images are remembered. Making a *long* dance on the model of a neighborhood movie, *that* is definitely remembered.

In the lakeside arboretum, performers row across the lake. Others safari across the campus and pitch tents. Six motorcycles thunder forth, eight horseback riders gallop down the hill, alternating noisy chaotic moments with quietly withdrawn ones. (How will the college's buildings-and-grounds department react to this tearing of the turf?) Scenes upon scenes for some six hours, sometimes seemingly connected, as often not as seemingly meant to be. Such tableaux, luminescent and unexpected in their movement images, are what I remember as being a landmark performance art departure from what is commonly called dance.

Commentators as well as Monk herself want us to appreciate the cinematic influence in *Needle-Brain Lloyd* that is indicated by the subtitle "A Live Movie." That contemporary artists are affected by cinematic techniques, that performance artists including modern dancers adapt such techniques and use film and video in multi-media presentations, is not surprising. They grew up engulfed by filmic images, powerful and as psychologically resident as any that Freud proposed, and many like Monk and Rainer took turns at film making.

A distinguished section of Monk's career is given to creating films, and it began early in the Sixties. She was never satisfied, I've heard her say, with the kinetic impulse alone, that preoccupied some Judsonites, nor with their disdain for spectacle and theatricality. She was drawn to visual imagery (including gesture) and its expressiveness, wanted to be painterly in her pieces, so the resources of film are naturally attractive. Sharp cutting from image to image, changing from remote to close-up, alternating slow and fast representations of time, and the like—these were incorporated into *Needle-Brain Lloyd* and other works. One of her earlier solos, *Break* (1964), was composed with cinematic effects in mind. Notable among Monk's films are *Quarry* (a 1978 documentary film of her 1976 opera, *Quarry*), *Ellis Island* (1981), *Turtle Dreams: Cabaret* (1983), and *Book of Days* (1988/89). Were fundraising less difficult, she says she would continue more regularly her role as filmmaker.

Modern dance of the Martha Graham era, that adhered to the traditional Aristotelian dramatic unities, had been "well-made" within rigorous space-time limits for the proscenium stage. Monk like others of her generation sought non-proscenium venues, creating works whose identity is defined more raggedly over various times and spaces. An example, bearing structural resemblances to *Needle-Brain Lloyd*, is *Juice* (1969).

Not having seen *Juice*, I draw from Don McDonagh's detailed description for conveying some sense of what the work is like. It is a big work; seventy-five or more performers, three different venues of New York's Guggenheim Museum, Barnard College's Minor Latham Playhouse's theater, and Monk's downtown loft, with music by Monk and others. Outside the museum, a woman rode a white horse (Monk is an equestrienne), and the audience after digesting the sight went inside to see white dressed dancers humming and moving in and out of sight along the Guggenheim's distinctive spiral ramp, "Like the overture to an opera," as McDonagh puts it. Women in different period costumes stood and rotated like store mannequins at different levels on the ascending ramp. Many incidents ensued, the white dressed dancers run down the ramp, stopping as a man cuts wood with an electric saw, and a woman "in black with a life mask of herself affixed to her stomach is carried to the second level, after which there is a blackout and the first scene ends."

Juice's second part, three weeks later at Barnard, is an ingeniously "reduced" version, hinting at the larger Guggenheim one through such devices as the reproduction of a painting in the museum. Four performers in red recited personal histories, not silent as in the museum version. And what had been "a stylized hike up the ramp was now broken down into the component pilgrimages of four individuals" represented by their improvised interactions. The third part, a week later at the loft, features the absence of live performers. The loft itself is theatrical enough, decorated with various items including costumes from the piece's first two sections, also a hobby horse that echoes the white horse at the museum. The dancers of the second section are seen on videotape, offering more autobiographies. This final section, McDonagh writes, "represented the complete compression of the performing material into the natural, and untheatrical personalities of the performers from which the piece had developed."

This account of *Juice*, called a "theater cantata" by Monk (other works called "epics," "operas," "oratorios"), while admittedly too thin here to enable you to "see" the piece, does point to certain aspects of Monk's aesthetic. The piling-on of images is done confidently because, as I understand her, the motive is not simply to shock nor to imitate cinema, but because a desired "clarity" or "luminosity" results, as she puts it, from the images "rubbing against each other." I guess that she means that each image becomes more luminous through contrasting juxtapositions, and that an overall clarity (of concept, of image, of both?) blesses the entire process. Maybe "clarity" means "jutting out" enough to be provocative, in stirring our minds to probe the images's potential meanings. If so, this is one of those intriguing stage-points where artist and audience getting together is something of a toss-up.

Another aspect of Monk's aesthetic is its rigorous structure, ordered complexity. If her tableaux sometimes have a casual look, it is the deliberate effect of a very uncasual stratagem. Works like *Juice* [and later large ones such as *Vessel* (1971), *Quarry* (1976), *Recent Ruins* (1979), *Specimen Days: A Civil War Opera* (1981)], and *Atlas: An Opera in Three Parts* (1991) impressively attest to their inventor's genius in managing a "zillion" details while keeping the enveloping configuration intact.

The music in these works, and again the voice, whether of Jew's harp or keyboards, and whether of hums, chants, keenings, muezzins's calls, create an atmosphere so distinctive of Monk's works, yet so hard to describe. A recent obituary notice of the Polish theater artist, Henry K. Tomaszewski, mentions that his "dreamlike wordless presentations" influenced American artists such as Meredith Monk and Robert Wilson, and "dreamlike" does get at the Monkian atmosphere (she is the dreamer in *Quarry*).

Sympathetic commentators have made the point, abundantly supported in my own experience, that Monk's works are oddly personal yet impersonal, here—now yet nowhere—notime. Many factors contribute to this, the music prominently in its wordless echoes of other and ancient cultures, so that, even when contemporary America, say, is the ostensible subject, the Monkian musical atmosphere dissolves it into some transcendent, timeless, unnameable tableau.

There is also the communal/ritualistic aspect. Calling her company in the Sixties "The House" suggests the idea of family, an idea or image, that besides sustaining a working group, lends itself to Monk's way of "mythically" blending ours and past societies into a haunted and haunting simultaneity. She told her ADF audience a few years ago that the "globular" or "spherical" surrounding of the body interests her more than the fixed balletic position. That helps to explain movement preferences, but to me it also suggests how the communal/familial fills in around oneself, is part of the globular surrounding referred to. House and family are often Monkian motifs, presenting domestic scenes like an ill child or others at the family table.

When I saw Monk's more recent *Magic Frequencies* at New York's Joyce Theatre in November 1999, she had surrounded herself with a genuinely extended family—and at the table. She and a man open the show, called by her a "science-fiction chamber opera," by setting a table, sitting at opposite ends while chomping corn on the cob, and "dialoging" with each other in nonsensical sounds—"affectionate monosyllables, all in Monk-style solfege," to quote Michael Feingold, *Village Voice* drama critic. The audience was audibly amused when three green-clad extraterrestrial creatures entered, comically curious about the couple of earthlings at the table and about the corn on the cob. Before long, they join the chomping, big-style.

Other scenes include a couple going shopping, satires on television news reporting, and some dancing. One observer's impression: "In one lovely episode, in which the company pairs off for a waltz, Monk is left to dance alone: she holds up her arms to create an invisible companion and sways back and forth until another performer lifts her up in a close embrace. Together they trace slow circles across the stage, like the exhausted winners of a marathon dancing contest, faces buried in each other's hair, Monk's legs dangling in the air."

A grim scene has a man dying surrounded by family, and its connections with the other scenes require your interpretations. Interviewed, Monk explains that some episodes in *Magic Frequencies* referred to a kind of "demonic" or "evil" energy underlying our daily lives that numbs us to violence, to each other, to death. "Visitations" are central concepts in the work; by extraterrestrials and ancestral ghosts around the deathbed, hovering toward some kind of potential relating. "Finally, in the shopping scene, I wanted the visitation to come from within. When you see someone on the street or in the subway, you may recognize him even though you've never met before." The frequencies that connect us, beyond our ordinary sensory capacities at deeper levels, I think we are to infer, are truly "magical."

The dominant theme of *Magic Frequencies* is death. Lamenting death-dodging in America, by artists included, Monk said, after the 1999 production closed, that she planned to tour it in different American cities for encouraging blunter confrontations of death and its meanings. "Even though the whole piece isn't about death," she observes, "you could say it has the point of view of someone who has just died, or of an outsider, or even of an extraterrestrial…we're going to invite people from local hospices to talk with us about death, especially about dying at home." This leads directly to an abiding concern of Monk's for spirituality, but first a quick notice of a certain issue.

In addition to dance and drama critics, music critics as expected also attended *Magic Frequencies*, and one of them tagged it, as commentators over the years have labeled Monk's work, as "minimalism." He writes about her "signature techniques" or "wordless vocalizations that combine a Minimalist simplicity and repetition with an appealingly complex, interlocking rhythmic counterpoint." Monk has often disavowed the "minimalist" label, contrasting those like Steve Reich and Philip Glass who came from conservatory backgrounds and went for a circular musical form of pattern and overpattern, with herself coming from a singing background. "Vocally," she says, "I was working maximally." So don't confuse her use of repetition, derived from folk music and functioning as a kind of ground bass from which the voice could skip around, with what Reich, Glass, and others known as minimalists are doing.

Relevant to this matter of Minimalism is a recent article by art critic Michael Kimmelman on Dan Flavin and Donald Judd, in particular about their sculptures and other creations in former army barracks in desolate Marfa, Texas. Minimalism, as illustrated by Judd, Flavin, and others, Kimmelman notes is a label artists dislike when it is taken to mean simple-mindedness. But Minimalism, he argues, is all about *concentration*; "Concentration makes simple things suddenly seem momentous."

Elaborate this equating minimalism with aesthetic concentration and, thinking of how over her career Monk experimented with getting viewers to change perspectives, to concentrate on the looks and sounds of things, to see them thus transformed, we might then have a more acceptable rationale for calling Monk a minimalist.

Death is no late-comer to Monk's topshelf concerns, appearing in her 1966 *16 Millimeter Earrings* that includes among its spectacular details a film of a doll-effigy of Monk fatally burning while Monk herself "dies" into a trunk. It ends with Monk rising from the trunk, naked and singing "Greensleeves," leaving us with a strikingly new take on the theme of death and re-birth.

In a 1998 interview, Monk reflected on her thirty-plus years of producing well in excess of one hundred works. References are made to her Jewish/ Eastern European family background, to her involvement with Shambhala, a form of Tibetan Buddhist worship, and to the fact that the performers in her recent piece, *A Celebration Service,* read sacred texts ranging from Hasidic and Chinese to Osage Indian, Zen Buddhist, Ethiopean, and Christian. She refers to her *Atlas: An Opera in Three Parts* (for 29 performers when staged in 1991 at Houston Grand Opera), *Volcano Songs* (1993 musical composition for 2 performers), *American Archaeology #1* (1994 piece for 70 performers at New York's Roosevelt Island, and to *The Politics of Quiet: A Music Theater Oratorio* (1996 musical theater piece staged in Copenhagen).

These references are summoned in support of her identifying "spiritual- ity" as a major if often oblique refrain throughout her works. She admits to nervousness in talking about it, is quick to separate it from escapist "goody goody" angelicism, and I think would agree that, apart from such attributes as "revitalization, regeneration, enlightened awareness" and the like, she leaves it mostly undefined, respecting the mysteries that never quite lift from the foggy bottom of deep emotional experience.

However one tries to nudge closer to the meaning of "spirituality" in Monk's works, I believe one thing is clear, it is not explicitly confessional. I'm impressed, when perusing her interviews, how often she replies "I wasn't thinking of that," "I wasn't there," "Actually, I came at it differently from what you suggest," or "It's the work of my imagination, you know." Autobiography seems not directly reflected in her imaginative inventions. Rather, those inventions look like the constructed mainstays of her autobiography.

Whether the invention be *Vessel* that relates to Joan of Arc, or *Education of the Girlchild* that is a left-field sort of look at youth, age, and finality, or *Quarry* that has WWII and the Holocaust in mind, or *Specimen Days* that refers to the American Civil War, the off-stage Meredith Monk seems mostly absent. Not her preoccupying concerns or interests, of course, since they command the scenes.

To say that her interests in the spiritual linkages between ours and other times and cultures, interests responsible for thinking of her creations as "mythic/archaeological," reflect a spiritual quest on her part is not to suppose that we can discover her hiding out in those works; it is rather that her spiritual quest is artistically defined and pursued through those creations. No dance artist more than Monk, I think, better exemplifies how spiritual questing is an ongoing artistic process.

Years ago a New Mexico friend, long unseen, responded to my effusive greetings "How wonderful to see you again, so long a time!" with "Next time, don't come so far. Instead, just send me your latest book." What he meant, I supposed, was at that life-juncture I mattered more to him in print than in the flesh; my thoughts, more than my smiles and slaps on the back. I think Meredith Monk would appreciate this, maybe even reward me with a smile and slap on the back.

Emphasizing the spiritual constant throughout her long career and asking how can a "sacred space" be created anywhere today, she sustains most originally the spirit of modern dance as exemplified, say, by Duncan, St. Denis, Graham, Limón, Dunham, Primus, Hawkins, Ailey, and Jamison. As Monk appreciates in asking how can she and others forward that tradition within a contemporary skeptical climate, risks are involved. The vague and various meanings of "spiritual" pose a problem. If not depending on traditional symbols and props, which modern dancers tend to avoid, how do you insure spirituality being actually *seen* by your audiences? And even if your intention is espied, how to make it and your production of it an authentic match?

On seeing the New York performance of *A Celebration Service*, described as a non-denominational religious celebration, I was not alone in finding it quiet and low-keyed compared to earlier works concerned with spiritual themes of quest, death, transcendence, re-birth. Not much movement by twelve performers/singers and two text readers, some small processionals and re-groupings, and more a cappella singing over a steady droning, and interspersed with readings from sacred texts. The spirituality, I thought, was while subdued certainly unmistakable. But, illustrating the risks involved and understood by Monk, one reviewer was put off by its Connecticut performance, calling it "spiritual pretense" and trendy/chic New Age stuff. The reviewer's main complaint seemed to be that the use of texts (Sufi, Plains Indians, etc.) amounted to "insincere" sampling for performance purposes. Whether Monk's intention was indicted here as insincere as well as the performance is not clear, but to leave that as suspect, I must say, is really risky business so far as reviewing is concerned.

Monk's piece *Facing North* (1990) happened to go unmentioned in the 1998 *Dance Magazine* interview where she reflected on her career and its theme of spirituality. She was working on this while also preparing *Atlas* (1991) (that took, she says, about five years to produce), setting in motion several other explicitly spiritual works of the 1990s to follow. For me, watching it at ADF in 1996, it proved more effective than *A Celebration Service*, more theatrical and, meeting my own apparent biases, through its formal qualities managed the "obliqueness" with which spirituality gets freshly communicated.

The scene of *Facing North* is like an Alaskan or Arctic desert, white bleak expanse. Monk and her co-performer, Robert Een, resembling Eskimos or Inuits, protectively clad with outerware and expected fur hats and mittens, dot the landscape like two lost wanderers. (They might cause you to recall Vladimir and Estragon in Beckett's *Waiting for Godot*.) They play symbolically with miniature props, dialogue in Monkian song-language, clump about and at times break into movements deliberately abrupt and awkward that come across as fuzzy, funny manifestations of two innocent well-meaning human creatures casting about in a virginal barrenness.

Monk has characterized *Facing North* as "a chamber music/theater piece about a barren wilderness and the fortitude and tenderness of two people surviving within it." It could also be "a tribute to our ancestors or to all the people and creatures who have ever lived in the north; or it could be an homage to the land itself. Or perhaps it could be an appreciation and acknowledgement of the north in all of us." Some observers, responding to the multiple-meaning stimulations of the unfolding tableau, judge it a "late-twentieth century version of traditional, stylized, deeply enigmatic Asian drama."

Monk says of *Facing North*'s musical forms that she made them, for her and Een, "So interrelated that if one of us falls down, then the whole thing falls down...where we're throwing notes in the air. It's like being on a tightrope with no clothes on and we never know if we're going to make it through. Every time." Elaborating on the speed of the vocal exchanges, where the body outruns the thinking, where getting adequate breath is almost impossible, she says "I think it's the closest thing to meditation, a speeded-up meditation, that I've ever experienced."

I can't say that I caught the meditative experience that she describes, but the effect made by the gestures, songs and moves of these two arctic waifs, with their clownish overtones, was sufficiently touching, and mysterious to be, in my glossary, spiritual. Its 1996 ADF performance received an ovation, although the next day a festival dance student confessed to me her puzzlement about its being called a dance, and we agreed on that while also agreeing, whatever you called it, that it was both entertainment and something more than that; the "more," for lack of anything better we agreed was spiritual—also agreeing that we needed to explore the meaning of this at another unspecified time.

One can understand how in her new hour-plus work *Mercy*, premiered at

ADF 2001, Monk in collaboration with the installation artist Ann Hamilton has extended the "fortitude and tenderness" of the "survivors" in *Facing North* into the multi-dimensional realm of mercy and merciful behavior. More a series of dramatic tableaux than dance, it nevertheless depicts the various manifestations of mercy from the dancer's point of view, that of the human body. What to think about mercy? How to "physicalize" that thinking on stage?

Monk-as-voice, the voice that sings, and Hamilton-as-hand, the hand that draws—that can be a starting point. And voice and hand can begin the piece, at opposite ends of a Monkian trademark, a simple table. Then make them big, by projecting onto the large backdrop screen blown-up images of hand, mouth, and vocal chords. Technology is all-important in *Mercy* (which is probably an implied statement in itself given how modern technology can be as merciless as ever it is merciful), including a tiny video camera in Monk's mouth, another that pictures for backdrop projection Hamilton's hand guiding a pencil drawing of a long wavy line or sketching out the twelve stories of mercy that constitute the piece.

These stories or scenes are never literally told, so, as is Monk's habit, they are alluded to with deliberate ambiguity. A group of "lost" people ("refugees" on back stage sign directions) in raincoats and caps come on stage and are told "Come in" by the waiting woman, and as they are singly "admitted" entrance by her, thoughts come to mind of the Holocaust, or of Ellis Island, or of human misery in general and its need for merciful response. Another coldly spotlighted scene has a "cold" doctor peering down at seated Monk (back to us) and apparently "diagnosing" through glow-glasses her condition. A prisoner squats, rocks, and silently screams or shouts within his cell-like space. His asylum-like movements define this scene that also includes the arresting sight of Monk crawling towards him, hands on a sheet of paper, then lies on stomach while staring at him. He draws a hand on the paper, gives it to Monk now standing, who rips it apart. Other hand and mouth motifs, sometimes grotesque, occur throughout, as if the intention is to "objectify"—as in magnified projections on the backdrop screen—not only the workings but also the "meanings" of these bodily organs.

The whole piece has a kind of haunting monotone to it, Monk's music holding to a steady pulsing and occasionally broken by vocal plaints and yelps, as the movement occasionally breaks out from static and silent action. These abrupt break-outs or changes create an uneasy, erratic atmosphere, that is enhanced by the performers' repeating "Help!" and the backdrop often streaked with a deathly gray.

On my second seeing of *Mercy*, at Connecticut College, those horizontal streaks of gray reminded me of the Metropolitan Opera's bleached sets of some years ago that caused more than a little grumbling. But that modulating gray speaks the tone of what it is often like when mercy-needed and mercy-offered meet, a tone that is remarkably sustained in a remarkably complex and memorable work.

For her achievements as one of America's most original artists, Monk has been appropriately honored and awarded. In addition to Guggenheim Fellowships, a MacArthur Fellowship, Rockefeller Foundation Distinguished Choreography Award, the Samuel H. Scripps American Dance Festival Award for lifetime achievement in modern dance, among others, she has received Sarah Lawrence College's Distinguished Alumna award, and Honorary Doctorates from Bard College and the University of the Arts in Philadelphia. These awards pay tribute to a career that makes the mind a part of the show and the dancing body/voice in on the know.

Trisha Brown

Trisha Brown's friendly, fun-radiating eyes are suggestively loquacious. They look, as you look at them straight-on, like they're going roundabout or from left-field, asking impishly maybe something like "Want to see what's behind you?" In conversation, as you're about to ascend the next step of your own seriousness, those eyes can send you back down three flights at a time.

My *impressions* of Trisha Brown are based on her own words, others' words about her, many if not most of her dances either seen or reported, and my recent though limited conversations with her at ADF. She does impress!

"My personality," she smiled during an interview, "embraces elusive behavior." You're inclined to say, once acquainted with her, "How true that is!" Because her personality is seductive, charming in conversation that is one moment spontaneous and candid but at the next is hesitant and pensive, you can feel in her presence always on the edge of being ambushed. Her autobiographical observations encourage one to credit her "openness" and self-described "Wild-Child" adventuresomeness to origins in Aberdeen, Washington and West Coast untamed spaciousness, and credit her ever-editing intelligence to lifelong dance/arts professionalism. Interplay compared to straight play is trickier to identify, and the interplay of a refining intellect makes for a certain elusiveness: neither this nor that but rather both, somehow.

Brown's career, like most modern dancers', connects college and professional environments. A dance major and graduate of Mills College, then a dance teacher at Reed College, she later joined, along with Yvonne Rainer and Simone Forti, Anna Halprin's California workshop in the late Fifties. Thus began a professional career that would regularly engage university as well as downtown audiences for whom movement ideas count as much as movement technique. There is no Trisha Brown technique, she says, instead are Trisha Brown concepts, attitudes, and some secrets of movement; things for the thinking viewer, I add, not to be hit with passively but to look for actively.

Brown weighs her words, searches for *les mots justes* in conversation, and she can surprise you with her verbal choices, with how she thinks about an idea, a person, a dance. Easy it was not, to create dances as a new mother in the Sixties and surrounded by unmarried colleagues, and easy it was not, for her to find in interviews words other than "not easy" to describe her situation then. If the right words don't occur, she stops, smiles enigmatically, gestures light-heartedly while refusing a pedestrianly verbal even if convenient conversational exit. When I watch her dances, I guess that their moves and patterns have elicited the right words for her, or silently stood in for them.

From Halprin's California workshop, where she eagerly absorbed improvisational and task-oriented dance practices but where no permanent opportunities were offered, she moved to New York City to become a founding member of the Judson Dance Theater and of the Grand Union group. She liked Merce Cunningham's classes, and though to some of us she looks not unlike a Cunningham company dancer, she was not invited into his company. "The best thing that could have happened," she reflects, because it forced her to invent her own style of stage movement.

Brown's movement style is lithe and athletic, mirroring her gymnastic training and her older brother's early encouragement to "compete" with him in basketball or to aspire in their backyard to become a pole vaulter. Not surprising, then, that she and Steve Paxton composed an improvisational duet, *Lightfall* (1963), that was physically demanding, obviously risky. Videos of her early dancing show contact improvisation in development, movements that are weighty, falling, leaning on one another.

Brown tells an amusing story about her first dance *Trillium* (1962), a very physical solo involving a headstand and composed to an offbeat musical score by Simone Forti while at ADF at Connecticut College. ADF students lobbied for its showing that had been vetoed by the leadership, and Bessie Schönberg was appointed to explain to Brown why the absence of an identifiable logic in *Trillium* disqualified its being on the program. Sitting at a cafeteria table, Schönberg proclaimed: "You can't just use any order of things like you do in this dance. You can't, say, on this table just put the pepper shaker here, this ash tray there…well, actually, this is looking rather nice." So *Trillium* got shown, and Brown's career as a recognized "experimental" dancer had begun.

Replacing the look of the trained dancer of the modern dance establishment motivated Brown's dance inventions. "In the field of avant-garde dance, in which you make up *everything*, there is not much to go on," she observed, "so we had to ask ourselves things like 'What will the structure of the dance be?'… Some people at Judson took it at full tilt and just lived with whatever happened. I took it more slowly, starting with ordinary movement organized by game plan or task and working backwards to the world of decorative gestures."

Movements suggested by a task or game plan, as in her Sixties dance *A*

String, obviously replaced the look of the trained proscenium stage dancer. In its first part, "Homemade," Brown moved about insofar as a projector strapped to her back permitted, shooting pictures of herself around Judson Church's performance space. In the second part, "Motor," she took spins on a skateboard, followed by the spotlight of a motorbike, and in the third part, "Outside," she donned sweatpants and exercised. In her *Rulegame 5*, a group of five followed her instructions, in effect playing a game of walking, sliding, jumping (while talking to each other for assisting the process) along parallel floor strips. A few years later in 1969, she improvised *Yellowbelly*, telling the audience to heckle her, and dissatisfied with their response, told them "louder!" Wit, humor, outrageousness, daringness, novelty—the Judson movement trademarks—featured in Brown's works of the Sixties, works that increasingly fudged distinctions between dance and performance art.

Asking "What is dance?" or "What can dance be?" was, probing the human body's resources, to ask how movement could speak for itself, independently of narrative or expressive supports. But this did not mean independently of any and all context, because for Brown "structure and game plan" serve as the context that rescues choreographic choices from being sheerly arbitrary and the dance movements chosen from being utterly meaningless. Happy with being called an "abstract" choreographer, she emphasizes how a score or structure of spatial patterns, rhythms, etc. gives the movements a coherence that, while indifferent to story-telling or emotion-expressing, does not prohibit hints of such from easing into an audience's consciousness. And if you ask how she reconciles structure with improvisation, she has no reason to hesitate for a reply, because it's so simple—it's "structured improvisation."

Context is also supplied by careful and often arduous use of sets and props. Her career is partly defined through four decades of collaboration with Robert Rauschenberg, an impressive influence. Donald Judd and Nancy Graves are other collaborative visual artists, and it is not unusual for Brown's dancers to interact in startling ways with sets, moving or stationary, and to cope with tasks that utilize challenging props such as tightropes. This developed, got bigger, and her contexts became architectural in the 1970s.

Inspired by the buildings around her in New York City, Brown extended the concept of dance skyward, almost out of reach, in a series of creative episodes that are "site-specific" and "equipment-fitted" for walking down buildings, as in her 1970 *Man Walking Down the Side of a Building*, or walking the Whitney Museum's walls in her 1971 *Walking on the Wall*. These and other such works/activities/performances created an aesthetic stir because of their ingenuity and nail-biting riskiness, but also because they melted previously cemented ideas about movement in relation to gravity and about our perception of such. In the Whitney Museum episode, for example, although the performers were "walking," supported by harnesses and cables above the spectators, the illusion created was one of looking down on the act.

Structuring in Brown's dances often amounts to a re-structuring of our concepts or ideas about movement and our ways of perceiving/apprehending it. *Roof Piece* (1971) illustrates this, although just how is debatable. Eleven performers (dancers?) were perched on eleven roofs over a twelve-block area, and their task was to "transmit" certain gestures from the first to the next and finally to the eleventh, this taking some fifteen minutes, proceeding in a downtown direction; and then, reversing to an uptown direction and beginning with the eleventh performer re-transmitting those gestures back to the starter. As a spectator, you could not see the entire transmittal, although discrepancies between how the gestures looked at the beginning of the performance and at its conclusion were discernible.

The point of this? For one writer, "Brown is interested in the tension between the clarity of a movement idea and its physical distortion," and we can see how that might apply to *Roof Piece*. Another suggests that Brown set herself the task of "how to establish a visual and kinetic relationship between bodies widely separated from one another in space," and how that might apply to *Roof Piece* is quite apparent. Of course, the piece might also say something about how context complicates communication, how even simple gestures can, like gossip or rumors, get skewed when passed along. Or, *Roof Piece* might be conceived as a kind of "happening," and what happens at a happening? Who knows? Let's try it and see what happens! *That*, too, could be its point; provocatively staged movement tugging at our minds.

Looking back, as the new Millennium begins, Trisha Brown sees her achievements not as a seamless growth but as sequences of distinct creative cycles; symptomatic, I venture, of a restless psyche excited for the next and different adventure. Thus, in the Seventies, besides the dangerous wall-climbings and other "equipment pieces" (that must remain undiscussed here), she chose another method of invention for what are called her "accumulation" pieces.

Her solo *Accumulation* (1971) she describes as follows:

> ...four and a half minutes long and accompanied by the Grateful Dead's *Uncle John's Band.* Movement one, rotation of the fist with the thumb extended, was begun and repeated seven or eight times. Movement two was added and one and two were repeated eight times. Then movement three was added and one, two, and three were repeated, eventually bringing into play the entire body.... The second performance was in silence and 55 minutes long.... Both the dance and its structure were visible and bare-bone simple. None of the movements had any significance beyond what they were. And I never felt more alive, more expressive or more exposed in performance.

Gerald E. Myers

Brown called such 1970s performance pieces, including *Primary Accumulation* and *Group Primary Accumulation,* "object-like" dances that became accumulative material for further dances. Working with objects, props, sets, scores, and "pure" movements themselves imagined as space-time objects, all on behalf of composing "object-like" dances, apparently satisfied a choreographic longing to create something identifiable and enduring "outside" of oneself. Whatever the inner transient sources of the creative process, the manipulation of movements, often according to mathematical or abstract game plans, resulted in a kind of "thing out there." Dances like *Locus* (1975) and *Pyramid* (1975) seem to satisfy a dancer's yearning to author works that, like paintings, buildings, and sculptures, exist objectively and beyond the brief life of a performance. Could be, too, that lamenting how so many "inner dances" by emotionally absorbed choreographers fail translation into outer visibility, she sought the kind that yields its all to a sufficiently searching stare.

Brown wants audiences to appreciate her dances through their structures, and the number of these "getting it" has grown. But when they don't, when the game plan is too private or esoteric, when the palindrome nature of *Son of Gone Fishin'* (1981), say, goes unnoticed, audiences may still relish the surface qualities. Brown's own dance style, of movements initiated peripherally, arms flung or swung around the head and body (sometimes called "floppy") rather than from a tight center, has always been an attraction, stimulating the adjectival imaginations of critics and writers.

About Brown's solo *Water Motor* (1978), where she strikes a familiar lengthened backwards slouch, Deborah Jowitt wrote:

> She seems to be changing directions or speed or weight every other second, and she doesn't stop to let your eye glom onto any positions. Here are some useful words: slip, twist [I note that Brown once said that the Sixties dance fad "the twist" had been a good influence], lurch, startle, shrug, slide, sidle, duck, hurl, but don't imagine that you can apply them one at a time. And remember that in the long run everything flows into everything else. The dance is so delightfully slippery to your eyes—try to hold a live fish—that when she begins to repeat her opening phrase you can't believe that you'd be able to notice a thing like that.

Brown has her own adjectives for describing her dance and different career phases, such as uninflected, eccentric, fluid, valiant, and zero. With her elaborations, these words work as illuminating labels, showing her to be, in my terms, a "poetic engineer" or, in hers, "a bricklayer with a sense of humor." Her dances that are meticulously organized or structured, that can be graphed or notated, can also be dissected and scanned like, say, any of Louise Gluck's complex poems. The details are engineered but interpreted poetically.

She calls her cycle of works "fluid" that culminated in the 1983 collaboration with Robert Rauschenberg and composer Laurie Anderson, *Set and Reset*; seven dancers executing flowing or swinging arms and legs, lolloping quarter or half turns of the body. The "valiant" series, on the other hand, of *Astral Convertible* (1989), *Newark* (1987), and *Lateral Pass* (1985), features powerful and geometrically figured movements, gestures, or interruptions of flow. Gender differences are highlighted in *Newark*, for example, with very strong moves choreographed for the men, also providing an outlet for Brown's own athleticism. The duets, employing falls and balances, are meant to show gender similarities as well as differences. Gymnastic partnering continues as Rauschenberg's set-panel drops to curtain them on stage.

Musical collaborations have enlisted Brown's versatility and experimentalism in recent years. And, if I have it straight, the 1990s and the years just ahead represent for her a "back to zero" phase, where creativity is credited more prominently to unconscious processes than to specific tasks or structured game plans. Her *For M.G.: The Movie* is a key though dense work in the latest cycle. In any event, collaborations with opera, jazz, and avant-garde music feature her most recent work.

In 1994, Brown widened her collaborations with Robert Rauschenberg to include his costume design and sets, his electronic score, and his concept of her solo dance *If You Couldn't See Me*. A comparatively brief piece, it is performed throughout with her back to the audience. So, given this plus a diaphanous costume that bares back and arms, with side slits that leave legs free, your spectator eyes are full of a woman's backside, tall and muscularly alive, moving angularly to and fro. Rauschenberg's music and soft side-lighting add to its feeling of remoteness, of seeing or sort-of-seeing a woman, yes, but abstracted.

This back-to-audience solo will also be remembered for being modified in 1996 into a duet for herself and Mikhail Baryshnikov. Appropriately titled *If You Could See Me*, Brown still dances facing upstage but Baryshnikov performs facing audience and displaying what we would see if Brown performed facing us. Sparely costumed with waist-to-feet white panels that echo Brown's appearance, he performs movements that copy hers for frontal viewing. This tour-de-force takes on added interest, of course, from being performed by two admirable dancers, though beyond their performing prime and with one of them adapting classical ballet training to modern/idiosyncratic. And Rauschenberg's electronic score in its repetitions contributes to a kind of mechanical abstractness and novelty on stage that, for some of us, is strangely evocative.

In 1986, Brown performed in and choreographed for a production of

Bizet's *Carmen* directed by Lina Wertmuller. This, she says, led her to work on character delineation, more concerned, for example, with masculinity and gender differentiation. The ensuing musical collaborations, including her *M.O.* to Bach's "A Musical Offering" and *Twelve Ton Rose* to Webern's opuses (when, she says, she was "working on magic" and making movements to dissolve like film) stimulated extensive research on Brown's part in music and musical history. She notes her current immersion in formalizing dance and movement relations to musical inventions, past and present. Directing a 1998 hour-long production of Monteverdi's *L'Orfeo*, that opened in Brussels and toured Europe and later to New York, she blended movement, music, and text into a work of operatic theater that won enthusiastic critical approval. The collaboration, with Italian composer Salvatore Sciarrino and his opera *Luci Mie Traditrici*, promises to be more sheerly narrative/dramatic than her previous ones.

Brown's creations are sometimes dubbed "cerebral" because her intentions, as are occasionally indicated by program notes and interviews, are typically buried in rather than publicly mounted on the movements. We have noted how her use of structure illustrates this, and it is also to be noted in her use of the body, for example in *M.O.* to Bach's "A Musical Offering." She told an interviewer that when she began this work, no matter what she did Bach's music made her moves look old-fashioned, like Isadora Duncan revived, so she worked "on what the lower body...can do," beyond, she says, its supportive and transporting functions, giving it an "aesthetic purpose the same as the arms have."

Another distinctive bodily strategy used by Brown has been noted by Anna Kisselgoff in reviewing Brown's *Foray Foret*. She notes how Brown invents recurring movement motifs like bringing "a hand to her cheek...pushing her jaw from side to side" that are not immediately intelligible. Kisselgoff makes us aware of Brown's intention, of de-conventionalizing gesture and movement through such motifs.

This use of de-conventionalized movement is worth noticing because many contemporary dancers also employ it. Hand gestures, especially head-oriented, like pulling the edges of the mouth, pushing up under the chin, or waving vaguely around the ears, occur in much avant-garde dancing. Why use gesture, that in daily life we would readily understand, in dead-end ways that leave us baffled? Because, I venture, choreographers like Brown find them interesting in themselves, also because they create movement-situations that as "problems" initiate movement sequences that otherwise would not have been considered. Maybe, too, the de-naturalized gesture deconstructs the act of recognition into exciting flutters of uncertainty when confronted by the familiar rendered novel.

Some observers have found more reliance on the dancers' bodies, than on abstract structures, for generating movements in Brown's recent jazz collaborations such as *The Trilogy* with composer Dave Douglas. The dancing energy, as might be expected, is turned up in the falls, jumps, quick foot work, alternations between unison and sequential movements, punctuated thumps and silences, in response to Douglas's jazz-flavored score.

Again, the "real" and the "abstract" mixture of Brown's aesthetic impresses in this three-section work. The movements of ten dancers echoing jitterbugging or lindy-hopping look improvised and "real" enough, yet they are deliberately not quite the real thing but abstracted/stylized from what one would have seen in Harlem's Savoy Ballroom. Terry Winters's three sets for the different sections—a backdrop of curlicues and lines, a pole holding cymbal-like discs, and a backdrop of many panels displaying the curlicues and lines of the first one—add a distinct abstractness to the piece. As does Jennifer Tipton's tempered lighting effects.

Brown and Douglas agreed, in a public conversation held at ADF's 2000 summer season, that *The Trilogy* had been a collaborative challenge. For the composer, the band was not to be a time-keeper, with a consistent boom, boom, boom, so the dancers were requested not to count. But for the dancers, who were required to sustain an uncomfortable speed and abrupt movement changes, they *had* to count even if silently. The anecdotes of this collaboration are often funny, usually instructive.

For those of us fond of jazz music and dancing, *The Trilogy* is a memorable landmark work. It raised questions for some observers, whether Douglas's score is real jazz or only jazz-influenced and whether Brown's choreography is as "jazzy" as might be expected. So how to treat jazz, as we are reminded by the recent thrashing about in reaction to Ken Burns's leviathan documentary series *Jazz*, will probably frustrate anyone, however gifted, hoping to satisfy everyone.

What is striking, that emerged in our ADF conversation, is Brown's comment that in researching and preparing for *The Trilogy*'s successive sections— "Five Part Weather Invention," "Rapture to Leon James," and "Groove and Countermove"—she discovered that she had been "dancing African-American" all her life. Remembering her early social dancing, now realizing its African origins, also the sources of long-favored "isolated" and "natural" bodily movements, it felt like "going home" to collaborate in jazz with Dave Douglas. Moreover, working on jazz motifs re-enlivened the issues of how to set limits or frameworks within which improvisation stands out, or otherwise gets lost through being scattered chaotically.

Bearing Brown's trademarks, the "meaning" of *The Trilogy* and its parts is enigmatic. She says, in a delightful phrase, that she "loves to play at dancing

Gerald E. Myers

on the edge between meaning and non-meaning." On the occasion that she said this, it followed some remarks on the limits of pure dance, of the limitations of the human body itself—"only one head, one front, one back…"—for making it and its movements into an object. I get from this the idea that for Brown the body's limitations allow the experimental choreographer to almost attain specified meanings but not quite, instead an odd place between meanings and non-meanings. Correct or not, true or not to her intentions, I thank her for the idea that seems to me useful in thinking about the nature of modern dance.

In her mid-sixties, Brown maintains an intense schedule, accepting commissions right and left, and accepting the rigors of seven months or more of international touring. She has received the gamut of awards and honors, including the MacArthur Foundation "genius" designation, the Scripps/ADF lifetime award, and Honorary Membership in the American Academy of Arts and Letters.

In addition to being hosted for performances and colloquia by numerous colleges and universities, Brown has recently received honorary doctorates from Skidmore and Bates Colleges. Such recognition, along with her continuing interactions with academia, one likes to believe, indicates an appreciation of how Trisha Brown's life in dance is equally a life of the curious and inquiring mind.

Twyla Tharp

"Dance is a microcosm of society," said Twyla Tharp, and on the occasion some years ago when I heard her say this she was concerned about the social role of dance. Everybody should dance, for their own good and for the good of society, and in addition to simply enjoying the activity, she contended that children, for example, can learn from dancing the values of cooperation, trust, and democracy; they can become sensitive to dance's moral implications, the ways in which it presents issues of justice, right and wrong. Although she didn't elaborate her meaning here, I think she meant at least that dance, like all the arts, but in its own distinctively physical mode, is inherently a social and hence morally involved activity.

The occasion was her receiving the Samuel H. Scripps American Dance Festival annual lifetime achievement award in 1990, and to emphasize her point about dance's sociability, she declined the award's routine invitation to perform in the theater as a part of the ceremony. Instead, she proposed holding a square dance in a Duke University gym, and in celebration of her award she joined an audience that enthusiastically responded to the caller's instructions to promenade and allemande. It was a hot evening, sweat pouring off the dancers hot-stepping it to the fiddlers and banjo, and in the social middle of it all was Tharp, swinging her partners, circling left, circling right, often pulling them into her faster pace. There she was! Performing with rather than for her audience that was gathered to honor her distinguished contributions to dance.

Because of all the issues that congregate in Tharp's career, it is itself a microcosm of modern dance's career, and a prominent instance of such issues is the problematic relationship of performer and audience. As we saw previously, modern dance has seemed trapped in a never-ending dilemma, wanting a popularity that it never quite trusts. She confesses her own susceptibility to this dilemma in her fine autobiography *Push Comes to Shove* (1992), being always attentive to audience reactions and often attending to these more than to the dance performances, for example, while collaborating with the Joffrey Ballet. Yet she was eventually dismayed by the popular success of her 1973 hit *Duece Coupe* to the music of the Beach Boys. When audience bravos depended on loud music, bright lights, spectacular scenery and sexy performers, she was troubled.

Catering to audiences was never the temptation, but pleasing them with quality dancing, who can quarrel with that? Especially when, as in Tharp's case, you go the extra miles, with lecture-demonstrations and community projects, towards making audiences better acquainted with the art. The depth of her interest in interesting audiences was made clearer to me when moderating a public conversation with her. I had mentioned to her that, in watching her re-stage her legendary *The One Hundreds* with a Durham, North Carolina community, I was reminded of the amount of community-related programming she had conducted; not all her creative endeavors were like *In the Upper Room* (1986) or *Brahms/Handel* (1984, with Jerome Robbins) that are associated with New York's ballet glamour-halls. She asked me to call this specifically to our audience's attention and because of the almost passionate nature of her remarks on behalf of connecting with audiences, I think to call "audience education" her objective is not quite right; "audience partnership" is more accurate. In Tharp's ideal world, audiences would be co-conspirators in the performances.

The American intelligentsia in the 1960s, Tharp sensed when she began her career, viewed dance as merely light entertainment, not deserving serious attention, and women could make it in dance, as she wryly put it, just because there was no profit in stopping them. She has done everything in her power to correct this view of the art, and one such effort was her 1970 *The One Hundreds* that she revives to this day. Whether in London, New York, or North Carolina, this work recruits 100 community volunteers (most of them untrained dancers) to join Tharp's leader-dancers, two of whom begin by performing together 100 different brief movements. Then five dancers together do 20 of the 100 movements, and for the big finale the 100 volunteers together each do one of the 100 movements for 11 seconds. This "community" dance feat (for a "feet-feat" it is!) acquaints actual and potential audiences with how a dance can be created, with how a choreographer relates to her artistic medium, and for Tharp this is an essential step towards understanding the art and why it deserves serious attention. (That 100 community volunteers are willing to yield so much time and energy for 11 seconds of communal fame may indicate a boatload of seriousness to start with.)

Given the premise of my jottings throughout about the importance of understanding modern dance philosophies, because how the choreographers think about what they're doing is an inevitable feature of their creative process (no matter how intuitive it may also be), I naturally groan a little when reading Tobi Tobias, back in 1970 (so in the meantime maybe she's modified the viewpoint) cautioning Tharp that informing audiences is not needed because her philosophy "is not what determines the impact of her work. Twyla simply [Oh, would that it were so simple] makes movement that is new and exciting. What anyone, including herself, thinks about it is probably incidental. (Although Twyla, being brainily oriented, would most likely disagree.)" Tharp, as I understand her, has always disagreed with this, continuing her lecture-demonstrations, giving informative interviews, etc. Perhaps as keenly aware as any modern dancer of the fact that no art is more mystifying to the public than concert dance, as she writes in her autobiography, and maybe more committed than others to "demystification," she once finished a dance, *Sue's Leg* in 1970, for public viewing and instruction and I'm quite sure that many viewers went away shaking their heads about the physical and mental complexities that went into this dance's creation.

Tharp is herself something of a microcosm, a petite movie of the kind of physical energy and choreographic imagination that course the history of modern dance. She is a small, sinewy dynamo with more motor-drive packed into a single human frame that I've ever witnessed. She comes at the world with head forward, maybe in a sweat suit, chin up, and eyes that stare with the fixing power of laser beams. Given the athletic biases that her body insinuates, it is not surprising that she has choreographed for ice-skater John Curry, a duet bit for Peter Martins of the New York City Ballet and Lynn Swann the former football star of the Pittsburgh Steelers, and after boxing lessons from Mike Tyson's trainer incorporated pugilistic moves on the dance stage. So you see clenched-fisted dancers in her 1975 *Ocean's Motion*, Kevin O'Day as a boxing champion in her 1998 (appropriately named) *Everlast*, and ballet luminary Ethan Stiefel on the cover of a 1999 *Dance Magazine* posing as a boxer. She once greeted me, as I'm sure numerous others, with "I've got a great left cross" as she struck a boxing posture. What did I do? Grinned and ducked!

Equally striking is the agility of her mind. All who know her attest to her mental acuteness and how that shapes her choreography. She seems always mentally on point, speaks immediately and directly to the issue, wastes few words, and loves to challenge you as much to keep up with her verbal repartee as with her dizzying sequences of dance steps. Her dancers, many of whom have been longtime associates and who receive her regular tributes, must own various assets but at the top of the list is *intelligence*.

The intelligence shared by the choreographer and her dancers, at its core, is the ability to recognize how and when a movement idea or motive is adequately embodied. Born in Indiana in 1941, reared in the Los Angeles area, graduated from Barnard College, Tharp joined the Paul Taylor Company in 1963 for a short time—and her comments about Taylor emphasize her early "bottom-line" valuation of the dancer's embodiment. She recalls in her autobiography how Taylor's own dancing "prowled" with a "feline grace"; how his solos in dances like *Aureole* and *Junction* featured "the deep coil of his body," how standing on one leg he could curl the rest of his body towards the center and then extend his body astonishingly far outwards, adding up to an exceptional "completeness" of a movement episode. You see this and you see a dancer's intelligence working, and if you don't at least sense it working then you don't see *this*, I mean what Tharp saw.

A dancer's intelligence, at basis, shows itself by the kinds of movements that take it in and by the kinds of "takes" it makes on movements. "You have to think," Tharp tells her dancers, "what the movements are about," and this one, she illustrates, "is about bringing the head as far down on the shin as possible," and this one is "about hitting something as hard as possible and having something left over." Working in 1969 on *Medley*, a dance outdoors for some 60 dancers or more at ADF/Connecticut College and based on running, walking and skipping, she recalls how hard "I tried to get this work *out of the head and into the body*" (my italics).

Tharp as a youngster had experience with ballet, tap, baton twirling, and modern dance, and as an adult studied ballet with Margaret Craske and Richard Thomas, jazz with Luigi and Matt Mattox, and modern with Martha Graham, Erick Hawkins, Alwin Nikolais, and Merce Cunningham. But from the beginning and through it all, it seems, what occupied her was "almost a scientific investigation of the body—the engineering of the movement, the timing, the different way you could sense the coordinations, the rhythms, and the compositing of what the body could physically do." Then followed an interest in the motivation, including emotional, of movement; and, for Tharp, the only satisfactory movement source is "the gut." She says, "I've always danced from the inside. I've always *danced according to what my body could understand*" (my italics). And to understand what your body can understand, let's add, calls for a special kind of intelligence, of a kind too often missing whether on or off the dance stage.

Learning what kind of dancing your body understands, and that promises an original niche for itself in the concert dance world, requires experimentation and lots of it. Because of her quick success, becoming a celebrity in "climbing to the top" of the dance-word ladder, a box-office attraction, award-winner many times over, she looked to some observers like a fall-back from, say, the radical experimentalism of the Sixties epitomized by the Judsonites. So not failing to remember appreciatively her own performance and choreographic excursions is important.

Content with crawling before walking, and fully aware of crawling's risks, Tharp debuted in 1965 with a 3-minute piece called *Tank-Dive*. (Tharp's dance titles are riddles with answers, this alluding to her thinking that she was diving off a platform without much chance of success; although one wonders whether she really was so dubious, given her early and startling confidence, as stated in her autobiography, that she would eventually hit it big and choreograph for New York's leading ballet companies.) Danced to Petula Clark's "Downtown" and lighted by Jennifer Tipton, the piece and entire evening took but several minutes. No one reviewed it, and, looking back, Tharp is grateful for her relative obscurity until about 1970, forcing her to locate her own idiom.

When one reads about or recalls Tharp's dances of the Sixties, they often seem to resemble the Judsonites—playing with the absurd in costumes and props, erratic or no use of music, departure from the proscenium stage for gymnasium and outdoors, and on occasion seemingly ambivalent towards audiences. In *Re-Moves* (1966), a 3-woman dance, each performer wears a glove on one hand only and a sneaker on one foot only. They pace methodically and hand a stopwatch to each other, carry eggs that smash to the floor. It looked pretty bare, and Tharp will call such dances "minimal," explaining that some American artists like herself were driven to "bare bones" in reaction to the extravagant abundance in the United States. (Another instance, note, of where Tharp socially contextualizes a dance that others may see only in isolation.) It was a revelation, for me anyway, to read Tharp in her autobiography describing *Re-Moves*, made during the Vietnam War, as concerned with death, costumed darkly and starkly nun-like, punctuated with mindless gestures that built into a "hypnotic babble."

No one especially liked it, she writes, but for many it was interesting, got attention. A feature of her dancing that also got attention was the deadpan, detached, who cares faces of the dancer. A reviewer of Tharp's 1965 dances *Cede Blue Lake* and *Unprocessed*, the first described as a kind of silent ritual that used a slide and the second having a billowing cellophane canopy that eventually engulfed things, noted "Miss Tharp, stony-faced but loose-limbed." Some called the Tharpian attitude, whether facial or in overall body language, "cool" or of a temperature akin to the gathering cultural climate at the time. Tharp quotes, presumably amused by it, reviewer Clive Barnes writing "Miss Tharp is so cool she could use a refrigerator for central heating."

Tharp's minimalist experiments of the 1960s resembled the Judsonites in some respects but otherwise differed radically. She was not out to redefine dance, to mark the art as problematic, to abandon tradition including Duncan, Graham, and Cunningham altogether. Her goal was to create (yes, "craft") first-rate dances and to attract audiences, whether on stage, in gyms, or meadows, for enjoying them. She told an ADF audience some years ago that when she was beginning her choreographic career her three "beacons" were Merce Cunningham's *How to Pass, Kick, Fall and Run*, George Balanchine's

Agon, and Martha Graham's *Primitive Mysteries*. She did not explain why, other than saying that these dances worked as models for her, and not because they were necessarily "the best." One guesses, because each of the dances cited was arguably an acknowledged aesthetic "breakthrough" when premiered, that she found them inspirationally instructive, reinforcing her own choreographic rebelliousness that nevertheless recognized its continuity with artistic forerunners.

Tharp was in fact severely critical of Judson aesthetics. She disagreed with what she took to be their view that skilled difficult dance movements are seductive, cheap. Where Yvonne Rainer said "no" (to spectacle, etc.), Tharp said "yes," thinking that despite their championing nudity and other challenges to convention the Judsonites were quite puritanical, preferring a kind of austerity rather than fully enjoying the "juice of moving." If you *danced* rather than just walked or ran, she said, you had "sold out" according to the Judson philosophy. So, as she and her dancers increasingly strove for "well-made" dances that drew upon tap, ballet, modern, and jazz, while considering themselves a small communal and feminist group, they were "kicked out," she writes, by the Judsonites for being "hopelessly commercial."

A landmark event for Tharp was making *The Fugue* in 1970. It was premiered at the Amherst campus of the University of Massachusetts during a Tharp residency there (another of the numerous colleges/universities that collaborated with her, that helped in promoting an American intellectual awareness of modern dance). Tharp has described The Fugue as consisting of 20 variations on a 20-count theme, and though it is done in silence, its theme was suggested by the structure of Bach's "Musical Offering." One can cite this as a particularly interesting example of Tharp's lifetime exploration of musical stimulation, working to or with an extraordinary mix of composers in jazz, classical, rock, country, and contemporary avant-garde. Her penchant for finding structural ideas in dance from music, whether Jelly Roll Morton, Brahms, or Philip Glass, point us to why she so admired Balanchine, also why music and musical concepts influence her choreographic aesthetics as contrasted with many of her contemporaries whose stimulation came from the visual arts.

The Fugue is its own music, since as a piece where tap style is recognizable, the three dancers stamp out complex rhythms on a miked stage, their sounds being a loud and distinctive feature of the dance. When I saw it a few years ago at Jacob's Pillow, and knowing something about Tharp's fondness for its structured complexity and the intellectual labor she invested in its creation, I managed to catch enough of that for rewarded watching. With access to her charts and graphs, her explanation of how the piece was diagrammed, I might well have responded more fully to what looked to me like determined performing of an abstract stylized form of tap, "a dancer's dance."

But I can understand why some critics find *The Fugue* "atmospheric" and not sheerly abstract; why some felt its earlier version with women in black and stamping the floor with boots was "eerie and menacing," whereas a later version with three men seemed "lighter and more congenial." (Another discussed issue provoked by Tharp's career arises here, though more often apropos of her 1982 *Nine Sinatra Songs*, is her dance-attitude towards sex, romance and male-female relationships.) Atmosphere or no atmosphere, given Tharp's affection for *The Fugue*, one wants to love it, too. Already a great success with some of her masterworks such as *The Bix Pieces*, *Deuce Coupe*, and *Sue's Leg* achieved, though exhausted from the frustrated experiences of directing the musical *Singin' in the Rain* in 1985, she realized that *The Fugue* of some fifteen years earlier was her favorite dance.

She liked its simplicity, a three-section "pure" movement piece that succeeded independently of costumes, music, lights, scenery, because it was performed by "committed" dancers working intelligently through the dance's structure that she realized later was actually *canonic*. And though what has been said about it makes it seem terribly abstract and intellectual, she writes that its theme was developed in the open air on a hillside so for her its associations are sensual, certain counts of the dance twisted around blackberry bushes and others involved dropping to kneel on the sloping inclines.

Her fondness for *The Fugue*, I think she tells us, is mainly due to its being a destination, a realization of a goal, of constructing a "pure" dance. For some, like her dancer Tom Rawe, this was "classical" dance. He explained its being his favorite because he had always wanted to be a classical dancer, "and *The Fugue* is the most classical thing I do."

Now that the "bare bones" of concert dance as represented by The Fugue had been displayed, Tharp asked, "Okay, now what?" To move to a new stage, not because audiences may have failed always to "get" the design, structure, or bare bones, because she took that for granted ("only Balanchine would have gotten it"), but because now she was ready to give those bones some choreographic elaborations.

Tharp's creative output in the 1970s was phenomenal, inventing or involved in some forty works or close to one-third of her total inventory to date. In addition to those already mentioned, the productions included jazz-focused such as *Eight Jelly Rolls* (1971) to Jelly Roll Morton's music and *Baker's Dozen* (1979) to Willie "the Lion" Smith; ballet-focused such as *Mozart Sonata* (1971) to Mozart and *As Time Goes By* (1973) to Haydn; hybrid-formed like *The Raggedy Dances* (1972) to Scott Joplin and Mozart, and *Push Comes to Shove* (1976) to Joseph Lamb and Haydn; pop and country like *Once More Frank* (1976) to Sinatra and *Cacklin' Hen* (1977) to Richard Peaslee's arrangement of country music. The variety of these works attests to Tharp's determination to "do it all," also precluding facile pigeonholing of her choreographic record.

The dance world, gazing at Tharp's mix of jazz, ballet, tap, country, and pop that often seemed to blend Hollywood, Broadway, and television with the concert stage, quickly acknowledged her as the regal seamstress of the classical and vernacular. *Deuce Coupe*, a collaboration between the Joffrey Ballet and Tharp's company that was hailed by some critics as the hit of the 1973 ballet season, is an example. Its assemblage of elements—modified ballet steps, adapted jazz/social moves, familiar Beach Boys tunes like "Papa Ooh Man Man," "Little Deuce Coupe," and "Cuddle Up," graffiti paintings for a backdrop, and non-stop dancing by what looks like a bunch of grown kids—shot audiences out of their seats applauding. The critic Marcia Siegel doubtless spoke for many in writing that your own growing-up in America was tapped into by the dance and that amid the slapstick and action avalanche Tharp seemed to be reflecting seriously, maybe at times sadly, about adolescence. (She was criticized on occasion for too often allowing her adolescent concern for adolescence an ungainly access to the concert stage.)

So *Deuce Coupe* and other dances that recollect the music and culture say, of the Fifties or earlier days have nostalgia working for them. But of course these are no "dance alongs," no audiences can even kinaesthetically follow the dancers' rapid-fire movement sequences. The beauty of Tharp's choreography and her dancers' execution of it is her re-tailoring of older music, dances, and images in exciting new forms and combinations that feel *now…and then.*

There is an unbanal sense in which one can say that Tharp is a "child of her times" in blending so distinctively the classical and vernacular, the refined and the popular. Post-WWII America had witnessed the Vietnam War, campus sit-ins. Woodstock, assassinations, increased immigration, and new artistic/cultural influences and fusions, civil rights struggles, and legislation, all of which were forcing an American revolution of values. Pop culture, whether in movies, TV, live stage, or in print, lighted up all these changes like "wake-up" fireworks, one result of which was to plop pop culture center-stage on American campuses for serious study. When this happened, former confidence in "high vs. low" art/culture went limp. The distinction itself came in for heavy academic analyses and America's intellectual spies, one presumes, were on the lookout for any subversive examples. You can be sure that, in addition to those who took notice of her in reviews and articles, many more were in those college-educated audiences of the Sixties and Seventies applauding Twyla Tharp's dismantling of the old high vs. low art concept. She was recognized as an intellectual ally in this respect, was often invited to campuses, I believe, as such, and for the intellectual interest being shown in concert dance she deserves much credit.

Pointing to the intellectual as is our habit because our intent is not for a moment to forget that Tharp's success is due to the action-excitement of her dancing. For her admirers, her style is absolutely exhilarating. They can respond to a Tharp dance like Tharp herself to a solo performed by Sara Rudner in *Deuce Coupe*. It left the audience in a "breathless heat," writes Tharp, like what she felt as a young girl after watching torrid love scenes in her mother's drive-in movie facility. (Tharp told us some years ago that if such opportunities had been open to women, she would have chosen to be a filmmaker, and the influence of the movie screen at her mother's facility, including the "double" comic/sad, etc. nature of Charlie Chaplin and Buster Keaton, would be interesting to track thorough her choreography and physical performing traits.)

What is most memorable about Tharp's dancing and that makes it so active and exciting, I believe, although indebted here and there to Balanchine, Bob Fosse, Vernon and Irene Castle, and others (seen, researched, or studied with), originates in a distinctly personal, idiosyncratic moving style all her own. This is what changed and expanded the modern dance vocabulary as she kept unraveling that style through the 1980s and 1990s to the present. For a starter, I as a non-dancer would say to one who is unfamiliar with Tharp that, when doing her "signature" movements, she looks to me like someone at a party spontaneously improvising in such unexpected, eye-catching ways that everyone stops to watch, fascinated by the hip swings, back bends, shoulder shrugs, arm flings, heel-and-toe exchanges, on top of which rides a face fronting almost confrontationally, seemingly asking "So what do you want to make of it?"

What grabs your attention is how many things, such little things like a hip tilt, a hand raised all five fingers stretched, or pelvic thrust and head laid back, succeed each other nonstop or simultaneously, alternating with hesitations or lazy rotations; the dancing body becomes a motion-picture show. Remarkable is the ceaseless flow, though disjointed and punctuated by different body-parts, of one movement into another; it really exemplifies John Martin's claim in the 1930s that such flow distinguishes modern dance from the static, episodic nature of traditional ballet. It becomes all the more remarkable when you learn the discipline involved, that the seemingly infinite variety of simultaneous and successive movements are "set," even more startling when choreographed for an ensemble of such, that ballet, jazz, modern and social steps have been chosen and refigured on behalf of a casual, improvised performance look. Where does it originate? From thousands of hours, often alone, Tharp reports, experimenting and experimenting. Her personal style, transferred to her dancers, is often called "floppy," "twitchy," "slouchy," "jazzy," etc. Tom Rawe, one of her dancers, told an interviewer, "We might do something that looks like a shoulder shimmy, but that shimmy is actually precisely given to us as two circles and a pump. But you can't go around explaining all the time, 'Hey, folks, I'm not loose and floppy.'"

Despite the style's idiodosyncracy, it translates well enough on the bodies of others, whether the Hubbard Street Dance Company doing the Golden Section of *The Catherine Wheel* (1981), *Sue's Leg* (1975), or *Nine Sinatra Songs* (1982), or Mikhail Baryshnikov in *Push Comes to Shove* (1976). In this celebrated piece, Baryshnikov sleekly costumed with derby hat and looking like a jazzy Fosse dancer (although Fred Astaire was apparently the model in Tharp's mind) and two women dance to some ragtime that is followed by a Haydn symphony. Baryshnikov does the Tharpian alternations, jump, turn, slouch, freeze, play with hat and ooze street-casual. The two women join the slouching play, the hat getting passed to each other. The stage becomes complicated when the Haydn music takes over. Sixteen women replace Baryshnikov and the two women in a complex series of floor patterns, and this leads to the others returning and eventually thirty dancers on stage for a "roaring" finale that replaces patterns with calculated partyish disorder. The Tharpian transformation has kept the classical Baryshnikov recognizable, but just barely. (There is no suggestion here that Tharp's dances are all look alikes, since of course her success is due not only to her highly original performing mode but to a choreographic virtuosity that contextualizes it differently, subdues it within balletic, ballroom, folk/social styles, and that increasingly, she says, is receptive to her dancers' own individual styles.)

Tharp observed in a talk at ADF that she entrusted dances like *Sue's Leg* and *Nine Sinatra Songs* to Hubbard Street dance company only because she trusted them to do the works correctly as staged by former star Tharp dancer Shelly Washington, "Because, you know, those dances are about a lot *more* than steps." The more involves a special Tharpian *attitude*, I thought. When she was recently asked to define "greatness" in a dancer, she mused, "a commitment that goes beyond sincerity. English does not supply the right description for greatness—you just feel it." *Attitude*, I thought. When Ethan Stiefel struggled for characterization in taking Baryshnikov's part in *Push Comes to Shove*, Tharp told him "You gotta think scumbag. It's too wholesome." So he imagined himself in his derby hat to be pimping the two ballerinas.

Attitude, yes indeed. When Deborah Jowitt once praised a performance of Deuce Coupe, enthusiastic about seeing "*people* up there dancing," I twisted this into "with Tharp, it's not so much people-as-bodies as it is bodies-as-people dancing." Personhood here is in the body, a matter of attitude, bodily, that is. When we talked in 1999 about her new piece, *Grosse Sonate*, to the challenging Beethoven Piano Sonata (the "Hammerklavier"), about Beethoven's artistic commitment with its sense of music's *moral* implications and of Tharp's companion-sense of dance's moral dimensions, again "attitude" I thought. When she said in the text included in *The Bix Pieces* (1972), what would have excited the philosopher Ludwig Wittgenstein, that "aesthetics and ethics are the same," I was led to connect and locate in the *attitude* the kind of dancing that is great, more than steps, personal, and so intensely aesthetically committed that it becomes morally implicated as well.

Tharp's performing attitude facially, I've always felt, is enigmatic, and any interpretation of it has to be found in how her body slouches, leans, catapults, and so on. And you feel the power of the impulses in that performing body even when subtly contained. Highlights in her autobiography include her remarks, when working on *In the Upper Room*, about "power women," about dancing so powerfully that only women can do it, about how the notion or feeling had developed in her own body. An inward womanly power, so when applauding *In the Upper Room*, remember now its true source.

I emphasize this because Tharp illustrates how a distinguished dancer's mind and body remarkably coalesce—in an overall attitude that works the coalescence. The *physical* dancing attitude that is *simultaneously* casual vs. disciplined, scumbag vs. haughty, impulse left vs. impulse right, up vs. down, contrapuntal vs. harmonic, slouch vs. strut—and so on—is the same *mental* attitude that is *simultaneously* ethical vs. aesthetic, pacific vs. aggressive, Appollonian vs. Dionysian, and so on. We talked publicly in 1999 about the latter tension, between the impulse towards controlled form and the urge towards emotional formless surging ("the gut") as famously formulated in Nietzsche's *The Birth of Tragedy*, apropos of Tharp's feelings about no longer simply reinforcing (for dramatic purposes) but now tempering or reconciling opposites in her later works in the 1990s such as *Grosse Sonate*. And I presume that her working towards a choreographic reconciliation of sorts between these polarities occurs as well in 2000 with the more recent *Mozart Clarinet Quintet K.581* and (the jazz collaboration with composer Donald Knaack) *Surfer at the River Styx*.

Tharp writes in her autobiography that her impulse had always been to counterpoise dual elements, and she sensed that, as in fugues, you can get a "fullness" by taking on the opposites simultaneously. This is the attitude I see in her "multiple-action" performing style and in her verbal conceptualizations of such. We have not thus far mentioned the comic, funny, chuckle-making movements that are sprinkled through her dances and that most critics have pointed us to.

These are mostly dancers' in-jokes, flaunted aberrations of steps and gestures, a head or rump in the wrong place, often not just laughable but witty. I appreciate Deborah Jowitt's perceptive phrase "seriously funny" in characterizing this feature of Tharp's works; it captures the co-existent opposites in the dance and in the attitude that created it. I can't imagine Tharp ever being totally unserious. Just one case in point is her bristling at the statement that she was parodying ballet, replying that she never parodied (too unserious and irresponsible); she *used*, she says, not *presented* ballet in her vocabulary mix. Observers have described Tharp's performing attitude as "throwaway" or what I might call "shrug-off." This kind of seeming indifference has been so prominent as maybe to thrill the rather desperate Jean Baudrillard who has called upon artists, because of postmodernism's alleged loss of meaning and desire, to dramatize indifference, make a stake of it. But though the Tharpian attitude may contain indifference, it's much too serious and concerned to be only that. The attitude contains a "fullness" with its opposites, and that's why it ends up—*enigmatic*.

During the late 1970s and 1980s, in addition to authoring new successes such as *Brahms' Paganini* (1980), *Bach Partita* (1983), *In the Upper Room* (1986) and choreographing for films like *Hair* (1979), *Ragtime* (1980), *Amadeus* (1984), and *White Nights* (1985), Tharp turned out works of a more narrative and autobiographical sort. Observers had commented that her earlier output had been impersonal, mostly a "floppy" mix of classical and vernacular movements underpinned by meticulously/mathematically diagrammed patterns and sequences. This may be true, yet for me there was always a "personal" radiation from Tharp and her dancers in their "committed" focus and concentration, and I guess that this results from doing your damndest to meet the strict demands of the diagrams even if the blueprint is invisible to the audience. It serves as the dancers' "motivator," urging their moves with the sort of focus, intent, or purpose that audiences sense appreciatively (as contrasted with "aimless" wanderings on stage), whether consciously or not.

We share a Quaker Heritage, so I asked Tharp if it had significantly influenced her life and work, and she indicated "yes" but seemingly disinclined, at that moment anyway, to elaborate. Thinking that the Quaker background might be relevant to her more explicitly narrational/autobiographical dances, I looked again at her autobiography. There seems to be a connection with her important 1979 *Baker's Dozen* (music by Willie "the Lion" Smith). The dancers are presented as couples, trios, quartets, and sextets, executing astonishing lifts and partnering bits, with tensions shown between individuals and groups, then ends as one harmonious ensemble. With references to American commercialism and Hollywood-type wastefulness, the dance is said to represent an ideal society. Tharp associates its assuring audiences that Biblical order is indeed possible, an assurance that made it her company's signature piece, with what is pictured by the American Quaker folk-painter Edward Hicks, in the almost 100 versions (during the 1830s and 1840s) of his well-known "The Peaceable Kingdom" where wolves, lion, lambs, etc. lie down together.

After *Baker's Dozen*, she writes, she wanted to dramatize herself, now a single mother wondering about her origins, so she created *When We Were Very Young* (with text and narration by Thomas Babe, music by John Simon) in 1980. Depicting a dysfunctional family, it struck some as emotionally profound, others as melodramatic. Two years later, she produced *The Catherine Wheel* (exploring what this title suggests conveys some of the undercurrents here). This, while a very different dance, seems again concerned with that family's problems. Anger, loneliness, depression and their accompaniments quite openly fuel the choreography and performing.

Tharp emphasizes this when, looking like a college professor at the lectern, she delivers a first-rate lecture, wonderfully organized and video/film illustrated, on "My Life and Times in Jazz." Almost 40 of the approximately 130 dances that she has choreographed since 1965, she says, are jazz-based. Her carefully researched interpretations of American jazz history, as an "outsider's" art, as dance and not just music, both spontaneous and disciplined at times, both exciting and stoic, etc., are correlated with her "maturing" emotions (anger prominently included) as expressed in *Eight Jelly Rolls* with its eight women jazzin' it up in bare-backed black tuxedo-costumes to the music of that outsider and complexity-of-opposites himself, Jelly Roll Morton (and his Red Hot Peppers). Key movements in the jazz dances are explained, often related autobiographically, as in *The Bix Pieces* (to Bix Beiderbecke and Thelonious Monk) that includes a narrator for indicating subtext references to her father's death, to the continuity made between that and her son's birth. She calls it a dance of remembering.

So are others like *Nine Sinatra Songs* (whether called pop or jazz), because in her autobiography she reports that in her Quaker family "Look at me" was never said because it was too immodest; what was said instead was "Look at what I've done," leaving young Twyla with an "inner emptiness"—and a lingering mother-directed anger. This is lingered on in the autobiography, and since Mother hated Frank Sinatra's music ("always sang flat"), what better revenge than to make lush romantic duets to Sinatra's records? So *Nine Sinatra Songs* tells a kind of Tharp story (easier for audiences, she notes, to follow than *When We Were Very Young* and *The Catherine Wheel*) and the successive dance vignettes, each drawing plentiful applause, to songs like "Stranger in the Night," "One for the Road," "All the Way," "That's Life," and "I Did it My Way," accompany appropriately. May be the most gorgeous dance revenge we'll ever have!

When you listen to Tharp talking about her choreographic output, so extensive and varied, to her interesting "takes" on her dances that often differ with critics ("That dance is not a new interest in partnering, I've been into that previously," "The audience didn't laugh at that piece because it was funny, rather because it made them uncomfortable," reminding me of a similar comment made by Donald McKayle when I was troubled by an audience laughing at the "wrong" place in his *Rainbow 'Round My Shoulder*)—you are struck by her immediate recall of the dances and how they compare. Continuity as well as difference is often pointed to, and on my own I venture that the anger and frame of mind released in *When We Were Very Young* and *The Catherine Wheel* connect with the early *Disperse* (1967) in which a child's chair gets smashed and *Jam* (1967) that exhibits "flailing around" and generally angry dynamics.

It would be a treat to hear Tharp identify for us, at length, the enduring continuities throughout her four decades of making dances. We know of course about her continuing to explore ballet, as shown for example by *Brahms Paganini* (1993) and a "big" ballet—*Variations on a Theme by Haydn* (2000), besides the already-mentioned *Grosse Sonate, Mozart Clarinet Quintet K.581,* and *The Beethoven Seventh.* And exploring jazz as in *Jump Start* (music by Wynton Marsalis, 1995), *Roy's Joys* (Roy Eldridge music, 1997), and *Surfer at the River Styx* (Donald Knaack music, 2000). And sustaining the folk/social interest in the recent *Westerly Round* (2001) square dance to Mark O'Connor's "Call of the Mocking Bird"; that calls to mind Tharp's writing in her autobiography that both she and Rudolph Nureyev were rooted in folk dance where real "raw movement" had been learned.

But more, one would welcome her telling not only how the lifts (where physical may equal emotional support), partnering, steps, and choreographic blueprints compare, say, between *The Double Cross* (1975), *The Catherine Wheel,* and *In the Upper Room,* but also whether, despite their obvious differences, underlying themes or concerns overlap. One wonders whether the apparent theme, mortality and its (mythic) transcendence, of *Surfing at the River Styx* connects with *Sweet Fields* (1996) to Shaker songs and music, a work that I much regret having missed. My wondering here, and less about the mentioned examples than about possible overarching thematic continuities, originated with Tharp's talks at ADF in 1999 and 2000 where she lamented the condition of contemporary aesthetics. She is interested, she said, in reviving the concept of Beauty that, as she well understands, is never mentioned now, is so old-fashioned it's dead, and you would have to scour many campuses before you could come upon a lecturer in aesthetics uttering "Beauty."

One might guess from those talks that the "hard-edge" Twyla Tharp had mellowed somewhat, that not only was she further melting the lines between classical ballet, modern, jazz, tap, and folk/social but that a softening of tensions, a reconciliation that tempers but without wholly eliminating her perennial opposites discussed above, is now in progress. If so, I suspect that it is hardly a brand-new movement for her but rather something that she has been into for a very long time, and, as she once said "forevermore."

No concert dancer, I suggest, has made the art more accessible than Tharp, an art deceptive in its looking so sheerly physical yet produced by such complexity of thought, gut, and practice. Tharp's dancing is exciting, yes, because it is physical-to-the-hilt but also, for me, because her "village" of moves—shoulder shrugs, off-center runs, marching west with head southward, etc., is like a ragbag of eccentric mingling in search of more mingling, even with those on pointe and to the manor born. You can be stimulated to "take" after "take" by those eccentric moves, and that is exciting. And it is something shared with Tharp whose "take" on a moment in *In the Upper Room* where the men hoist the women "as a mass" is: "As the men hoist high, I see communities building barns."

Continuity is not easy, especially when as in Tharp's case your dance company once bonded is disbanded, your collaborations with other companies and organizations are on and off. The money is elusive, and the national cultural climate is chilly. One presumes that the rare quality of her works insures their endurance. In 1990, the Twyla Tharp Foundation Archives were donated to Ohio State University, a dance campus stronghold. A recipient of the MacArthur Foundation "genius" award, a Honorary Member of the American Academy of Arts and Sciences, and at last count recipient of 17 honorary doctorates, she ought to have the backing needed for the future. One hopes that the intellectual world, to which she has contributed so richly, will figure importantly in providing current support and in preserving her legacy.

Gerald E. Myers

A Letter

New London
December '01

Dear Mrs. C.—

How I like you liking my jottings on Meredith Monk, Trisha Brown, and Twyla Tharp! And how puffed up I feel, sensing your monthly warming to modern dance as an adaptable art. Are you ready to tell?

Women, as these three demonstrate, are still conspicuous energizers of the art, whatever the challenges that endure. And, needless to tell you, when their contributions are recounted, how their wit and intelligence are to be underscored.

Lousie Steinman—in a book you'd do justice to, Mrs. C.—quotes Trisha Brown (in effect, all three): "*Without thinking*, there are just physical feats" (my italics).

Modern dance, say it again, is thoughtful dancing, with all the risks pertaining thereunto, and thanks to Monk, Brown, and Tharp for giving us such. Were my task not formidable enough, Pina Bausch would be thanked here, too, but, Mrs. C., among all that's been written about Bausch, take a look at Johannes Birringer's book, *Theater, Theory, Postmodernism*.

Of course, discussing these dance artists all in the same breath, as a group of women, is an old issue-raiser. Again, that issue won't go away. I didn't intend it as such, my jottings "flowed" that way. How sexist or gender-divided is the field?

Two women who have studied the field and this issue are Ann Daly and Judith Lynne Hanna. I send you to their ideas on the subject, referring to ballet as well as modern dance. Their assessments are backed by considerable historical and sociological information.

Sometime, you must unwrap your thoughts for me on how myth and ritual rely on a culture's folk/vernacular elements. It could thicken our understanding of what female (as well as male) dance artists have contributed to contemporary dance.

The other day I heard, from America's Rock, Rhythm, and Doo Wop pop music era, "Two Silhouettes on the Shade" sung by The Innocents. How I wished you were with me, longed for your reaction. Without that, I fear I'll never know you. Do you understand?

Good night, Mrs. Calabash, wherever you are,
GEM

P.S.: You've asked me several times why I have selected some modern dancers but not others for discussion in these jottings. I believe that most informed persons would agree that those I've included ought to be, but instead of those I've not discussed? How to explain the omission? Actually, what distresses me most is not the omission of well-known names but the *many* lesser-known dancers and persons in the field who have been friends, often helpful to me in various ways, including how to write about the art. The vitality of the art depends on these "unpublic" fine and dedicated dancers. When I consulted Billy Taylor on an ADF booklet on dance and jazz, I sympathized with his wanting to avoid a "great name" approach. They might have expected my mentioning them to you, but on the other hand, finding one's name on a "list" is less than thrilling.

It's better not to attempt a rationale for you on this highly selective rumination of mine. Mrs. C., in the end it becomes, alas, rather arbitrary, can't be avoided. I don't deliberately seek the arbitrary, but can't avoid its inevitablity though regrettable.

Pilobolus

In 1979, Annabelle Gamson, a dynamically persuasive performer/recon-structivist of Isadora Duncan's dances, produced a four-day series of pro-grams by dancers and companies at the Brooklyn Academy of Music titled "From Isadora to Pilobolus." This was of personal interest because one year earlier I happened to be present when Gamson eloquently complimented the dance troupe Pilobolus for their recent achievements.

The earlier occasion, June 1978, was the opening of ADF at its new facili-ties at Duke University after its lengthy stay at Connecticut College. In the program that appropriately followed greetings and remarks on the societal importance of the arts by Duke president Terry Sanford, Gamson and Pilobolus performed along with the José Limón Dance Company doing *The Moor's Pavane* and the Paul Taylor company doing *Aureole*. With Gamson's "bringing back" Duncan and Mary Wigman works, the evening was a wonder-ful historical and aesthetic mix. Pilobolus presented *Ciona*, the dance they had premiered at ADF/Connecticut College in 1973.

This was an early Pilobolus signature piece. The six dancers, four men and two women in unitards, executed movement sequences visually startling, one after the other. Although subject to revision, the first word that occurs to the observer for describing the performance is "gymnastic." The dancers create an elongating line by leaning on and extending out from each other. They make eye-catching circular patterns, do high partnering lifts, form successive sculptural groupings.

Sometimes they pause facing each other, then lean away sloping architec-turally backwards, ingenious mutual hand-holdings and leveraged limbs keeping them from falling. A single dancer leaps or falls into the other's arms, and they leapfrog over each other in a horizontal line. Characterization and humor are apparent, an "odd man out" looking comically lost and puz-zled on the floor while the rest do their thing. There is cart-wheeling and across-the-stage motoring accomplished by partners alternately rolling each other up and across their hips and then "pedaling" on the floor. And there is the memorable Pilobolus image of six dancers looking like one hydra-headed creature, four stacked on and sticking out, and arms and hands outstretched, from two visually shrouded standing men.

The image is, say, of a kind of human fungus. A confidently chosen image here because Pilobolus is first the name of a rural fungus, tiny but potent (said to be capable of scattering its spores a tall man's length), and now names one of America's leading modern dance companies—Pilobolus Dance Theatre, based in small town Washington Depot, Connecticut. They choreograph and perform solos, duets, and individually within their ensemble pieces, yet they retain the fungus image with which they began, of a multi-appendaged single entity.

For ADF's 1978 kick-off programs in North Carolina, Pilobolus also performed some of their best-known works including *Pseudophodia* (1974), *Shizen* (1978), *Untitled* (1975), and (ADF commissioned/premiered) *Molly's Not Dead* (1978). The first mentioned is a solo choreographed and originally performed by Jonathan Wolken, a founding company member and co-artistic director, that is describable as gymnastic acrobatic. It features stage-crossings via back and front rolls/somersaults, physically demanding wavelike risings and fallings to the floor, abrupt up-from-the floor jumps and turns, striking bodily sculpturing, rapid and "freeze" movement alterations, slow-motion back rolls exiting into the wings for its conclusion.

Shizen, choreographed and originally performed by Alison Chase (co-Artistic Director) and company co-Founder Moses Pendleton, depicts two nearly nude "creaturely" figures in tenderly erotic embraces. Softly lighted and with Eastern flute music, it is more a prolonged mood than an intensely emotional piece. Familiar Pilobolus movements occur such as rumps up and legs taut while leaning forward on hands ("monkey-like"), and two-tiered structurings (one figure on the other's shoulders, their arms extended and, moving effectively in unison). The ingenious intertwinings of the two bodies has also become a Pilobolus imprint, and here the seeming blending into a single body brings to mind Aristophanes's imagining that the sexual urge is the longing of split halves for primordial reunion. For the critic Arlene Croce, *Shizen* is a "pure object of contemplation," "a decisive advance in Pilobolus style," a "movement from prose to poetry."

Untitled, also shown at ADF's 1978 first North Carolina season, is an audience favorite, a visual frolic in the Pilobolus repertoire. Two genteel ladies, gowned and hatted, are presented on stage but then, to audience gasps and chuckles, they abruptly zoom up to some 12 feet, revealing under their gowns the two bare-legged men who had stood up to produce the zoom effect and then to "walk" the aloft women, as it were, about the stage on male stilts. Two formally dressed men enter, are startled by the women's height, comically examine under their skirt, and become flirtatious. There are fine "picture" moments, the two women leaning backwards from their heights, then to be lowered to seating level by their under-the-skirt male supporters.

A "birthing" episode occurs, when the men finally emerge from under the gowns, and other incidents are suggested. But what dominate are not representations so much as the movement styles. Interesting partnering occurs, along with lovely sculptured manipulations of the women's costumes. What I call the "peasant" walk, often used by Pilobolus, is prominent, a "heavy" methodical forward-leaning walking by the men as they push the women along. And deserving notice are the "controlled tensions" of the male bodies as two men "fight," the stilted women quiet in the background, using slow suspensions and hovering jumps. The audience is left to its own devices for interpreting the piece that ends, after several other "episodes," with the two women quietly rocking with the four men dormant on the floor.

Molly's Not Dead, premiered by ADF at Duke's Page Auditorium in 1978, became an audience delight because of the raucous mix that is distinctively Pilobolus. Nearly nude in unitards, to traditional music, the six dancers perform hokey communal explorations (including visual) of each other and the world around them. There is the customary show of curiosity, of searching looks and gestures, one figure horseback-astride another and waving arms while scout-peering about, and the fungus-like constellation where from a centered middle dancer the other two swing like loose limbs. They are, again, bizarre creaturely figures who sneeze, voice utterances, lark, and mutually confront both aggressively and cautiously.

Lots of chuckles, too. In one tangled bodily duet, the audience giggles in puzzlement about which man's expansive buttocks they're looking at. There is audience-gratifying "rump shaking" as also occurs in *Ciona*. (Audiences, we found, liked the movement phenomenon in some of Talley Beatty's dances when we toured ADF's Black Tradition in Modern Dance project, so it pleased us no end to see a sign on a nightclub in Asheville, North Carolina that read "Rump-Shaking Contest Saturday Nights.") There are the deliberately awkward duet-walkings where one dancer carries another like an anatomy part, and there are such satisfying moments as when the two women stand out facing front on their men's knees and, extending airily into space while male-supported, wave their arms lyrically.

There are the Pilobolus exaggerated struts, the eye-arresting two tiered partnering, sometimes as three couples, and their humor of uncertainty expressed and re-expressed here by a male carrying a woman in his arms, announcing to the audience "Pa, Molly's dead," followed by "Molly's not dead, she's only sleeping." Much of the comedy in the piece, as Deborah Jowitt observed, is due to its raunchiness—heads and crotches together, women's "buttocks under the men's chins, their backs forming the men's paunches, their heads dangling between the men's legs like scrotums." Unoffended audiences chuckle at the "innocence" of it all, at the prelapsarian environment created by Pilobolus where the odd personalities of *Molly's Not Dead* suggest their own definitions of the human condition through "sniffing" each other out via successive bodily entanglements and disengagements.

It was for these and other achievements (notably solos, of a different tone by Alison Chase, Michael Tracy, Martha Clarke, Moses Pendelton, Robby Barnett and Jonathan Wolken) that Annabelle Gamson appreciated the Pilobolus troupe's North Carolina performances. I remember her saying to them something like "You are the hot property today," and my wondering then "For how long, how long?" (Now, more than 25 years later, there's no end is sight.) So, Gamson in 1979 linked her own heroine Isadora Duncan with the "hot" raunchy troupe of the late 1970s in a program series "From Isadora to Pilobolus." This was in fact an adaptation or follow-up to what Charles and Stephanie Reinhart, ADF's co-directors, had done in long championing Pilobolus and in mixing them programmatically in 1978 with the likes of Erick Hawkins, José Limón, Paul Taylor, Merce Cunningham, Trisha Brown, Twyla Tharp, and others.

But how, actually, are we to link Isadora and the Pils (as they are affectionately called), to locate this troupe in modern dance history? A small puzzle here because, as Charles Reinhart and others have noted, the Pils are not readily identifiable branches of some modern dance family tree. The founding members were Dartmouth undergraduates, untrained in dance but motivated to an interest in it after taking a class at Dartmouth taught by Alison Chase. She had come from U.C.L.A. with a M.A. in dance, and had studied with Merce Cunningham, Mia Slavenska, and Murray Louis.

The latter, with Alwin Nikolais, sponsored the Pils' initial New York City performance in 1972, and some have viewed them as a Louis/Nikolais offshoot. But the Pils and others, acknowledging the sometimes shared look of "biomorphic creatures," point to the distinct "fungus" style of the Pils as well as their avoidance of Bauhaus-type technology and costumes disguising the performers' bodies. Also, they are more traditional in their theatrical pieces (especially since the 1980s) such as *Return to Maria La Baja* (1984), *The Golden Bowl* (1987), *Sweet Purgatory* (1991), *A Selection* (1999), and *Davenen* (2000). Stories or narratives of a sort are often on or just below the performance surface, and the Pils tend to share, I think, a Martha Graham-like impulse for movements that are psychological probings even if done more slyly, or outrageously.

We can (and with their help) begin a placing of Pilobolus within the modern dance tradition, but it is important to remember, as Peter Schickele

(P.D.Q. Bach) put it when presenting the Pils the Samuel H. Scripps American Dance Festival Award for lifetime achievement in June 2000, how they came "out of left field" to become an artistic alternative to convention, a modification of tradition. As Dartmouth undergraduates, these innovators were living through the effects of the Vietnam War, the Civil Rights struggles, societal churnings leading to youthful revaluations of conventional careers and lifestyles. It was in this cultural climate, that encouraged "alternativeness" that Moses Pendleton (a literature major), Johathan Wolken (a philosophy major), and Robby Barnett (an art history major)—all possessing (untrained) athletic abilities—after graduating founded (with one other who later left) Pilobolus in 1971. Lee Harris, the fourth Pilobolus co-founder, soon left and was replaced by Michael Tracy (a pre-medical student with high school gymnastic experience).

It began as an all-male, collegiate, heterosexual small group living together hand-to-mouth and, to their own surprise, actually developing an unfinanced dance/movement collective. Two years later, they were joined by Alison Chase, their former dance teacher, and Martha Clarke who had studied with Graham, Limón, Cunningham and Anthony Tudor, at Juilliard and ADF/Connecticut, then performed with the Anna Sokolow Dance Company. Chase and Clarke brought new perspectives to group deliberations, reflecting their dance training and interest in theater as well as dance, choreographing in 1973 a duet, *Cameo*, noticeably different in its look from the men's previous creations. They also brought first-rate performing personalities to the ensemble pieces. It is hard even now for those of us who have followed the Pils since the early Seventies not to insert the faces and moves of Chase and Clarke when looking at their successive replacements'; hastily adding, however, that the Pils' continuing success is of course largely due to those talented dancers successively joining the company.

Chase continued as a company artistic director and choreographer in addition to independent projects, her role at Dartmouth in triggering it all of course never forgotten. She recently conducted a workshop with the Radio City Rockettes, described to me by an observer as "fascinating"; a new piece, *Rockobolus*, choreographed for the Rockettes by Pilobolus is in the works.

Martha Clarke left Pilobolus in 1979, forming the company Crowsnest for producing her more individualistically conceived versions of dance theater. She had been influential in creating the Pils' *Monkshood Farewell* (1974), described as a transitional work for the Pils by being a "fantasy piece" that veered more towards theatricality. Inspired by Hieronymous Bosch's picture *Garden of Delights*, the work is a wild series of "episodes," including resemblances to medieval joustings. Interestingly, some years later Clarke conceived and directed *The Garden of Earthly Delights*, a dance-theater "hit," again inspired by Bosch's painting. Robert Brustein, calling this superior to most of what New York offered, wrote that it "shows us theater in the art of regenerating itself, exploring realms...beyond realism, beyond representation, entering the very source of creation itself."

Given the kinds of issues that Pilobolus raises, I am surprised that my review (admittedly more casual than systematic) of dance writings about the troupe comes up with fewer than anticipated. One issue is their treatment of sex and gender roles, an issue I have sometimes heard put to the company's directors in public discussion for the ADF community including students. The Pils appreciate its being a "touchy" subject, and they recall earlier times, at a MIT lecture/demonstration for instance, before they realized what was politically correct, volunteering theories about "male and female energy" distinctions that dismayed their audience. And they remember the men's debates preceding the admission of Chase and Clarke into the previously all-male company.

Some observers, while praising Chase's and Clarke's contributions to the troupe, detected theirs to be a not-quite-at-home presence. Someone said, Alison Chase recalls, that when she and Martha Clarke joined the men, it set modern dance back ten years. This might be traced to the troupe's male majority regarded by some as collegiate jocks, larking gymnasts, raunchy clowns, acrobatic mimes, and the like. More likely, some observers questioned the performance roles of the women, being thrown and carried upside down, roles assigned them in the dance's narratives. On the other hand, Judith Lynne Hanna praises *Untitled*, a work capable of raising conservative eyebrows, for being "definitely contemporary" in its images of "the masculinized female and feminized male, intimacy and rivalry between women, competition among men...sexual jealousies, costume and identity...." And the Pils' *Ritualistic Day Two*, with everyone topless and moving similarly, is viewed as erasing gender distinctions.

For their part, I judge from their responses in ADF forums, the Pils see no sexual or gender issue. Wolken, Barnett, and Tracy who regularly represent the troupe are unassuming, friendly/outgoing, bright and sensitive, cordial and sharp, seemingly free of gender hang-ups, so one sympathizes when they wince at anyone's suggesting they are fungus sexists. They have clearly learned how not to assume it as their issue, sometimes tossing back to a challenging questioner their own inquiry, intimating that maybe the interrogator suffers from his/her own hang-up here.

Another issue or topic that does generate fruitful exchanges between the Pils and audiences is this: How does "collective" creativity work, and is it really to be recommended? What is it like for a company of six to committee-

Gerald E. Myers

choreograph? Like "six radios, all on different stations at the same time," Alison Chase once commented. It works so well, Robby Barnett says, that he and colleagues wonder why more companies don't create collectively/collaboratively, because the six-radio dissonance or wrangling so often produces richer sounds than issue from a single voice. We conjecture here that as Arnold Schoenberg claimed his 12-tone music "liberates dissonance," the Pils could argue that their six-tone dissonance liberates choreography.

And there are collaborative collaborations, as in the jazz music/dance collaboration with the composer Maria Schneider called *The Hand That Mocked, The Heart That Fed* (1998); the collaboration with author/artist Maurice Sendak and children's writer Arthur Yorinks, a dramatic take on WWII and the Holocaust called *A Selection* (1999); and producing with Frank London and the Klezmatics a movement exploration of prayer and spirituality titled *Davenen* (2000). The latter two works represent the Pils' continuing interest in dramatic dance theater. And despite enormous differences between the two, the 1998 dance-jazz music collaboration wakened my memory of the raucous *Black and Blue*, to the music of Stormin' Norman, choreographed by Alison Chase and Moses Pendleton eighteen years earlier.

My private name for Pilobolus is The Brainy Bunch; referring to the original group as well as the sextet collaborative that has continued since Clarke's departure in 1979 and Pendleton's in 1991 to form his spectacular performing company Momix. They bring an intellectual sophistication into theatrical dance. As I learned in the early 1980s in panel discussions with Pendleton and later with the others, they articulate their theory and practice impressively, often with gatling-gun rapidity but always pointedly, thoughtfully.

So an intellectual kind of oversight, by highly charged minds, is provided by their committee-choreography. I gather, from listening to their public statements, that the group intelligence operates in pre-thinking a prospective work but also prominently in editing its initial phases into the final edition. My impression is that they tend to create a piece by first simply "making" something—specific movements, postural images, bodily sculpturings, etc.—and then together decide whether it has the potential for generating appropriate sequences; and this process gets repeated, phase-by-phase.

When they began as untrained aspiring dance artists, they seem to have worked by initially "making" whatever their bodily impulses, native physical abilities, and restless intuitions together incited. Jonathan Wolken has called what they do an "energy circus," a description perhaps as applicable to their creative process as to some of their products. They seem not to have started with grandiose theories of Space, Time, Art, Life, Universe; nor even with small-cap blueprints, rather with just "making" something, then huddling on whether and how to take it further.

The process as described involves lots of give-and-take between the Pils, lots of intuitive decisions (but always in the context of an extensive intellectual/artistic group background and experience), and beyond this maybe much can't be said. It is a kind of "stumbling forward," says Wolken, to get agreement and hard to explain why and when you get it. It's work but it's also fun, he adds, because "it's pulling the knowable out of the unknowable."

The riskiness of the process, as the Pils let us know, is down-the-line confusion; of evaluation, of meaning, of intention. And among themselves, not only on the audience's side. The reason they called the dance *Untitled* was their inability to agree on a title, a dance that they originally conceived, from the start to finish, as quite serious until its initial audience responded with guffaws. So they want you to know that often genuine disagreement occurs among themselves as their own audiences; such is the nature of artistic invention.

Little risk is involved in immediately accessible solos such as Pendleton's marvelous herky-jerky nimble-limbed *Momix* (1980), or the favorite of kids and adults alike, the group piece *Walklyndon* (1971) with its hilarious collision-walkings and other antic encounters, or the laugh-making *The Empty Suitor* (1980) with its acrobatic frantic scrambling over rolling tubes. The more sheerly gymnastic/acrobatic dances and the more obviously vaudevillian ones are about as clear as one may request.

My impression, from reading critics and watching audiences, is that the "confusion" risk (of meaning, intention, evaluation) is lessened where the pieces are more diminutive (solos, duets) and choreographically attributed not to the entire group but primarily to one or two. Thus, Alison Chase's *Moonblind* (1978) solo, with its gymnastic (and physically demanding) inside-out bodily configurations, can raise questions about the character being depicted by the female dancer, but given the "physical-on-parade" here such questions seem quite secondary. Similar remarks apply, say, to Chase's choreographed solo *Femme Noire* (1999), a humorous sendup of the femme fatale, and to her entertaining *Uno, Dos Trays* (1999), that has a waitress flirting with male customers. But program notes help the observer with Chase's recent ambitious *Monkey and the White Bone Demon* (2001), inspired by writings of a 16th century Chinese poet and that, among other danced "episodes," portrays a Buddhist monk saved by a monkey.

Insofar as Pilobolus is generally dedicated to "ambiguity" of expression (not to be confused with "confusion"), almost any of their works whether attributed choreographically to all or just one or two, can stimulate you to "thinking it over." This is true of their classic *Day Two* (1980), created for the Olympics at Lake Placid, a kind of country music romp featuring variations and complex sequences of Pils-type moves for six dancers, that ends with them nearly nude emerging from under waterslick floor coverings. They grandly slide their curtain calls over these to audience bravos and clappings. Great fun, yes, but because there is so much more than fun here—sexual anxieties and torture racks as seen by one observer, for instance—there is also plenty to ponder, in the good old modern dance tradition.

Return to Maria La Baja (1984) is another complex work, attributed to Barnett and Chase. It was inspired by Gabriel Garcia Marquez's novella, *The Tale of Innocent Erendira and Her Horrible Grandmother.* Not all audiences are prepared to sit comfortably through the systematic maltreatment of the young girl by her grandmother (who looked to me remarkably like Jonathan Winters in one of his impersonation/character acts). This is a densely danced/acted narrative, plenty of freaky moments, that needs several re-seeings for catching the innuendoes. For one reviewer, despite the interpretive challenges, "the success of *Return to Maria La Baja*...demonstrates that Pilobolus techniques provide exactly the kind of physical vocabulary the imagistic theater of the late 1960s always longed to possess." And the comment is added that the Pils' physicality, that settles at times for tricks, works best when serving dramatically powerful scenarios such as *Return.*

Physicality in the service of expressive ambiguity, a Pils trademark, guarantees diversity of critical reactions. This, it would appear, has facilitated rather than hindered their popularity. So a piece like *Particle Zoo* (1989), with its interpretive options, continues as a repertory staple. *Gnomen* (Barnett, Wolken, 1997), an emotionally charged and hardly surface-clear work, performed by four men, arouses a range of differing critical responses. *Aeros* (1996), that features alien creatures and a downed pilot trying to relate, is comic but also sufficiently violent to worry the sensitivities and interpretations of some observers. (But, says Wolken in its defense, humor and sweetness are also its ingredients.) Risks of interpretation continue with dramatic narratives such as *A Selection*, dealing with the Holocaust, and *Davenen*, depicting prayer and characteristics of spirituality. How to characterize the "deformed" menacing central figure in the former, and how to respond to the (surprising) charge that the latter is anti-Semitic?

Pilobolus relishes ambiguity, outlaws specific meanings, leaving "solutions" to those observers wanting or needing such. And, whether by partial or total committee-choreography, they often achieve their goal through the kind of creative process mentioned above, a making-and-editing of sequences or collages of movement images. So you get a "progression" of images (and maybe suggested meanings), but the progression as a collage is usually deliberately disjointed or non-linear. Given other contingencies, this may or not satisfy the critic. Reacting to the Pils' *Quatrejeux* (1994) and *Collideoscope* (1994), Tobi Tobias wrote in *New York* magazine that "ideas are dropped before they're even halfway developed; the piece is a compendium of unexamined, unnutured notions, lackadaiscally arranged."

Non-linear or disjointed serial layering of images (like any creative strategy) is vulnerable. Another critic who finds it so is Joan Acocella, reviewing a performance by Pina Bausch (a European, highly innovative and influential dance/theater choreographer/director; another, alas, who could not be added to these jottings) whose creative method bears some resemblance to Pilobolus's. Although mainly favorable in her comments, Acocella writes: "More than anything else, I would have asked that Bausch try developmental rather than serial form—just try it, and see if she couldn't make her art describe a longer span, and be intelligent between scenes as well as within scenes."

I guess the issue is not really about whether ambiguity is good or not, since presumably all the arts woo and embrace it like one of Apollo's messengers. I thought of this recently when glimpsing the exhibit of magnified photos of firefighters and others witnessing the September 11 World Trade Center destruction. The very specificity of the faces causes immediate emotional effects and associated thoughts, of who they are, what they did next after the photo was taken, and so on. But the specificity of the photos spent itself in arousing emotions of sympathy, etc., no momentum left over for the kind of "mentally creative" exploring that is stimulated by artistic ambiguities—that is, when they are done "right," this becoming the real issue.

One way of rendering ambiguity kinder and gentler, whether in the act of creating an art work or observing it critically, is interpreting it metaphorically. Treating dances as non-verbal metaphors, as critics sometimes do, can transform their ambiguities from dead-ends to open roads. Jennifer Dunning, for example, helps our thoughtful seeing of the Pils' *Sweet Dreams* (Michael Tracy, 2000) by calling its overall effect a "metaphorical world." Although that world, and thus the metaphor, remains mainly unspecified, she helps us, by referring to the dance's decor that looks (barely) like a walled city with what looks (barely) like an odd-shaped moon overhead, to view the piece as occurring in a "dreamy" kind of landscape. Given the appropriate atmospheric score here by composer Paul Sullivan, and sounds of the children's song "Lullaby and Goodnight," it is for Dunning (she persuades me, too) an "aural" landscape as well.

When I saw *Sweet Dreams*, it had the mysterious, enigmatic look and feel of many a Pilobolus theatrical dance. A woman and three men, perhaps in her dreams, interact with Pils-type moves, some slow motion and others livelier and light-hearted, sometimes as three-on-one or as two couples. She seems both a cohesive and divisive force, in this surreal moonlit landscape, an object also of male curiosity/perplexity. It ends with two men making themselves into a kind of bed that rocks her as she reclines on it. An enigmatic sequence of images in an other-worldly site, with an enigmatic finale that befits dreams, especially sweet ones.

But whether in this or any of the Pilobolus dances of deliberate ambiguities, what always merits first attention is the "gymnastic" technique that, apart from the costumes and sets and music, is the distinctive source of those ambiguities. Since the original Pils were not trained gymnasts, nor do their dances composed for dramatic purposes resemble gymnastic exercises done for their own sakes, they prefer other terms such as "multi-body theater" and "body-linkage" technique. (This also, if elaborated, distinguishes Pilobolus from the Judsonites and Contact Improvisation; the Pils were never anti-theater/spectacle, nor satisfied with unstylized ordinary movements, were rather striving beyond improvisation for the well-crafted product.)

The linked-body technique whereby they create such illusions as a three-headed man chasing a woman, and the like, involves bodies hanging from and over each other, "glued" to one another, and growing amoeba-like out of an initial fungus. As Jonathan Wolken tells us so aptly, you can create a multi-personality character within a three-person linked body that chases itself, shadows itself, expands, dissolves, and so on. What the Pils have shown over the years is the limitless range of startling images that multi-body theater can generate, as well as the associated startling ambiguities that stimulate interpretations metaphorical or otherwise.

The technique, as the Pils employ it, I suggest, not only produces ambiguity but often *simultaneously* produces beginning penetrations of that ambiguity, hints of where you may locate some emotional and conceptual sense of it. I mean to underscore the technique's experiential effects on the observer that are rich and immediate, that are ambiguous, yes, but already—before your post-performance thought-out formulations (metaphorical or whatever) occur—the ambiguity seems pointed to partial clarifications just ahead. Something like this kind of experience, of how ambiguity can be experienced during a performance, I suppose, is what we mean in calling movement-images "resonant." And resonant are the Pils' whether they be of a Ciona-like multi-body sculpturing or of a four-figure embracing as in *Sweet Dreams*.

The point is that, not later but immediately while the performance occurs, one often identifies the movements for what they are, as ambiguous yet simultaneously suggesting initial clarifications. We need to say something like this if, as in my own case, we remain true to how and what we experience as audiences. The ambiguity *at the very outset* of our watching need not be totally opaque, which is my claim for "mind-bending" enigmatic dances typical of Pilobolus and modern dance generally. Insofar as metaphors are compressed similes or comparisons, our point is that the dance movements, with all their equivocations, are often first identified for what they are, not for how they compare with something else; hence, are not to be called metaphors. This possibly connects with what Twyla Tharp meant in writing that dance for her is like boxing for Joyce Carol Oates; of all the sports, boxing is not "played" like a game, is not a metaphor. Dance to me, Tharp asserts, is the same—"simply the thing itself."

Essential to this technique as used expressively/narratively by the Pils is what I call "personalizing" the movement images. This can apply to a solo's moves as in *Moonblind*, to the body linkages in *Gnomen*, to the huddled images well as central characters in *A Selection* and *Davenen*. Pilobolus treats its movement images anthropomorphically, and anthropopathically. For me, the "creaturely" characters in Pilobolus dances are rarely so alien or sub-human as not to appear akin to my fellow-creatures, maybe on a bender or in a psychic traffic jam, behaving so as to light up the human condition one way or another. This technique, an "in-between" original, between dance and non-dance, between gymnastics and theater, between the abstract and the expressive, becomes a novel movement strategy for inducing novel audience experiences that in turn induce novel conceptualizations; in short, the technique significantly expands human experience beyond its quotidian expectations.

Something like the preceding analysis, I like to think, helps to explain the Pils' extraordinary popularity. In addition, one must note how their "methodical" workmanlike approach contributes to their success. Any picture of them as a larking group of ex-collegiates improvising their way to the concert stage is ludicrous. They labor hard to make everything "fit" like a glove, costumes, sets, movements, characterization, and music. They have used a variety of music, classical, jazz, popular, and commissioned. They cite, for instance, Paul Sullivan, whose scores and electronic compositions are often used, as a treasured sound/music resource. If like myself you are repeatedly impressed by how the music fits with their pieces, you are not surprised to learn that the happy fit results from labor not accident; that, for example, the scores of the two Czech composers (Haas and Krasa) were cut, edited, and re-worked to fit the tone-climate of *A Selection*.

Another manifestation of the "methodical" Pilobolus style is how the performers seem typically focused or concentrating. This is all-important because, whether consciously realized or not, audiences relate to this positively, but are restless when the performers appear to be mindlessly shuffling about. Although audience engagement is a Pilobolus priority, they rarely "mug" or try to ingratiate themselves. This may be what Jack Arnold, a former Pils dancer, meant some years ago when moderating at ADF a Pils post-performance discussion, in suggesting that Pilobolus dancers are not "presentational," do not, as we might put it, preen for their public. They seem too busy with each other and the complications of inter-locking bodies to play directly to their audiences.

Still another instance of the "methodical" is the rhythm/pacing of their dances. Typical movements are held postures, one dancer standing out her entire body into space from another's supporting floor-based legs, and then slowly unfolding the position while gradually lessening the tension in both bodies. This makes for slow, methodical walks and lifts, sculptural formings and dissolvings, that you can follow quite clearly, as compared with the difficulties of visually registering rapid step-based dancing. And, given dancers' proclivities for uniting mind and body, these sequential formings and dissolvings of linked bodies often seem like physical manifestations of thought-processes themselves. Wolken wasn't kidding in saying "We go wherever our thoughts go."

Such considerations, I hope, go towards explaining the kind of "rags to riches" story represented by the Pilobolus career, that began next to a cow-pasture and, enjoying that fungus capability of tossing its spores not merely over a cow but across international boundaries, is seen now as a thriving enterprise. I estimate, based on their year 2000 information, that the company has produced since 1971 a body of some 70 to 80 works.

The company tours selections from these plus new ones half the year, and during 2000–2001 they presented 101 performances in 47 cities across the United States and in 3 foreign countries. They performed in a variety of venues and, as a rarity in the field, attracting enthusiastic audiences young and adult alike. Remarkably, in their 14th season at Manhattan's Joyce Theater, during a four-week run they sold 98% of the house capacity; their national box office averages 91% of all available tickets.

The Pilobolus popularity serves modern dance well, making the art all the more accessible. The possible worry that such popularity compromises modern dance's non-commercial mission is countered by arguing that the Pils show how a larger than suspected audience exists "out there" for the art; moreover, let's not get carried away, their kind of success falls far short of commercialism.

As of 2001, there are special projects such as a commissioned work for the Winter Olympic Games in Utah. In addition, the Pilobolus Institute or educational division spent 17 weeks on the road, presenting more than 230 classes and 30 performances to participants ranging in age from 6 to 80. Included also were a residency at Yale in the Theater Studies program, multi-day workshops in St. Louis and New Orleans, and variously located Pilobolus-in-Schools programs.

For its success, Pilobolus can thank the appreciation shown by both youngsters and adults for the special wit and braininess that preside over their multiple projects, and over the novel physicality and movement featured in their dance/theatrical works. In a tradition "From Isadora to Pilobolus" they have produced their own original proofs of how dance blends body and mind like no other art.

Bill T. Jones

The Blob!—That slimy horror film monster of the late Fifties, Bill T. Jones tells us, paralyzed his childhood body with fear. But when he acted out the monster for his classmates—"reduced the Blob to movement"—hanging onto tables and chairs and slurping around the classroom, the "kids squealed with laughter and disbelief," and for himself in the process something about the Blob became even lovable.

Metamorphose the Blob into various forms of Life's Challenges, and Jones's dance career can look like a series of personal movement conquests, his audiences perhaps at times squealing with laughter and disbelief but probably more often with wonder and fascination. Moving now into his fifties, three decades of stellar dancing and creativity behind him, Jones is a hard act to follow, narratively. Besides his solo works and (totaling more than 50) those for the Bill T. Jones/Arnie Zane and Company (Zane was company co-founder and Jones's partner until his death in 1988), he has created commissioned pieces for numerous modern and ballet companies including the Alvin Ailey American Dance Theater, Boston Ballet, Lyon Opera Ballet, and Berlin Opera Ballet.

Since 1990, when he choreographed Sir Michael Tippet's *New Year* directed by Sir Peter Hall for the Houston Grand Opera and the Glyndenbourne Festival, Jones's engagements with theatrical and other collaborative projects have proliferated. For example, that same year he conceived, choreographed, and co-directed *Mother of Three Sons* (a Leroy Jenkins opera), performed at the Munich Biennale, New York City Opera, and the Houston Grand Opera. In 1994, he directed Derek Walcott's *Dream on Monkey Mountain* for the Guthrie Theater in Minneapolis.

A year later, he directed and performed in *Degga*, a collaborative piece with Max Roach and Toni Morrison at Lincoln Center's Alice Tully Hall. In 1996, he worked with Laurie Anderson (and to her music) in *Bill and Laurie: About the Rounds*, and the following year he did a joint piece with the writer Bell Hooks. Another Lincoln Center collaboration (premiered at New York's City Center in 1999) was *How! Do! We! Do!*, with Jessye Norman. And a few days ago, at Alice Tully Hall, I saw his much-anticipated collaboration, "A Visionary

Fusion of Dance and Music," with the Orion String Quartet and members of Lincoln Center's Chamber Music Society; premiering three new works.

Television viewers have seen his *Fever Swamp*, filmed for PBS's "Great Performances" series in 1989. That series, three years later, showed a documentary on his *Last Supper at Uncle Tom's Cabin/The Promised Land*. Jones and Gretchen Bender co-directed his *Still/Here* for television, and the making of this work was the focus of a documentary by Bill Moyers and David Grubin, *Bill T. Jones: Still/Here with Bill Moyers* that PBS aired in 1997. His work is featured in the Blackslide documentary *I'll Make Me a World: A Century of African-American Arts*, aired in 1999. He is interviewed in ADF's *Free to Dance: The African American Presence in Modern Dance*, that also shows excerpts from his *D-Man In the Waters*, aired by PBS in 2001.

In 1994, Jones received a MacArthur "genius" Fellowship, was pictured on *Time* magazine cover, and was profiled in *The New Yorker* by Henry L. Gates, Jr. His autobiography or memoir *Last Night on Earth* appeared in 1995. A children's book, *Dance*, written by Jones and photographer Susan Kuklin was published in 1998. For his contributions that have made him an international celebrity, one of our most distinguished modern dance choreographers and performers, Jones has been regularly honored by the dance/theatrical worlds. In addition, attesting to how his career has aroused American intellectual attention, he has received honorary doctorates from the Art Institute of Chicago, Bard College, The Juilliard School, and Swarthmore College, and the SUNY Binghampton Distinguished Alumni Award. He occupied the 1998 Robert Gwathmey Chair at the Cooper Union for the Advancement of Art and Sciences.

His career, studded with marquees around the world bearing his name, is all the more remarkable when you note its origins. He was the tenth of twelve children, born in 1952 in Florida to an African American migrant worker family that soon moved to upstate New York. How he coped with family complexities, shared chores as a youngster in the orchards and potato fields, starred as a sprinter in high school (like an African American dance predecessor, Alvin McDuffie, who at the University of Michigan had almost made the USA Olympic track/sprint team, and who in the late 1980s inspired our ADF Black Tradition in Modern Dance project), entered SUNY Binghampton in 1970 where he met his lover/partner Arnie Zane—all this and much more are brilliantly recounted in Jones's memoir *Last Night on Earth*; recommended reading!

Bill T. Jones and Arnie Zane—you couldn't ask for a more unlikely duet, which with a modern dance career in mind is very good, it being the art created and sustained by "unlikelys." Reviewers and they themselves in the Seventies and Eighties described Jones as tall, black, muscular, beautiful, a composed "silky" mover, and Zane (b. 1948) was white, short, wiry, Jewish-Italian, an abrupt "worried" mover. Neither was a thoroughly trained dancer or identified with a particular school or technique, Zane's first specialty being photography. Jones tells how, in his sampling different styles and techniques for discovering his own idiom, he sometimes found a class exercise difficult, surprising those who assumed because black he was a "natural" dancer able to do anything.

Their eventual success was due to their originalities/oddities that grabbed attention, but what also contributed was their early openness to influences of all sorts. They aimed to be sophisticated, through early travels to Amsterdam and California, through exposure to Dada, Surrealism, Constructivism, Merce Cunningham and John Cage, the Judson movement, Contact Improvisation, and the worlds of contemporary poetry, music, and literature. They aimed high yet performed in the mid-Seventies with neighborhood kids in Binghampton and, like most modern dancers, harbored doubts about showbiz and sheer entertainment.

In a 1983 review of their jazz collaboration, *Intuitive Momentum*, with drummer Max Roach and pianist Connie Crothers (imposing decor by Robert Longo), Sally Banes commented on the choreographic structure—second half of the dance reversing the opening, accumulation from duet to trio to quintet, etc.—but found special interest in Jones/Zane partnering:

> They somersault, flip, jump, and slide, using one another's shoulders, hips, or hands as levers.... Their synchrony is more like that of ballroom dancers than ballet partners, as they separate to break into individual turns and then casually make contact on the beat. Their partnering looks so easy and so absolutely right that when they dance with the rest of the group the proliferation of tumbles and catches and leaps looks strained in contrast.

But missed in the piece, she added, was the "talking" that they usually did so effectively. Words or texts spoken while performing had become a trademark of their solos and duets; this reflected Jones's bent for poetry, also for what was a major aesthetic premise—"I have made dancing a partner to language." As a youngster, after seeing the film *West Side Story*, he threw himself in the air while walking home but more like Michael Jordan than Jerome Robbins, because then "Who knew that a body could talk?" That bodies talk, want talk, inspire talk—that talk (whether understandable or enigmatic and Dada-like) can be intensely physical, an essential ingredient in thoughtful dancing—something like this, I think, was a starting-point for Jones's dancing.

Marcia Siegel provides a helpful formulation in reviewing Jones's solo *Floating the Tongue* (1978), writing that you can see his process of following a train of "movement-thought" as he performs the piece. Movement-thought it is, proceeding as he repeats improvised movement sequences while talking, to himself or the audience, about family, contemporary culture, sex, or the performance itself. The talk, depending on the particular dance, can be confrontational, humorous, revelatory, inspirational, puzzling, etc.

Jones tells us that *Floating the Tongue* was less a dance story than an exercise inspired by his mother's praying ("the first theater I ever saw"), taking its title from Buddhist meditations that focus on floating the tongue freely in the mouth. Performing the piece took him into a trancelike state that "granted me access to new levels of emotion and meaning." He quotes the critic Arlene Croce whose reaction was "He works himself into a tizzy." His reaction, "I was hurt by this, and offended."

The ambivalence of intimacy, its switching between consenting and fighting, featured not only the Jones/Zane personal relationship but also their dance aesthetic. As Jones tells it, *tension* energized their love, took it to new places, and this vitality of tension (confrontational about race, sex, audiences, etc., often "in your face", but along with its happier opposites) is indispensable for vibrant choreography and performance. A special tension in their working relationship was between Jones's impulse towards highly personal/autobiographical dances and Zane's preference for more objective/formalistic ones. So you did well, in watching their dances, to look for Zane-insisted structural devices (like block-by-block disassembling and reconstructing a wall of 150 cinder blocks in their 1980 piece (*Blauvelt Mountain*) and Jones-inspired texts autobiographically imprinted. There are structured strategies that involve tasks, along with "talking," like placing and re-placing flags on stage in Jones's solos such as *Progresso* (1978) or repeating and adding to movement sequences as in *Echo* (1979) and *Addition* (1979).

The venerable modern dance risk, of tempting while frustrating audience understanding, Jones was more than willing to run in verbally frosting the movements enigmatically. Given the nature of their gestures, movements, and words, no structural strategies no matter how ingeniously invented or rigorously implemented guaranteed against audience frustration. This is shown by a 1983 review of the company's Los Angeles performance of *Fever Swamp* (1983 piece commissioned by the Alvin Ailey American Dance Theater) and *Blauvelt Mountain*. Donna Perlmutter was excited by *Fever Swamp*'s "rock minimalism," its display of balletic spins, "dervish whirling, assorted falls, and pogo-stick bouncing"; a dancey dance and a spectacle propelled by Peter Gordon's percussive "raw art-rock" score.

But Perlmutter found *Blauvelt Mountain* frustrating. This evening-length work that represents one section of a Jones/Zane autobiographical trilogy "is not necessarily for public consumption...the creators of this work must take greater pleasure in it than could an audience not privy to their secret codes." She questioned whether the audience cared about the personal thought processes presented on stage through "occasional armlocks and word-association games," through "coded" movement patterns "marked by Jones's big, majestic strides and Zane's quirky little broken runs."

Blauvelt Mountain, in its creators' minds, was a landmark work in blending a rigorous structuralism with "personal introspective poetry." Whether they were surprised or not by a reviewer's reaction to it, they were indeed by a friend's praising it as a "truly beautiful homoerotic work." Part of it homoerotic, yes, but they deemed it much more than that or any pas de deux; it was a dance-place "where the strategies of our relationship and our art making were delineated even as commingled. We were serious. We had fun. We fought like hell."

Jones participated in ADF's 1981 "emerging choreographers" project in North Carolina, presenting a group piece, *Social Intercourse: Pilgrim's Progress.* He thought of this as a fusion of the traditional and new wave, for them a farewell wave to the minimalism of postmodernism of the Seventies and a forward move towards a complex dance theater that used text, multiple media, and all the trimmings of lights, costumes, sets, etc. that constitute spectacle. Jones wrote the lyrics for *Social Intercourse* about the "mental life of a New Yorker." Joe Hannon was the arranger, Randy Gunn, a "perennially pale rocker," with his electric bass the sole musician. Jones's three sisters were a chanting Greek chorus.

What you saw, Jones reports, were four persons including himself "dressed in black, lurching, strutting, rushing from upstage to down, obsessively performing fragments of athletic partnering and dance movements peppered with semaphoric arm gestures against the chanted sound score." This contained spoken lines like *Go! Wash down, zip up! I am the judge. These are your rights. What is the law? What are my rights?* The dancing was upright and aggressive, with hip wiggles and head tosses, sometimes karate-like; and an "insistent eroticism expressed through embraces, clinches, counterclinches, and the nihilistic smashing of one face against the other in gender-based variations of kissing."

Jones also performed a "largely improvised solo" at the 1991 ADF. Its text was as tense as it gets, one contradiction after another. *I love women,* then *I hate women. I love white people,* then *I hate white people. I'd like to kiss you,* then *I'd like to tear your fucking heart out. Why didn't you leave us in Africa?,* then *I'm so thankful for the opportunity to be here.* That "angry" solo, with its movements and gestures accompanying such spoken lines, as Jones remembers, shocked many—I know because I was there, my introduction to Jones and his work.

When ADF began its Black Tradition in Modern Dance programming in the mid-Eighties, and I as one of its point persons was busy learning about black modern dance past and present, the name Bill T. Jones when mentioned by my African American colleagues seemed almost always associated with controversy. The source of this was apparently Jones's behavior at a landmark Black Dance conference in 1983 at the Brooklyn Academy of Music. At this novel gathering of black dancers intended to celebrate their collective achievements, Jones was reported to have offended many of them by declaring that he wanted to be known as an artist first, a black man second, thus seeming to divorce his artistry from the American "black experience."

That was all I knew about it until reading Henry Gates's profile of Jones in *The New Yorker.* Jones says there that at the 1983 conference he did indeed, as a young upstart, announce that he was an artist first, a black person second. But where he offended was mentioning Merce Cunningham and Alvin Ailey among his favorite choreographers, but omitting his former teacher Percy Borde (at SUNY Binghampton) and husband of Pearl Primus who was present, listening. "I can almost picture her," he tells Gates, "coming down and turning three times and cursing me.... I showed respect for her. I'd done nothing wrong." This was all the more interesting because, in my various conversations with Pearl Primus in the years prior to her death in 1994, Jones's name had never come up.

The Jones/Zane enterprise seemed to live off controversy. It was criticized for being too "personalized," and apart from being considered repugnant by some, the professional judgment could be made that their charismatic performances dwarfed the choreography. Whereas its overt gayness was generally an asset, Jones's aggressive eroticism ("exhibitionism," some naturally called it), that in good surrealistic tradition could eroticize anything and everything in explosive fantasies, did offend many. Interestingly, Jones was chided on one occasion by critic Lynn Garafola in her review of his 1989 *Absence* (a dance referring to Zane's death the year before) for "pulling his sexual punches" by facing the dancers upstage and "neutralizing the subversiveness of cross-dressing" through making it comic when the bulky Lawrence Goldhuber dons a skirt. And while some applauded the diversity of physical types in the company, illustrated up front by Jones, Zane, and Goldhuber, others regretted the perceived absence of such diversity among the (allegedly, "all of them thin") women.

The "too personal" criticism was rebutted somewhat by the Jones/Zane piece *Freedom of Information* in 1984; its success led to an Asian tour sponsored by the United States Information Agency. More conceptual than personal, Jones says, this work combines a reporting of a downed plane with movements ranging from "flinging and falling" bodies, some movements taken from ballet and "fractured" contact-improvisationally, to crawlings and barking like dogs. What did it all mean? Hard to say, a subject for another time, but for Jones it represented concerns of community and society rather than self. It was also, more simply, a version of an "endurance dance."

Secret Pastures, also in 1984, made a splash and in doing so set off new controversies. A spectacular collaboration with artist Keith Haring, costumer Willi Smith, and rock musician Peter Gordon, it was described by Deborah Jowitt as "the first dance work of any consequence to acknowledge the influence of MTV on our perception." Its promise of kinetic, musical, and visual excitement brought out the audiences including Madonna and Andy Warhol. Some saw social implications in it, about the black man's place in a white arts world, though Jones told an interviewer that it is mainly a non-narrational excuse for dancing. He had hoped that the "downtown" dance world would recognize that below its surface are the postmodern abstract exercises preferred by the downtowners. Some surely did, but for others the "splashy" graffiti *Secret Pastures* looked like commercialism in leaps and jumps.

Inevitably, there was the question of taste. This surfaced noticeably with the Jones/Zane production in 1985 of *How to Walk an Elephant*, the first section of a projected Animal Trilogy. It was in Jones's words a work that "quoted freely" from Balanchine's signature ballet *Serenade* but for some observers it was an offensive parody. Black bodies had substantially replaced white ones, Balanchine's movement flow had been altered with "rambunctious angularity," smaller dancers supported bigger partners, a long-limbed black man performed an arabesque that in *Serenade* is done by a lovely white woman, and so on. Jones insists on his admiration for Balanchine and *Serenade*, that the theory and practice of modern dancer Senta Driver had actually inspired the take-off, and in moving the art along experimentally, "This was how we walked the elephant of dance history."

Through it all, one controversy supplanting another and despite or because of such, the Jones/Zane hike kept accelerating to the summit. Any explanation of their success has to mention the rare mix of imagination and intelligence that informs both their choreography and performance. Deborah Jowitt spoke for many observers in 1981 by praising "the air of *intellectual* engagement and *purposeful* vitality" (my italics) in their dancing. Henry Gates, distinctly impressed by Jones's cultural literacy and his quick alternations between black vernacular and sophisticated speech, agreed that he would have made a fine English professor; adding, in a model of understatement, "To all his projects he brings a searching intelligence. But the world does not love him only for his mind."

That searching intelligence shows up in all sorts of ways, in the concept of a piece, its formal organization, choice of music, theatrical strategies, and more, but what I emphasize here is the gestural quality of Jones's work. Here I echo various critics and Jones himself in stressing the importance of gesture. When I watch his solos I see a dancer "thinking" his progression through the piece, his movement choices coming across like linguistic phrasings that he has created/discovered along the way. He really meant it in saying he had made dancing a partner to language, and in all or most of his works that I've seen, whether solos or ensembles, he seems to have searched for something like Alwin Nikolais's "unique gesture" movement that "speaks" to and for a particular moment uniquely.

Jones says of his 1992 self-portrait solo *Last Night on Earth* (on which his book of the same title is based) that his gestures are "emphatic, quizzical and crude," and after describing them—"mouth stretches open," "right index finger enters," etc.—concludes "I am dancing about sex with no consequences." Jones's mother prays in his 1990 epic *Last Supper at Uncle Tom's Cabin/The Promised Land*, and he standing next to her performs isolated movements in joints, back, shoulders, and hips. But understand, "it is not *interpreting* her words at all. I'm responding to the cadences, rise and fall of her voice, her breath, the rhythm which is there. I'm trying to underline: do you see what a poet she is?" His shuddering movements are not interpretations (certainly not illustrations); they are gestural and meaningful on their own. The gestures, subtle or explicit or in your face, give his dances their thoughtful, purposeful qualities. For me, never more so than in his solo *Etude*, performed to a Beethoven quartet at 1999 ADF, where the thoughts of an aging dancer about his relationship to the art seem kinaesthetically and visually to unfold though not spelled out, just suggested.

A "laid-back" cocktail lounge kind of atmosphere fills the stage in *Out Some Place* (1999), a collaboration of Jones and the jazz composer Fred Hersch. When seeing this at the 1999 ADF, and, associating Jones with more abstract (though expressive) than literal gestures, we sat up when the dancers looked about prominently holding cocktail glasses in hand. Asked about this, Jones replied that it was a gestural "pathway" for the audience to a place/scene they could understand. Dances have to mean something, he has said, especially these days when cynicism and "spiritual fatigue" reign, so gestural pathways as audience guidelines to meanings are important.

When comparing movement to language, we need to remember that both words and actions can be meaningful in a variety of ways, including meanings that are only suggestive, indefinite, absurd, nonsensical. *Ursonate* (1996), a work co-choreographed with Darla Villani, forces our recognizing this. This piece, with two air mattresses for propping a startling stew of dance styles is performed to a phonetic poem "Ursonate" by the Dadaist Kurt Schwitters that is magnificently performed on tape by Christopher Butterfield. Anna

Kisselgoff, who told her readers to run not walk to see and hear it, noting Jones's longtime relating speech and movement, illuminates our point here. Schwitters sought in his sound poem, she writes, a "wordless language" yet with its own logic. To hear Mr. Butterfield "roll his r's, spew out grunts and syllables in an astonishing non-verbal way" is to grasp, she suggests, how questing the "'transrational' acquires a meaning of its own."

So grunted syllabic nonsense can be meaningful, affecting our feelings and at some level our understanding. Jones's accompanying movements, according to Pamela Sommers, make perfect sense. "After a while," she writes, "the snakelike tongues, undulating torsos, myriad isolations of body parts, leapfroggings and back flips accumulate into a kind of physical hieroglyphics." Again, the fascination of the movement hieroglyphics comes from the sense of following a train of movement-thought, of a kind of mentality, (uniquely) appropriate to Schwitter's poem, made visible. (It is worth noting that finding movement meaningful is often something that just "happens" to you, which is good since you don't have to work for it, but on occasion—as these jottings insist throughout—working to find it is good, too.)

The gestural in Jones's works is of course not reducible to handshakes and hat-tipping. One usually discerns gestural movements in a Jones dance that sometimes clues audience understanding, other times only teases it. In *Some Songs* (1996) to songs by Jacques Brel, there is an odd "limp" walk by a woman dancer, "skewed" balances by others on one leg, or one dancer lifting another's arm in rapid succession.

In *War Between the States* (1993), to a Charles Ives score, you see "military" type strides and movement scurrying that intimates mass/group hysteria. There are provocative arm "salute" motifs that are varied into soft up and down wavings in *After Black Room*. And here, too, what I call gestural even though unspecified compared, say, to handshakes, holding cocktail glasses, or salutes—are quietly dramatic episodes when, for example, one dancer standing on a cylinder relates to/looks at (enigmatically) another sitting below him on the floor. *In Red Room* (1987), "shivering" gestures of the dancer while extending his arms, or the legs in black knee-length tights "wobbling," and "silent mouthing"—all such get you to wondering.

Gesture, broadly conceived, as any movement(s) that asserts to you "Something may be meant here," is, in my view of Jones's dances, wrapped up with his intense physicality. A *New York Times* photo of him academically gowned suddenly lunging to his feet in an impromptu dance step, after receiving an honorary degree at The Juilliard School's commencement, to applause from his surprised colleagues on the platform, is the kind of response I've seen from him on other occasions. He seems ever poised to pounce, seeming to experience every stimulus including ideas as a physical impulse. I think the physical impulse is his motivator, and insofar as modern dance audiences can get closer to the art by getting a feel for what motivates its creators, this is a Jonesian feature worth some gossip.

Jones's physicality and its dance representations, it's safe to say, account for much of his success and popularity; it makes for compelling theatrical dancing. Photos of him and Zane in *Rotary Action* (1982), their last major duet before Zane's death six years later, are fine witnesses to this. With the physical impulse consorts a sense of its worth. The solo *Last Night on Earth* is a kind of dance-homage to the whole body, with its successive spoken lines *My eyes are not my enemy, My tongue is not my enemy, My dick is not my enemy.* Some might call Jonesian eroticism narcissistic but you could call it a passionate apology on behalf of the human body.

Soon (1988, to music by Kurt Weill and Bessie Smith, revived 1996) is one of my favorite pieces, and when I told this to Jones he smiled, saying "Ah, you are a romantic." An erotic/loving duet that can be danced by any two dancers, it was originally done by Jones and a woman though conceived by him as "fictionalizing" his former relationship with the deceased Zane. Jones and Arthur Aviles performed when I first saw it, and I was struck by the capacity of its intense physicality to intimate subtle as well as stronger characteristics of the duo's relationship. The rapid flow of the movement, with rolls, leaps, etc. over and around each other, the larger dancer carried at times by the smaller and any number of partnering variations, made a continuous line of gestural movements telling a duo's romantic mini-story. No text, just very physical.

D-Man in the Waters (1989), another favorite and better known and often acknowledged as a modern dance masterpiece, a memorial piece to a former company dancer, to a rippling Mendelssohn Octet, is perhaps the most physically demanding ensemble work in Jones's repertoire. I've heard him say, shaking his head, after jumping ecstatically at how the company had just performed it, that one can't do that sort of work on a regular basis. Swimming against death, to live beyond loneliness with communal support, is one way of conceiving *D-Man in the Waters*. Swimming movements, dives, leaps, and slides on watered flooring speed by breathtakingly. Provocative walking/processionals with subtle suggestive variations give a pensive air to the ensemble's exits and entrances. There is fisted arm-waving, a dancer's two hands held tight into the body's waist, and what look like in-place preparations for a flying dive. Gestures everywhere and mostly displayed through relentless surge upon surge of energetic "swimming"/dancing. I think at the end something like, "this isn't just about struggling life upstream, it's about swimming against you-know-what, and right now *D-man* looks a winner."

When Arnie Zane died of AIDS in 1988 and Bill T. Jones learned that he was HIV-positive (and would not until some years later have another partner, Bjorn Amelan, who would design sets and co-administer company affairs), the tragic loss, Jones said, changed his world. His work "began to speak more as that of a black man. And of a gay man, too." He was someone "who never really had to be a black artist until the other member was dead." His personal journey, he said, had originated in the avant-garde Sixties and Seventies and with it the idea of artist first, black man second. "And now [1989] I do say that I am a black artist, because all of those things are very important in my healing, to understand more carefully and completely who I am."

This shift to a "black artist" identification by Jones can be viewed as significant yet not inconsistent with what had preceded. Reading his *Last Night on Earth* leaves one impressed by his loyal ties to family, involving mother and sisters in his works, the constant references to them and thus the African American history borne within himself. What is dancing? He has often said, for myself it is trying to define who I am in the light of racism, sexual discrimination, and other challenges personal and cultural. His earlier social/political rappings can be interpreted less as political activism than as artistic confrontations of issues on behalf of maturely defining his personal identity. And I think about his creating *Negroes for Sale*, one of his earliest ventures in 1974, to music by Bessie Smith (and Tibetan temple chants), and it's Bessie Smith again eighteen years later for the dance *Last Night on Earth*. So presuming a non-accidental continuity between the pre- and post-1988 Bill T. Jones is no accident, either.

The shift to being publicly "the black artist" occurs, after pieces like *Forsythia* and *Absence* in 1989, in 1990 with the 3.5 hour epic *Last Supper at Uncle Tom's Cabin/The Promised Land*. Less dance than a deliberately disjointed 4-section play, *Cabin* theatrically explores Jones's questions: "Was Uncle Tom a disgrace to his race? A romanticization of servitude? Was he as a Christ-like figure a precursor of Dr. Martin Luther King or Gandhi? Is this high-minded, propagandistic literary work of any relevance to us today?"

The first section "deconstructs" Harriet Beecher Stowe's novel with zany portraits of Uncle Tom, Little Eva, Simon Legree and others, with ominous overtones in the dramatic action and Julius Hemphill's music. The second section recreates Eliza as a "multidimensional polemic," including a "historical Eliza" (who with her pelvis-originated loping movements "Alvin Ailey would have recognized") amid battering-ram actions/episodes. Bill's mother, Estella Jones, leads a prayer in an *Entr'Acte: The Prayer*. Section three, *The Supper*, brings the whole company on stage looking like Leonardo's *Last Supper*, and what transpires is an "orgy of inchoate imagery" or "kind of religious Dada." Another entr'acte has a local minister, rabbi, or priest coming on stage to cope with Jones's insistent queries: Is homosexuality a sin?, What is faith?, Is Christianity a slave religion?, and more. The fourth section, *The Promised Land*, its action much too dense for attempted summary here, ends with what can be distinctly remembered, all fifty or more (numbers depending on local presenters' success in recruiting performers additional to Jones's small company), conspicuously diverse in shape/size, age, and race, surge naked into the footlights.

Jones writes that *Cabin*—with musical history indicated in Julius Hemphill's score, excerpts included from writings of Sojourner Truth and Le Roi Jones as well as Stowe, and its bewildering mix of dramatizations via "nonlinear juxtapositions of iconographic events"—aimed at *disorientation* for effect and wherein resides its truth. This I can believe, because it left my head swimming after its performance on tour at Wesleyan University.

For Jones, the nude group-surge at the end was a "visual manifestation of my profound sense of belonging. This was my portrait of us." It could not really succeed, he muses, but it did not fail; moreover, "I believe that the communal nature of [*Cabin*] was revolutionary in the world of dance." And I take it that part of his meaning here is that *Cabin*, in "absurdly" revisiting history through disorienting contemporary lenses, amalgamates African American and other unbranded types of experience into one commonality/humanity.

Last Supper at Uncle Tom's Cabin/The Promised Land is one of those works in theatrical modern dance that especially pique intellectual interest in the art. Like *Finnegan's Wake* or *Waiting For Godot*, it promises endless insights if one could repeatedly study it. Because of its subject matter, its density attracts scholarly/academic detective-type interpretations, and one can imagine the amount of "search-for-its-meanings" literature that would ensue if its live performances were always available for re-readings.

Still/Here (1994) is another such work, in some respects exceeding *Cabin* as a commotion-stirrer. Theatrical but more dancey than *Cabin*, it is a two-section "communal" encounter with (not just *about*) disease and death, mortality. It grew out of fourteen Survival Workshops, two of them for children, conducted by Jones in eleven cities. Participants, diversely representative, ranged in age from 11 to 74 and faced life-threatening situations. Demonstrating his own reliance on gesture for reflecting inner states of mood, etc., he asked the participants to "choreograph a rudimentary portrait of themselves. We linked our gestures round-robin style."

The first section, *Still*, using the participants' words and gestures, represents their "inner worlds," and the mood here is heightened by Kenneth Fragelle's songs, and vocals performed by folksinger Odetta. Gretchen Bender's ambitious video work, a prominent ingredient, includes three bluish screens that move slowly downstage to display a participant/survivor's face. (I seem to recall that the portable video screens, throughout, were more distracting on the stage at BAM than when performed at ADF/North Carolina.) For Jones, the introductory video image suggested a "spirit world" and thus "poeticized" the video technology presence.

He told a journalist that whereas *Still* is the survivor's inner world, the second section *Here* "parallels the sensation of leaving one's doctor office with life-altering news, compelled to ride the New York City subway." Rock guitarist Vernon Reid's music, Liz Prince's blood-colored costumes, Bender's video images of big human hearts pulsating, and Jones's choreography mark prominent changes from *Still*. In that first section, for instance, individual performers were habitually watched by the group, but in *Here* dancers are all running and active simultaneously with individuals doing their thing; compared to *Still*, this is an "agitated" stage. Jones not performing is seen only like a "message in a bottle" on video smiling, speaking, gesturing. At the end, with survivor/participant video images showing "still here," life going on defiantly if rockily as on a New York subway train, we can "get" Jones's view of the dance as being about life and affirmation—"We don't need another work about death."

Still/Here by itself, for its imaginative and technically ingenious presentation of the kind of profound experience that all the arts circle like vultures, is a major modern dance event. It has also been appreciated as a further shift in Jones's dance aesthetic, beyond the "black identity" issues of *Last Supper at Uncle Tom's Cabin/The Promised Land* towards an even broader concept of commonality/humanity. But its reputation got a huge if odd boost by a "non-review review" by Arlene Croce. She called *Still/Here* with its terminally ill participants, and productions that use performers with "obvious problems" (e.g., overweight, sickled feet, physical deformities, etc.) "victim art." Unable, she wrote, to review objectively performers for whom you feel sorry or hopeless, she had to sit out *Still/Here*. By including dying persons in his art, Jones was truly "undiscussable," beyond the reach of criticism.

We were touring Minnesota with ADF's Black Tradition in Modern Dance project, featuring performances by the Dayton Contemporary Dance Company and commentaries by our humanities team, in the early winter of 1995 shortly after Croce's article in *The New Yorker* appeared, and also but a few weeks after *Still/Here*'s performance at the University of Minnesota's Northrup Auditorium. We were surprised by how often our reactions to both were asked for, how we fitted them into our "story" of African American contributions to modern dance. Without re-opening a complex multi-sided controversy, a couple of remarks only I'd like to deposit here.

The historically "uneasy" relationship between black concert dancers and white dance critics (hard to find black critics) was one of our Black Tradition themes. And Arlene Croce's (influential) role, because of what she had written, negatively, about Donald McKayle's *Rainbow 'Round My Shoulder* and Alvin Ailey's *Revelations*—back in the mid-Seventies—did concern us. Our commentary approach to public audiences, however, was not to focus on a single critic unless asked to but to look generally at how black dancers had been critically received, roughly from the 1920s to the present. The gulf often glimpsed between the aesthetic of many black dancers and that of critics like Croce was/is troublesome.

What tended to get lost, I think, in the astonishing avalanche of discussion about Croce and so-called "victim art" was this: Croce's lament was actually less about *Still/Here* than about the *fin-de-siècle* plight of criticism generally as she perceived it. A lot more than Bill T. Jones is assembled in her article "Discussing the Undiscussable" for going gloomy over America's cultural climate in the Nineties; as she put it, "I do not remember a time when the critic has seemed more expendable than now."

Still/Here was just the last-straw symptom of a cultural decay that she, and not alone of course, saw menacing what few objective criteria were left for the poor critic to tool with. Let's not forget, then, that among what was put to the test by *Still/Here* was the health of dance criticism itself. Is it terminally ill, taking the bad news to the subway, vanished—or still here?

Recent prominent works by Jones that observers have noted for being less confrontational and less talky, maybe indicating a firmed-up personal identity, include *We Set Out Early...The Visibility Was Poor* (1997), *Out Some Place* (1999), Jones's experimental 80-minute solo *The Breathing Show* (1999), *The Table Project* (2001, theatrical product of a 4-year residency project at C. C.N.Y.'s Aaron Davis Hall, with untrained dancers from Harlem), and three pieces (2002) in collaboration with Lincoln Center's Chamber Music Society—*Black Suzanne, World Without/In*, and *Verbum*. In discussing these works and his career, Jones emphasizes a new focus on goals like beauty and commonality. Once (in my own words) it was "Can you see me, Bill T. Jones?" Now it is "Me seen, come see what I find Beautiful." And for him the shift from fighting onstage with audiences for an identity amid racial and sexual prejudice to a more contemplative posture involves, in his paraphrasing Martha Graham, "putting his faith in an art that does not lie."

All serious artists can be presumed to be concerned about authenticity—until proven guilty—but none in my observational acquaintance matches Jones for being preoccupied with it. I've heard him allude to it with various formulations and usually, I take it, pertaining to a performer's relationship to himself, his audience, his art. "Is it a lie? Is it the truth?" I've heard him exclaim. He repeats his worries, having eroticized these relationships, about "seducing" audiences through "lies, cheap tricks, hiding imperfections and mistakes." Jones as a performer is in the double-bind of wanting and not wanting to seduce his audience one way or another, so the superego of authenticity hovers, won't let up.

This concern was evident also at 1997 ADF in a lively panel discussion exchange (reminiscent of the entr'acte in *Last Supper/The Promised Land*) between Jones and Dr. Michael Eric Dyson (author of *Between God and Gangsta Rap, Race Rules,* and books on Malcolm X and Martin Luther King, Jr.). The topic was "spirituality in dance." Dyson, a self-described Detroit Baptist minister (but also distinguished scholar/author/lecturer), sympathetically but firmly defended religious faith against Jones's theological skepticism and placing his own faith in art. A similar exchange, between Jones and Reverend Dr. Calvin D. Butts, occurred at Aaron Davis Hall in Harlem in December 1999. According to attendee Irene Sturla, "Jones and Butts agreed on the intricate role spirituality plays in art."

If your faith/spirituality is in your art, and your art is Martha Grahams' that does (ought?) not lie but requires an authenticity triumphant over self-deception and other-seduction at every creative and performative turn, then you've assumed a heavy burden indeed. Small wonder it becomes preoccupying, a self-imposed Sysiphean task.

Sysiphus is the title of a Jones 1980 solo. It combines monologues (of memories) and gestural movements and, consistent with its title, employs repetitive movement strategies. It calls for taking a chance and commenting on some situation "in the most honest way I can," and the desired emotions will occur if the material, Jones says, is "real"; to be "honest" and "real" in performance is an artist's "moral responsibility."

Watching concert dancers sweating physically and morally on stage, noting their post-performance frowns and reservations about how they did, no matter how many bouquets, I find my admiration of them connecting with a wistful feeling that they attempt something ultimately impossible. I happen to relish this feeling, and its picturing a leotardian world of Platonic ideals that are unattainable yet have to be pursued. It's a metaphysical picture though framed in feeling, one that lingers for me after all I've seen or drawn from Bill T. Jones's life and career. "It's impossible to succeed, but we did not fail."

A Letter

New London
January '02

Dear Mrs. C.—

There I was, crowned and feathered to celebrate a centennial correspondence, our *affaire* epistolary, and you deliver me the unbelievable!

Vita and George—those muses of our year together, those young hearts these jottings were meant to reassure, those wonderful dancing kids—they've turned their backs on modern dance? Because I've convinced them that it's too brainy, too intellectual, too difficult an art? And you and Vanessa are helpless to change their minds? *Incroyable*! You didn't say I shot myself in the foot, but that's exactly where I'm looking. I'm walking wounded, you must know.

I was swelling with the intention—were Vita and George still listening—of embroidering on a couple of observations by the dance/cultural critic, Terry Teachout. They make the dance's intellectual ingredient seem natural, easily absorbable into plain enjoyment of a performance.

Teachout intersects dance (painting, and arts generally) and the humanities when observing that, "passionately" believing in the value of connoisseurship and getting informed, "The more I *know*, the more I see" (my italics). Getting informed and furnishing one's mind with appropriate concepts and attitudes, let's rejoice, typically result not from library secludings but from seeing and re-seeing dances. Teachout, confessing his past uncertainties about Mark Morris's choreography, attests to this. "I kept on looking [at Morris's works], and thinking about what I saw," and eventually "I felt more in tune with what Morris was trying to do."

It's like that, I wanted to expound on for you all, like homework-at-the-performance. But too late obviously. Not even a farewell from those kids. Tell them Mrs. C....

You still intend to save these jottings? Why? I don't understand. No matter. I'll finish up as envisaged. Do with them as you will. Who knows? Who knows who might replace Vita and George to be persuaded by my apologia for modern dance? Are you persuaded? You never tell.

Where are you on it, Mrs. C.?

Goodnight, goodnight, Mrs. Calabash,
Wherever you are.
GEM

A Second Letter

Club
New York
April '02

Dear Mrs. Calabash:

This comes to you in haste. Why? Because I had the best conversation with you last evening while half-awake half-asleep. You asked me the best questions, so I hasten to record them before forgetting. You know how quickly dreams become black holes.

You came here. You were waiting by the long Empire mirror.

GEM: *There* you are!

Mrs. C.: I've been here, or was I early?

GEM: Thank you for listening all these months.

Mrs. C.: Reading. You've been too conscientious. So much dance education. Who deserves it?

GEM: Some benefit? Effort wasted?

Mrs. C.: Something's missing. Have you a dance aesthetics shelved somewhere? Pull out, show me?

GEM: Where to begin? You turn the key this time, I'll follow.

Mrs. C.: We…writers…they are subalterns straggling after epiphanies. Maureen Howard says it, about how as a novelist she makes a "flagrant display of herself," not in a tell-all exhibit but "in the rhythm of a sentence, the shape of a paragraph…." Comparable in dance?

GEM: Could we look back at my jottings? No? Then savor Edwin Denby's telling how a dancer's *leap* is a "whole story with a beginning, a middle and an end." You want epiphany? Denby sends you to Alicia Markova's soaring leap. At the leap's peak she must be completely still, "revealing the calm of that still moment," and if not, we judge with Ms. Howard that in a "flagrant display" of herself she reveals her technical inadequacy as a classical dancer.

Qualities of movement, Mrs. C., the rhythm, shape, and dynamics of a movement, are the epiphanies dancers pray for. Dancers are blown away by a certain tilt in the neck, a special ripple in the arms. Remember Alwin Nikolais on this kind of thing? Think of Isadora Duncan's sighing over the years it took to learn how to make one little gesture. So she knew, she said, how long it would take to learn to write one "simple, beautiful sentence." Words, movements, pigment, sounds, marble, steal, bronze—they're all materials for the artists to *qualitize.*

Mrs. C.: "The body is All!"—you're quite certain that the dance world taught you this? Does your aesthetics groan, just a little, even a half-tone, under the weight of this?

GEM: Never enough about the human body! Still pondering the ramifications of a book's thesis recently read, about how silent films spread "the American myth," dispersed globally our popular culture. Paula Marantz Cohen, the book's author, hypothesizes that film associated the body with comedy, landscape with the Westerns, and the face with melodrama. In its image of the body, she argues, film portrayed it as "independent" of usual constraints, even of time and space (e.g., Harry Houdini's "miraculous" escapes, Buster Keaton and Charlie Chaplin as bodies-in-extraordinary-actions). Like film, we say, dance "liberates" the body in our ways of thinking about it, and no style promotes such liberation more effectively than modern dance.

Mrs. C.: Your recitation, what you call "jottings," makes much of modern dancers' ambivalence about popularity. They seem quick to distrust it. Is this in the altar of their aesthetics, or yours?

GEM: If altered, maybe. I think of the art's beginnings and of the thousands of modern dancers today who are seen only by devotees. Obscured from the big public eye, they perform in cramped venues across the land, in areas like New York's Chelsea and Greenwich Village, often in downtown lofts. These "loft" performances are small, intimate, poetic, chamber-music occasions where audiences and performers close in together.

My wife Martha and a professional dance friend not long ago had an experience to remember of watching a Merce Cunningham rehearsal in his Village studio. Largely due to the space's intimacy, they were more emotionally affected by this than many formal theater events attended.

Small is good! Thinking this was reinforced by things said after *Peanuts* creator/cartoonist Charles Schulz died. The *Peanuts* characters like Snoopy are of course diminutive, but the "small" in the cartoons to be noticed, as George Saunders makes us aware, is how much gets expressed—within the cartoon's four panels. The Charlie Brown world is a really complex one, presenting issues that are emotional, conceptual, moral, etc. Besides only four panels for representing all this, other small-making features, as Saunders tells it, are the presences of kids only, a single neighborhood, only round heads, and the like. But of course such cartoon economies of scale work in this instance for, not against, popularity.

But you can't distribute modern dance in daily newspapers, nor even in videos that equal for full-bodied vitality the real thing that is the live performance. We need in our "hyped" culture, that genuflects to Blockbuster events (consider the multi-million dollar movie advertisements that help to make box office competitions a regular part of the evening news), to preserve pockets of intimate artistry.

Touring ADF's Black Tradition project, we met people who often wished, given the enjoyment of those attending, that the audiences had been larger. That can always be wished for. But discard we must the presumption that it's no good if it fails to generate a mob scene. So long as people feel deprived and edgy because of empty seats or midget spaces, they represent a culture that, ironically, edges itself towards empty seats except for midget imaginations.

Still, a caveat here. Modern dancers need all the marketing help they can get, and it's evident that a potentially much larger audience for the art exists "out there." No one serves them or the art well by praising smallness that implies satisfaction with the status quo, or worse.

Remember, too, that early modern dancers, despite their anxieties about popularity's possible downside, sometimes played to large crowds. That was true of Denishawn in the 1920s for instance. It was true of Helen Tamiris. She performed a series of dances in *Promised Land*, a festival-type story of the Mormons, their migration to Utah, etc., that played for 3.5 weeks in Salt Lake City in 1947. It is reported that an average of 10,000 persons per night attended. After this, Tamiris took her choreographic skills to Hollywood for the film version of *Up in Central Park*.

But—Mrs. C.—I have to believe that productions like Salt Lake City's, on that scale, so transform the "lofty" character of modern dance that it is barely recognizable. Let concert dance grow as it can and will, but if it loses touch with its loft-like intimacy, we'll have lost too much and we'll understand why the art's practitioners have worried about the costs of commercialism.

Mrs. C.: Never one for popularity, always endorsed Stendhal's "happy few," so let me say, "Welcome, welcome, modern dance, to my artist's attic." But will it stay there? Aren't you also leading me to believe, Herr Professor, that the art has long left the attic, down the fire-escape into the streets, everywhere? So popular?

GEM: It's on the edges of the campus, of pop culture, like contemporary poetry—Merwin's, Dove's, Ashberry's, Gould's, Pinsky's—it's never farther than a stone's throw yet of a familiarity not so familiar.

No question but that concert dance "exploded" after WWII. In 1965, about 37 professional dance companies existed. Today, there are almost 700 such companies. More than 400 of these are modern/concert, other than traditional ballet, social, folk, etc. If contemporary non-professional troupes are included, the number vastly exceeds 400. Dance is offered in the majority of America's 3,000-plus universities/colleges (and often at the secondary school level, too). Detailed listings include the National Dance Association's of over 500 programs in two and four-year institutions, the American College Dance Festival Association's of over 400 institutions, and *Dance Magazine*'s directory of over 550 college dance programs. So, accordingly, have the largely college-educated audiences increased for the art.

Mrs. C.: An appeal on behalf of the artist, is *dying* to be heard here. Why do you neglect the *intuitive* extolling the intellectual? Something's missing.

GEM: Institutions are like the qualities of movement we mentioned a moment ago. Like the still or "lyric" quality of a Makarova's leap, an intuition occurs embedded in a context without which it would not be an intuition. That context includes one's rationality, knowledge, experience, etc. If, say, I'm thinking about A, B, and C and wondering what results if A=B and B=C, I then "see" (mind's eye) or intuit the result that is A=C. "Seeing" that A=C here is just intuitive, not more discursive or serial reasoning involving ifs, ands, and buts.

Mrs. C.: Yes, now I do like that.

GEM: And you think your favorite, Moore, would agree?

Mr. C.: I do.

GEM: The intuitive and intellectual work together, absolutely depend on each other if they seem to conflict, it's not because they inhabit one and the same mind at the same time. It's rather a conflict between two kinds of persons, one of whom is content with something, say, created or judged. If asked why, she replies "I intuit it." But Pilates or whoever may not want to leave it like that, he's not content with it so asks questions about it, brings in fresh information, and so on, and that process is called "intellectualizing." Such common conflicts are to be negotiated if possible, not by pitting intention versus intellect but by getting the two persons to realize, first, "where the other is coming from."

Intuition and intellect—Mrs. C.—think of them as Aesthetics' Siamese Twins. Defying your best-intentioned surgical operations.

Bernard Holland supports my case here. He writes of Pierre Boulez's recording of Scriabin's music: "The slightly mad find their most eloquent spokesmen in the ranks of the eminently sane."

It would be absurd to demand artists to create glaringly intellectual works. Like you—Mrs. C.—I don't like such.

A dance company that I much admire is the French troupe, Compagnie Maguy Marin. But I was disappointed by their piece *Waterzooi* performed at

1994 ADF. Why? Because it seemed an attempt to bring alive through dance Descartes's theories about human emotion. The movements (words, gestures, etc.) seemed to me dulled by trying to illustrate complex ideas. Neither the dance nor Descartes were given a lift here.

Different, however, is what Jack Anderson saw in John Jasperse's choreography in *Waving to you from here* (1997). In his review titled "Making the Movements Spring From Thoughts," Anderson writes that it "magically made dancing resemble thinking," every action seemed the result of a thought or memory, a "remarkable blending of mind and matter."

I like that kind of work, too, adding that for me Jasperse's piece owes its surprising mirroring of movement and thought to its being less a dancey than a dramatic/action (performance art) work.

Alas, I guess there'll always be those for whom intellectualism, philosophy, and abstract thinking kill dance dead in its tracks. I visualize their idea of the intellectual as resembling Mabel Dwight's 1932 lithograph "Abstract Thinking." It pictures three tired, hatted men juxtaposed on a subway car seat, looking "out of it," lost not so much in as out of thought. Or perhaps Gustav Klimt's "Philosophy," a mural of naked bodies intertwined in "the endless cycle of birth, procreation and death."

Mrs. C.: Are you exhausted?

GEM: Exhausted.

A Third Letter

Club
New York
April '02

Mrs. C.—

You returned. But to another room in the club. You'd never believe that room's name, and I will not wreck the promise to myself not to mention it. I thanked you for yesterday's conversation, which was like a dream come true. You looked somewhat remote though, never removed your hat, the Robin Hood one.

Last night, after the watchman locked the front, you did return, and though remote you were generous in interviewing my conscious sleeper.

Mrs. C.: Something's missing. The "other side" of your position on intellectualism and dance. Those materials you loaned me, I looked them over, and I confess to sympathizing with Arlene Croce who is quoted as saying, "I never saw a good ballet that made me *think*" (my italics). What say you?

GEM: That's good. I'm thinking.

Mrs. C.: Anna Kisselgoff is a joy. I was nonplussed, you must have known, learning that she had to review a ballet by William Forsythe for his Frankfurt company, that he actually named it *Woolf Phrase* with unbelievable! quotations from that literary dinosaur, *Mrs. Dalloway*.

It's all so brainy (some fun, too), Kisselgoff says, so much so that she cautions us, "Forget the theories and watch the movement." His "intellectual spring boards," for her and for us as she rightly suspects, "can come across as irritating or incomprehensible."

Woolf Phrase—what a clumsy mix it must be. Not for me to see. What say you?

GEM: Croce and Kisselgoff, those two distinguished critics, would probably elaborate those remarks such that mine as well as your agreement would fall into place. I only balk at such remarks when they seem symptomatic of an attitude—call it anti-academic, anti-intellectual, anti-stuffy, whatever—

that is greeted by an excess of relieved smiles in the dance world.

A writer I much admire is John Lahr, so you may appreciate my squirming a bit at his writing, about the musical *Contact* and its choreographer/director Susan Stroman, that "dance, which is about resonances and not reason, allows an audience to be more playful…free to fill in the emotional outlines of each gesture." Maybe unintended, but the fragrance of this (and the text from which this is excerpted) says to me, "Dance! Thank God for its being an art that settles for resonances, leaves for once our reason alone." Great to have it for our relaxed and free-loving entertaining moments, a rest-away from those other more serious and mind-demanding arts.

Edwin Denby wrote an essay, "Against Meaning in Ballet," noting that he sympathized with the "anti-intellectualism" of friends who also loved ballet. But he could not himself adopt that attitude because "I find my interest in the kind of meaning a ballet has leads me to an interest in choreography and dance technique."

Odd! No one confesses to being straight-out anti-intellectual. No one expects advocates in the other arts, including the non-verbal ones like painting, sculpture/architecture, photography, and music, to advise turning off thoughts and theories while viewing/listening. No one seriously denies Denby's point that intellectual interests can take you to the guts of an art. Yet, and I speak from years of looking/listening, throughout the dance world—teachers, students, critics, the artists themselves, their fans—an uneasiness too often stirs when intellectual interests are introduced.

Mrs. C.: You don't understand it, do you?

GEM: Maybe because, as Denby said, the creative and critical viewpoints and their respective pleasures are at opposite poles. Maybe because everyone in the dance world, pulling for and identifying with the "creative" dancer who is sorely in need of a societal recognition commonly bestowed on artist in other fields, resists the critical/intellectual posture of the opposite pole. Because to do otherwise might appear to leave the creative dance artist stranded.

Mrs. C.: Is the critic (or whoever) adopting the creative rather than the critical side of Denby's opposites when advising audiences not to worry about meanings in dance?

GEM: No one seriously denies meanings in dance. Apparent denials turn out to be attempts to relax audiences, encourage their attendance. To make them comfortable with the fact that dances have no single meanings, that the point of watching a dance is not to solve a puzzle in a game called "Name that meaning!"

And comfortable with the fact that all interpretations are touched with subjectivity, even those proposed by the artists themselves. But, I am *uncomfortable* with the suggestion that all judgments about an art work and its worth are equally good or bad. Some interpretations/judgments, about meanings and worth, are better than others because they are more informed, judicious, relevant, and so on. Many members of our touring audiences, who thanked us for talking about dance theories, philosophies, ideas, etc., agreed that some interpretations improve over others and that intellectual interests assist rather than cripple the improvement process.

If anyone had told Beethoven that music lacked meanings, he would have had that person committed. Debussy's response, if you told him that you like "La Mer" and precisely because of its absence of meaning? Maybe "I can't believe my ears" or "You don't believe mine."

What is architecture? An "art of constructing meaning, among other things," writes Herbert Muscamp. Written in the aftermath of the September 11th destruction of the World Trade Center, Muscamp's article offers eloquent reading. What he says about the "fragility of meaning," as what the history of architecture throughout the ages demonstrates, is especially provocative.

The artist Elizabeth Murray, looking at Jan Vermeer's picture *Young Woman with a Water Jug*, responds that though it is just a simple domestic scene "I get a very strong feeling of some meaning beyond just the facts of the oriental rug, the map, the jug."

Like all arts, concert dances typically inspire in the observer a "very strong feeling of some meaning" *beyond* just those movement facts on stage. And though in our theater seats we may be more or less unconscious of it, that "strong feeling" gets us on board *thinking* our way towards those meanings sensed beyond, yonder.

Mrs. C.: Yonder? I must go.

GEM: Thank you. Good night, wherever you go.

A Fourth Letter

Club
New York
April '02

Dear Mrs. C.—

After you left last night, there was a 3-alarm fire near Grand Central Terminal. Sirens and horn blasts racing up Madison Ave. and fading a little on 42nd St. Couldn't sleep, so dressed and took the elevator down to the reading room. Couldn't concentrate. Troubled a bit, I think, by your abrupt departure last night. You got restless about meanings in dance; you probably are saying "something's missing." So I went back upstairs, head on pillow, eyes shut, and thank you, Mrs. C., for then showing up—for one more go at it.

GEM: You're generous, patient. Even when you hide your sighs but not your skeptical eyes. You're very meaningful to me.

Mrs. C.: I realize that 20th century thought has obsessed more with Meaning than any other single concept. It is quite synonymous with Modernism since, shall we say, 1910?

GEM: 1913?

Mrs. C.: I allow myself the (unjustified, I'm sure) opinion that, after it's all sorted out, from your Logical Positivists to Deconstructionists, artists are seen to handle "meaning and the meaningful" better than the intellectuals, and I don't exclude here the likes of Bertie Russell and I.A. Richards.

GEM: We don't handle meaning in dance well if we try to extract it from some allegedly unique capacity of dance. Though that's a tempting direction.

I warmed the other day to Ken Johnson's responses to a New York photography show, of 1850's photos of ships, factories, and Crimean War battlefield "all bathed in ethereal light." They make him feel, he reports, "a strange sadness, a sense of lost time that only photography can evoke with such poignant specificity."

He may be right, depending on how specific you make "specificity" here.

Gerald E. Myers

Would an authentic printed menu from the Titanic's dining room serve as effective a poignant reminder of the ship as does a photo of it?

Think of how Jasper Johns is reminded of his friend Frank O'Hara. A few years before O'Hara died in 1966, Johns made a plaster cast of O'Hara's left foot. After O'Hara's death, he created a sculpture *Memory Piece (Frank O'Hara)* that attaches the plaster cast to the lid of a 3-drawer box containing sand. When the lid is opened, you see the plaster foot attached inside it, each time it's closed down it makes a new imprint in the sand. The sculpture, Russell Ferguson writes, keeps O'Hara's physical footprint in the world "in an echo of the way his poetry lives on in the minds of his readers."

That seems sufficiently poignant, and specific, too.

If a dance uniqueness exists, in conveying meanings, it must reside somehow in the special capacities of the human body and its movements. But for me, the interesting issues about meanings arise apropos of dancers that seem (like Vermeer's picture seemed to Elizabeth Murray) to mean something beyond the obvious movement facts onstage. So we're back to meanings sensed beyond, "yonder."

Mrs. C.: Yonder again!

GEM: Don't leave!

Mrs. C.: How quaint. Yonder! Is that Southern talk?

GEM: When meaning in dance is like Mona Lisa's smile! The Italians, Sandra Blakeslee informs us, have a word for that smile—"sfumato" meaning "blurry, ambiguous and up to the imagination." Let us add "fascinating, tantalizing, intriguing," and the like. The kind of meaningful dances that I prefer are of the "sfumato" variety.

Two articles by the critic Jack Anderson expound on "sfumato" dancing. He writes in "What Touches the Heart Can Puzzle the Mind" that dance's capacity "to be simultaneously forceful in impact and vague in meaning is one reason dance is a gloriously mysterious art." He similarly observes in "Puzzles in Dance That Tickle the Imagination" that the skillful choreographer knows how to seize our attention while developing imagery that stimulates thought. Two dances illustrating this, and are the occasion for his article, he says, are *Grass*, by the Swedish choreographer Mats Ek and *Vespers* by the African American choreographer Ulysses Dove.

When we toured ADF's Black Tradition project, the Dayton Contemporary Dance company sometimes performed *Vespers*. Always certain to engage the audiences, and one of my favorite works, *Vespers* fits Anderson's description perfectly. It pounds out one "mysterious" moment after another, to Mikel Rouse's nonstop drumming/murmuring/pulsating/percussive score.

It is performed by six women in black costumes who at times sit in a vertical line of chairs, simultaneously and successively with exquisite timing, run agitatedly singly and in pairs—and dangerously, precise timing required else violent collisions. The dancers' full-out dancing, their fierce concentration/purposefulness, their erotic exposures of thighs by abrupt yanks of their dresses, and their wild combo of group and individual movements make it riveting throughout, and mysterious.

Ulysses Dove, the choreographer, told the Dayton dancers in rehearsal that the inspiration for *Vespers* was his recollections of what he had heard, sounds made by women out of sight in a room doing some kind of communal activity after the regular (black) church services were completed. *Vespers* is Dove's keyhole vision of the goings-on in that room. Worshiping, embracing divinity, amplifying church services by trance-inducing dancing (both aggressive and tender), these six women hypnotize us and each other in this fervent ceremonial of numbingly manicured hysteria.

Mrs. C.: I don't think I'd like it. Something is missing. *Why* do you like *Vespers* so much?

GEM: Try again. Mona Lisa. The "sfumato" effect. How that effect is created. Think of how a dance performance outspeeds our vision, how it is for the viewer riding the rapids of dance sequences. So much can happen as time swoons!

In music too, of course, and via a performance phenomenon shared with dance that is given insightful formulation by Bernard Holland. In commenting on the "duel" of flute and electronic sounds in Bruno Maderna's "Musica su deu dimensioni," he says that a frame is created within in which "details reinvent themselves from moment to moment." In *Vespers*, too, the movements seem to reinvent themselves from moment to moment. Leaping on or off a chair when repeated seems neither totally new or wholly familiar but reinvented. As such, they take on modulated, reinvented meanings.

Mrs. C.: I asked, did I hear, Why?

GEM: Why I like exciting by mysterious dances is my liking the "sfumato" experience they give me. These kinds of experiences are special and deserve our careful attention. They arrest our awareness, perplex it enough so we sense meanings yonder, are then led to *think* our way towards some conception of those meanings.

Consider it this way: dance (and art generally) add to our experience inventories, and the "sfumato" experiences are neither totally new nor wholly familiar, and if "reinvented" is not quite appropriate, maybe "novel" will do. They're different from the same old sorrow, pleasure, etc. We applaud the artist who modifies tradition through her individual talent and we ought to congratulate ourselves on the modifications of our perennial feelings/emotions that such talented art produces in us.

If we were ideal audiences, we would commend these art-produced novel experiences for stimulating what I may call the conceptualization process, and we would eagerly sign up for process participation. We would stop, pay attention to these experiences while in our theater seats, and without loss of attention to the stage. We would let the "suggestions of meaning" play with our thinking, and now and then one thought will emerge as the happiest. That thought is a conceptualization (not a "solution" in a meaning game) of meanings only vaguely sensed before. And it is a destination, however temporary or permanent, of the process that began in "feeling very strongly" that yonder are meanings that we're somehow stimulated to pursue and caption.

This conceptualization process, from registering the original felt experiences that stimulate thinking about meanings to an eventual conceptualization/formulation, is a bona fide intellectual process. I emphasize this, because in the kind of dance aesthetics that I find congenial, the "intellectual" is not confined to technical, historical, anthropological, sociological, etc., studies of dance. An intellectual contribution is made by dance performances as they occur, that contribution being the conceptualization process set in motion.

The aesthetics I find congenial is Michael Kimmelman's when he writes that what we want from art, what we get from the best art, is "to be moved and made to *think*" (my italics).

Whatever be the detailed nature of the process by which he came to the conceptualizations, Edwin Denby came up with two of the finest examples I know. In thinking about Martha Graham's *Herodiade* and *Deaths and Entrances*, he notes that both dances happen in a room of some kind, and that when Graham "suggests in her gesture a great space about her it is, so to speak, the intellectual horizon of the character she depicts." Specifically about *Herodiade*, Denby writes: "The secret of the piece lies much more in the complex and completely individualized elegance of the heroine than it does in the classic allusions of her gesture. *Her elegance of motion is her private integrity*" (my italics).

If we were ideal audiences, we would gladly participate in the conceptualization process hoping for such happy conceptual destinations as Denby reached. It is downright sad that so many persons leave the theater without feeling the lure of that process, much less participation in it. And it's sad that anti-intellectualist sentiments encourage a crowded loss of such opportunities "to feel and think" appropriately in response to great works of art.

When we become ideal audiences, we'll be inspired by Denby's example, of knowing that our forays into conceptualizing our experiences, when "right," are equally conceptualizations of the dance performance (or art work). Those conceptualizations point both to the art work and to our response to it.

We can't overlook the fact that Denby's conceptualizations are poetic, their own meanings capable of being probed. And, upon reflection, could it be otherwise? Given the nature of the experiences that incite the conceptualization process, what kinds of meanings and what kinds of concepts can those meanings accept, other than poetic? It's hard to imagine how any formulation to be called "literal" could begin to do the trick. The poetry is the reward at the end of the intellectual trail.

I call this conceptualization process "ichthyo-poetic," meaning that it is a process of "fishing for the poetic concepts" that best fit our special responses to the art work. Searching the meanings of these experiences—that's poetic fishing, don't you think!

Mrs. C.: Yeats would seem an appropriate mention here. Why is he missing in your dance poetics?

GEM: Mrs. C., you're fading...fading out...out...out.

P.S.: I neglected to mention, Mrs. C., what I know animates you daily, that spiritual hide-out you reserve for yourself. Many dancers share this trait with you while occasionally crediting their art for sustaining it. So for your perusal and for lingering, these impressions into mutual memories of our *pas de deux*...

Because modern dancers—Isadora Duncan, Ruth St. Denis, Martha Graham, Katherine Dunham, José Limón, Erick Hawkins, Alvin Ailey, Judith Jamison, Merce Cunningham, Meredith Monk, and endlessly, others—have all in one way or another pointed to the "spiritual" dimension of their art, this invites exploration. Since modern dance is generally acknowledged to aim at "more" than entertainment alone, perhaps such exploration will reveal that the "more" and the "spiritual" coincide.

We at ADF, impressed while conducting our Black Tradition project by how prominently spirituality figures in African American artist circles, and by how it overlaps with modern dance's history as just indicated above, floated possible programming ideas on "spirituality in modern dance." Reactions ranged from "Great!" to "Good!" to "Okay" to "What?" The muted "Okays" and exclaimed "Whats?" defy facile explanations. It is surprising how many and varied reasons from such wide-ranging origins—cultural, religious, economic, psychological, aesthetic, personal, etc.—will surface for being skeptical about a proposal like ours.

Howard Cotter notices this, with respect not to dance but to art. Considering an exhibit of drawings by Rudolph Steiner, and how they get associated with philosophers like Hegel and Schopenhauer, and with artists like Mondrian, Kandinsky, and Joseph Beuys, Cotter appreciates how the "spiritual" might will be attributed to Steiner's and these artists' works. "But these days," he observes, "any talk about the 'spiritual in art' tends to make everyone squirm a little."

Exploring what dancers have meant by calling what they do an involvement of the spiritual might interest audiences, bring them closer to the art. So might help the art, couldn't hurt? Natalia Makarova writes in her autobiography about how she was trained "to sense a movement, no matter how simple, and to fill it with *spiritual meaning*" (my italics). Exploring this leads to a comparison of Russian with Western dance traditions, of classical ballet with modern dance, as well as scrutinizing more closely what is meant by calling a physical movement "spiritual."

Speaking of ballet, I came upon some novel comments about Degas. Knowing, Mrs. C., that he is one of your favorites (though, as I recall, you prize his pictures of horses more than dancers) I paid special attention to what Toni Bentley, former New York City Ballet ballerina, has written about his dance portraits. She claims that Degas was at best when portraying dancers not dancing but tying a pointe-shoe, stretching a leg, waiting. Also, unlike the 19th century image of the ballerina as an unearthly, ethereal creature, "Degas's dancers," Bentley writes, "have their feet securely on the ground, literally and *spiritually*" (my italics). So not without your collaboration, I hope, I'm set to espy that physically anchored spirituality when next looking at Degas's dancers.

Art's eternal entanglement with spirituality ought to be obvious. But, ignoring ancient history, names of spiritually-tilted artists that come randomly to mind are Blake, Bernard Tschumi, Franz Marc and the Blue Rider group, Rothko, Al Held, John Frederick Kensett, Strindberg, Bruckner, Messiaen, Duke Ellington, John Coltrane, John Tavener, Michaelangelo Antonini, and endlessly, others.

The relationship is exemplified by the life and career of Marsden Hartley (the "Maine Painter"). His painting *Shells by the Sea*, an image of shells against a dark mottled background, is conceptualized by one observer as conveying as much by what seems absent as by what is visible. The "small mundane" shells seem suspended in a "Zen-like emptiness," the painting in melding the real and the abstract "was precisely what Hartley had come to understand as the essence of spirituality."

No noun in the English language is used more timidly than "spirituality." An omnipresent cultural jinni, it must be, that instructs us "If you must use the word, toss it and run." Since it is not for me to define your notion of spirituality, nor is this the proper place for my confessional, I can at least take from Marsden Hartley the barest starting-point in advocating programmatic looks at modern dance's spiritual tradition. For Hartley, it seems, the spiritual means a kind of experience where one's being feels precariously suspended in a vast emptiness, a reality backed up against indecipherable abstractness. From there, perhaps, the possibility of further possibilities? A little matter of experience, that is, wedged within boundless mystery.

The mysterious or inexplicable centrally characterizes the kind of dance experiences, described above, that initiate the viewer's conceptualization process. We already know, from what dancers have said, that in all likelihood spirituality will appear one way or another in their conceptualizations of dancing's significance. But it all deserves exploration.

Tell me what and how you feel about spirituality, you make me an intimate confidant. Dance artists and audiences as intimate confidants, it doesn't get more ideal than that! Have them tell us about themselves on spirituality. No need to worry, we still have the art being served between us. Intimacy never occurs uncompromised no matter what kind of embrace.

Swear to heaven! I feel a drowning mind, I *never* meant to *end* on *intimacy*.

Good night, Mrs. Calabash,
Wherever you are—
GEM

Notes

A Rolling Recollection
Eric Bentley, *What is Theatre?* (1956), p. 34.

Isadora Risking It
M. E. W. Sherwood, *The Art of Entertaining* (1892), p. 260.
Elias Howe's *Complete Ball-Room Hand Book* (1858), p. 67.
Report of the American Society of Professors of Dancing from January 19, 1879 to September 8, 1893 (1894), p. 99.
"current vogue of 'line dancing'": This current dance fashion is culturally useful in community-building if William McNeill's thesis, that military drill and dancing "together in time" ("muscle-bonding") leads to communal bonding, is true. See his *Keeping Together in Time: Dance and Drill in Human History* (1995).
Anna Pavlova quoted by Ann Daly in *Done Into Dance: Isadora Duncan in America* (1995), p. 75.
See also Deborah Jowitt, *Time and the Dancing Image* (1988), p. 69–102.

Rating Her Risks
Sample quotes from Amsterdam: See Lillian Loewenthal, "Isadora Duncan in the Netherlands," *Dance Chronicle* (vol. 3, no. 3, 1979–1980), p. 227–253.
Duncan and *Tristan und Isolde*: Carl Van Vechten, "Duncan Concerts in New York," in Paul Magriel, ed., *Isadora Duncan* (1947), p. 23–24.
Sol Hurok and Duncan: Quoted by Lydia Joel, "Finding Isadora," *Dance Magazine* (June 1969), p. 51.
Duncan and *Ausdruckstanz*: Karl Toepfer, *Empire of Ecstasy: Nudity and Movement in German Body Culture, 1910–1935* (1997), p. 146.
Duncan and Stanislavsky: John Martin, "Isadora Duncan and Basic Dance," in Magriel, p. 8.
Soul in movement: Ann Daly, *Done Into Dance: Isadora Duncan in America* (1995), p. 30
"flow" of movement in modern dance: See John Martin, *The Modern Dance* (1933), p. 31 ff., p. 58 ff.
Duncan and audience reaction: Irma Duncan, "Isadora Duncan—Pioneer in the Art of Dance," *Dance Magazine* (June 1969), p. 55.
See the recent interesting study of Isadora Duncan, *Isadora: A Sensational Life*, by Peter Kurth (2001).

A Letter (January '01)
St. Denis's introduction to dance: In *Ruth St. Denis, An Unfinished Life* (1939), p. 16–17.
"The orthodox churches": St. Denis, *Unfinished Life*, p. 106.
"flesh has its own wisdom": St. Denis, *Unfinished Life*, p. 367.

Miss Ruth
Radha: St. Denis, *Ruth St. Denis, An Unfinished Life*, p. 57.
Edinburgh: St. Denis, *Unfinished Life*, p. 129.
Nautc: St. Denis, *Unfinished Life*, p. 135.
Her touring success: St. Denis, *Unfinished Life*, p. 130.

Ted Shawn

Eastern culture: St. Denis, *Unfinished Life*, p. 139.
Shawn "sobbing": See St. Denis, *Unfinished Life*, p. 136.
Shawn on *Incense*: See Walter Terry, *Ted Shawn: Father of American Dance* (1976), p. 43–44.
St. Denis on *Incense*'s audience: St. Denis, *Unfinished Life*, p. 137.
St. Denis and Shawn "religious" aesthetic: See Terry, *Ted Shawn*, p. 16.
St. Denis church performance: Unfortunately, my newspaper clipping reporting the Winchester,
    Massachusetts, church performance is missing date and name of paper.
Shawn quoting Nietzsche: Ted Shawn, *Gods Who Dance* (1929), p. 3.
"America's new God": Shawn, *Gods*, p. 16–17.
Shawn's "kind of dancers": Shawn, *Gods*, p. 16.

Denishawn

Denishawn respectability, "from good families": See Terry, *Ted Shawn*, p. 68–69.
Tango craze and "orgy": Mr. and Mrs. Vernon Castle, *Modern Dancing* (1914), p. 37, 39.
Shawn and Hampton Institute: See John O. Perpener, III, *African-American Concert Dance: The
    Harlem Renaissance and Beyond* (2001), p. 83–84.
Shawn the American Optimist: Quote from Shawn, *Gods*, p. 16.
St. Denis and "rumor": *Ruth St. Denis, An Unfinished Life* (1939), p. 306.
St. Denis at Adelphi College: St. Denis quote from Kamae A. Miller, ed., *Wisdom Comes Dancing:
    Selected Writings of Ruth St. Denis on Dance, Spirituality, and the Body* (1997), p. 198.
Margaret H'Doubler: See the recent definitive *Moving Lessons: Margaret H'Doubler and the
    Beginning of Dance in American Education*, by Janice Ross (2000).
Modern dance's entry into higher education: See Nancy Lee Ruyter, *Reformers and Visionaries:
    The Americanization of the Art of Dance* (1979), esp. p. 77–107; see also Naima Prevots, *American
    Pageantry: A Movement Art & Democracy* (1990), p. 131–152.
Charles W. Eliot quote: From Frederick Rudolph, *Curriculum: A History of the American
    Undergraduate Course of Study Since 1636* (1977), p. 140–141.

Dance on Campus

"career of the fine arts": Rudolph, *Curriculum*, p. 141.
Wesleyan 1925, Yale 1936: Rudolph, *Curriculum*, p. 141.
U.S.C. and "trauma": Rudolph, *Curriculum*, p. 267.
Shawn and Springfield College: Ted Shawn, *One Thousand and One Night Stands* (1960), p.
    240–246.
Shawn "first American" male dancer: Shawn, *One Thousand*, p. 240–241.
Greek *molpe*: Walter Terry, *Ted Shawn: Father of American Dance* (1976), p. 5.
Kinetic Molpai and men dancing: For this and fuller description, see *Don McDonagh, The Complete
    Guide to Modern Dance* (1976), p. 38–39.
Shawn on *Allegresse*: Shawn, *One Thousand*, p. 207.

Body-Wrapping

Duchamp: Quoted by Paul Crowther, *The Language of Twentieth-Century Art: A Conceptual History*
    (1997), p. 171.
Clive Barnes on Hawkins: Clive Barnes, "The Problem of Hawkins." *The New York Times* (March
    21, 1971).
Hawkins on *Naked Leopard*: Erick Hawkins, *The Body is a Clear Place and Other Statements on Dance*
    (1992), p. 97–98.

A Letter (March '01)

William McNeill, *Keeping Together in Time: Dance and Drill in Human History* (1995), see book's
    back cover, also p. 94.

Body-Democratization

Gautier on Elssler: Quoted by Cyril Beaumont, *A Miscellany for Dancers* (1934), p. 58.

Larson, etc.: See Margaret Lloyd, *The Borzoi Book of Modern Dance* (1949), p. 227, 322.

"once written about Larson": Lloyd, *Borzoi Book*, p. 227.

Anna Halprin on H'Doubler: Quoted in Jean Morrison Brown, ed., *The Vision of Modern Dance* (1979), p. 128.

"wherever there is life": Margaret H'Doubler, *Dance: A Creative Experience* (1940), p. 102.

"Little by little": H'Doubler, *Creative Experience*, p. 104.

"mind becomes intellect" and "in this stage": H'Doubler, *Creative Experience*, p., 105–106.

Martha Graham

"1926" described: David Brownstone and Irene Franck, *Timelines of the 20th Century: A Chronology of 7,500 Key Events, Discoveries, and People that Shaped Our Century* (1996), p. 116–119.

Martha Graham in 1926: See Agnes De Mille, *Martha: The Life and Work of Martha Graham* (1956, 1991), p. 82.

For more on Martha Graham, see Don McDonagh, *Martha Graham: A Biography* (1974); see also Walter Terry, *Frontiers of Life: The Life of Martha Graham* (1975).

Graham at Denishawn, etc.: For more such biographical details, see Trudy Garfunkel, *Letter to the World: The Life and Dances of Martha Graham* (1995).

"Martha Graham recalled": An interview with Douglas M. Davis in *The National Observer* (December 30, 1968), p. 18.

Graham recalling "one little old lady": In remarks by Martha Graham at May 15, 1976, meeting of the National Council on the Arts, where Graham was honored on her 50th choreographic anniversary year.

Louis Horst on *Lamentation*: See Janet Soares, *Louis Horst: Musician in a Dancer's World* (1992), p. 85.

The Stage is Graham's

Sophie Maslow quote: From Marian Horosko, *Martha Graham: The Evolution of Her Dance Theory and Training, 1926–1991* (1991), p. 53.

Stravinsky's *Apollon Musagète*: See George Balanchine and Francis Mason, *Balanchine's Complete Stories of Great Ballets* (1977), p. 28.

Deborah Jowitt on Graham: Deborah Jowitt, "The Monumental Martha," *The New York Times* (April 29, 1973).

Graham on "American" dance: Quoted from company *Pressbook* (n.d., circa 1936) by concert management Frances Hawkins, publishing Herbert Brodsky.

Graham's "modern dance…freedom of women in America": From Graham interview with Emily Coleman, "Martha Graham Still Leaps Forward," *New York Times Magazine* (April 9, 1961).

Graham "I was through with character dancing": Quoted from Margaret Lloyd, *The Borzoi Book of Modern Dance* (1949), p. 49–50.

Graham's *Letter to the World*: See Trudy Garfunkel, *The Life and Times of Martha Graham* (1995), p. 56.

Fokine and Graham: Quoted by Janet Soares, *Louis Horst: Musician in a Dancer's World* (1992), p. 97.

Fokine on modern dance, "ugly girl": Quoted by Deborah Jowitt, *Time and the Dancing Image* (1988), p. 152. I and others occasionally heard Walter Terry quoting Fokine with these words.

Louis, Too

Louis Horst, *Pre-Classic Dance Forms* (1953), Foreword by Henry Gilfond. Horst's courses in pre-classic court dances of the 16th century and their music—pavane, minuet, etc.—were designed to stimulate a sense of compositional form; and badly needed, in Horst's judgment.

Horst "a consciousness of form": In Louis Horst, *Modern Dance Forms in Relation to the Other Modern Arts*, ed. Janet Mansfield Soares (1987), p. 8.

Horst, "to compose" and quoting Klee: Horst, *Modern Dance Forms*, p. 21, 23.

Horst's influence: For more, see Ernestine Stodelle (and Barbara Morgan's photographs), *The Story of Louis Horst and the American Dance* (1964), a tribute booklet for Horst.

Graham-Based Thoughts on Dance

John Martin on Graham in the Forties: John Martin, *The Dance* (1946), p. 133.

Dance and fine arts (Sparshott): In Francis Sparshott, *Off the Ground: First Steps to a Philosophical Consideration of the Dance* (1988), p. 24.

Agnes De Mille on Graham's "new way of thinking": Quoted in *Martha Graham and Her Dance Company*, Program Booklet (n.d., circa mid 1950s).

John Martin, "substance" of dance: John Martin, *The Modern Dance* (1933), p. 6–7.

Martin, "impatient with the layman,": Martin, *Modern Dance*, p.11.

Martin, "few audience issues": Martin, *Modern Dance*, p. 11–12.

Martin, "no conscious use of metakinesis": Martin, *Modern Dance*, p. 15. For recent attention to Martin's concept of "metakinesis," see the critic Jack Anderson's new Introduction to John Martin's *The Dance in Theory* (1965, 1989).

Bessie Schönberg's recollection of Graham: Quoted in Marian Horosko, *Martha Graham: The Evolution of Her Dance Theory and Training, 1926–1991* (1991), p. 28.

Sophie Maslow's recollection of Graham's classes: Quoted in Horosko, *Martha Graham*, p. 52.

Frances Herridge on *Night Journey*: For these quotes and fuller description of *Night Journey*, from which I have drawn here, see Frances Herridge, "Martha Graham Dances her 'Night Journey'," *PM* (February 1948).

Lloyd on *Night Journey*: Margaret Lloyd, *The Borzoi Book of Modern Dance* (1949), p. 45.

Balanchine, "to say dryly": See Deborah Jowitt, *Time and the Dancing Image* (1988), p. 240.

Review quote of *Clytemnestra*: Robert Coleman's Theater, *New York Mirror* (April 2, 1958).

Mindy Aloff on Graham Technique: Mindy Aloff, *The New Republic* (September 11, 1995), p. 30 ff.

Doris Humphrey

"course on Doris Humphrey": In Marcia B. Siegel, *Days on Earth: The Dance of Doris Humphrey* (1987), Preface xi.

"person drawn to dance...unintellectual": Doris Humphrey, *The Art of Making Dances*, ed. Barbara Pollack (1959), p. 17.

Humphrey quote on Fokine: Humphrey, *The Art*, p. 18.

Humphrey quote, "It seems to me": Humphrey, *The Art*, p. 18.

Humphrey, "For my taste": Humphrey, *The Art*, p. 111

Quote about Humphrey, "had yet to find the way": In Margaret Lloyd, *The Borzoi Book of Modern Dance* (1949), p. 84.

For more on Humphrey's dance philosophy, see John Martin, *The Dance* (1946), p. 124.

Marcia Siegel on early Humphrey films: Siegel, *Days on Earth*, p. 85.

"contrasting Humphrey and Graham": This is taken from Agnes De Mille's *Martha: The Life and Work of Martha Graham* (1956, 1991), p. 78 ff.

"broke her heart": De Mille, *Martha*, p. 70.

Thinking With Humphrey

On metaphor and concertos, see the review by the always insightful Edward Rothstein of Joseph Kerman's *Concerto Conversations* (1999) in *The New York Times* (October 30, 1999).

Pauline Koner on *The Visit*: See Pauline Koner, *Solitary Song* (1989), p. 161.

Kisselgoff on *Lamentation*: Anna Kisselgoff, "A Classical Approach to the Graham Karma," *The New York Times* (October 26, 1999).

Humphrey, "to express the essence": Doris Humphrey, *The Art of Making Dances*, ed. Barbara Pollack (1959), p. 116.

Humphrey, "You cannot philosophize": Humphrey, *The Art*, p. 36.

Katherine Dunham and Pearl Primus

Dunham and Primus: For more on this and the general subject of the black presence in modern dance, see our American Dance Festival (ADF) publications (with their bibliographies), *The Black Tradition in American Modern Dance*, ed. Gerald E. Myers (1988) and *African American*

Genius in Modern Dance, ed. Gerald E. Myers (1993). See also John Perpener's *African-American Concert Dance: The Harlem Renaissance and Beyond* (2001).

John Martin on Dunham Broadway debut: Quoted by Zita Allen in ADF's *Black Tradition*, p. 28.

Dunham, "She had to create a new dance technique": Bill Moore in ADF's *Black Tradition*, p. 17.

Dunham Technique, "more than just 'dance' as bodily executions": For this and more on Dunham Technique, see Albirda Rose, *Dunham Technique A Way of Life* (1990), p. 23.

New Dance Group: For a full account of the New Dance group and modern dance at the time, see Ellen Graff, *Stepping Left: Dance and Politics in New York City, 1928–1942* (1997).

Primus, "people use their bodies": Quoted by Kariamu Welsh Asante, ed., *African Dance: An Artistic, Historical and Philosophical Inquiry* (1998), p. 6.

Primus, on African professional dancing: Quoted by Asante, *African Dance*, p. 7–8.

For more on Primus and her legacy, see Beverly Hillsman Barber, "Pearl Primus: Rebuilding America's Cultural Infrastructure," in ADF's *African American Genius*, p. 9–12.

A Project—Dancers Modern and Black

ADF's "goal of supporting modern dance": For a history of the American Dance Festival (ADF), see Jack Anderson, *The American Dance Festival* (1987).

Touring Rainbow and Black Classics

McKayle, "woman, the inspirer,": Donald McKayle, "The Act of Theater," in *The Modern Dance: Seven Statements of Belief*, ed. Selma Jeanne Cohen (1965, 1966), p. 59.

Joe Nash on *The Stack-Up*: Joe Nash, "Talley Beatty," in ADF's *African American Genius in Modern Dance*, ed. Gerald E. Myers (1993), p. 15.

My description of *Mourner's Bench*: Taken from my "ADF—Home of An Art Form," in ADF's *Reflections on the Home of An Art Form, 1934–1998* (1998), p. 25–26.

ADF's Black Tradition project: Much of its character and objectives is shown in ADF's film/TV series *Free to Dance: The African American Presence in Modern Dance* that aired nationally on PBS in June 2001.

Role of African American women in dance: See *Dance Women/Living Legends* (n.d.), produced by 651, An Arts Center; Aaron Davis Hall; and New Jersey Performing Arts Center.

Erick Hawkins

Kisselgoff's obituary notice for Hawkins: "Erick Hawkins, a Pioneering Choreographer of American Dance, Is Dead at 85." *The New York Times* (November 24, 1994).

Hawkins, "ballet is woman," etc.: See Erick Hawkins, "Pure Poetry," in *The Modern Dance: Seven Statements of Belief*, ed. Selma Jeanne Cohen (1965, 1966), p. 39–51.

Hawkins on Isadora Duncan: In Cohen, *Seven Statements*, p. 41.

Beverly Brown on Duncan and Hawkins: Beverly Brown, "Training to Dance With Erick Hawkins," in *Erick Hawkins: Theory and Training* (1979), p. 10 ; see also p. 8–28.

Mabel Todd, "living the whole body": Mabel E. Todd, *The Thinking Body: A Study of the Balancing Forces of Dynamic Man* (1937), p. 1.

Lucia Dlugoszewski on Northrop and Asian thought: Said in ADF talks, among others.

Hawkins led-workshop: Quoted by Mark Woodworth, "Sensing Nature's Flow, Hawkins Teaches up a Storm—Showers of Dance-Poems!", *Dance Magazine* (October 1972), p. 28.

Hawkins on movement quality: In Cohen, p. 39. I once stressed the significance of movement qualities for dancers in my "Do You See What the Critics See?", in ADF's *Philosophical Essays on Dance*, eds. Gordon Fancher and Gerald E. Myers (1981), p. 33–68.

Barnes, 1973, on Hawkins: Clive Barnes review, "Modern Goes Classic—and Vice Versa; Dance." *The New York Times* (June 17, 1973).

Jowitt, 1997, on Hawkins: Deborah Jowitt, "Call if found." *Village Voice* (March 18, 1997).

McDonagh on Hawkins: Don McDonagh, *The Rise and Fall and Rise of Modern Dance* (1970, 1990), p. 24–25.

Hawkins on *Naked Leopard*: Erick Hawkins, *The Body is a Clear Place and Other Statements on Dance* (1992), p. 97.

Naked Leopard, "innocence of the sensuous": Mark Woodworth, "Opening the Eye of Nature," *On the Dance of Erick Hawkins* (n.d.), p. 15.

Siegel, "philosophically, Hawkins": Marcia B. Siegel, *The Shapes of Change: Images of American Dance* (1979), p. 318–319. See also Siegel's provocative remarks about Hawkins's *Here and Now with Watchers* in Marcia B. Siegel, *Watching the Day Go By* (1977) p. 227–228.

Prevots reviewing Hawkins: Naima Prevots, "When History Records Great American Artists of the 20th Century, Hawkins will be at the Top of the List," *Washington Dance View* (December 1981–January 1982).

Hawkins, Heyoka and "clowning": Hawkins quoted in Prevots, "When History Records."

Kisselgoff, "Ethics and aesthetics": Anna Kisselgoff review, *The New York Times* (February 2, 1995).

Alwin Nikolais

Nikolais reviews, "In the Nikolais scheme": P.W. Manchester, "Nikolais Equates Dance with Color, Sound, and Design," *Christian Science Monitor* (February 18, 1961).

Nikolais review, "seemed of little movement": Jacqueline Maskey review, *Dance Magazine* (June 1966), p. 32, 80.

Nikolais review, "pure sensory luxury,": Doris Hering, *Dance Magazine* (February 1970), p. 83–85.

Nikolais review, "at the still point": William Glenesk, "The Still Point," *Dance Magazine* (April 1965), p. 39–40.

For more on Nikolais's career, see Marcia B. Siegel, ed., "Nik: A Documentary," *Dance Perspectives* (Winter 1971). See also Sali Ann Kriegsman, *Modern Dance in America: The Bennington Years* (1981), p. 252–255.

Nikolais, Holm, and Colorado: For more on this, see Margaret Lloyd, *The Borzoi Book of Modern Dance* (1949), p. 157 ff.

"at its demise in 1983": Unpublished notes by Claudia Gitelman. Recently, Claudia Gitelman has published the important *Dancing With Principle: Hanya Holm in Colorado, 1941–1983* (2001). In addition to telling how the Holm/Colorado College Summer School of the Dance contributed to modern dance and its place in American education, the book includes fresh information about Nikolais' work with Hanya Holm.

Nikolais's 1968 award, his comments: in *Dance Magazine* (June 1968), p. 41.

Nikolais's reaction to *Trend*: Quoted in Kriegsman, *The Bennington Years*, p. 165.

Nikolais's paper "The New Dimension of Dance," in *Impulse Magazine*, ed. Marian Van Tuyl (1958), p. 43–46.

Nikolais, "He is ready to raise the self": in *Impulse Magazine*, p. 43–46.

Louis, "With an artist like Graham": Murray Louis, "Thoughts: Murray Louis on Alwin Nikolais," *Dance Magazine* (December 1979), p. 56–65. See also in same issue of the magazine Ruth E. Grauert, "Nik's Own Son et Lumière Show," p. 56–69; also her recent "Alwin Nikolais" in *America Dancing* (n.d.), Performing Arts Education Department, The John F. Kennedy Center for the Performing Arts (booklet).

Nikolais on Prodigal Son theme: In his "No Man From Mars," in *The Modern Dance: Seven Statements of Belief*, ed. Selma Jeanne Cohen (1965, 1966), p. 63–77.

Louis, "I couldn't understand": Murray Louis, *Inside Dance*: Essays (1980), p. 25.

"His [Nikolais's] developments": In program brochure, Nikolais/Louis 25-year Retrospective (1992), Rutgers Art Center.

Murray Louis promises to sustain the Nikolais legacy with several documentary/publication projects currently under development.

Merce Cunningham

Cage, "Haiku requires of us": In Richard Kostelanetz, ed., *John Cage: An Anthology* (1968, 1991), p. 90.

Review of *Way Station*: Byron Woods, "The Body Electric: Merce Cunningham Troupe Explores, Discovers," *The News and Observer*, Raleigh, NC, (July 14, 2001).

Henry Cowell, "Cage's method of employing the I Ching": In Kostelanetz, *John Cage*, p. 99.

Remy Charlip on *Suite by Chance*: In Richard Kostelanetz, ed., *Merce Cunningham: Dancing in Space and Time* (1992), p. 41.

Cunningham's use of Life Forms: See *Art Performs Life: Merce Cunningham, Meredith Monk, Bill T. Jones*, Walker Art Center (1998), p. 21.

For the most comprehensive and authoritative review of Cunningham's career, see David Vaughan, *Merce Cunningham: Fifty Years*, 1997.

1944 "Cage argued that modern dance": In Kostelanetz, *Merce Cunningham*, p. 21–24.

Cunningham, "the moving becomes clear if the space and time": In Kostelanetz, *Merce Cunningham*, p. 37–39.

Kostelanetz, "talking with Cage": Kostelanetz, *John Cage*, p. 29.

Gombrich's aphorism: E.H. Gombrich, *Art and Illusion: A Study In the Psychology of Pictorial Representation* (1960), p. 86.

Cunningham's invoking Gertude Stein: See James Waring's comments in Kostelanetz, *Merce Cunningham*, p. 30; see also Earle Brown's comments, p. 62.

Cunningham, "dancing is a spiritual exercise": In Kostelanetz, *Merce Cunningham*, p. 39.

Paul Taylor

Taylor on *From Sea to Shining Sea*: Paul Taylor, *Private Domain* (1987), p. 234–235.

Taylor on *American Genesis*: Taylor, *Private Domain*, p. 332–333.

Kisselgoff, Taylor's "heavy-duty pieces": Anna Kisselgoff, "Dance Review: Paul Taylor: Heavy-Duty and Lite," *The New York Times* (October 13, 1995).

Shapiro on *Company B*: Laura Shapiro review, "This Time, One From Heart," *Newsweek* (November 11, 1999), p. 68–69.

Taylor on Graham and male dancing: Taylor, *Private Domain*, p. 85.

Taylor, "Merce danced his own roles dramatically": Taylor, *Private Domain*, p. 49.

For more on Taylor's relation to the Judson and "post-modern" dancers, see Don Daniels, "Paul Taylor and the Post-Moderns," *Ballet Review* (Summer 1981), p. 66–83.

Taylor's influence: For a few interesting references to Antony Tudor and Paul Taylor, see Judith Chazin-Bennahum, *The Ballets of Antony Tudor: Studies in Psyche and Satire* (1994).

Taylor, defining modern dance: Taylor, *Private Domain*, p. 68.

Big Bertha, etc.: For more on interpretive issues relating to Taylor's dances, see Jack Anderson, *Choreography Observed* (1987), p. 164–165.

Siegel, on *Public Domain*: Marcia Siegel, *At The Vanishing Point* (1967), p. 207–208.

Polaris: Arlene Croce, Going to the Dance (1982), p. 33.

Taylor, "the finest choreography": Paul Taylor, "Down with Choreography," in *The Modern Dance: Seven Statements of Belief*, ed. Selma Jeanne Cohen (1965, 1966), p. 91–92.

Taylor, "I grew up watching for": Taylor, *Private Domain*, p. 31. For more on Taylor's career and collaborations, see Lillie F. Rosen, "Talking with Paul Taylor," *Dance Scope* (vol. 3., nos. 2–3, 1979); Jack Anderson, "Choreographic Fox: Paul Taylor," *Dance Magazine* (April 1980), p. 68–74.

Taylor, "discovering how to hold still": Taylor, *Private Domain*, p. 77.

Taylor, "The most communicative dances": Taylor, *Private Domain*, p. 31.

Taylor, "For instance, the light turn": Taylor, *Private Domain*, p. 77.

Taylor, "she is not merely moving to a different spot": Taylor, *Private Domain*, p. 78.

Taylor, "By failing to find": Taylor, *Private Domain*, p. 80.

Croce, 1982 review: Arlene Croce, *Going to The Dance* (1982), p. 31.

Taylor on *Aureole*: Taylor, *Private Domain*, p. 135–136, 141.

Taylor, "No matter how often I've practiced it": Taylor, *Private Domain*, p. 136.

Taylor, "yet for all its success": Taylor, *Private Domain*, p. 141.

Taylor, "By alternating contradiction with": Taylor, *Private Domain*, p. 103.

Reinhart on *Esplanade*: Charles L. Reinhart, "Paul Taylor 70th: A Birthday Remembrance," in *Dance Magazine* (July 2000), p. 41–42.

Taylor, "A dancer's true voice" and "must be inundated": Taylor, *Private Domain*, p. 331.

Anna Halprin

H'Doubler, University of Wisconsin: See again the definitive study of Margaret H'Doubler by Janice Ross, *Moving Lessons: Margaret H'Doubler and the Beginning of Dance in American Education* (2000).

"H'Doubler and Halprin were not drawn": For more on this, see an interview with Anna Halprin by Vera Maletic, "The Process is the Purpose," *Dance Scope* (Fall/Winter 1967–1968), p. 12.

Halprin, "the stress in movement": Quoted in Maletic, "The Process," p. 12.

Denby, "heavy accents and strained postures": Quoted in Marcia Siegel, *Days on Earth: The Dance of Doris Humphrey* (1987), p. 228.

Halprin, "feeling unrelated": Quoted in Rose Hartman, "Talking with Anna Halprin," *Dance Scope*, (Fall/Winter 1977–78), p. 61–62.

Halprin, "I've always accepted": In Maletic, "The Process," p. 18.

Halprin, "seeking a sense of her body": See Maletic, "The Process," p. 18.

Perls, Reich, etc.: For more on Gestalist theory and practice that is relevant here, see Joen Fagan and Irma Lee Sheperd, eds., *What is Gestalt Therapy?* (1970).

Halprin, "feeling more comfortable in the theater": See Anna Halprin, *Moving Toward Life: Five Decades of Transformative Dance*, ed. Rachel Kaplan (1995), p. 245.

Halprin, "I began to chart movements": "Yvonne Rainer Interviews Anna Halprin," in Halprin, p. 81.

Halprin on *Five-Legged Stool*: Halprin, *Moving Toward Life*, p. 83.

Barnes, "Finally, people enter": Clive Barnes review, "Dance: The Ultimate in Bare Stages," *The New York Times*, April 24, 1967.

Halprin, "changing her first name": Halprin, *Moving Toward Life*, p. 75.

Halprin, "In 1981, I began to create": Halprin, *Moving Toward Life*, p. 67–68.

Ross on Planetary Dance: Janice Ross, "A Day of Dancing, by the Hundreds, on Hitler's Grave," *The New York Times* (September 3, 1995).

Halprin, "the modern dance movement was 'real'": Halprin, *Moving Toward Life*, p. 248.

Halprin, "He was a Hasidic Jew": Halprin, *Moving Toward Life*, p. 246.

Judson

Rainer's "No": Quoted in Sally Banes, *Terpsichore in Sneakers: post-modern dance* (1980), p. 43.

McDonagh, "A woman stands with profile": Don McDonagh, *The Complete Guide to Modern Dance* (1976), p. 447.

Rainer, *Trio A*: See Yvonne Rainer, *Yvonne Rainer Work, 1961–1973* (The Press of the Nova Scotia College of Art and Design; NYU Press 1974).

Rainer, "Conceived *Trio A* out of": See Rainer's comments quoted in Jean Morrison Brown, ed., *The Vision of Modern Dance* (1979), p. 141–150.

Rainer, "The goal to be moved by something": in Brown, *The Vision*, p. 146.

Cage, "there is in Rauschenberg": John Cage, *Silence* (1961), p. 103.

Rainer, "I was more involved": in Brown, *The Vision*, p. 145.

Rainer, "movement as task": in Brown, *The Vision*, p. 147.

Rainer, "The irony here": in Brown, *The Vision*, p. 147.

Rainer, "My *Trio A* dealt": Brown, *The Vision*, p. 149.

Banes citing Heidegger: Banes, *Terpsichore*, p. 49–50; Heidegger quoted, p. 50.

Rainer, "the risks involved": Whether Rainer was always consistent about self-effacement, etc., raises issues discussed, for example, by Mark Franko. See his "Some Notes on Yvonne Rainer, Modernism, Politics, Emotion, Performance, and the Aftermath," in *Meaning in Motion*, ed. Jane Desmond (1997), p. 289–304.

Paxton, "the most embarrassing moments": Steve Paxton interview with Nancy Stark Smith, in *Contact Quarterly: A Vehicle for Moving Ideas* (Winter 1989), p. 18.

Gordon's *Random Breakfast*: My description here is indebted to Don McDonagh's in his *The Complete Guide to Modern Dance* (1976), p. 379.

Gordon, "artworks that analyze" and "accumulates and organizes": Banes, *Terpsichore*, p. 109.

Gordon, "I am this thing": David Gordon interview by Amanda Smith, in *Dance Magazine* (February 1981), p. 74–78.

Kisselgoff, "can save this white elephant of a ballet": Anna Kisselgoff review, *The New York Times* (October 26, 2000).

Tobias, on Childs's *Radial Courses*: Tobi Tobias review, *New York Magazine* (October 10, 2000), p. 105–106.

"Design is the art that is hidden": Philip Nobel, "Design is the Art that is Hidden in Plain Sight," *The New York Times* (November 27, 2000), p. 23.

Paxton, Baryshnikov, etc.: Mike Wallace, interviewing Mikhail Baryshnikov on the TV weekly *60 Minutes*, called the Judson style "minimalist and intellectual." This program, which I saw November 28, 2000, showed Baryshnikov performing an excerpt from Paxton's *Flat*. For more on this, see (with Baryshnikov pictured in *Flat*) Wendy Perron's helpful comments in *Dance Magazine* (November 2000), p. 54–59. My use of occasional quotes here is indebted to Perron's observations.

Novack, "trying to realize a re-definition": Cynthia J. Novack, *Sharing the Dance: Contact Improvisation and American Culture* (1990), p. 3.

Novack, "the responsive body": Novack, *Sharing the Dance*, p. 189.

Novack, "represents honesty, reality": Novack, *Sharing the Dance*, p. 186.

Nelson, "Actually, for me": Lisa Nelson, "Improvisation and the Sense of Imagination," *Contact Quarterly* (Summer/Fall 1992), p. 47–50 (discussion with Daniel Lepkoff and Lisa Nelson).

Paxton, "isn't mental so much as": Steve Paxton, "Trance Script," *Contact Quarterly* (Winter 1989), p. 14–21 (interview with Nancy Stark Smith).

Paxton, "choreographer's job is the traffic cop's": Remarks made at ADF in 1994.

Baryshnikov and Perron on Deborah Hay: Quotes from Perron, *Dance Magazine*, p. 57.

Hay "describes innate skills": Deborah Hay, *My Body, the Buddhist* (2000), p. xxv, xxx.

A Letter (October '01)

Joseph Kerman, *Concerto Conversations* (1999), p.2.

Deborah Gans, "Table Talk: A Discussion of Michael Graves' Set for the Ballet Fire," *The Princeton Journal: Thematic Studies in Architecture, Ritual* (vol. 1, 1983), p. 58. This is an informative, provocative discussion, taking Michael Graves' theater set for Laura Dean's dance *Fire* as its occasion.

Susan Sontag, Interview: "On Art and Consciousness," *Performing Arts Journal* (Fall 1977), p. 31.

Carly Simon, "How Lyrics Work," *Doubletalk* (Spring 2001), p. 14.

Meredith Monk

Review of "Solo Landscapes": James R. Oestreich review, "Sounds of Almost Wordless Songs" *The New York Times* (July 20, 2000).

The demonstration I saw at Connecticut College was in the Fall, 2000.

Rockwell review: John Rockwell, "Music: Meredith Monk," *The New York Times* (January 21, 1979).

"When Monk began her career": For more on Monk's career, see Deborah Jowitt, ed., *Meredith Monk* (1997); *Art Performs Life: Merce Cunningham/Meredith Monk/Bill T. Jones*, Walker Art Center (1998), p. 66–115; George Dorris, "Meredith Monk," *Fifty Contemporary Choreographers*, ed. Martha Bremser (1999), p. 159–164.

Monk on Broadway: See the account, to which I am indebted here, by Frances Herridge, "Meredith Monk Comes to Broadway," *Dance Magazine* (February 15, 1969).

McDonagh on *Juice*: Don McDonagh, *The Complete Guide to Modern Dance* (1976), p. 416–417.

Monk, "images rubbing against each other": In comments by Monk at ADF in 1996.

Tomaszewski obituary notice: William H. Honan, *The New York Times* (October 23, 2001), p. a21.

Monk's way of "mythically": My comments here are based not only on what has been printed but also on her 1996 talks at ADF.

Feingold on *Magic Fequencies*: Michael Feingold, "Momentary Musicals," *Village Voice* (November 16, 1998).

Magic Frequencies, "In one lovely episode": Mark Robinson, interview with Monk in Theater (vol. 30, no. 2, 2000); my quotes and emphases on *Magic Frequencies* taken from this interview.

Music critic, minimalism, "wordless vocalizations": Review by music critic Allan Koznin, *The New York Times* (November 4, 1999).

Kimmelman, on Flavin and Judd: Michael Kimmelman, "The Last Great Art of the 20th Century," *The New York Times* (February 4, 2001).

1998 interview: By Gia Kourlas, "A Verb, Not a Noun," *Dance Magazine* (April 1998), p. 72–75.

Subsequent reference by Monk to "sacred space": Kourlas, p. 72–75.

One reviewer of *A Celebration Service*: Review in the *New London Day* (April 30, 1999).

Monk, *Facing North*, "A chamber music/theater piece": Quoted in Jowitt, *Meredith Monk*, p. 168. See also Jowitt's fine description of *Facing North*, p. 167–170.

Facing North a "late-twentieth century version": Tobi Tobias review, *New York Magazine* (February 24, 1992).

A splendid photo of *Facing North* appears in *Danspace Project 25 Years* (1999), p. 63.

Monk, on musical forms in *Facing North*: Quoted in Monk interview with Jamake Highwater, in *Art Performs Life*, p. 88.

Trisha Brown

Brown, "My personality embraces elusive": Trisha Brown interview with Charles Reinhart at ADF in 1993.

Brown, and A. Livet. "Trisha Brown." Edited Transcript of an Interview with Trisha Brown, in *Contemporary Dance*, p. 44–54.

Brown, Trisha. "Trisha Brown: An Interview." In *The 20th Century Performance Reader*. Ed. Michael Huxley and Noel Witts, 1996. p. 119–128.

Brown's career: For biographical information, see "Trisha Brown: An Interview," chapter 14 of *The 20th Century Perfomance Reader*, ed. Michael Huxley and Noel Witts, (London: Routledge, 1996). See also Marianne Goldberg's essay on Brown in *Fifty Contemporary Choreographers*, ed. Martha Bremser (1999), p. 37–42.

"no Trisha Brown Technique": In 1993 ADF interview.

Brown, "the best thing that could have happened": In 1993 interview at ADF.

Brown and Schönberg, "You can't just use": 1993 interview at ADF.

Brown, "In the field of avant-garde dance": Quoted by Debra Cash, "The New Wave in Modern Dance" (also about Lucinda Childs and Laura Dean), *Saturday Review* (March 1982), p. 34–38.

Brown's dances *A String, Rulegame 5*, etc.: For my description here, I am indebted to Marcia Marks's review in *Dance Magazine*, May 1966, p. 62–63.

Brown, "dance-structure": For more on dance structure, improvisation, etc., see Sally R. Sommer, "Trisha Brown Making Dances," *Dance Scope* (Spring/Summer, 1972), p. 7–18.

"Brown is interested in the tension between": Sally Banes, in the *International Encyclopedia of Dance*, Selma Jeanne Cohen, founding ed. (1998, 2003), p. 543.

"Brown set herself the task of": Roger Copeland, "The 'Post-Modern' Choreography of Trisha Brown," *The New York Times* (January 4, 1976).

Brown on *Accumulation*: Trisha Brown, "Trisha Brown: An Interview," *The 20th Century Performance Reader*, ed. by Michael Huxley and Noel Witts, p. 121–122.

Jowitt, "She seems to be changing directions": Deborah Jowitt, "Not All Explosions are Violent." Review in *Village Voice* (June 12, 1978).

Brown "calls her cycle of works": For more on Brown's successive career "cycles," see the fine discussion by Marianne Goldberg in *Fifty Contemporary Choreographers*, p. 37–42. And on Brown's career, see Lisa Brunel and Trisha Brown, *Trisha Brown* (1987), with Brown's drawings exhibited.

Brown, "what I did to develop a vocabulary": Interview with William Harris, "Trisha Brown Takes Up the Challenge of Bach," *The New York Times* (July 16, 1995).

Kisselgoff on *Foray Foret*: Anna Kisselgoff, "Trisha Brown: Simplicity Within Complexity," *The New York Times* (March 3, 1991). Compare this feature of Brown's artistry, say, with Sol Lewitt's as discussed by Jeffrey Kastner, "A Playful Geometer Makes the Complex Seem So Simple," *The New York Times* (December 3, 2000).

Brown "loves to play," etc.: Brown's remarks in 1997 ADF talks.

Twyla Tharp

Tharp, "Dance is a microcosm of society": In remarks at ADF 1990.

Tharp, on popularity, *Deuce Coupe*, etc.: See Twyla Tharp, *Push Comes to Shove* (1992), p. 110, 185.

"The depth of her interest in interesting audiences": The episode referred to here was her talk at ADF 1999.

"The American intelligentsia in the 1960s": See Tharp, *Push*, p. 155.

The One Hundreds: For an illuminating discussion of this work, see Marcia Siegel, "In Twyla's Company," *The Hudson Review* (Winter 1999), p. 735–742.

"Tobi Tobias in 1970": Tobi Tobias, "Twyla Tharp," *Dance Scope* (Spring 1970), p. 10; and see on this Tharp, *Push*, p. 199.

Tharp, on Paul Taylor's dancing: Tharp, *Push*, p. 65.

Tharp to her dancers "You have to think": This is quoted by Tobias, p. 6–17.

"I tried to get this work out of the head": Tharp, *Push*, p. 120.

"Scientific investigation of the body" and "the gut": Quoted in Selma Jeanne Cohen, ed., *Dance as a Theatre Art* (2nd edition, 1992), p. 233.

"What my body could understand": In Barbara Zuck, "Tywla in Ohio," *Dance Magazine* (January 1992), p. 53.

Tharp's dances of the Sixties: See Don McDonagh, *The Complete Guide to Modern Dance* (1976); see also Michael Robertson, "Twyla Tharp and the Logical Outcome of Abundance," *Dance Magazine* (March 1980).

Tharp on *Re-Moves*: Tharp, *Push*, p. 89.

Cede Blue Lake, etc. reviewed: Reviewed by Marcia Marks in *Dance Magazine* (January 1966), p. 58–59.

Clive Barnes quote, "so cool": Quoted by Tharp, *Push*, p. 90.

Tharp on Judson aesthetic: Tharp, *Push*, p. 87, 110. For more on comparison with Judson, see Susan Leigh Foster, *Reading Dancing: Bodies and Subjects in Contemporary American Dance* (1986), p. 220–227. See also Deborah Jowitt, untitled lecture transcripts on radical choreographers of the 1960s and 1970s, in Anne Livet, ed., *Contemporary Dance* (1978), p. 146.

Tharp, on *The Fugue*, Bach, etc.: See Tharp, *Push*, p. 132.

Examples of reactions by critics include Arlene Croce, *Afterimages* (1977), p. 390 ff; Marcia Siegel, *The Tail of the Dragon* (1991), p. 104, 165; Tobi Tobias, "Tharp on Broadway," *Dance Magazine* (July 1980), p. 62.

Nine Sinatra Songs, Tharp and gender roles: On this issue, see Susan Manning, "The Female Dancer and the Male Gaze: Feminist Critiques of Early Modern Dance," in Jane Desmond, ed., *Meaning in Motion: New Cultural Studies of Dance* (1997), p. 153–166. See also Elizabeth Dempster, "Women Writing the Body: Let's Watch a Little How She Dances," in Ellen W. Goellner and Jacqueline Shea Murphy, eds., *Bodies of the Text* (1995), p. 21–28; Judith Lynne Hanna, *Dance, Sex, and Gender: Signs of Identity, Dominance, Defiance, and Desire* (1988), p. 179, 215.

The Fugue, Tharp's favorite: Tharp, *Push*, p. 300.

The Fugue actually "sensual": Tharp, *Push*, p. 34.

Tom Rawe and *The Fugue*: Quoted by Michael Robertson, "Twyla Tharp and the Logical Outcome of Abundance," *Dance Magazine* (March 1980), p. 72.

Tharp's "creative output": For a chronology of Tharp's career through 1997, see Dale Harris and editor Martha Bremser, *Fifty Contemporary Choreographers* (1999), p. 221–223.

Deuce Coupe: Instructive characterizations of this dance are provided by Arlene Croce, *Afterimages*, (1977), p. 13–19; and Marcia Siegel, *Watching the Dance Go By* (1977), p. 46–47.

Tharp and "high vs. low" art distinctions: Not everyone was thrilled by Tharp's fusion of classical and vernacular that menaces high-low art distinctions. Clive Barnes was one such example, for which see Siegel, p. 46–47.

Sara Rudner and "breathless heat": Tharp, *Push*, p. 184.

Tharp, wanting to be a filmmaker: Comments made by Tharp at ADF in 1999.

Tom Rawe and "floppy" style: Quoted by Robertson, "Twyla Tharp," p. 70.

Fred Astaire the model for male role in *Push Comes to Shove*: Tharp, *Push*, p. 218.

Push Comes to Shove: I refreshed my memory of this dance by looking at a tape of it and at the summary given it in Nancy Reynolds and Susan Reimer-Torn, *Dance Classics: A Viewer's Guide to the Best-Loved Ballets and Modern Dance* (1980, 1991), p. 283–285.

Tharp on "greatness": Wendy Perron interview, "Tharp: Still Pushing the Boundaries," *Dance Magazine* (March 2001), p. 46.

Tharp, Stiefel, "scumbag": Harris Green, "ABT's Method Dance," *Dance Magazine* (November 1999), p. 57.

Jowitt on *Deuce Coupe*: Quoted in Tharp, *Push*, p. 185.

The Bix Pieces and "Aesthetics and ethics are the same": Reprinted in Selma Jeanne Cohen, *Dance as a Theatre Art: Source Readings in Dance History From 1581 to the Present* (1974, 1992), p. 230.

In The Upper Room and "power women": Tharp, *Push*, p. 304, 306, 307.

"impulse to counterpoise dual elements": Tharp, *Push*, p. 301.

Jowitt's "seriously funny": I think Deborah Jowitt's locution "seriously funny" for Tharp's works occurs in another place, but her point is phrased only slightly differently in her *The Dance* (1985), in responding to Tharp's *When We Were Very Young* (1980).

Jean Baudrillard: See his interview in *Flash Art* (October/November 1986), p. 54–55.

Tharp on *Baker's Dozen*: Tharp, *Push*, p. 245–247.

The Catherine Wheel: I recommend for analysis/description of this dance what Marcia Siegel writes in *The Tail of the Dragon* (1991), p. 157–160, 182–183. This book includes other excellent discussions of Tharp's dances.

"My Life and Times in Jazz": Lecture given by Tharp at ADF 2000.

Motives for *Nine Sinatra Songs*: Tharp, *Push*, p. 270.

"easier to follow": Tharp, *Push*, p. 274.

Disperse (1967) reference: Tharp, *Push*, p. 101–102.

Jam (1967) reference: According to Sara Rudner's recollections, in *Robertson*, p. 72.

Like Rudolph Nureyev, "rooted in folk dance": Tharp, *Push*, p. 326.

Tharp on *In the Upper Room*: Tharp, *Push*, p. 306.

A Letter (December '01)

Louise Steinman, *The Knowing Body: The Artist as Storyteller in Performance* (1995), p. 12. This fine book, besides its insights on Trisha Brown and Meredith Monk, is a highly original commentary/intepretation of modern dance and contemporary performance art.

Johannes Birringer, *Theatre, Theory, Postmodernism* (1991). This is a stimulating look at Pina Bausch and the contemporary scene. See especially p. 132–146.

Ann Daly, "The Balanchine Woman: Of Humming Birds and Channel Swmmers," *The Drama Review* (Spring 1987), p. 8–22.

Judith Lynne Hanna, "Patterns of Dominance: Men, Women, and Homosexuality in Dance," *The Drama Review* (Spring 1987), p. 22–48.

Pilobolus

Croce on *Shizen*: Arlene Croce, *Going to the Dance* (1982), p. 51.

Jowitt on *Molly's Not Dead*: Deborah Jowitt, *Time and the Dancing Image* (1988), p. 365.

New York 1972 performance: See Jack Anderson's review of this first New York City performance by Pilobolus at The Space, in *Dance Magazine*, January 1973, p. 79–80.

"It began as an all-male": On Pilobolus beginnings, see Iris Fanger, "Pilobolus," in *Dance Magazine* (July 1974), p. 38–42; see also Elvi Moore, "Talking with Pilobolus," *Dance Scope* (Spring/Summer 1976), p. 56–66.

The beginnings and Pilobolus historical record are covered by Johnathan Wolken, Robby Barnett, and Michael Tracy in an ADF video-interview, with Charles Reinhart, in 1996.

For the best photos of Pilobolus up to 1978, that illustrate some of the desciptions offered in our discussion, see Tim Matson, *Pilobolus* (1978). See also Deborah Jowitt, *Time and the Dancing Image* (1988), p. 362, for a description of the film made in 1973 of Pilobolus – *Pilobolus and Joan*, by Ed Emshwiller.

Martha Clarke, "fantasy piece," etc.: See Iris Fanger, *Dance Magazine* (July 1974), p. 40.

Brustein on Clarke: Robert Brustein, *The New Republic* (February 16, 1985), p. 26.

Alison Chase, "set modern dance back ten years": Remarks by Chase at ADF 1991.

Praises for *Untitled*: Judith Lynne Hanna, *Dance, Sex and Gender* (1988), p. 199.

On *Ritualistic Day Two*: See Hanna, *Dance, Sex*, p. 214. See also Jennifer Dunning, "Women Depicted in Dance Come in Many Guises Today," *The New York Times* (September 9, 1984).

"six radios, all on different stations": Quoted in Martha Bremser, ed., *Fifty Contemporary Choreographers* (1999), p. 193.

Robby Barnett's remarks on merits of collaborative choreography: Made at 1991 ADF talk.

Jonathan Wolken, "stumbling forward": Comments made at 1999 ADF talk.

"inability to agree on title for *Untitled*": Robby Barnett comments at 1991 ADF talk.

Chase's *Monkey and the White Bone Demon*: See the favorable review of this dance by Anna Kisselgoff, *The New York Times* (July 5, 2001).

Day Two "as seen by one observer": See Elizabeth Zimmer's "mixed" review of this dance, *Dance Magazine* (May 1982), p. 149–150.

The success of *Return to Maria La Baja*: Review by Sally R. Sommer, *Dance Magazine* (June 1985), p. 20–21.

Wolken on *Aeros*: 1996 ADF interview with Charles Reinhart.

See Jack Anderson's reviews of *A Selection* and *Davenen* in *The New York Times*, July 7, 1999 and July 4, 2001, respectively.

On the issue of anti-Semitism, see Iris Dorbian, "Choreography's Mind-body Problem," *Forward* (December 1, 2000). See also Jennifer Dunning "Gimmicks and Games to Create Dancegoers," *The New York Times* (July 6, 2001).

Tobi Tobias 1994 review: In *New York Magazine* (July 18, 1994), p. 55.

Joan Acocella on Pina Bausch: In *The New Yorker* (January 14, 2002), p. 80–82.

Whether ambiguity is good or not: Consistent with what they have said on other occasions, the Pils and especially Jonathan Wolken emphasized in June 2000 ADF talk how they work for a tension between specificity and ambiguity, how in the end they aim for the kind of mix that tilts toward ambiguity.

Dunning review of *Sweet Dreams*: See Jennifer Dunning's review, *The New York Times* (June 30, 2000). See also Susan Broili's review in *The [Durham] Herald-Sun* (June 17, 2000). I owe her review my reference here to the song "Lullaby and Goodnight."

Wolken, "you can create a multi-personality": Johnathan Wolken in talk at 1996 ADF.

Tharp, metaphor, her quoting Joyce Carol Oates: See Twyla Tharp, *Push* (1992), p. 250.

Did it not take me too far afield, I would have discussed here the philosopher Francis Sparshott's way of looking at gymnastics vs. dance. He quotes T.S. Eliot's claim that whereas acrobatics appeals to the mind (judging the skill required), dancing appeals to the senses, to immediate appreciation rather than to judgement. Responding to this would be too lengthy for inclusion here; so would it be to Sparshott's writing that "Gymnastics lacks metaphor. What you see is what you get.... Gymnastics comprises movements of body; dance comprises movements of a person." See Francis Sparshott, *Off the Ground: First Steps to a Philosophical Consideration of the Dance* (1988), p. 321–323.

Pilobolus, variety of music, "fitting" the choreography: Jonathan Wolken explained at length the "painstaking" process used to "fit" the music to the dance, at 1999 ADF talk.

Current and future projects: Information here taken from *News of Pilobolus Dance Theatre* (No. 11, Fall/Winter, 2001–2002).

Bill T. Jones

"The Blob" See Bill. T. Jones's autobiography (with Peggy Gillespie), *Last Night on Earth* (1995), p. 37.

"His career": Henry L. Gates's *The New Yorker* (November 21, 1994) profile of Jones contains some biographical facts not included in Jones's own *Last Night on Earth*. See also Donald Hutera's review of Jones's career in Martha Bremser, ed., *Fifty Contemporary Choreographers* (1999), p. 123–128. The many interviews of Jones over the years tend to cite the same prominent facts though occasionally yielding a novelty.

Jones and Zane, careers described: For examples of such descriptions, see Burt Supree, "The Daily Fact of Absence," in *Body Against Body: The Dance and Other Collaborations of Bill T. Jones and Arnie Zane*, eds. Elizabeth Zimmer and Susan Quasha (1989), p. 123–125. This is the best collection of texts, essays, and photos. And see Julinda Lewis, "Making Dances From the Soul," *Dance Magazine* (November 1981), p. 70–71. See also the interviews with Jones by Ann Daly and Thelma Golden in *Art Performs Life: Merce Cunningham, Meredith Monk, and Bill T. Jones*, Walker Art Center (1998), p. 118–136. Also, on Zane's legacy, see Ann Daly, "Turning A Photographer's Vision Into Choreography," *The New York Times* (June 27, 1999), p. 28–29.

"surprising those who assumed because 'black' therefore a 'natural' dancer": Jones, *Last Night*, p. 99, 107.

Influences on Jones: See sources mentioned above. See also, regarding Contact Improvisation, Cynthia Novack, *Sharing the Dance: Contact Improvisation and American Culture* (1990), p. 75, 110, 149, 178.

"Harbored doubts about showbiz": Jones, *Last Night*, p. 107, 115, 151.

Banes review of *Intuitive Momentum*: Sally Banes's review, *Dance Magazine* (June 1983), p. 36.

"I have made dancing a partner to language": Jones, *Last Night*, p. 108.

"Who knew that a body could talk?": Jones, *Last Night*, p. 65.

Siegel on *Floating the Tongue*: Marcia Siegel, *The Tail of the Dragon: New Dance, 1976–1982* (1991), p. 65–66.

Jones on *Floating the Tongue*, and Croce: Jones, *Last Night*, p. 140–141.

Jones/Zane *Tension*: In addition to Jones's *Last Night*, see Ann Daly interview with Jones in *Art Performs Life*, p. 119.

Fever Swamp: For the origin of this dance's title and Arlene Croce's influence, see Jones, *Last Night*, p. 165–166.

Donna Perlmutter review: In *Dance Magazine* (August 1983), p. 36–37.

Jones/Zane autobiographical trilogy: The first section of the trilogy was *Monkey Run Road* (1979) and the third was *Valley Cottage* (1981). See Julinda Lewis, "Making Dances from the Soul," *Dance Magazine* (November 1981), p. 70–71, for a description of their performance of *Valley Cottage*.

Blauvelt Mountain, a "landmark work": See Zimmer and Quasha, *Body Against Body*, p. 62–63 (with photos). See also Deborah Jowitt's upbeat remarks about *Blauvelt Mountain*, that contrast with Perlmutter's, in *Body Against Body*, p. 62.

"truly beautiful homoerotic work": Jones, *Last Night*, p. 48; see also p. 145–149 for Jones's fuller analysis of *Blauvelt Mountain*, etc.

Social Intercourse and "a farewell wave to the minimalism of the Seventies": For the changes perceived by Jones between the 70s and 80s, see his *Last Night*, p. 161 ff. See also his "frankly" expressed reservations, at a 1983 panel, about the "postmodernism" of the 60s and 70s, as quoted by Cynthia J. Novack, *Sharing the Dance* (1990), p. 224–225. Jones recalls that when he first met Alvin Ailey, whom he much admired, he asked Ailey for his opinion of "postmodern" choreographers. Ailey replied, "I like them when they dance," and Jones seems to have joined Ailey in that sentiment.

Social Intercourse: See Jones's own illuminating description of the work in *Last Night*, p. 163–164.

1981 solo, "contradiction after another": Jones, *Last Night*, p. 165.

1983—Jones, Primus, and Black Dance: See Henry L. Gates, Jr., *The New Yorker* (November 21, 1994), p. 123.

Lynn Garafola review of *Absence*: In *Dance Magazine* (July 1989), p. 54–55. Jack Anderson's article "Portraits of Gay Men with No Apologies", though not referring to Bill T. Jones, is of interest here; in *The New York Times* (January 10, 1993).

"others regretted the perceived absence of diversity among the women": See Ann Cooper Albright, *Choreographing Differences: The Body and Identity in Contemporary Dance* (1997), p. 72. ("Even companies such as the Bill T. Jones and Arnie Zane Dance Company who pride themselves on the diversity of their dancers, rarely have much variation among the women dancers (all of whom are quite slim).")

Freedom of Information on "endurance dance": See Ann Daly interview, *Art Performs Life*, p. 121. Also see Jones, *Last Night*, p. 168 ff.

Secret Pastures: See photos in Zimmer and Quasha, *Body Against Body*, Deborah Jowitt quoted in *Last Night*, p. 173, and Jones's comments on same page.

For a "social" interpretation of *Sweet Pastures*, see Donald Hutera, in Martha Bremser, ed., *Fifty Contemporary Choreographers* (1999), p. 124.

How to Walk an Elephant: For more on this dance, including one critic's negative reaction, see Jones, *Last Night*, p. 166–167. See also for an interesting gloss on this dance, including its gender-role implications, Judith Lynne Hanna, *Dance, Sex and Gender* (1988), p. 234–235. See also Hanna's comments about Jones's *Shared Distance* (1981), p.212. See also Ann Daly, "Classical Ballet: Discourse of Difference," in Jane C. Desmond, ed., *Meaning in Motion: New Cultural Studies in Dance* (1997), p.117.

Deborah Jowitt praising "the air of intellectual engagement": In her *The Dance* (1985), p. 190.

The quote by Gates, "To all his projects": In his *The New Yorker* profile of Jones (1994), p. 114.

Mother's praying and "are not interpretations": For this, see Ann Daly interview in *Art Performs Life*, p. 122.

Out Some Place, "holding cocktail glasses": "Dances have to mean something," Jones stated in a pre-performance talk at ADF 1997, adding that choreographers need to give their audiences "pathways" to the meanings. So, as said to interviewer Shayna Samuels, the cocktail glasses, etc. are such a "pathway." Samuels interview in *Dance Magazine* (May 1999), p. 22.

Anna Kisselgoff review of *Ursonate*: "A Dadaist Display For Eyes And Ears," in *The New York Times* (June 13, 1996). On "meaningful nonsense" that connects here, see John Lowney, "Langston Hughes and the 'Nonsense' of Bebop," in *American Literature* (June 2000), p. 357–385.

Pamela Sommers on *Ursonate*: In *The Washington Post* (April 15, 1996). For more on the movement features of *Ursonate*, see Deborah Jowitt's review, *Village Voice* (July 2, 1996).

Juilliard School commencement photo: In *The New York Times* (May 22, 1999).

Rotary Action: For a vivid sense of this piece's physicality, see the photos in Zimmer and Quasha, *Body Against Body*.

Zane's death and Jones on "becoming a black/gay artist": Jones's comments occured in an interview with Eric K. Washington, "Sculpture in Flight: A Conversation with Bill T. Jones," *Transition* (no. 62, 1992), p. 191–194.

Jones's comments are quoted, where I found them, in Marcie Wallace's essay, "The Autochoreography of an Ex-Snow Queen: Dance, Desire and the Black Masculine in Melvin Dixon's Vanishing Rooms," in *Novel Gazing: Queer Readings in Fiction*, ed. Eve Kosovsky Sedgwick (1997), p. 379–400. This is recommended reading, for what it says about the similarity of Melvin Dixon's novel to Jones's life, and for its surrounding insightful observations.

"Now I do say that I am a Black artist": Said by Jones at panel discussion at Black Choreographers Moving Toward the 21st Century (BCM) Festival, November 1989, quoted in *Black Choreographers Moving*, compiled by Halifu Osumare and edited by Julinda Lewis-Ferguson (1991), p. 95.

On *Last Supper at Uncle Tom's Cabin/The Promised Land* and the questions it is meant to raise, see Jones, *Last Night*, p. 209. My description of this work owes much to *Last Night*, p. 197–223.

"my profound sense of belonging": See, Jones, *Last Night*, p. 223.

"Communal nature of *Cabin* was 'revolutionary'": Jones, *Last Night*, p. 251.

The piece "piques intellectual interest": See, as examples of scholarly interest in *Last Supper at Uncle Tom's Cabin*, Jacqueline Shea Murphy, "Unrest and Uncle Tom: Bill T. Jones/Arnie Zane

Dance Company's *Last Supper at Uncle Tom's Cabin/The Promised Land*," in *Bodies of the Text: Dance as Theory, Literature as Dance*, eds. Ellen W. Goellner and Jacqueline Shea Murphy (1995), p. 81–107; and Randy Martin, "Overreading The Promised Land: Toward a Narrative of Context in Dance," in his *Critical Moves: Dance Studies in Theory and Politics* (1998), p. 55–107. This essay had appeared earlier in Susan Leigh Foster, ed., *Corporealities* (1996), p. 177–199.

For more on Survival Workshops, see Jones, *Last Night*, p. 252–253.

My description of *Still/Here* owes much if not most to Jones, *Last Night*, p. 249–268.

"He told to a journalist about *Still/Here*": Told to Terry Truco in interview, "Bold Work that Honors Survival," in *The New York Times* (November 27, 1994).

Still/Here and critical responses: Reviews of the piece seem to have been generally favorable from high to moderate praise, including those in *Village Voice*, *The New York Times*, and *New York Magazine*.

Croce on *Still/Here*: See Arlene Croce, *Writing In the Dark: Dancing in The New Yorker* (2000), p. 708–709. Her original article "Discussing the Undiscussabble" appears here, p. 708–719.

Croce on McKayle and Ailey: See Croce, *Writing in the Dark*, p. 22–29.

Croce's "I do not remember a time when": Croce, *Writing in the Dark*, p. 719.

"Recent prominent works by Jones": Reviews of these works are readily available, but it may help to note that *The Table Project* is reviewed by Jennifer Dunning, *The New York Times* (May 15, 2001). And for Jones's new focus on beauty, see Kevin Giordano "Discussing Beauty with Bill T. Over Tea," *Dance Magazine* (October 1998), p. 36. Also, in a similar vein, see Wendy Perron, "Bill T. Searches for Beauty, and a New Home [i.e., in Harlem]," *The New York Times* (January 27, 2002).

Jones's shift to "a more contemplative posture": See, for what "contemplative" seems to mean more fully for Jones, his short article about his garden and its significance for him, "The Ground Beneath His Feet" (with photos by Marilyn Thompson) in *Talk* magazine (August 2000), p. 106–107.

Jones and authenticity: Jones, *Last Night*, p. 245.

Rev. Butts and Jones: See Irene Sturla, "How Do People Create?", in *Attitude: The Dancer's Magazine* (Spring 2000), p. 5. Notes taken by a friend of mine, attending the session, agree with Sturla's account of the Jones and Rev. Butts discussion, including the maternal "spiritual" influence on Jones that is also vividly described throughout *Last Night on Earth*.

Sysiphus: For more on this dance, see Jones's comments in interview with Julinda Lewis, "Making Dances from the Soul," *Dance Magazine* (November 1981), p. 70–71.

Note: I have resisted here (as I have throughout these jottings though not wholly successfully) the (strong) temptation to name other contemporary dancers (and writers, scholars, critics, teachers, etc.) who naturally come to mind when writing about Bill T. Jones and his interests in autobiography, black identity, the black tradition in modern dance, gay artistry, etc. But merely mentioning names, however well-intentioned, seems to me to be a disservice. Better unmentioned than to be found on a laundry list. For more on African American connections, however, I do refer the reader to the recent and excellent book, *African-American Concert Dance: The Harlem Renaissance and Beyond* (with full bibliography), by John O. Perpener, III (2001).

A Letter (January '02)

Terry Teachout, "When a Full-Time Critic Keeps His Opinions to Himself," *The Chronicle of Higher Education* (March 13, 1998), p. 86; also Terry Teachout, "Dance Chronicle: Going A Lot to the Mark Morris Dance Group," *Partisan Review* (Spring 2000), p. 283.

A Second Letter (April '02)

Maureen Howard, "The Enduring Commitment of a Faithful Storyteller" (in "Writers on Writing" series), *The New York Times* (Feburary 14, 2000), p. 1–2.

Edwin Denby, *Looking at the Dance* (1968), p. 24 ff.

Qualities of movement and Isadora Duncan: For an interesting discussion of issues here, and that indirectly relate to Maureen Howard's observations, see Iris Fanger's "Fixing in Language a Ceaseless Flow," *The New York Times* (November 19, 2000). My remarks here on Duncan and quotes are based on Fanger's article.

Paula Marantz Cohen, *Silent Film and The Triumph of the American Myth* (2001). See Edward Rothstein's discussion of the book, *The New York Times* (June 12, 2001).

Peanuts, etc.: See George Saunders's "Strip Mind," *The New York Times Magazine* (January 7, 2001), p. 52–53.

On Helen Tamiris and the *Promised Land*: Unfortunately I have misplaced my source for the data here but am confident, because of how it has been recorded, that I have it here true to its source. I *think* the information may have been on a Salt Lake City brochure of some sort.

"Explosion" of modern dance: The comparative numbers for 1965 and 1999 were supplied by the dance service organization, *Dance/USA*.

Bernard Holland on Pierre Boulez and Scriabin: Bernard Holland, "Music: Translating a Language of Ecstasy," *The New York Times* (August 8, 1999).

On Maguy Marin and *Waterzooi*: For a more positive and fuller response to this work, see Anna Kisselgoff's aptly titled "A Philosopher's Words Translated Into Action," *The New York Times* (July 25, 1994).

Jack Anderson's review of Jasperse's *Waving to You From Here*, in *The New York Times* (April 29, 1997).

On Klimt's "Philosophy": See Hilarie M. Sheets, "Books in Brief" column, *The New York Times* (October 28, 2001) (review of Colin B. Bailey's *Gustav Klimt: Modernism in the Making*).

A Third Letter (April '02)

Arlene Croce, quoted by Terry Teachout, "Art For Pleasure's Sake," his review of Croce's *Writing in the Dark*, in *The New York Times* (November 19, 2000).

Anna Kisselgoff's review of Forsythe's *Woolf Phrase*, in *The New York Times* (December 17, 2001).

John Lahr, "Gotta Dance," *The New Yorker* (October 18 and 25, 1999), p. 239–240.

Edwin Denby, "Against Meaning in Ballet," in *Looking At The Dance* (1968), p. 31.

Edwin Denby, on "creative and critical viewpoints" with comments made by Don McDonagh, Arlene Croce, and Georges Dorris: "A Conversation with Edwin Denby," *Ballet Review* (vol. 2, no. 5, 1969) (the "conversation" includes Don McDonagh, Arlene Croce, and George Dorris).

Herbert Muscamp, on meaning in architecture: "Filling the Void: a Chance to Soar," *The New York Times* (September 30, 2001).

Elizabeth Murray: Reported and quoted by Michael Kimmelman in his *Portraits: Talking With Artists at the Met, the Modern, the Louvre, and Elsewhere* (1998), p. 26.

A Fourth Letter (April '02)

Ken Johnson, art review: "For Those In Search of Calm, an Armory Full of Modernists," *The New York Times* (February 22, 2002).

Russell Ferguson on O'Hara and Johns: In Ferguson's *In Memory of My Feelings: Frank O'Hara and American Art* (1999), p. 133.

Sandra Blakeslee: See the intriguing brief article, "What is It with Mona Lisa's Smile? It's You," *The New York Times* (November 21, 2000).

Jack Anderson's pieces "What Touches the Heart" and "Puzzles in Dance That Tickle the Imagination" appear in *The New York Times*, August 10, 1997 and August 16, 1992, respectively.

Bernard Holland on Maderna's music: "The Language of Postwar Composers," *The New York Times* (November 25, 1995).

"made to *think*": Michael Kimmelman, art review, *The New York Times* (February 14, 1997).

Denby on *Herodiade*: In his *Looking at the Dance* (1968), p. 322–323. After connecting with Denby here, I wanted to compare what others might have said about *Herodiade* and in process came upon Deborah Jowitt's citing and praising the first of my two Denby quotes here. I'm naturally pleased to find myself in such distinguished company. See Deborah Jowitt, *Time and the Dancing Image* (1988), p.212.

P.S.

Holland Cotter on Steiner: "The Puzzling Road Maps of a Philosopher's Mind," *The New York Times* (March 13, 1998).

Makarova and spirituality: Natalia Makarova, *A Dance Autobiography* (1980). This is reviewed by Gabrielle Annan, *Times Literary Supplement* (April 4, 1998), p. 386. I take Makarova's statement as quoted by Annan.

Toni Bentley, "What's Wrong With Degas?", in *Art and Antiques* (November 1987), p. 70–75, 126.

Marsden Hartley: See Townsend Ludington, *Seeking the Spiritual: The Paintings of Marsden Hartley* (1998), p. 78.

Sources

"A Party at the Plaza, Dance Magazine's Annual Award Party." Transcript of the award ceremony. Plaza Hotel. April 22, 1968. *Dance Magazine* June 1968. Photos by Jack Mitchell.

Acocella, Joan. On Pina Bausch. In *The New Yorker* January 14, 2002: 80–82.

Albright, Ann Cooper. *Choreographing Differences: The Body and Identity in Contemporary Dance.* Middletown, CT: Wesleyan University Press, 1997.

Allen, Lewis. *Strange Fruit* (1939). Performed by Billie Holiday. New York, 1948.

Aloff, Mindy. On Graham Technique. *The New Republic* 11 September 1995: 30 ff.

"Alwin In Wonderland." *Time Magazine* 20 May 1966.

Anderson, Jack. "Choreographic Fox: Paul Taylor." *Dance Magazine* April 1980: 68–74.

Anderson, Jack. *Choreography Observed.* Iowa City: University of Iowa Press, 1987.

Anderson, Jack. "Dark Theme Ushers In Pilobolus." Rev. of *A Selection*, by Robby Barnett, Michael Tracy, and Jonathan Wolken. *The New York Times* 7 July 1999.

Anderson, Jack. "Introduction." In *The Dance in Theory*. By John Martin. Princeton: Princeton Book Co., 1965, 1989.

Anderson, Jack. "Portraits of Gay Men with No Apologies." *The New York Times* 10 January 1993.

Anderson, Jack. "Puzzles in Dance That Tickle the Imagination." *The New York Times* 10 August 1997.

Anderson, Jack. Rev. of Pilobolus's first New York City performance at The Space 1972. *Dance Magazine* January 1973: 79–80.

Anderson, Jack. Rev. of *Waving to You From Here*, by John Jasperse. *The New York Times* 29 April 1997.

Anderson, Jack. "Spiritual Ecstasy and Klezmer Frenzy." Rev. of *Davenen*, by Robby Barnett and Jonathan Wolken. *The New York Times* 4 July 2001.

Anderson, Jack. *The American Dance Festival.* Durham: Duke University Press, 1987.

Anderson, Jack. "What Touches the Heart Can Puzzle the Mind." Rev. of Trisha Brown and Angelin Preljocaj. *The New York Times* 16 August 1992.

Balanchine, George and Francis Mason. *Balanchine's Complete Stories of Great Ballets.* Garden City, NY: Doubleday & Co., Inc., 1977.

Banes, Sally. Rev. of *Intuitive Momentum. Dance Magazine* June 1983: 36.

Banes, Sally. *Terpsichore in Sneakers: post-modern dance.* Boston: Houghton Miffliin, 1980.

Barber, Beverly Hillsman. "Pearl Primus: Rebuilding America's Cultural Infrastructure." In *African American Genius in Modern Dance*. Ed. Gerald E. Myers. Durham: American Dance Festival, 1993. 9–12.

Barnes, Clive. "The Ultimate in Bare Stages." *The New York Times* 24 April 1967.

Barnes, Clive. "Modern Goes Classic—and Vice Versa; Dance." On Erick Hawkins. *The New York Times* 17 June 1973.

Barnes, Clive. "The Problem of Hawkins." *The New York Times* 21 March 1971.

Barnett, Robby. Comments at ADF talk. Durham, NC. 26 June 1991.

Baudrillard, Jean. Interview with Twyla Tharp. *Flash Art* October/November 1986: 54–55.

Beaumont, Cyrill. *A Miscellany for Dancers.* London: C.W. Beaumont, 1934.

Bentley, Eric. *What is Theatre?.* Boston: Beacon Press, 1956.

Bentley, Toni. "What's Wrong With Degas?" *Art and Antiques* November 1987: 70–75, 126.

Blakeslee, Sandra. "What is It with Mona Lisa's Smile? It's You." *The New York Times* 21 November 2000.

Birringer, Johannes. *Theatre, Theory, Postmodernism.* Bloomington: Indiana University Press, 1991.

Broili, Susan. Rev. of *Sweet Dreams. The [Durham] Herald-Sun* 17 June 2000.

Brown, Beverly. "Training to Dance with Erick Hawkins." In *Erick Hawkins: Theory and Training.* By Richard Lorber. New York: American Dance Guild, 1979.

Brown, Jean Morrison, ed. *The Vision of Modern Dance.* Hightstown: Princeton Book Co., 1979.

Brown, Trisha. Remarks made at ADF talks in 1997. Durham, NC.

Brown, Trisha. "Trisha Brown: An Interview." In *The 20th Century Performance Reader.* Ed. Michael Huxley and Noel Witts, London: Routledge, 1996: 119–128.

Brown, Trisha and A. Livet. "Trisha Brown." Edited Transcript of an Interview with Trisha Brown." In *Contemporary Dance.* Ed. A. Livet. New York: Abbeville, 1978: 44–54.

Brown, Trisha and Lisa Brunel. *Trisha Brown.* Paris: Editions Bougé, 1987.

Brown, Trisha and Schönberg, "You can't just use." Interview at ADF in 1993. Durham, NC.

Brownstone, David and Irene Franck. *Timelines of the 20th Century: A Chronology of 7,500 Key Events, Discoveries, and People that Shaped Our Century.* Boston: Little, Brown, 1996.

Brustein, Robert. Rev. of Martha Clarke. *The New Republic* 16 February 1985: 26.

Cage, John. *Silence.* Middletown, CT: Wesleyan University Press, 1961.

Cash, Debra. "The New Wave in Modern Dance." *Saturday Review* March 1982: 34–38.

Castle, Irene and Vernon. *Modern Dancing.* New York: The World Syndicate Co., published by arrangement with Harper & Brothers, 1914.

Chase, Alison. Remarks by Chase at ADF in 1991. Durham, NC.

Chazin-Bennahum, Judith. *The Ballets of Antony Tudor: Studies In Psyche and Satire.* New York: Oxford University Press, 1994.

Cohen, Paula Marantz. *Silent Film and The Triumph of the American Myth.* New York: Oxford University Press, 2001.

Cohen, Selma Jeanne, ed. *International Encyclopedia of Dance: A Project of Dance Perspectives Foundation, Inc.* New York: Oxford University Press, 1998, 2003.

Coleman, Emily. "Martha Graham Still Leaps Forward." *New York Times Magazine* 9 April 1961.

Coleman, Robert. Rev. of Martha Graham's *Clytemnestra. New York Mirror* 2 April 1958.

Copeland, Rodger. "The 'Post-Modern' Choreography of Trisha Brown." *The New York Times* 4 January 1976.

Cotter, Holland. "The Puzzling Road Maps of a Philosopher's Mind." *The New York Times* 13 March 1998.

Cowell, Henry. "Cage's method of employing the I Ching." In *John Cage: An Anthology.* Ed. Richard Kostelanetz, New York: Da Capo Press, 1968, 1991.

Croce, Arlene. *Afterimages.* New York: Knopf, 1977.

Croce, Arlene. *Going to the Dance.* New York: Knopf: Distributed by Random House, 1982.

Croce, Arlene. *Writing In the Dark: Dancing in The New Yorker.* New York: Farrar, Straus and Giroux, 2000.

Crowther, Paul. *The Language of Twentieth-Century Art: A Conceptual History.* New Haven: Yale University Press, 1997.

Cunningham, Merce, Meredith Monk and Bill T. Jones. *Art Performs Life: Merce Cunningham/ Meredith Monk/Bill T. Jones.* New York: Walker Art Center, 1998.

Daly, Ann. "Classical Ballet: Discourse of Difference." In *Meaning in Motion: New Cultural Studies in Dance.* Ed. Jane C. Desmond. Durham: Duke University Press, 1997: 117.

Daly, Ann. *Done Into Dance: Isadora Duncan in America.* Bloomington: Indiana University Press, 1995.

Daly, Ann "The Balanchine Woman: Of Humming Birds and Channel Swimmers." *The Drama Review* Spring 1987: 8–22.

Daly, Ann. "Turning A Photographer's Vision Into Choreography." Rev. of *Continuous Replay: The Photographs of Arnie Zane,* by Arnie Zane. *The New York Times* 27 June 1999: 28–29.

Dance Women/Living Legends (n.d.), produced by 651, An Arts Center; Aaron Davis Hall; and New Jersey Performing Arts Center.

Daniels, Don. "Paul Taylor and the Post-Moderns." *Ballet Review* Summer 1981: 66–83.

Danspace Project—25 Years. Photo by Tom Brazil. New York: Danspace Project, 1999: 63.

Davis, Douglas M. Interview with Martha Graham. *The National Observer*, 30 December 1968: 18.

De Mille, Agnes. *Martha: The Life and Work of Martha Graham.* New York: Random House, 1956, 1991.

Dempster, Elizabeth. "Women Writing the Body: Let's Watch a Little How She Dances." In *Bodies of the Text: Dance as Theory, Literature as Dance.* By Ellen W. Goellner and Jacqueline Shea Murphy, eds. New Brunswick, NJ: Rutgers University Press, 1995: 21–28.

Denby, Edwin. "Against Meaning in Ballet." In *Looking At The Dance.* New York: Horizon Press, 1968.

Denby, Edwin. *Looking At The Dance.* New York: Horizon Press, 1968.

Denby, Edwin. "A Conversation with Edwin Denby." *Ballet Review* vol. 2, no. 5, 1969.

Dlugoszewski, Lucia. On Northrop and Asian thought at American Dance Festival talk. Durham, NC.

Dorbian, Iris. "Choreography's Mind-body Problem." *Forward* 1 December 2000.

Dorris, George. "Meredith Monk." In *Fifty Contemporary Choreographers.* Ed. Martha Bremser. New York: Routledge, 1999.

Duncan, Irma. "Isadora Duncan—Pioneer in the Art of Dance." *Dance Magazine* June 1969: 55.

Dunning, Jennifer. "A Cityscape So Wondrous Strange." *The New York Times* 30 June 2000.

Dunning, Jennifer. "Dance Notes." *The New York Times* 3 September 2001.

Dunning, Jennifer. "Gimmicks and Games to Create Dancegoers; People Aren't Born Loving Pas de Deux, So the Art of Persuasion Grows Complex." *The New York Times* 6 July 2001.

Dunning, Jennifer. "Who Needs Training? Nondancers Make a Case." *The New York Times* 15 May 2001.

Dunning, Jennifer. "Women Depicted in Dance Come in Many Guises Today." *The New York Times* 9 September 1984.

Fagan, Joen and Irma Lee Sheperd, eds., *What is Gestalt Therapy?* New York: Harper & Row, 1970.

Fanger, Iris. "Fixing in Language a Ceaseless Flow." *The New York Times* 19 November 2000.

Fanger, Iris. "Pilobolus." *Dance Magazine* July 1974: 38–42.

Fanger, Iris. Rev. of Martha Clarke. *Dance Magazine* July 1974: 40.

Feingold, Michael. "Momentary Musicals." *Village Voice* 16 November 1998.

Ferguson, Russell. In *Memory of My Feelings: Frank O'Hara and American Art.* Los Angeles: Museum of Contemporary Art, 1999.

Foster, Susan Leigh, ed. *Corporealities: Dancing, Knowledge, Culture and Power.* New York: Routledge, 1996.

Foster, Susan Leigh. *Reading Dancing: Bodies and Subjects in Contemporary American Dance.* Berkeley: University of California, 1986.

Franko, Mark. "Some Notes on Yvonne Rainer, Modernism, Politics, Emotion, Performance, and the Aftermath." In *Meaning in Motion: New Cultural Studies of Dance.* Ed. Jane Desmond Durham: Duke University Press, 1997: 289–304.

Free to Dance: The African American Presence in Modern Dance. Dir. Madison Davis Lacy. PBS. American Dance Festival, The John F. Kennedy Center for the Performing Arts, and Thirteen/WNET, New York. June 2001.

Gans, Deborah. "Table Talk: A Discussion of Michael Graves' Set for the Ballet Fire." *The Princeton Journal: Thematic Studies in Architecture, Ritual,* vol. 1 (1983): 58.

Garafola, Lynn. Rev. of *Absence. Dance Magazine* July 1989: 54–55.

Garfunkel, Trudy. *Letter to the World: The Life and Dances of Martha Graham.* Boston: Little, Brown and Company, 1995.

Gates, Jr., Henry L. On Jones, Primus, and Black Dance. *The New Yorker* 21 November 1994: 114 & 123.

Gilfond, Henry. "Foreword." In *Pre-Classic Dance Forms*. By Louis Horst. New York: Kamin Dance Publishers, 1953.

Giordano, Kevin. "Discussing Beauty with Bill T. Over Tea." *Dance Magazine* October 1998: 36.

Gitelman, Claudia. *Dancing With Principle: Hanya Holm in Colorado, 1941–1983*. Boulder, CO: University Press of Colorado, 2001.

Gitelman, Claudia. Unpublished notes.

Glenesk, William. "The Still Point." *Dance Magazine* April 1965: 39–40.

Goldberg, Marianne. "Trisha Brown." In *Fifty Contemporary Choreographers*. Ed. Martha Bremser. London & New York: Routledge, 1999.

Gombrich, E.H. *Art and Illusion: A Study In the Psychology of Pictorial Representation*. New York: Pantheon Books, 1960.

Graham, Martha. National Council on the Arts ceremony honoring Graham's 50th choreographic anniversary year. Washington, DC. 15 May 1976.

Graff, Ellen. *Stepping Left: Dance and Politics in New York City, 1928–1942*. Durham: Duke University Press, 1997.

Grauert, Ruth E. "Alwin Nikolais." In *America Dancing* (n.d.), Performing Arts Education Department, The John F. Kennedy Center for the Performing Arts.

Grauert, Ruth E. "Nik's Own Son et Lumière Show." *Dance Magazine* December 1979: 56–69.

Green, Harris. "ABT's Method Dance." *Dance Magazine* November 1999: 57.

Halprin, Anna. *Moving Toward Life: Five Decades of Transformative Dance*. Ed. Rachel Kaplan. Middletown, CT: Wesleyan University Press, 1995.

Hanna, Judith Lynne. *Dance, Sex and Gender: Signs of Identity, Dominance, Defiance, and Desire*. Chicago: University of Chicago Press, 1988.

Hanna, Judith Lynne. "Patterns of Dominance: Men, Women, and Homosexuality in Dance." *The Drama Review* Spring 1987: 22–48.

Harris, William. Interview with Trisha Brown. "Trisha Brown Takes Up the Challenge of Bach." *The New York Times* 16 July 1995.

Harris, Dale & Martha Bremsler. "Twyla Tharp." In *Fifty Contemporary Choreographers*. Ed. Martha Bremser. London & New York: Routledge, 1999: 217–223.

Hartman, Rose. "Talking with Anna Halprin." *Dance Scope* Fall/Winter (1977–78): 61–62.

Hawkins, Erick. "Pure Poetry." In *The Modern Dance: Seven Statements of Belief*. Ed. Selma Jeanne Cohen. Middletown, CT: Wesleyan University Press, 1965, 1966: 39-51.

Hawkins, Erick. *The Body is a Clear Place and Other Statements on Dance*. Pennington, NJ. Princeton Book Co., 1992.

Hay, Deborah. *My Body, the Buddhist*. Hanover, NH: University Press of New England: Wesleyan University Press, 2000.

H'Doubler, Margaret. *Dance: A Creative Experience*. Madison: University of Wisconsin Press, 1940.

Hering, Doirs. On Alwin Nikolais. *Dance Magazine* February 1970: 83–85.

Herridge, Frances, "Martha Graham Dances her 'Night Journey'." *PM* February 1948.

Herridge, Frances. "Meredith Monk Comes to Broadway." *Dance Magazine* 15 February 1969.

Holland, Bernard. "The Language of Postwar Composers." *The New York Times* 25 November 1995.

Holland, Bernard. "Translating a Language of Ecstasy." *The New York Times* 8 August 1999.

Honan, William H. Tomaszewski obituary notice. *The New York Times* 23 October 2001: a21.

Horosko, Marian. *Martha Graham: The Evolution of Her Dance Theory and Training, 1926–1991*. Chicago: A Capella Books, 1991.

Horst, Louis. *Modern Dance Forms in Relation to the Other Modern Arts*. Ed. Caroll Russell. Princeton: Princeton Book Co., 1987, 1961.

How, Elias. *Complete Ball-Room Hand Book*. Boston: A. Williams, 1858.

Howard, Maureen. "The Enduring Commitment of a Faithful Storyteller." In "Writers on Writing" series. *The New York Times* 14 February 2000: 1–2.

Humphrey, Doris. *The Art of Making Dances*. New York: Grove Press, 1959.

Joel, Lydia. "Finding Isadora." *Dance Magazine* June 1969: 51.

Johnson, Ken. "For Those In Search of Calm, an Armory Full of Modernists." *The New York Times* 22 February 2002.

Jones, Bill T. Remarks made at a pre-performance talk at ADF in 1997.

Jones, Bill T. "The Ground Beneath His Feet" (with photos by Marilyn Thompson). In *Talk* August 2000: 106–107.

Jones, Bill T. and Peggy Gillespie. *Last Night on Earth.* New York: Pantheon Books, 1995.

Jowitt, Deborah. "Call If Found." *Village Voice* 18 March 1997.

Jowitt, Deborah. *Meredith Monk.* Baltimore: John Hopkins University Press, 1997.

Jowitt, Deborah. "Not All Explosions are Violent." *Village Voice* 12 June 1978: 67.

Jowitt, Deborah. Rev. of *Ursonate, Village Voice* 2 July 1996.

Jowitt, Deborah. *The Dance In Mind: Profiles and Reviews* 1976–1983. Boston: D.R. Godine, 1985.

Jowitt, Deborah. "The Monumental Martha." *The New York Times* 29 April 1973.

Jowitt, Deborah. *Time and the Dancing Image.* New York: W. Morrow, 1988.

Jowitt, Deborah. Untitled lecture transcripts on radical choreographers of the 1960s and 1970s. *Contemporary Dance.* Ed. Anne Livet. New York: Abbeville Press, 1978.

Juilliard School commencement photo. In *The New York Times* 22 May 1999.

Kastner, Jeffrey. "A Playful Geometer Makes the Complex Seem So Simple." *The New York Times* 3 December 2000.

Kennedy, A.L. *Original Bliss.* New York: Vintage, 1998, 1997.

Kerman, Joseph. *Concerto Conversations.* Cambridge: Harvard University Press, 1999.

Kimmelman, Michael. *Portraits: Talking With Artists at the Met, the Modern, the Louvre, and Elsewhere.* New York: Random House, 1998.

Kimmelman, Michael. Art review. *The New York Times* 14 February 1997.

Kimmelman, Michael. "The Last Great Art of the 20th Century." *The New York Times* 4 February 2001.

Kisselgoff, Anna. "A Classical Approach to the Graham Karma." *The New York Times* 26 October 1999.

Kisselgoff, Anna. "A Dadaist Display For Eyes And Ears." *The New York Times* 13 June 1996.

Kisselgoff, Anna. "A Monkey Saves a Monk, Who Thereby Is Made Wiser." *The New York Times* 5 July 2001.

Kisselgoff, Anna. "A Philosopher's Words Translated Into Action." *The New York Times* 25 July 1994.

Kisselgoff, Anna. "Brainy with a Contemporary Sense of Fun." *The New York Times* 17 December 2001.

Kisselgoff, Anna. Rev. of *Bayadere. The New York Times* 26 October 2000.

Kisselgoff, Anna. "Erick Hawkins, a Pioneering Choreographer of American Dance, Is Dead at 85." *The New York Times* 24 November 1994.

Kisselgoff, Anna. "Ethics and Aesthetics." *The New York Times* 2 February 1995.

Kisselgoff, Anna. "Paul Taylor: Heavy-Duty and Lite." *The New York Times* 13 October 1995.

Kisselgoff Anna. "Trisha Brown: Simplicity Within Complexity." *The New York Times* 3 March 1991.

Koner, Pauline. *Solitary Song.* Durham: Duke University Press, 1989.

Kostelanetz, Richard, ed. *John Cage: An Anthology.* New York: Da Capo Press, 1968, 1991.

Kostelanetz, Richard, ed. *Merce Cunningham: Dancing in Space and Time.* New York: Da Capo Press, 1992.

Kourlas, Gia. Interview with Meredith Monk. "A Verb, Not a Noun." *Dance Magazine* April 1998: 72–75.

Koznin, Allan. Rev. of Monk's music. *The New York Times* 4 November 1999.

Kriegsman, Sali Ann. *Modern Dance in America: The Bennington Years.* Boston: GK Hall, 1981.

Kurth, Peter. *Isadora: A Sensational Life.* Boston: Little, Brown, 2001.

Lahr, John. "Gotta Dance." *The New Yorker* October 18 and 25, 1999: 239–240.

Lewis, Julinda. "Making Dances from the Soul." *Dance Magazine* November 1981: 70–71.

Lloyd, Margaret. *The Borzoi Book of Modern Dance.* New York: Alfred A. Knopf, 1949.

Loewenthal, Lillian. "Isadora Duncan in the Netherlands." *Dance Chronicle* vol. 3, no. 3 1979–1980: 227–253.

Louis, Murray. *Inside Dance: Essays.* New York: St. Martin's Press, 1980.

Louis, Murray. "Thoughts: Murray Louis on Alwin Nikolais." *Dance Magazine* December 1979: 56–65.

Lowney, John. "Langston Hughes and the 'Nonsense' of Bebop." In *American Literature* (June 2000). Ed. Houston Baker. Durham, Duke University Press, 2001. vol. 72, no. 2: 357–385.

Ludington, Townsend. *Seeking the Spiritual: The Paintings of Marsden Hartley.* Ithaca: Cornell University Press, 1998.

Makarova, Natalia. *A Dance Autobiography.* London: A. and C. Black, 1980.

Maletic, Vera. "The Process is the Purpose." *Dance Scope* Fall/Winter (1967–1968): 12.

Manchester, P.W. "Nikolais Equates Dance with Color, Sound, and Design." *Christian Science Monitor* 18 February 1961.

Manning, Susan. "The Female Dancer and the Male Gaze: Feminist Critiques of Early Modern Dance." In *Meaning in Motion: New Cultural Studies of Dance.* Ed. Jane Desmond. Durham: Duke University Press, 1997: 153–166.

Marks, Marcia. Rev. of *Cede Blue Lake* and Tharp choreography. *Dance Magazine* January 1966: 58–59.

Marks, Marcia. "Trisha Brown and Deborah Hay, Judson Memorial Church. March 29, 1966." *Dance Magazine* May 1966: 62–63.

Martha Graham and Her Dance Company, Program Booklet (n.d., circa mid 1950s).

Martha Graham Dance Company Pressbook (n.d., circa 1936). Ed. by concert management Frances Hawkins, publishing Herbert Brodsky.

Martin, John. "Isadora Duncan and Basic Dance." In *Isadora Duncan.* Ed. Paul Magriel. New York: H. Holt & Co., 1947: 8.

Martin, John. "Muscling in-Male Performers and Choreographers Monopolizing the Modern Field." *The New York Times* 17 December 1961.

Martin, John. *The Dance.* New York: Tudor Publishing, 1946.

Martin, John. *The Modern Dance.* New York: A. S. Barnes & Co., 1933.

Martin, John. Rev. of Martha Graham. *The New York Times* 27 May 1928.

Martin, John. Rev. of Martha Graham's performances in 1928. *The New York Times* 13 February 1928.

Martin, Randy. *Critical Moves: Dance Studies in Theory and Politics.* Durham: Duke University Press, 1998.

Maskey, Jacqueline. Rev. of Alwin Nikolais. *Dance Magazine* June 1966: 32, 80.

Matheson, Katy. "Twyla Tharp (1941–)—*The Bix Pieces* and Excerpt from a Lecture-Demonstration." In *Dance as a Theatre Art: Source Readings in Dance History From 1581 to the Present.* Eds. Selma Jeanne Cohen and Katy Matheson. Princeton, NJ: Princeton Book Co., 1974. New York: Dodd, Mead and Company, Inc., 1992: 230.

Matson, Tim. *Pilobolus.* New York: Random House, 1978.

McDonagh, Don. *Martha Graham: A Biography.* Newton Abbot, England: David & Charles, 1974.

McDonagh, Don. *The Complete Guide to Modern Dance.* Garden City, NY: Doubleday & Co., Inc., 1976.

McDonagh, Don. *The Rise and Fall and Rise of Modern Dance.* Pennington, NJ: Chicago Review Press, 1990.

McKayle, Donald. "The Act of Theater." In *The Modern Dance: Seven Statements of Belief.* Ed. Selma Jeanne Cohen. Middletown, CT: Wesleyan University Press, 1965, 1966: 59.

McNeill, William Hardy. *Keeping Together in Time: Dance and Drill in Human History.* Cambridge: Harvard University Press, 1995.

Monk, Meredith. Comments made at ADF in 1996. Durham, NC.

Moore, Elvi. "Talking with Pilobolus." *Dance Scope* Spring/Summer 1976: 56–66.

Murphy, Jacqueline Shea, "Unrest and Uncle Tom: Bill T. Jones/Arnie Zane Dance Company's *Last Supper at Uncle Tom's Cabin/The Promised Land.*" In *Bodies of the Text: Dance as Theory,*

Literature as Dance. Eds. Ellen W. Goellner and Jacqueline Shea Murphy. New Brunswick, NJ: Rutgers University Press, 1995: 81–107.

Muscamp, Herbert. "Filling the Void: a Chance to Soar." *The New York Times* 30 September 2001.

Myers, Gerald E., ed. *African American Genius in Modern Dance.* Durham: American Dance Festival, 1993.

Myers, Gerald E. "Do You See What the Critics See?" In American Dance Festival's *Philosophical Essays on Dance.* Ed. Gordon Fancher and Gerald E. Myers. Brooklyn: Dance Horizons, 1981. 33–68.

Myers, Gerald E., ed. *Reflections on the Home of An Art Form: American Dance Festival 65th Anniversary, 1934–1998.* Durham: American Dance Festival, 1998.

Myers, Gerald E., ed. *The Black Tradition in American Modern Dance.* Durham, NC: American Dance Festival, 1988.

Nash, Joe. "Talley Beatty." In *African American Genius in Modern Dance.* Ed. Gerald E. Myers. Durham: American Dance Festival, 1993: 15.

Nelson, Lisa. Interview with Daniel Lepkoff. "Improvisation and the Sense of Imagination." *Contact Quarterly,* Summer/Fall 1992: 47–50.

News of Pilobolus Dance Theatre no. 11, Fall/Winter (2001–2002).

Nikolais, Alwin. "The New Dimension of Dance." In *Impulse Magazine.* Ed. Marian Van Tuyl. San Francisco: Impulse Publications, 1958: 43–46.

Nikolais/Louis 25-year Retrospective Program Brochure. Rutgers Art Center, 1992.

Nobel, Phillip. "Design is the Art that is Hidden in Plain Sight." *The New York Times* 27 November 2000.

Novack, Cynthia J. *Sharing the Dance: Contact Improvisation and American Culture.* Madison: University of Wisconsin Press, 1990.

Oestreich, James R. "Sounds of Almost Wordless Songs." *The New York Times* 20 July 2000.

Osumare, Halifu and Julinda Lewis-Ferguson, ed. *Black Choreographers Moving: A National Dialogue.* Berkley: Expansion Arts Series, 1991.

Paxton, Steve. Remarks made at ADF in 1994. Durham, NC.

Perlmutter, Donna. Review. In *Dance Magazine* August 1983: 36–37.

Perpener, III, John O. *African-American Concert Dance: The Harlem Renaissance and Beyond.* Urbana: University of Illinois Press, 2001.

Perron, Wendy. Baryshnikov and Perron on Deborah Hay. *Dance Magazine* November 2000: 54–59.

Perron, Wendy. "Bill T. Searches for Beauty, and a New Home [i.e., in Harlem]." *The New York Times* 27 January 2002.

Perron, Wendy. "Tharp: Still Pushing the Boundaries." *Dance Magazine* March 2001: 46.

Pollack, Barbara, ed. *The Art of Making Dance.* By Doris Humphrey. New York: Reinhart, 1959.

Prevots, Naima. *American Pageantry: A Movement Art & Democracy.* Ann Arbor: UMI Research Press, 1990.

Prevots, Naima. "When History Records Great American Artists of the 20th Century, Hawkins will be at the Top of the List." *Washington Dance View* December 1981 – January 1982.

Quasha, Susan and Elizabeth Zimmer, eds. *Body Against Body: The Dance and Other Collaborations of Bill T. Jones and Arnie Zane.* Barrytown, New York: Station Hill Press, 1989.

Rainer, Yvonne. On *Trio A.* In *The Vision of Modern Dance.* Ed. Jean Morrison Brown. Hightstown, NJ: Princeton Book Co., 1998. 141–150.

Rainer, Yvonne. *Yvonne Rainer, Work, 1961–1973.* The Press of the Nova Scotia College of Art and Design with New York, NYU Press, 1974.

Reimer-Torn, Susan and Nancy Reynolds. *Dance Classics: A Viewer's Guide to the Best-Loved Ballets and Modern Dance.* Chicago: A Capella Books, 1980, 1991.

Reinhart, Charles. Interview with Robby Barnett, Michael Tracy, and Jonathan Wolken. At ADF in 1996. Durham, NC.

Reinhart, Charles. Interview with Trisha Brown. American Dance Festival. Durham, NC. 1993.

Reinhart, Charles L. "Paul Taylor 70th: A Birthday Remembrance." *Dance Magazine* July 2000: 41–42.

Report of the American Society of Professors of Dancing from January 19, 1879 to September 8, 1893. Amsterdam, New York: The Morning Sentinel, 1894.

Rev. of A Celebration Service. In the New London Day April 30, 1999.

Robertson, Michael. "Twyla Tharp and the Logical Outcome of Abundance." Dance Magazine March 1980: 72.

Robinson, Mark. Interview with Meredith Monk. In Theater vol. 30, no. 2, 2000.

Rockwell, John. "Meredith Monk." The New York Times 21 January 1979.

Rose, Albirda. Dunham Technique: A Way of Life. Dubuque, IA: Kendall/Hunt Publishing Co., 1990.

Rosen, Lillie F. "Talking with Paul Taylor." Dance Scope vol. 3., no. 2–3 (1979).

Ross, Janice. "A Day of Dancing, by the Hundreds, on Hitler's Grave." The New York Times 3 September 1995.

Ross, Janice. Moving Lessons: Margaret H'Doubler and the Beginning of Dance in American Education. Madison: University of Wisconsin Press, 2000.

Rothstein, Edward. "Shelf Life; The Concert as a Metaphor for the Individual in Society." Rev. of Concerto Conversations by Joseph Jerman. The New York Times 30 October 1999.

Rothstein, Edward. Rev. of Silent Film and The Triumph of the American Myth by Paula Marantz Cohen. The New York Times 12 June 2001.

Rudolph, Frederick. Curriculum: A History of the American Undergraduate Course of Study Since 1636. San Francisco: Jossey-Bass Publishers, 1977.

Ruyter, Nancy Lee. Reformers and Visionaries: The Americanization of the Art of Dance. New York: Dance Horizons, 1979.

Samuels, Shayna. Interview with Bill T. Jones. In Dance Magazine May 1999: 22.

Saunders, George. "Strip Mind." The New York Times Magazine January 7, 2001: 52–53.

Soares, Janet. Louis Horst: Musician in a Dancer's World. Durham: Duke University Press, 1992.

Shapiro, Laura. "This Time, One From the Heart." Newsweek November 11, 1991: 68–69.

Shawn, Ted. Gods Who Dance. New York: E.P. Dutton & Co., 1929.

Shawn, Ted with Gray Poole. One Thousand and One Night Stands. Garden City, NY: Doubleday & Co., Inc., 1960.

Sheets, Hilarie M. "Books in Brief: Nonfiction; Naked Under the Gold." The New York Times 28 October 2001.

Sherwood, M.E.W. The Art of Entertaining. New York: Dodd, Mead and Company, 1892.

Siegel, Marcia B. At The Vanishing Point; A Critic Looks at Dance. New York: Saturday Review Press, 1972.

Siegel, Marcia B. Days on Earth: The Dance of Doris Humphrey. New Haven: Yale University Press, 1987.

Siegel, Marcia B. "In Twyla's Company." The Hudson Review Winter 1999: 735–742.

Siegel, Marcia B., ed. "Nik: A Documentary." Dance Perspectives Winter 1971.

Siegel, Marcia B. The Shapes of Change: Images of American Dance. Boston: Houghton Mifflin, 1979.

Siegel, Marcia B. The Tail of the Dragon: New Dance. Durham: Duke University Press, 1991.

Siegel, Marcia B. Watching the Day Go By. Boston: Houghton Mifflin, 1977.

Simon, Carly. "How Lyrics Work." Doubletalk, Spring 2001: 14.

Smith, Amanda. Interview with David Gordon. Dance Magazine February 1981: 74–78.

Smith, Nancy Stark. "Trance Script." Contact Quarterly: A Vehicle for Moving Ideas Winter 1989: 14–21. Sommers, Pamela. Rev. of Ursonate. The Washington Post 15 April 1996.

Sommer, Sally R. Rev. of Return to Maria La Baja. Dance Magazine June 1985: 20–21.

Sommer, Sally R. "Trisha Brown Making Dances." Dance Scope Spring/Summer, 1972: 7–18.

Sontag, Susan. Interview: "On Art and Consciousness." Performing Arts Journal Fall (1977): 31.

Sparshott, Francis. Off the Ground: First Steps to a Philosophical Consideration of the Dance. Princeton: Princeton University Press, 1988.

Steinman, Louise. The Knowing Body: The Artist as Storyteller in Contemporary Performance. Berkeley: North Atlantic Books, 1995.

St. Denis, Ruth. Ruth St. Denis, An Unfinished Life. New York: Harper & Brothers, 1939.

St. Denis, Ruth. "St. Ruth at Adelphi College." In Wisdom Comes Dancing: Selected Writings of Ruth

St. Denis on Dance, Spirituality, and the Body. Ed. Kamae A. Miller. Seattle: PeaceWorks, 1997: 198.

Stodelle, Ernestine. *The First Frontier: The Story of Louis Horst and the American Dance.* Cheshire: E. Stodelle, 1964.

Sturla, Irene. "How Do People Create?" *Attitude: The Dancer's Magazine* Spring 2000: 5.

Supree, Burt. "The Daily Fact of Absence." In *Body Against Body: The Dance and Other Collaborations of Bill T. Jones and Arnie Zane,* Eds. Elizabeth Zimmer and Susan Quasha. Barrytown, NY: Station Hill Press, 1989: 123-125.

Taylor, Paul. "Down with Choreography." In *The Modern Dance: Seven Statements of Belief.* Ed. Selma Jeanne Cohen. Middletown, CT: Wesleyan University Press, 1965, 1966: 91–92.

Taylor, Paul. *Private Domain.* New York: Knopf, 1987.

Teachout, Terry. "Art For Pleasure's Sake." Rev. of *Writing in the Dark,* by Arlene Croce. *The New York Times* 19 November 2000.

Teachout, Terry. "Dance Chronicle: Going A Lot to the Mark Morris Dance Group." *Partisan Review* Spring 2000: 283.

Teachout, Terry. "When a Full-Time Critic Keeps His Opinions to Himself." *The Chronicle of Higher Education* 13 March 1998: 86.

Terry, Walter. *Frontiers of Life: The Life of Martha Graham.* New York: Crowell, 1975.

Terry, Walter. *Ted Shawn: Father of American Dance.* New York: Dial Press, 1976.

Tharp, Twyla. "My Life and Times in Jazz." Lecture given by Tharp at the ADF in 2000. Durham, NC.

Tharp, Twyla. *Push Comes to Shove.* New York: Bantam, 1992.

Tharp, Twlya. Comments made at ADF in 1999. Durham, NC.

"The Grecian System of Physical Culture for Women" Advertisement. *Harper's Bazaar; A Monthly Magazine for Women.* February 1903.

Tobias, Tobi. Rev. of *Facing North* by Meredith Monk. *New York Magazine* February 24, 1992.

Tobias, Tobi. Rev. of Pilobolus. *New York Magazine* July 18, 1994: 55.

Tobias, Tobi. Rev. of *Radial Courses* by Lucinda Childs. *New York Magazine* October 10, 2000: 105–106.

Tobias, Tobi. "Tharp on Broadway." *Dance Magazine* July 1980: 62.

Tobias, Tobi. "Twyla Tharp." *Dance Scope* Spring 1970: 10.

Todd, Mabel E. *The Thinking Body: A Study of the Balancing Forces of Dynamic Man.* Brooklyn: Dance Horizons, 1937.

Toepfer, Karl. *Empire of Ecstasy: Nudity and Movement in German Body Culture, 1910–1935.* Berkeley: University of California Press, 1997.

Trucco, Terry. "Bold Work that Honors Survival." Rev. of *Still/Here,* by Bill T. Jones. *The New York Times* 27 November 1994.

Van de Velde, Theodore H. *Ideal Marriage.* New York: Ballantine Books, 1975.

Vaughan, David. *Merce Cunningham: Fifty Years.* New York: Aperture, 1997.

Vechten, Carl Van. "Duncan Concerts in New York." In *Isadora Duncan.* Ed. Paul Magriel. New York: H. Holt & Co., 1947. 23–24.

Wallace, Marcie. "The Autochoreography of an Ex-Snow Queen: Dance, Desire and the Black Masculine in Melvin Dixon's Vanishing Rooms." In *Novel Gazing: Queer Readings in Fiction.* Ed. Eve Kosovsky Sedgwick. Durham: Duke University Press, 1997: 379–400

Wallace, Mike. Interview with Mikhail Baryshnikov and excerpt of Baryshnikov performing segment of Paxton's *Flat. 60 Minutes* 28 November 2000.

Washington, Eric K. "Sculpture in Flight: A Conversation with Bill T. Jones." *Transition* no. 62, 1992: 191–194.

Welsh, Kariamu Asante, ed. *African Dance: An Artistic, Historical and Philosophical Inquiry.* Trenton: Africa World Press, 1998.

Wilson, Florence Yoder. "A Famous Dancer Talks on Artistic Types." *Needlecraft—The Magazine of Home Arts* January 1931.

Wolken, Jonathan. On *Aeros.* Interview with Charles Reinhart at ADF in 1996. Durham, NC.

Wolken, Jonathan. Comments made at ADF. Durham, NC. 26 June 1999.

Wolken, Jonathan. Remarks made at ADF Post-Performance Discussion. Durham, NC. 7 June 1996.

Wolken, Jonathan and Piloblous. Remarks made by Wolken and the group about how they work for a tension between specificity and ambiguity, how in the end they aim for the kind of mix that tilts toward ambiguity. Re-emphasized at an ADF talk in June 2000.

Woods, Byron. "The Body Electric: Merce Cunningham Troupe Explores, Discovers." *The News and Observer*, Raleigh, NC 14 July 2001.

Woodworth, Mark. "Sensing Nature's Flow, Hawkins Teaches up a Storm—Showers of Dance-Poems!" *Dance Magazine* October 1972: 28.

Woodworth, Mark. "Opening the Eye of Nature." In *5 Essays On the Dance of Erick Hawkins*. By Mark Woodworth, Parker Tyler, Lucia Dlugoszewski, Beverly Brown, Robert Sabin, and M L Gordon North. New York: Foundation for Modern Dance, 1970–1979: 15.

Zimmer, Elizabeth. Rev. of *Day Two*. *Dance Magazine* May 1982: 149–150.

Zuck, Barbara. "Tywla in Ohio." *Dance Magazine* January 1992: 53.

Index

Moore, Bill: 90, 245
Moore, G.E.: 65, 229
Morris, Mark: 224, 256, 267
Morris, Robert: 135, 143
Morrison, Toni: 209
Morton, Jelly Roll: 183-184, 190
Motherwell, Robert: 96
Moyers, Bill: 210
Mozart, Wolfgang Amadeus: 66, 184, 188, 191
Murray, Elizabeth: 233, 235, 257
Muscamp, Herbert: 233, 257, 265
Myers, Martha: 65, 105

Nash, Joe: 70, 86, 91, 245, 265
Nelson, Lisa: 152, 249, 265
Nielsen, Lavinia: 63
Nietzsche, Friedrich: 8, 14, 23, 62-63, 188, 242
Nijinsky, Vaslav: 5
Nikolais, Alwin: 102-104, 106, 114, 181, 198, 216, 227, 246, 262, 264-265
Noguchi, Isamu: 56-57
Nordoff, Paul: 49
Norman, Jessye: 209
Northrop, F.S.C.: 95-96, 101, 245, 261
Novack, Cynthia J.: 151-152, 249, 254, 265
Nureyev, Rudolph: 129, 191, 252

Oates, Joyce Carol: 206, 253
O'Connor, Mark: 191
O'Day, Kevin: 180
Odetta: 220
O'Hara, Frank: 235, 257, 261
Owens, Jesse: 60

Parks, Rosa: 73
Parsons, David: 35
Patton, M.: 124
Pavlova, Anna: 5-6, 241
Paxton, Steven: 142-145, 148-153, 170, 248-249, 265, 267
Peaslee, Richard: 184
Pendleton, Moses: 196, 199, 201-202
Perlmutter, Donna: 212, 254, 265
Perls, Dr. Fritz: 134, 136-137, 248
Perpener, John: 71, 242, 245, 256, 265
Perron, Wendy: 153, 249, 252, 256, 265
Petipa, Marius: 146
Picasso, Pablo: 49, 60
Pilates, Joseph: 229
Pinsky, Robert: 228
Pinter, Harold: 148

Plato: 8, 23
Pollock, Jackson: 3, 54
Pomare, Eleo: 82, 88
Pound, Ezra: 30, 40, 49
Powell, William: 149
Prevots, Naima: 99, 242, 246, 265
Primus, Pearl: 70-73, 75-79, 81-82, 84, 165, 214, 244-245, 254, 259, 261
Prince, Liz: 221
Rainer, Yvonne: 139, 141-147, 151-152, 160, 169, 183, 248, 261, 265
Rambert, Marie: 5
Rauschenberg, Robert: 114, 119, 127, 129, 143, 149, 171, 174, 248
Ravel, Maurice: 39, 63
Rawe, Tom: 184, 186, 251-252
Rawlings, John: 129
Reich, Steve: 163
Reich, Wilhelm: 134, 248
Reid, Vernon: 221
Reinhart, Charles: 1, 84, 104, 130, 159, 198, 247, 250, 252-253, 265, 268
Reinhart, Stephanie: 1, 198
Reitz, Dana: 148
Richards, I.A.: 66, 234
Riley, Terry: 135
Roach, Max: 92, 209, 211
Robbins, Jerome: 148, 179, 211
Robinson, Cleo Parker: 2, 88
Rockwell, John: 158, 249, 266
Rodin, Auguste: 5
Rogers, Buck: 105, 107
Rorem, Ned: 157
Ross, Betsy: 123
Ross, Janice: 138-139, 242, 248, 266
Rothko, Mark: 54, 239
Rouse, Mikel: 235
Rudner, Sara: 148, 186, 252
Rudolph, Frederick: 22, 242, 266
Rushing, Jimmy: 86
Russell, Bertrand: 234

Sanford, Terry: 195
Sartre, Jean-Paul: 150
Satie, Erik: 39, 115, 121
Saunders, George: 227, 257, 266
Schickele, Peter: 198
Schiller, Friedrich: 52
Schlemmer, Oskar: 104-105
Schneider, Maria: 201
Schoenberg, Arnold: 49, 115, 201
Schönberg, Bessie: 55, 170, 244, 250, 260
Schopenhauer, Arthur: 238

Gerald E. Myers